ARIZONA

ARIZONA

A PANORAMIC HISTORY OF A FRONTIER STATE

MARSHALL TRIMBLE

Foreword by Barry M. Goldwater

DOUBLEDAY & COMPANY, INC., GARDEN CITY, NEW YORK

1977

Library of Congress Cataloging in Publication Data

Trimble, Marshall.
  Arizona: a panoramic history of a frontier State.

  Bibliography.
  Includes index.
  1. Arizona—History.   I. Title.
F811.T73   979.1
ISBN: 0-385-12806-1 Trade
      0-385-14064-9 Prebound

Library of Congress Catalog Card Number 76-45265

FOREWORD

Marshall Trimble has written a very comprehensive history of Arizona which he calls ARIZONA: A PANORAMIC HISTORY OF A FRONTIER STATE. From the very beginning until the last page, he covers in a comprehensive and well-written way the entire history of Arizona from the earliest days to the present.

It would be necessary to read four or five books to get the exposure to Arizona's history that Mr. Trimble has accomplished in this one. I find this to be one of the main attributes of this work; so many times people are reluctant to delve into history, even extremely interesting history, because of the mass of details that some authors are prone to use to get their story across. There is much to be said for the extremely complete history, but there is also a lot in favor of a book that one can carry around and peruse from time to time. During the course of that perusal, a person can come up with an understanding of the history of a region and also, I dare say, an ability to discuss it with others who are interested. As an example, Mr. Trimble has a most interesting chapter on the California Column which made Arizona a participant in the War Between the States. While this subject has been written about many times, it has never been handled in quite the way that I read it in his approach, and I'm sure that anyone will enjoy having an understanding of what prompted the Column and what it accomplished in our state.

I recommend the reading of this book to anyone who is interested in the history of Arizona both before statehood and even before we became a territory. I'm sure any reader will get as much benefit from it as I have.

BARRY M. GOLDWATER

ACKNOWLEDGMENTS

History is an interpretation of events in the way we and our contemporaries perceive, or, as one noted buff stated, "What is history but a fable agreed upon?" Even though we do have certain data and documented information from which to draw, recording historical events is likened to asking witnesses to describe an accident; there are as many versions as there are viewers.

Some writers do take certain liberties with historical material—the "when the truth interferes with the legend I'll take the legend" or "if this wasn't the way it happened, it's the way it should have happened" syndrome. The novelist and filmmaker may take this to the extreme by interjecting bizarre plots or torrid love scenes to spice up the story for public consumption. The feeling, of course, is that the truth may be too placid to be marketable. On the other hand, the purist will use only that information which he can document and footnote. He will gain respect in his field, but unfortunately, he is playing to a limited audience. Still others write in such a manner that truth, as they interpret it, is held to, and yet the material accentuates the character and style of the times about which one is writing. One shouldn't necessarily have to be a student or historian to enjoy it. It was my intention to write that kind of book.

To write a one-volume history of Arizona is a difficult task. There is such a diversity of subjects to cover that it is impossible to give fair and equal treatment to all. Therefore I have chosen a composite of material that I have found people to be interested in over the years I have been associated with teaching and public speaking on the subject. My listeners range from newcomers and students to old-time natives and hobbyists.

To accomplish a task such as this is rarely the work of one person. In reflecting back over the past three years when this endeavor began, I am grateful to the many experts in the field who have been of assistance or have exerted an influence upon this work. Dr. Pat Copeland of Scottsdale Community College advised me on and read the geology section. Gary Shaffer and Dennis Massion of that same institution offered many helpful suggestions in the writing of the anthropology and natural history sections. Dee Rae Bayless, Virginia Waterman, Jess Pogue, Rex Orme, Jim and Betty Swanson of the Scottsdale School District and Barbara Wilford of the Maricopa County Community College District spent many hours advising and reading. Arizona history professor Don Ellis of Mesa Community College read the manuscript, offering much helpful criticism. There were others too numerous to mention who were a constant source of encouragement. I will not list them for fear of omitting some.

I would like to thank Bob Breinholt of Doubleday & Company for his assistance, which went "above and beyond the normal call of duty" in getting this work to the right people. A special thanks goes out to Aaron and Ruth Cohen, owners of the Guidon Book Store in Scottsdale, Arizona. I doubt that I could have accomplished this task without their generous help and support.

Like all his many disciples and students, I have stood in awe of Dr. C. Leland Sonnichsen from our first meeting. I first read his classic, *Billy King's Tombstone,* when I was a lad of about eight and I still consider it to be one of the best books ever written about Arizona. Grass-roots historian, man of letters, gifted speaker, and teacher, Dr. Sonnichsen's contribution to the history and lore of the Southwest has been significant indeed.

To my mentor, Bert Fireman, who first introduced me to the formal study of Arizona history, I also owe a great debt of appreciation. Several years ago I audaciously walked into the maestro's office and informed him of my intentions of becoming a teacher and writer of Arizona history. Bidding that I follow, he led me through the stacks of the Arizona Room at the Hayden Library pulling out volume after volume, at the same time telling me to make note of the title and author of each. "So you want to be a teacher and writer," he chided. "When you finish reading these come back and see me and I'll pull some more." That was a long time ago and I'm still reading.

My father, Ira "Happy" Trimble, was the first to sharpen my appetite for Southwestern lore, filling my mind with stories of his youth along the Mexican border. As a young man in the early 1900s he ranged from Langtry, Texas, to Scottsdale, Arizona. I do believe he did nothing but collect anecdotes during his formative years to pass along to me in mine.

Much of my work during the past few years has been involved with taping and filming Arizona pioneers for the Maricopa County Community College District. Bits and pieces of their reminiscences are located throughout the latter stages of this work. To sit and chat with those wonderful people has been a labor of love that I shall always cherish.

These writers and pioneers have been my teachers, but I take full responsibility for the accuracy of the material herein. If there is error, the fault is mine.

Last, and the most important thanks of all, to Gena, for understanding.

It is to all the above that this work is most respectfully dedicated.

MARSHALL TRIMBLE
September 1976

CONTENTS

MAPS

PROLOGUE

This land has a name today. It is marked on maps and most of it has been explored by man. A few generations ago, no more than the blinking of an eye in the geological epoch, it was a part of the great unknown, inhabited only by wild animals and aborigines. To the Spanish it became known as the Pimería Alta, the land of the upper Pima people, or Apachería, the land of the Apache. The Americans would call it Arizona.

INTRODUCTION

"No country that I have yet visited presents so many striking anomalies as Arizona. With millions of acres of the finest arable lands, there was not at the time of our visit, a single farm under cultivation in the Territory; with the richest gold and silver mines, paper-money is the common currency; with forts innumerable, there is scarcely any protection to life and property; with extensive pastures, there is little or no stock; with the finest natural roads, travelling is beset with difficulties; with rivers through every valley, a stranger may die of thirst. . . . In January one enjoys the luxury of a bath as under a tropical sun, and sleeps under double blankets at night. There are towns without inhabitants, and deserts extensively populated; vegetation where there is no soil, and soil where there is no vegetation. Snow is seen where it is never seen to fall, and ice forms where it never snows. There are Indians the most docile in North America, yet travelers are murdered daily by Indians the most barbarous on earth. The Mexicans have driven the Papagoes from their southern homes, and now seek protection from the Apaches in the Papago villages. . . . Mines without miners and forts without soldiers are common. Politicians without policy, traders without trade, store-keepers without stores, teamsters without teams, and all without means, form the mass of the white population."

J. Ross Browne, *Adventures in the Apache Country*, 1864.

They came to the land from all points on the compass. From the south came the conquistadores, searching in vain for a golden dream. Following in their footsteps came the zealous missionaries, who brought to the natives not only Christianity, but also the rudiments of ranching and farming. Then came the Americans, searching at first for beaver and other fur-bearing animals. Others came to take from the land, stripping the mountains of the rich mineral-laden ore. The backwash of the California gold rush brought Argonauts in search of a new bonanza. Some traversed the inhospitable deserts while others traveled by ship to the mouth of the Colorado River, then by steamer up that river to ports such as Yuma, Ehrenberg, and Hardyville. From Utah, Mormon missionaries migrated southward into the valley of the Little Colorado River. Eventually these industrious settlers would migrate all the way into Mexico, farming land heretofore thought to be so poor that "you couldn't even raise hell on it." From the East came people from all walks of life. They traveled by stagecoach, wagon, railroad, horseback, and some even came afoot. They came, all of them, in search of a dream in one form or another. For some it was health—the dry, hot desert air might restore life again to crippled lungs and limbs. Others came for a new start, or as Bret Harte said, "a fresh deal all around." In the final analysis, it was really the West that brought them, the love of adventure, the wild, free life. Many left their blood upon the land, but where they died, others followed and somehow survived.

The era passed all too quickly; it was over almost before it started. The last frontier was ended, there would be no more Wests to win. Dreamers from later generations could only lament the West that was past. For them there would be no virgin lands left to conquer, and no matter how hard they tried to re-create those times past, they were gone forever.

Arizona is one of the fastest-growing states in the nation. Over 2 million people live in the state. Each year thousands more come to visit to bask in the warm desert sunshine, escaping the cold, inclement weather that grips most of the country during the winter season. Others come to see firsthand a land seen previously only through the eyes of a photographer.

Arizona is a land of free-spirited people, both young and old. Newcomers shuck their old ties and traditions as the new life-style of the great open country engulfs their bodies and souls. Natives have only to go someplace else periodically to keep a proper perspective of their home state. With the advent of air conditioning the hot desert lands have become livable all year long. No longer do citizens have to pack up their belongings and head for the cool pines of Horsethief Basin or other similar mountain retreats out of necessity, though many still do for pleasure and recreation. Burlap sack refrigerators, screened porches, and sleeping outside during the hot summer months are things of the past, though many still suffer from "heat frustration" during the months of June through September. The oversized "bathtubs" found in the back yards of thousands of desert dwellers have done much to thwart this malady.

Ma Nature was a generous old lady and she must have taken a special interest in Arizona. Stirring her caldron of beautiful creations she treated the land as her own special laboratory, conjuring up the most versatile piece of handiwork in North America.

Among all the geographic areas of the United States, the Southwest in general and Arizona in particular is blessed with a panoramic beauty that almost defies description. Only a limited number of poets, painters, and photographers have been able to do justice to her splendor. Geologically and geographically Arizona displays the grand design and tremendous forces of nature. The landscape changes dramatically from the wind-sculptured sands of the Sonoran Desert, where the average annual rainfall is only 3 inches, to the lush green meadows of the White Mountains, where more than 30 inches of moisture is recorded each year. The climate is so diverse that many times during the year the state records both the hottest and coldest spot in the nation on the same day. The sporting enthusiast could conceivably spend the morning snow skiing on the peaks above Flagstaff, and the afternoon water skiing on one of the many lakes that impound the Salt River 150 miles to the south.

Climate zones range from desert to above timberline. It is possible to take an automobile ride from Tucson to the top of Mount Lemmon and pass through transition zones ranging from Sonoran Desert to Canadian Rockies, all in about twenty minutes. To gain an even better perspective of the land one might begin a day's journey in the low Sonoran Desert near Yuma, where the elevation is 137 feet, spend midday in the high desert above Phoenix, and continue on to the forested mountains of the Mogollon Rim country, past the San Francisco Peaks, where majestic pinnacles reach a height of 12,611 feet, and on to the Grand Canyon. After viewing this great chasm with its sublime panoramic tapestry of color and beauty, the traveler might continue on to Monument Valley. Monument Valley, a vast land of serenity and splendor where one can scan the clear horizons some 70 miles away, presents a view of noble red rock formations sculptured by wind and rain that cannot be equaled anywhere in the world. The voyager might conclude this odyssey with a short walk down into Canyon de Chelly, an abyss of serenely peaceful canyons so remote that even today much of it remains unexplored. In the high, steep canyon walls one can still see the former dwellings of the ancient Anasazi Indians.

Great inundations and recent volcanism; mountain barriers and inhospitable deserts; hostile Apache and Navajo; this was the land that was sometimes known as the Pimería Alta, and sometimes called Apachería. In 1736, a Yaqui Indian led a Spanish trader to a rich lode of silver some 25 miles southwest of today's Nogales. The native silver, so pure that it was described as "soft as wax," was found in chunks weighing as much as 500 pounds each. In what became known as the Miracle of the Planchas de Plata, more than 10,000 pounds of the metal was taken out in a few months. The Spanish Crown had a law concerning such matters at the time; if a discovery was judged to be ore, a tax of only 20 per cent was levied. However, if it was judged a treasure, the king's share skyrocketed to 95 per cent. The choice was the king's to make and it should go without saying which way he decided. Legends still persist in southern Arizona that the padres in the area resisted this decision and hid what silver remained, giving birth to the still lingering tales of lost Jesuit treasures and mines in the area. This event occurred in a little valley called Arizonac. Historian James McClintock mentioned that Arizona was named after some springs near the area called by the Papago Indians "Aleh-Zon," which means "small spring." The notoriety of the discovery did popularize the area and the name; however, it was not until 1863 that the name "Arizona" became official.

From the time of the coming of the first white man to the region Arizona has been considered the Siberia of duty stations. When the reputed "Golden Cities of Cibola" turned into mud and wattle mirages, and the fabled Northwest Passage failed to materialize, the Spanish Crown gradually lost interest in the economically unproductive land. The area that was to become known as Arizona was relegated to the role of something to be dreaded when man crossed from the Rio Grande villages to California. Only the natives seemed at home in the inhospitable environment. Some of these, especially the nomadic Apache and Navajo, gave those early-day explorers and soldiers even more reason to dread the perilous expeditions into the land. General of the Army William Tecumseh Sherman, the man best remembered for the wide swath he and his army cut through Georgia, did the same to Arizona in a verbal manner when he remarked one day during one of his frequent acrimonious moods, "We went to war with Mexico to get Arizona, and now we should go to war with her again and make her take it back." On another occasion the general was informed that although the place was kind of hot, all she needed was more water and a better class of people, Sherman acridly replied, "That's all hell needs."

There were other complaints. Dick Wick Hall, the legendary "sage of Salome," told of a seven-year-old frog he knew of that had not yet learned how to swim. Legend has it that a soldier stationed at Fort Yuma died and went to hell. A few days later he sent word to his supply sergeant requesting blankets as he had become so acclimated to Yuma's weather that he feared he might catch his death of cold at his new duty station. Some anonymous philosopher spoke for countless travelers when he or she remarked, "Forty miles from wood, fifty miles from water, and ten feet from hell."

The first Anglo-American child born in Arizona was to make his initial outcry while floating on a raft down the Gila River on October 21, 1849. The family to whom the child was born was named Howard, and they named their son Gila, in honor of the river that carried them across the desert. Three years earlier, Lieutenant George Stoneman of the Mormon Battalion experimented with floating a homemade military craft down that same river, thus earning for himself the dubious title of first military skipper to attempt to navigate that stream. The raft sank, taking with it a few sacks of flour. Stoneman, who later rose to the rank of general (though not because of his navigational prowess), noted officially that "boating on the Gila was definitely not to be recommended to Washington."

Camels and steamboats once crossed paths on the Colorado River in what must have been one of the most unlikely encounters in the history of the arid Southwest. The year was 1858 and both conveyances were part of a noble experiment to improve transportation in the real estate just recently acquired by the United States government. The camels were merely fording the river at the time, not navigating it. The camel experiment, seemingly a more likely solution to travel in the Southwest than the riverboat, was destined for an early demise, while the paddle-wheeler would play a key role in the development of the Territory for the next twenty-five years.

During World War II, a German prisoner-of-war camp was located just east of Phoenix and a short distance from the Salt River. While planning an escape some of the prisoners were able to obtain a map of the region. Noting that the Salt joined the Gila west of Phoenix, the would-be escapees also noted that the Gila joined the Colorado River a short distance above the Mexican border. What they did not notice on their map was the number of dams that abounded in the Salt halting the free flow of water. Surmising that it would be a relatively simple task to drop a raft into the Salt, float to the Gila, from there to the Colorado, and thence to Mexico, plans were made and implemented. The idea of a river that runs dry was furthermost from the minds of these ardent young lads as they sneaked past the guards with their raft in hand. The looks of embarrassed chagrin when they dropped their boat into the sandy Salt no doubt did provide some comic relief to their ill-fated scheme.

As rivers run, or rather don't run in Arizona, the town of Wickenburg takes the award for grandiose optimism. On a bridge that crosses the normally dry Hassayampa River is a sign that righteously warns one and all there is to be "no fishing from the bridge." Perhaps the best-known bridge in the world, the fabled London Bridge, has been transplanted to the desert community of Lake Havasu City on the Colorado River.

There are still a few rather outdated statutes that abound in the lawbooks of Arizona. For example, it is against the law to shoot a camel in Arizona. It is also unlawful to ride a horse into a saloon in Prescott. Another law prohibits the locating of a house of ill repute at the entrance to a mining camp: evidently the residents were sensitive about first impressions. Selling whiskey to Indians in the 1870s was illegal, but American "ingenuity" had its champions in the town of Globe, where one resourceful merchant circumvented the technicalities of the law by giving a pint of whiskey free to any customer who purchased a potato for the sum of $2.00. In no time at all the shopkeeper found himself out of potatoes as the local Apache purchased every last one. The dilemma was soon resolved and the brisk business was resumed when the equally resourceful Indians returned the potatoes to the store for resale.

The fourteen counties of Arizona, with the exception of two, have Indian or Spanish names. The unique multi-cultural Southwestern vernacular of colorful metaphors given the communities and terrain lends a colorful flair to the region. Many of these names vividly describe the land, while others were, no doubt, named with tongue in cheek. Whatever the reason, most of them are still out there. They are the picturesquely whimsical Bonita, Bumble Bee, Bullhead City, Cornville, Cowlic, Cuckleburr, Dos Cabezas, El Mirage, Gunsight, Happy Jack, Horsehead Crossing, Jackrabbit, Jakes Corner, Jerked Beef Butte, Lousy Gulch, Punkin Center, Tortilla Flat, Total Wreck, Two Guns, Screwbean Spring, and Why. With names like that beckoning to one and all, a trip to each has to be a worthwhile experience, even for the native.

Oftentimes there is some confusion to newcomer and native alike between the name of a county and its namesake city. The town of Pima is not located in Pima County, but Graham County. The town of Navajo is in Apache County, while Fort Apache is located in Navajo County. Arizona even has a lost county to go with numerous "lost" mines. The county, named Pah-Ute, isn't really lost; rather it was taken away from the new Territory in 1866 by a callous Congress and given to Nevada.

The wind seldom blows slow at Winslow. Copperopolis was a metropolis that didn't metrop. Snowflake was not named after the inclement weather that sometimes frequents the area. It was named instead after one of the Mormon apostles, Erastus Snow, and early pioneer William Flake, both of whom founded the community in 1878. Oraibi, a Hopi village in Navajo County, is considered to be the oldest continuously inhabited community in the United States. Bush Valley, in the White Mountains, rests on an elevation of some 8,000 feet and is said to be the highest spot in the United States where farming is successful. Mount Lemmon, near Tucson, boasts that its skiing area is the southernmost in North America. The extreme northeast corner of Arizona marks the only point in the United States where four states meet. The states, making up the so-called "Four Corners," are Utah, Colorado, New Mexico, and Arizona. Bisbee is a picturesque mining community in the southern part of the state. Most of her homes are built on the steep hills that abound in the area. It has been said that children playing in the yard must be tethered by a rope to the house lest they fall onto their neighbor's roof below. According to Ripley, Bisbee High School is the only school in America that stands four stories high and has a ground-floor entrance to each level.

Like the changeless land that surrounds them, many Arizonans still cling to the old customs and ways. In the Arizona Strip country, north of the Grand Canyon, a group of industrious farmers manage to eke out a living from that inhospitable land. Reputed to be polygamists, they engage in communal efforts, not at all unlike the American pioneers during the Westward Movement. They share the toil and the wealth in one of the most remote, yet beautiful regions of the county. Littlefield, a small farm village in the same area, has the distinction of being the first Anglo-Saxon community in Arizona.

Pinetop, winter and summer playground for thousands of valley residents, was named for a tall, bushy-headed bartender who operated a saloon for the Black troopers stationed at Fort Apache. It was they who named both him and the town. Nearby, the town of Show Low received its christening when two friends, Marion Clark and Cordydon E. Cooley, felt the area was not large enough for both so they decided to play a winner-takes-all game of cards called seven-up to settle the matter of who would stay and who would move on. As the last hand was being dealt Cooley needed just a single point to win. At this juncture Clark is reputed to have said, "Show low and you win." Cooley drew the deuce of clubs, and throwing his cards on the table replied, "Show low it is." Clark moved up the creek to Pinetop and Cooley's place became known as Show Low.

Flagstaff, with its curious blending of cultures which range from traditional Navajo and Hopi to mod university student, is to the casual observer a one-street town loaded with neon signs and motels. Originally the city was a railroad construction camp. Later it was the cattle, sheep, lumber, and mercantile center for northern Arizona. Located at the foot of the state's highest range of mountains, Flagstaff claims to have the cleanest air of any city in the United States. Named by a party of immigrants in honor of a July 4, 1876, flag-raising ceremony, she is also the home of Northern Arizona University, the Museum of Northern Arizona, and the Lowell Observatory; the latter was where, in 1930, the planet Pluto was discovered.

Kingman, one of the fastest-growing communities in northern Arizona, owes its early existence to the Santa Fe Railroad and the rich mineral deposits that abounded in her surrounding mountains. Located near the site of Beale Springs, along the old camel trail, Kingman today relies heavily on the tourist and the recreational dollar. She is the gateway to Hoover Dam, Lake Mead, and the other lakes along the western boundary of the state. She is also, for Arizonans, the gateway to that "Babylon of the West," Las Vegas. Most of the communities that stretch across Interstate 40 and the Santa Fe railroad line, including Kingman, Seligman, Winslow, and Holbrook, were named for early railroad men or other businessmen.

Tucson, once known as the only walled city in America, served as a bastion against the hostile Apache bands in the early days. Captain John C. Cremony, however, apparently regarded the Old Pueblo with extreme disdain, for during a visit to that community in 1862 he noted the following in his memoirs: "Tucson is cursed by the presence of two or three hundred of the most infamous scoundrels it is possible to conceive. Innocent and unoffending men were shot down or bowie-knifed merely for the pleasure of witnessing their death agonies. Men walked the streets with double-barreled shotguns, hunting each other as sportsmen hunt for game. In the graveyard there were 47 graves of white men in 1860, and of that number only 2 had died natural deaths."

Situated on the Santa Cruz River, Tucson was reported to contain only two hundred inhabitants in 1865; two years later she was named territorial capital and by 1871 she was claiming three thousand residents, a newspaper, a brewery, two doctors, several saloons, and one bathtub. One observer recalled having seen whole blocks of adobe houses, the wooden framework being held together with strips of rawhide as nails were impossible to obtain. By the 1880s Tucson boasted a telephone, a telegraph, and a railroad. The ground on which the University of Arizona stands today was a gift from a philanthropic trio consisting of two gamblers and a saloonkeeper. The Old Pueblo remained the largest city in Arizona until the census of 1920, when she lost the lead to Phoenix. Today Tucson is a large metropolitan area; much to her credit she has not lost that multi-cultural Southwestern charm.

Scottsdale, described as a place with "thirty-odd tents and a half a dozen adobe houses" in the early 1900s changed from a small community with one class-B high school in the 1950s to a major metropolitan area in the 1970s. Paradise Valley, just north of Scotts-dale, was unreclaimed desert land in the 1940s. Today it is more aptly described as a "millionaires' ghetto."

The many rivers flowing out of the mountains down into the Salt River Valley made the area a natural for settlement. Some twenty miles north, near where the Verde River meets the Salt, was Fort McDowell. The Bradshaw Mountains to the northwest and the min-ing camp at Wickenburg were thriving on the gold and silver that were being extracted in great quantity. The first man to realize the opportunities of farming during this period was John Y. T. Smith, post sutler at Fort McDowell. Smith noted the wild hay growing abundantly in the area and immediately secured a contract to sup-ply the post. In 1867 he was operating a "hay camp" near where Fortieth Street meets the Salt in modern Phoenix. At that time the place was known as Smith's Station.

Jack Swilling, erstwhile adventurer, miner, and ex-Confederate soldier, learned from Smith the opportunities open to anyone who might care to settle in the valley. After observing ancient Hohokam canals branching out from the Salt, Swilling became convinced that these canals could be cleaned out and used again to irrigate in the same manner as those prehistoric natives had done several cen-turies before. A company called the Swilling Irrigation Canal Com-pany was organized in 1867, and the following year the first farm was established. On the corner of Twenty-fourth Street and Wash-ington Street today in Phoenix stands a small plaque commemo-rating the farmer, Frenchy Sawyer, and the occasion.

Before long a small village grew up along the river, and with size comes sophistication. The locals wanted a name and so a committee was selected to perform this memorable task. Swilling wanted to call the place Stonewall, in honor of his hero, the late Stonewall Jackson. Another seemingly more suitable name, Salina, was suggested because of the proximity to the Salt River, or Río Salina. The most colorful of this group of distinguished gentlemen gath-ered for the occasion was an Englishman dubiously known as "Lord" Darrell Duppa. Duppa was a world traveler, adventurer, scholar, and gifted elocutionist. He was also known to be a bibu-lous reprobate, a victim of demon rum. After listening to the others proclaim the merits of their choices, "Lord" Duppa rose and, draw-ing upon his erudite knowledge of the languages, waxed eloquently on the subject of the pre-Columbian peoples who once dwelt in the rich, fertile valley. He prophesied that another great civilization would spring phoenix-like from the ashes of the old. Duppa's act was apparently an impossible one to follow and "Smith's Station" gave way to "Phoenix."

Shortly after his famous name-bestowing speech, Duppa noted the small community on the south side of the Salt near Hayden's Ferry reminded him of a beautiful valley in Greece called the Vale of Tempe. Just how the mesquite-covered dusty village reminded "Lord" Duppa of some Grecian garden spot has never been recorded, but the name stuck. Duppa had struck again.

Phoenix continued to grow and prosper long after the mining camps and military posts were abandoned. On October 15, 1870, her citizens got together and selected an official townsite. City lots were expensive. Some sold for over a hundred dollars apiece. In 1889 the territorial capital was moved to this city on the Salt, where, through statehood, it has remained permanently.

This chronicle is not meant to be just a history of Arizona, but rather a folk or social history of its people. Many of them weren't soldiers, mining magnates, or politicians and therefore have been left out of the previous histories written of the state. Arizona is so closely linked to her territorial past that it is still possible to talk to pioneers who came here to start a new life in covered wagons. They are a vanishing breed. Most didn't become famous politicians or win medals on some foreign battlefield, nor did they become wealthy mining magnates. They are just a lot of people doing "the best they could." This is their story.

IN THE BEGINNING

SOME SCIENTISTS BELIEVE the age of the earth to be at least 4.5 billion years old. Arizona's Grand Canyon with its multitude of sedimentary layers presents to geologists a layer-by-layer record of the earth's history. In the inner gorge of this timeless chasm lie some of the oldest rocks known to man, dating back some 2.7 billion years. To say the Grand Canyon is magnificent seems a bit of an understatement. The first missionaries who viewed this monument to the powers of nature no doubt described it as one of God's finest creations. The modern cynic might mutter acidly that it looks like a bad case of soil erosion, while a cowboy might gaze into its vast abyss respectfully and quietly observe that it would be a "hell of a place to lose a cow."

Each new viewing offers a totally different perspective to the observer as the canyon reveals her many moods. During sunny and clear weather, or when afternoon thunderheads gather; sunrise or sunset; the morning after a snowstorm; looking down on the canyon from an airplane, or standing near her precipitous rim; the vista is an ever changing panorama of splendor and beauty.

The Grand Canyon of the Colorado was first navigated by a party of ten explorers led by a daring ex-Civil War major named John Wesley Powell in 1869. There had been other explorers on the Colorado, but none had ventured into the 150 miles of rapids and high canyon walls that Powell sought to penetrate. A man of in-

domitable spirit, Powell had lost his right arm at Shiloh when a
Minié ball smashed his elbow. Two years after the war ended, he
was able to secure funding from the government to explore the
West. In the summer of 1868, he and a party of friends scaled
Longs Peak in Colorado's Rocky Mountains. Looking off toward the
west he saw the rivers of the Western Slope converging on the Colorado River and became obsessed with exploring that vast unknown region.

The trip through the canyon took three months and was the first
of three such scientific expeditions taken by him. During the journey, three members of the party wandered off and were killed by
hostile Indians.

Keeping dry was a never-ending problem on the journey down
the river. Most of the time the men wore no clothing at all while in
the boats. Powell claimed that he was "fully clad" when he had
only his life preserver on. He soon had occasion to be thankful that
the party had not reverted to total nudity when going ashore. At
the campsites Powell could not resist scaling the nearby cliffs. Once
he found himself stuck on a high precipice and could not go up or
down. Hanging on by his one arm, Powell was finally rescued by
one of his companions, who gallantly stripped off his long johns and
lowered them down to the commander and hoisted him to safety.

Powell developed a sincere liking and respect for the Indians he
met on his expeditions. He learned several of their languages and
became a lifelong friend of the red man. In 1879 he founded the
Bureau of American Ethnology for the study of Indian culture.
From 1881 to 1894, Powell continued his scientific work as head of
the United States Geological Survey.

Powell's poignant description of the Grand Canyon in 1869 is as
timeless as the canyon itself:

> Wherever we look there is but a wilderness of rocks—deep gorges
> where the rivers are lost below cliffs and towers and pinnacles and ten
> thousand strangely carved forms in every direction, and beyond them
> mountains blending with the clouds.

The current theory on the formation of the Grand Canyon goes
back to the middle of the Cenozoic era, some 20 million years ago.
The stage was probably set by a low-lying plain and a great river
draining the Western Rockies, dropping down through the Four
Corners and going in a southwest direction. The river curved

around, following much of the channel of the Little Colorado River, but flowing in a southeast direction toward the Rio Grande.

Something, still unknown, lava flow or more uplift, dammed the river, forming a huge lake which ultimately covered most of what is today's Navajo reservation. The key to the riddle as to what caused this dam has not yet been discovered. When the lake waters overflowed the divide somewhere between Grand Canyon Village and Desert View they flooded down a little river flowing toward the Gulf of California. This resurgent stream has spent 9 million years cutting the Grand Canyon as we know it today.

Actually the region surrounding the Grand Canyon has not always been at today's 8,000-foot elevation. The land has been rising for the last 10 million years, while at the same time the great river has been able to maintain its cutting edge, creating the chasms that we see today.

Just as the earth today is constantly undergoing change, the past several hundred million years have brought about many diverse alterations in Arizona's landscape. Six hundred million years ago, during the Cambrian period, Arizona had an arid climate. Gradually during this period a sea moved into the northern and southeastern regions. From the Devonian period, 400 million years ago, to the Permian period, some 120 million years later, great seas rolled back and forth across the land, inundating it, then receding as the land rose once more. Mountains rose and eroded away during these same periods.

Reptiles were formed and developed during the Permopennsylvanian period, some 280 million years ago. During this same period while small lizardlike creatures were leaving their tracks in ancient Grand Canyon sand dunes, giant amphibians lived, fought, and died in the verdant swamps and marshes that abounded in the area.

The Petrified Forest, a stony epitaph to a living forest, is a legacy of the Triassic period. Contrary to popular myth, the tree forms were not turned to stone, they were permeated by minerals while buried beneath the sea for a million years or so. Thus the trees did not turn to stone; the stone merely turned into trees. This, the Mesozoic era, was also the time of the great sea turtles, dinosaurs, and crocodiles. During the Cretaceous period, 135 million years ago, the dinosaur became extinct and a sea advanced over the region, then retreated again as the land uplifted. This period saw the coming of flowering plants and to the west, the uplift of the Sierra Nevada.

About 100 million years ago a tremendous surge of mountain building and faulting began north of the Mogollon Rim, including the San Francisco Peaks and the White Mountains. It wasn't until the Cenozoic era that what was once a great block of sea bottom began to rise as climatic conditions changed radically, and this rise of sedimentary deposits thousands of feet thick created the Colorado Plateau. This elevated tract of immense proportions may have been as much as 2,000 feet higher at its zenith. At the southern edge of the plateau is a great precipitous escarpment stretching diagonally across the center of the state and into New Mexico. This raw edge of rock and faulted displacement that is the mighty backbone of Arizona was named for a former Spanish soldier-governor, Juan Ignacio Mogollon. Since that last great uplift the land has been in a state of erosion from wind and water, all a part of nature's grand design of things.

During the Cenozoic period a three-toed equine was developing on the grassy plains of today's American West. These dog-size critters were the forerunners of the horse. Changing climates forced their migration some 10 million years ago across the Bering Strait into the Eastern Hemisphere.

The vulcanism from the latter part of the Tertiary period (between 2 and 7 million years ago) has yielded great quantities of iron and manganese, while this same period is credited with little gold, silver, copper, lead, or zinc. These non-ferrous metals were distributed during the ancient Pre-Cambrian era, an immense time span that embraces all formations older than 600 million years.

Arizona's land areas are labeled according to whichever scientist happens to be doing the classifying. The geologist refers to the Basin and Range Province, the Mexican Highlands, and the Plateau Province. The geographer labels it the Basin and Range Lowlands, the Mountains, and the High Plateau.

The first thing that usually comes to mind when one thinks of Arizona is the beautiful deserts for which the state is noted. However, there is another part of Arizona that many tourists and winter visitors never see: the forests. There are more forests in the state than in Maine or Wisconsin, and nearly as many as in Michigan. Some 20 million acres, or 20 per cent of the land, is forested. The largest stand of ponderosa pine in the United States grows in the high country of Arizona. There are two places in the state where the mountains rise above timberline, the 2-million-year-old San Francisco Peaks, near Flagstaff, reaching a height of 12,611 feet, and the billion-year-old-plus Mount Baldy in the White Mountains, which rises to an altitude of 11,590 feet.

In 1889, long before the word became a part of our everyday language and there was a national awareness of the subject, the science of ecology was conceived and implemented by Dr. C. Hart Merriam in the forests of Arizona. Merriam, first chief of the United States Bureau of Biological Survey, proposed a theory of life zones based on the practical observation of zonation of vegetation in the mountains of the American West. It was commonly known that different climate zones exist and overlap from the foothills to the top of a mountain. Merriam and his party made a study that extended from the Painted Desert to the summit of the San Francisco Peaks, observing the interrelationships of plant and animal life. His observations were accurate enough and his life zones useful, even though his attempt to relate zonation to temperature was oversimplified. Merriam's life-zone theory is still applicable to Arizona, although a serious flaw in his theory was his attempt to universalize his lower life zones. Moisture becomes far more important than temperature in determining the type of vegetation in warmer regions. A system based on the relationships between temperature and precipitation is more realistic.

Man has benefited more from the forest than any other single resource. The trees have given him fuel, shelter, and food. The forest provides a home for many of nature's critters as well as a hold on the soil and the conservation of water. Today, in the hustle and bustle of life in the city with a fast-paced life-style, the forests provide an immeasurable service to mankind as therapy for the soul in search of a place to pause and reflect. In that forested "Sea of Tranquility," the mind can find solace and through this relationship with nature one can become reacquainted with what is real and eternal. Through this perspective man is better able to cope with himself.

The San Francisco Peaks number among their inhabitants members of the family of the world's longest-lived species: the bristlecone pine. Reaching an age of 4,600 years in the California Sierra, they are some 1,400 years older than the better-known sequoia. The bristlecone pines in the San Francisco Peaks are only about a thousand years old, having grown since about the time of the last great volcanic action in the area.

The largest native tree in Arizona is the Douglas fir. Rising in height up to 200 feet, it is the most important timber in the United States, although it accounts for only a small percentage of the trees cut in Arizona. Most of the timber cut in the state is the ponderosa pine, a coniferous tree which grows up to 150 feet and has a life span of approximately five hundred years.

Few places in the world are subject to as much lightning as the Mogollon Rim country, and for thousands of years nature followed her own course of action after a fire. Conifer seedlings such as spruce, Douglas fir, and ponderosa pine cannot survive in direct sunlight, as they must have a proper amount of filtered light to grow. After a fire young aspens would begin to grow first and provide a canopy for the conifers and the cycle would begin again. In time the conifers would overtake the aspens and the forest would be as it was some 150 years previous.

A strange phenomenon occurs in the Kofa Mountains, near Yuma. In the rocky crevices and canyons of these rugged mountains, palm trees are growing. These Washingtonia palms aren't found anywhere else in the area and nobody seems to know how they got there, though it has been suggested that birds carried seeds in from some distant oasis.

Many of the state's highest mountains were the result of molten rock cast up from the subterranean depths of the earth. In the San Francisco Peaks area lies one of the earth's major volcanic fields. In this region alone there are approximately 250 of these extinct cinder cones. Lying on the north side of the peaks today is an area about the size of an acre whose temperature remains at a steady 70 degrees and melts the winter snows that fall on it. It is believed that before tens of thousands of years of wind, rain, snow, and ice eroded those lofty pinnacles, the San Francisco Peaks reached a height of nearly 15,000 feet.

Basically there are three types of volcanoes; the shield, with its broad, easy flow; the composite, which flows and spews magma alternately; and the most violent, the cinder cone. This type may block up, build a tremendous amount of pressure, and then literally blow its top. When it blows the surrounding area shudders with a series of earthquakes, rocks and molten lava spew thousands of feet into the air, a violent air cushion is raised above the earth, and as the dust falls back to earth it can cause 100-mile-an-hour winds, wiping out entire forests. It can also lay igneous material over the terrain to a depth of a thousand feet. The explosion at Sunset Crater in A.D. 1064 is a good example. This, the most recent in the area, was witnessed by man. Prehistoric Indians lived in the area and archaeologists have been able to pinpoint the date of the explosion by studying the charred timbers in the burned-out pit houses. The ruins, called Wupatki, a Hopi word meaning "red ruins in black cinder," are today a national monument.

ARIZONA'S NATURAL
INHABITANTS

IN THE WEEKS FOLLOWING the winter rains the desert literally springs
to life as nature, in her inimitable creative genius, transposes the
desert into a tapestry of panoramic beauty. Cactus blossoms and
desert flowers burst forth with broad, bold, brush strokes of colors
upon the landscape. The sunscreenlike paloverde trees explode
with a profusion of gold, and the ironwood tree complements its
gray-green leaves with a crown of beautiful pale violet blossoms.
The flaming red torches atop the ocotillo, and the yucca with its
magnificent white candelabra dispel the myth held by some that
the desert is nothing but an intractable, barren, forbidding sea of
inhospitableness. They will bloom only briefly, for the long, hot
summer is not far behind and the hardy desert flora will have to
regroup their resources or "tighten up their belts" so to speak, and
through the cycles of change in the changeless land, they will cling
to life, fighting for survival every day of their existence. Only those
who have adapted to dry conditions have survived and can now
coexist within the prescribed boundaries of what outsiders consider
a "hostile environment." That is why they continue to abide while
others have long since become extinct.

The plant that comes to mind most frequently when one ponders
the flora of Arizona is the saguaro cactus. This stately lord of the
desert is one of the largest of the cactus family and almost without
exception unique to the state, as far as the United States is con-

cerned. Weighing some 15 to 20 tons, of which about 98 per cent is water, the saguaro reaches a height of over 50 feet and can live to a ripe old age of two hundred years.

The natives have harvested its reddish figlike fruit since prehistoric times. It is sweet-tasting, and it is possible to ferment the juices. The Papago celebrate their New Year at the harvest. In addition to eating the fruit they use the ribs of the giant cactus for the building of homes, traps, and baskets. Blooming in the summer months, the saguaro blossom is the official state flower.

The saguaro is a slow grower and at the age of 9 years it stands only 6 inches high. An adolescent burst occurs at about age 22 and the cactus may grow 2 inches in a year. By the time it reaches 80 it may be about 8 feet high and at 150 years it could grow to a height of 35 to 50 feet. Given plenty of moisture during wet seasons the saguaro will expand its girth, resembling some avaricious gourmet, storing up for the drier months ahead.

Considerably smaller and carrying a different type of spine is the barrel cactus. One species is the compass cactus, so called because of its habit of leaning toward the southwest. The barrel averages only 5 or 6 feet in height at maturity. Cactus candy is made from the pulp of the barrel by cutting the meat into squares and boiling it in water to remove the sap. The meat is then boiled in sugar syrup. When ready, it tastes somewhat like strawberry preserves. The barrel is also noted as a source of bitter-tasting moisture to the wayward wanderer lost in the desert.

In the country around the town of Ajo is another cactus which is largely confined to this one general area. The organ pipe cactus, so called because its arms branch out in a way not unlike the pipes of an organ, also produces a fruit that Indian food gatherers harvest. In many ways this cactus resembles the saguaro.

Prickly-pear cacti are found throughout the world. The name comes from the pear shape of the flat pads attached to the stem. During droughts the large spines and the tiny, almost invisible splinters can be singed off by fire and typically fed to the cattle. They also produce a dark red fruit that can be eaten by man.

Probably the most notorious of the cactus plants are the chollas, especially the jumping cactus. There are several species of these in the desert, all seemingly waiting to prick the unwary visitor. The barbed spines embed themselves in the skin and are most difficult to extract, many times leaving the sheath inside the skin, causing painful irritation. It is said that one has not really been initiated to the desert until one has removed cholla from self, dog, or horse.

The thorns on a desert plant are nature's way of preventing the plant from being fed upon by the many animals looking for food or moisture. Many thorny plants found in the desert are not cacti at all, such as the century plant, yucca, and Joshua tree, all of which are members of the lily family. The yucca is actually more closely related to the lowly garlic plant than to the cactus.

The agave plant, also referred to as the century plant, maguey, or mescal, closely resembles the yucca and the two are oftentimes confused. The century plant rosette grows next to the ground and looks like the bud of a giant artichoke. Pulque, tequila, and mescal are fermented or distilled from the agave plant and are Mexican national drinks.

Contrary to popular belief, the century plant does not live to be a hundred but has a life span of ten to seventy-five years. It blooms only once in its lifetime and spends that lifetime preparing for the grand occasion. When the time comes it sends up a stalk which might grow as much as a foot in a day, reaching a height of 15 to 30 feet. After blooming, its life's work done, the century plant usually shrivels up and dies.

Traditionally during the blooming period the Indians would take the bud of the flower stalk and cook it in a primitive barbecue pit of hot stones covered with dirt. When done it resembled a golden brown mush similar to sugared sweet potatoes. This mescal was used as a staple in the diet of the southwestern Indians. One of the primary missions of the U. S. Army in their conquest of Apachería during the latter part of the nineteenth century was to locate and destroy the hostile Apache's mescal caches.

The so-called monkey-tailed or devil's coachwhip is in reality the ocotillo. Ocotillo is Spanish for "coachwhip" and hence the name. It is neither akin to the cactus nor the lily family, but is related to the even stranger-looking Boojum tree of Mexico. Most of the year the ocotillo appears dead but following a rain it comes to life, sprouting thousands of tiny green leaves. As the weather dries the leaves evolve into sharp thorns protecting it from would-be desert gourmets. In the spring the ocotillo adorns its long, spiny limbs with a beautiful orange-red torchlike blossom. Today, as in the past, southwestern gardeners use ocotillo limbs woven into mesh wire to

keep out rabbits. When planted the limbs take root, creating a living fence.

The yucca with its long, pointed stems is in actuality an uncle to
the onion. The Indians used the yucca roots to make shampoo for
their hair and the stems were used in making sandals and twine.

The ways of nature are difficult to fathom and one of the most
unusual events of the plant and insect world involves the banana
yucca and the moth. The pollen from the yucca is too heavy to be
carried by the wind and therefore must be transported some other
way if cross-fertilization is to take place. The moth collects this pollen from one flower and injects her egg tube into a different flower,
depositing her eggs. She then packs the sticky pollen into the hole
to feed the larvae. Strangely, there are some thirty variations of
moths in Arizona, and with one or two exceptions, each has its own
particular yucca and will have nothing to do with any other species.
Starting life together in this harmonious fashion, the yucca and the
moth are each vital to the survival of the other. In the co-evolution
of two species any adapting which better guarantees the survival of
both will be selected.

Another member of the lily family, growing mostly in the high
desert above Wickenburg, is the Joshua tree, tallest member of the
desert yuccas. The Joshuas have a most unique appearance, their
living leaves appearing daggerlike on the ends of numerous twist-
ing arms. The arms and body covered with dead leaves give the
tree the look of a huge, hairy, abominable desert creature. The
Joshua is one of the indicator plants of the Mohave Desert.

The mesquite tree will grow almost anywhere in the state below
5,000 feet. Reaching a height of only about 30 feet, its roots may
grow twice that distance. The hard roots were used as fuel in the
early days by miners as they burned much like coal. Mesquite
beans are nourishing for both man and animal. They are not native
to the Sonoran Desert as they were transported from Texas during
the days of the cattle drives.

The state tree of Arizona is the paloverde tree. The paloverde
(Spanish for "green stick") is an unusual tree in that not only are
the leaves green but so are the limbs and trunk. Long, green nee-
dlelike stems protrude from the trunk and branches. The paloverde
comes to life each spring with a profusion of beautiful yellow
flowers. During periods of drought the leaves are shed so that less
water is lost, and the green stem, protected by a thick, waxy cover-

ing, continues the photosynthesis process in the absence of the leaves.

Arizona receives its moisture at two different times of the year, summer and winter.

The spectacular summer thunderstorms that send torrents of water, rock, and cactus down usually dry desert washes and the soft Pacific rains of the winter serve as a catalyst to the survival of most desert animals and reptiles. Getting their moisture from seeds and other forage, other desert critters can go their entire lifetime without a drink of water. Many plants are keyed to just one period of rainfall and hence only germinate either in the spring after cold winter rains or in the fall after warm summer rains.

One is not likely to see much life on the desert during daylight hours, especially during the hot summer months when the ground temperature can reach as high as 150°F. However, many animals which have escaped the harshness of the day begin their activities under the cloak of the darkness.

The wildlife in Arizona is as contrasting as her landscape, ranging from the desert animals along the Mexican border to the majestic wapiti, better known as the elk, in the high country. The elk or wapiti formerly ranged the open grasslands until an encroaching civilization drove them into the high forested mountains. In the 1890s the Merriam elk became totally extinct in Arizona. In 1913 about two hundred Roosevelt elk were brought in from Yellowstone Park and allowed to multiply. Today the herd numbers something near ten thousand. Their habitat today ranges above and below the Mogollon Rim, and in the White Mountains of Arizona. Weighing up to 750 pounds, with larger bulls weighing up to 1,000, the elk is the largest of the cloven-footed antlered wildlife found in the state. They are extremely adroit, gliding through the thick timber country, the large bulls laying their heads and antlers back and moving through the trees with ease. During winter storms they are frequently seen by travelers at lower elevations, grazing along major highways.

An important animal historically has been the beaver, made valuable because of the economic use of his pelt, especially for hatware. The first Anglo-Americans to enter Arizona did so in search of the Sonoran beaver. The beaver has been the nemesis of cattlemen and farmers because of his proclivity toward damming up streams and clogging irrigation ditches. There are still many beaver creating trout ponds today in the high meadows of Arizona. They also inhabit the waters of the Salt, Gila, and lower Colorado. Until recently a colony of beavers was living along the Santa Cruz in Tucson. However, the encroaching civilization has since swallowed them up.

The buffalo or bison is not native to Arizona although a few were shipped in from the Palo Duro and the Staked Plain country of west Texas in the early 1900s. Today there are some three hundred head located mostly at the Raymond Ranch east of Flagstaff and House Rock Valley, near the Utah border. The bull can weigh up to 2,000 pounds, while cows weigh only about half that much. They are characterized by their enormous torso and hump, contrasting with a much smaller rear. As for speed, they are most deceptive. Although from all outward appearances they are slow and bulky, the buffalo has the ability to accelerate to great speeds and has tremendous stamina. Obviously, a full-grown bison has few, if any, natural enemies in Arizona today.

There are three species of antelope in Arizona, the American antelope, the Mexican antelope, and an endangered species, the Sonoran. They are found on the open plains and plateaus of both northern and southern Arizona. They are nearly always found in bands and are characterized by their pronged horns and white rumps that flare up as they gracefully bound away. This flaglike display is caused by long white hairs on the rump patch that grow erect when the animal is excited. A small animal, the antelope weighs only about 80 to 100 pounds.

The white-tailed deer is a desert or semi-desert inhabitant, although whitetails also range into the higher elevations of the Mogollon Rim and the White Mountains. Vegetarians, they prefer the brushy hill country for both protection and forage. The white-tailed deer is characterized by its long tail with a bushy white underside that "flies like a flag" when the animal is in distress. Their natural enemies are lions, bobcats, coyotes, and during hunting season, man.

With the exception of some of the mountain ranges in southern Arizona, the mule deer habitat is statewide. The upper-elevation dwellers are called Rocky Mountain mule deer while the desert mule deer occupy the lower elevations. The two are similar except the desert species is leaner. Mule deer weigh up to 200 pounds, and as some hunters may attest, there are some even larger bucks found in the environs of the high country. The Kaibab Plateau, on the north rim of the Grand Canyon, is an isolated area some 30 by 60 miles. Kaibab is a Paiute word meaning "mountain lying down." The Kaibab mule deer, isolated on the Kaibab Plateau, can weigh up to 260 pounds. They are characterized by and derive their name from their large mulelike ears.

Perhaps the best-known of all the desert mammals is the ubiquitous coyote. They can be found anywhere in the state and are most active at night. Weighing from 20 to 40 pounds, their yapping and howling serenades are a familiar song to anyone who has spent a night in the desert. The coyote lives in family units and hunts in groups or teams. They are extremely fast and can outrun most dogs. Domestic animals, especially cats, are easy prey to the cagey coyotes, who pursue in relays, one giving chase while the others rest. They are an integral part of nature's plan, a combination of predator, scavenger, and vegetarian. As predators they eliminate the weak and diseased. As scavengers they clean up the remains of other dead animals, and as vegetarians they eat just about anything from melons to roots. They subsist mostly on rabbits, rodents, and birds. At home in any type of climate and terrain, the coyote is found in all the western states, Mexico, western Canada, and Alaska. Coyotes have even been seen in the Los Angeles area, apparently adapting well to urban life.

The gray fox is found throughout the state, especially in agricultural areas. They do most of their hunting at night. Weighing approximately 8 pounds, they are no match for dogs, and although the fox is a fast runner he usually seeks refuge in a small tree when dogs are in pursuit.

The kit fox ranges mostly in the hot sandy desert regions that stretch across the southern half of the state. Weighing only 3 to 5 pounds, they are the smallest species of foxes. The kit fox is characterized by a long, bushy tail and large ears. They subsist on rodents, birds, insects, and snakes. Their natural enemies are coyotes, bobcats, and eagles.

The ring-tailed cat is the only species of this Mexican family found north of the border. A confirmed recluse, this beautiful critter sleeps by day and hunts by night and is seldom seen by man. Preferring canyons, caves, and other broken country, the ring-tailed cat subsists mostly on mice, rats, and birds. Early-day prospectors tamed these so-called "miners' cats" to keep the rat and mice population to a minimum around the mining camps. These cats, foxes, and coyotes are all a tremendous friend of man especially in checking the rodent population.

The coatimundi strongly resembles the raccoon and ring-tailed cat and is oftentimes confused with one or the other. They are found mostly in southern Arizona's grasslands and wooded mountain regions. Expert climbers, these fleet-footed critters are active mostly during morning and evening hunting lizards, small mammals, and birds.

Preferring to live in the high plateaus and forested regions, the badger is also found in the deserts, where forage is good. Pound for pound the badger is one of the most ferocious animals in Arizona. They usually weigh from 12 to 15 pounds, although some do reach a weight of over 20 pounds. The badger is equipped with powerful legs and well-developed claws enabling him to tear into the refuges of his potential food supplies burrowed in the subterranean communities. They are usually most active during daylight hours, hunting rodents, especially ground squirrels, reptiles, birds, and fish. They have no natural enemies except perhaps the cougar and the black bear.

There are three subspecies of the mountain lion or cougar found in the state, the Kaibab, the Mexican, and the Yuma. The most common is the Mexican, found throughout the state except on the Kaibab Plateau and in the southwest corner. Next to the jaguar, the mountain lion is the largest and most powerful cat in North America. They prefer the isolated, rugged canyons away from their most dreaded enemies, man and his hunting dogs. The commonly seen Hollywood dramatization of cat attacking man is mythical, as only in the most rare and unusual of circumstances has a mountain lion ever attacked man. Reclusive and rarely seen, these, the largest of the unspotted cats, have a wide range and stalk their prey. Weighing anywhere from 120 to 225 pounds, they are clever hunters, subsisting on all types of wildlife and at times domestic animals.

Having the general appearance of an oversized domestic cat, minus the tail, the bobcat is found all over the state, although it prefers the densely wooded areas and the higher timber country. While they usually feed upon rabbits, rodents, snakes, and birds, they can kill animals as large as deer and antelope.

The black bear is found mostly in the timber and chaparral country of central and eastern Arizona. A social animal preferring the company of others of its species, it is most active during the fall, storing up fat for the winter sleep. Cubs are born, usually two to a sow, during this siesta. Black bears are excellent foragers, eating anything from garbage to putrefying meat, although they have a strong preference for berries, wild honey, and ants. They also have no natural enemies.

Inhabiting the central and southern portions of the state, especially the rugged, remote sections of the mountains, the javelina, with its acute sense of smell, is a most difficult specimen to observe. It weighs about 35 to 40 pounds when grown, although there have been some as large as 60 pounds. Even so, they are the state's smallest hoofed animals. Many tales have been told of the ferociousness of the javelina, although like most animals they are dangerous to man only when trying to defend themselves. During times of excitement the long, bristly hair stands on end from head to rump. When danger is sensed they release a musky odor as a warning to other javelinas in the area. Their diet consists mostly of cactus, plants, and fruits. An interesting phenomenon of the javelina is its proclivity for "rooting" or digging in the earth with its snout. Not a few hunters have discovered rich gold deposits embedded around the gums of the animal: the malleable yellow metal collected on its teeth while it was poking in or near some prospector's dream. Occasionally they are raised as pets but this doesn't always work out because of their unpredictable behavior.

The desert bighorn sheep at one time inhabited a large part of the Sonoran Desert up through the forest country, including the Grand Canyon. They provided a steady source of groceries for both the Indian and the early-day miner. In time their numbers were reduced to remnants existing only in the most remote sections. They did finally come under protection from the government and for many years no hunting was permitted. In recent years a limited number of permits have been issued. Today the bighorn sheep range the precipitous mountain ranges around the western border of the state. Another herd started in the Aravaipa Mountains near Safford in recent years has adapted to its new environs quite well.

The raccoon is found throughout Arizona except for the driest of desert areas. They prefer living in the bottom lands along streams and in the wooded highlands. They are nocturnal animals and do most of their prowling at night. Their food consists of just about anything from frogs to chickens to garden vegetables, and they are characterized by their desire to wash their food tediously during meals if water is available.

Living in colonies with extensive burrows and passageways, the kangaroo rat is found mostly at lower elevations and in desert regions. Most active at night, they are characterized by their long hind legs, short forelegs, and external fur-lined cheek pouches. These pouches are used for gathering food such as seeds. They are propelled by two powerful hind legs, and are guided by a long tail which acts as a rudder. They are not marsupial and therefore their pouch is not used in transporting their young. Perhaps the most unusual characteristic of kangaroo rats is they rarely drink water even when it is available. Preferring air-dried seeds to more succulent plants, the kangaroo rat creates moisture in its own body from these seeds through a chemical process during digestion. They have adapted extremely well to the arid climate and can go for months without free water. They have such an aversion to water that they prefer sand to water when bathing. Their natural enemies are numerous both on land and air. Their best defense against this legion of predators is a long, erratic jump that can extend 10 feet in flight. They can also change directions abruptly, throwing their pursuers off stride. The hopping style of transporting themselves is a distinct adaptation to existing in a sandy, loose soil.

There are four species of skunks found in Arizona. The spotted and striped skunks are found throughout the state, while the hog-nosed and hooded skunks are found in the southern and central portions. It should go without saying what comprises the skunk's arsenal of weaponry. Man and animal alike give them a wide berth, as all recognize this aromatic potency. Skunks seem to enjoy living close to humankind although it seems safe to conclude that man does not reciprocate this extension of friendship on the part of his bicolored neighbor.

There are several species and subspecies of chipmunks found in the state, inhabiting lands of contrasting terrain. They spend much of their time scampering along the ground foraging for food. They make their homes for the most part in burrows which contain a series of intricate subterranean towns.

Similar to and oftentimes confused with the chipmunk are the ground squirrels, of which there are some six species and thirteen subspecies found throughout the state. All are similar in nature, varying somewhat in color and markings. Stripes across the face of the chipmunk are a distinguishing feature that is absent on ground squirrels.

The muskrat is found along the river valleys of Arizona. Their lives are spent in or near water, where they subsist on anything from fish to frogs to vegetation. Their natural enemies are hawks, snakes, coyotes, and owls.

Cottontail rabbits are found throughout Arizona as they adapt well to all environments. They are seemingly quite romantic as they seem to reproduce whenever the spirit moves them. Litters can come at any time of the year, providing food is available: females apparently do not reproduce when forage is scarce. Characterized by a little ball of cottonlike fur on their rump, cottontail rabbits usually weigh about 3 pounds.

Jackrabbits are really hares and are larger than cottontails, although their habitat is much like that of their smaller cousin. They live in groups and are active in the early morning or late afternoon. An overpopulation of these vegetarians can be detrimental to nature; however, predators such as lions, cats, coyotes, and foxes maintain the ecological balance.

Unique and indigenous to Arizona is the Kaibab squirrel. Named for the plateau they inhabit, north of the Grand Canyon, they are distinguished by their long white tail and pugnacious but humorous disposition. Their scientific name is *Sciurus kaibabensis. Sciurus,* translated from Latin, literally means "shade tail." Actually the Kaibab squirrel inhabits a much smaller region than the Kaibab Plateau because it is dependent upon the tall stands of ponderosa pine which grow only at certain altitudes in that area. There was a time a few years ago when the Game and Fish Department unwisely okayed the killing of these squirrels. Shortly thereafter the Secretary of the Interior published a list of some sixteen endangered species in America, including the Kaibab squirrel. The Game and Fish Department immediately rescinded their order, much to the happiness of all conservationists.

There are many other squirrels in the forests, including the abert, spruce, rock, golden-mantled, and the colorado chipmunk, but none so unique as the Kaibab.

Bird life in Arizona ranges from duck and wild turkey in the northern areas to the abundant quail and dove of the central and southern sections.

The cactus wren gets its name from the flora in which it makes an oven-shaped nest, especially the cholla. They are the largest members of the wren family and are the Arizona state bird.

Literally hundreds of species of avian critters are found throughout the state, although special mention should be given to the nemesis of the rattlesnake, the roadrunner. They usually build their nest in a cactus or a paloverde tree and are characterized by their long tail, which acts as a rudder or stabilizer when speeding through the desert. When stopping, the tail flips up and serves as a brake. They can fly but only for short distances and for the most part are content to remain grounded. They subsist on other birds' eggs, lizards, and small- or medium-sized rattlers. The roadrunner will wear down the rattlesnake, who tires quickly. At the same time this desert bird will maneuver to keep the rattler out in the open where the hot sunlight will quickly kill the cold-blooded reptile. Afterward they will tenderize the meat by beating the snake on the rocks. This being done, the roadrunner will then swallow the meal in the usual manner, head first. Last seen of the snake will be the rattles protruding from the roadrunner's mouth.

The garbage man of the desert is the turkey buzzard, who gets his name from his featherless, red, wrinkled head. Rather awkward on the ground and not particularly graceful, the buzzard is a thing of eerie beauty as it glides through the desert sky looking to clean up the remnants of some other animal's kill. They are one of the desert's most prolific scavengers.

Some people consider the scorpion to be potentially the most dangerous of all desert life. There are some fifty species in North America, ranging from the merely menacing in appearance to the deadly. More than twenty of these have been recorded in Arizona. The scorpion dates back over a period of some 400 million years, the era that saw the rise and fall of the dinosaurs. Since then they have undergone little change in appearance. The most dangerous scorpion in the Southwest is the *Centruroides sculpturatus*. Seven people died in one year in Arizona from the sting of this scorpion. The venom of the larger scorpion such as the *Hadrurus arizonenis* is only 1/150 as potent as that of his smaller cousin. A sting from the larger scorpion causes only local swelling similar to that caused by a wasp or bee. The venom from the *sculpturatus* diffuses rapidly into the body tissues, attacking the nervous system, often producing convulsions and cardiac and respiratory difficulties. It is especially dangerous to small children. No fewer than fifty-four people died from scorpion sting during the years 1935 to 1949 in Arizona, although there has been only one death recorded since 1964. These are believed to be the only deadly scorpions in the Southwest, although there are several in Mexico. The *sculpturatus* species is found in the southern part of the state and in the bottom of the Grand Canyon.

Scorpions do not bite; they sting. The large pincers at the front are for holding their prey while they tear it apart with their jaws. The stinger is located at the tip of the tail. Recommended treatment for scorpion sting is to place an ice pack at the site of the sting. Old-timers recommend using ammonia when ice is not available. Medical care is, of course, advisable. In earlier days mothers used to cover infants' cribs with screen wire at night lest some scorpion crawl across the ceiling and fall into the bedding. The best rule to follow is to remember that the smaller the scorpion, the more deadly it is likely to be. The deadly *sculpturatus* is easily distinguished by its straw-colored slender-tailed body, about 2 inches in length, contrasting with the non-deadly type, which are usually larger and have a broader body. Scorpions are found under rocks in the desert, in wooded areas, and along ditch banks. As menacing as the scorpions are in both myth and reality, the fact is that the common honeybee is more dangerous, being responsible for more deaths than snakes or scorpions.

There are two poisonous spiders in Arizona that constitute a danger to man, the black widow and the brown recluse. They both enjoy locating in such fly-infested places as outdoor privies. People using these toilets, unaware that they are invading the sanctuary of these normally shy spiders, have been bitten in the most sensitive and unmentionable places.

There are many species of reptiles in Arizona. Most are harmless to man, though too often they are slaughtered out of man's innate fear of anything that crawls upon the ground. This chronicle will concentrate mainly on the reptiles which have, for one reason or another, gained notoriety in the Southwest as "the bad guys."

There are only two poisonous lizards in North America and only one poisonous lizard in the United States, and it resides in Arizona. Black and orange, feeling much like an Indian beaded belt, the reclusive Gila monster is a chunky lizard reaching a length of about 12 inches. Their food consists mostly of bird and reptile eggs and rodents. They are usually non-aggressive unless provoked; when one does bite, the jaws lock in such a way that the only way to free it from your body is literally to rip its teeth out. The teeth are constructed in the jaw in such a way as to make this easier than it sounds. Not being equipped with syringelike fangs, the Gila monster must salivate its poison into the wound as it tears the flesh. Therefore, it stands to reason that the faster it is removed, the better. Though it looks sluggish, the Gila monster is extremely quick when angered. They are especially fond of hens' eggs and in captivity they enjoy lounging in a pan of water for hours at a time.

The only poisonous snake found in Arizona that is not a member of the pit viper family is the Sonoran coral snake. The coral averages about 18 inches in length and has a tiny mouth, making it most difficult for it to bite an adult except in such areas as between the toes or fingers where it can open wide enough to take hold and chew. It is a relative of the cobra family and the venom is highly toxic. The North American coral and the harmless king snake bear a strong resemblance to one another because of similar coloration. Both species sport the colors black, red, and yellow. The coral snake has black, red, and yellow rings encircling its body. The red and yellow colors are always in contact or situated next to one another. Also its snout is black. It may sound rather corny but the best way for the novice to remember the difference is to memorize this little ditty: "Red on yellow kills a fellow." The king snake is also tricolored and appears to be similar except that the colors are not in the same arrangement as on the coral. Probably the best advice is never to antagonize or handle either kind.

There are some sixteen species of rattlesnakes in Arizona. All are cold-blooded and therefore hibernate in cold weather, becoming quite sluggish when the temperature drops. During spring and fall months they can be found sunning themselves out in the open, but during the hot months they confine their activities to cooler times of the day or night. Direct exposure to the hot sun will kill a rattler in a short time.

The species known as the sidewinder gets its name from the peculiar sidelike looping method of locomotion. The sandy habitat of the sidewinder has caused it to adapt to this unusual method of travel, which consists of thrusting the body forward sideways, then using the front part to act as an anchor to push the back half ahead. Averaging less than 2 feet in length, it is distinguished by two small horns above the eyes. The sidewinder doesn't need to coil to strike and is very quick. They are known to bury themselves in the sand, the only visible part being the head, while waiting for their prey.

The most notorious creature in the desert, both by reputation and folklore, is the western diamondback rattlesnake. Reaching a length of over 6 feet and at times known to be aggressive, this rattler accounts for the majority of deaths from snakebite in North America.

The jaw on the rattler is hinged in such a way as to allow it to open its mouth more than 180 degrees for biting, and it can also swallow an object five times the diameter of its neck. The fangs are as large as 1 inch long and can eject up to 75 per cent of the venom supply on a single bite. Baby rattlers are born alive and are deadly at birth. Also, a rattler will not be rendered harmless if defanged. It will simply grow another set.

Its diet consists mostly of rodents and small rabbits. It will eat twice its weight in a ten-day period. Once it bites its prey and injects the venom, the snake's digestive process is already taking place within the victim. The doomed critter will go off somewhere to die and the rattler, equipped with an acute sensory device, will follow some distance behind. When it locates the victim it will move around to the front and swallow it whole, taking always the head first.

Ninety per cent of the people bitten by rattlesnakes are bitten on the extremities. However, the mortality rate in treated cases is less than 1 per cent. It has been estimated that fewer than a hundred people are bitten annually in the United States.

The venom of the rattlesnake is quite complex, consisting of several qualities that work on the victim. Most people who die from snakebite actually expire from shock or blood poisoning. The venom consists of a constituent which deactivates the white corpuscles, allowing bacteria to enter the wound unhampered. There are also digestive enzymes which cause the flesh to deteriorate. Tetanus shots must also be given in case of snakebite.

The most dangerous member of the rattlesnake family is the Mohave. The Mohave is a desert rattler found at elevations over 1,000 feet, packing an arsenal of venom many times more deadly than its relatives.

Recent studies have done much to dispel old myths about rattlesnakes. Some of these results are listed as follows: they can and will strike above their head; they can bite in water; they can lift themselves from an upside-down vertical position and bite, making it unwise to hold them by the tail; they can strike only about half the distance of their body. J. Frank Dobie mentions in his book *Rattlesnakes* that about one in a hundred rattlers is of such mild-mannered temperament that it can actually be kept as a pet.

A professional golfer's swing has been measured at 27 miles per hour, while a rattlesnake strike has been timed at only 5½ miles per hour. Before one deduces that the rattler is slow on the draw, that 5½ miles per hour calculates to a speed of 8.1 feet per second. Much too fast for the average person to challenge.

Rattlesnakes are pit vipers and the two pits come equipped with sensitive "range finders" similar in nature to heat-seeking missiles which allow them to zero in on a warm object with uncanny accuracy. The pit contains two chambers, the back chamber separated from the front by a membrane full of nerve endings. These are special infrared sensing devices which give them excellent depth perception, perfectly gauging the distance and timing of the strike. On top of this, their eyes are very good. In tests, a blindfolded rattler would follow the movement of a warm object held some 6 feet away. When the object was moved, the snake would move but wouldn't strike. As soon as the object was brought within range, the rattler would strike immediately, and was right on target. Without the lethal venom and the keen sensory devices, the rattler would be at the mercy of all its adversaries. A mature rattler over two years old has only one enemy and that is man. With all the expert equipment that nature provided the rattlesnake, it still must crawl on the ground, thus rendering the young ones easy prey to hawks and other snakes and leaving the mature ones at the mercy of man.

The rattler, contrary to popular belief, doesn't always give a warning before striking. Another study was conducted recently on the rattles as a deterrent to an adversary. Two weasels were put in a cage with a rattler. The snake rattled furiously and the weasels maintained a safe distance. Next, a large bull snake was substituted for the rattler. The bull snake reared and struck furiously but the weasels attacked and devoured it almost immediately. The rattler was then placed back in the cage, this time minus the rattles. Without this warning device, the rattler was soon devoured by the weasels, no doubt lending proof to the idea that the rattling is a most effective scare tactic in warding off enemies. Incidentally, the number of rattles on a snake does not give one an accurate reading of the snake's age. They merely indicate the number of times the snake has shed its skin, as each time it sheds, a new rattle appears. Sometimes rattles are broken off, and sometimes a snake will shed more than once a year.

The reaction to snakebite will differ from person to person, as there are many things to consider, including the species of snake, whether it has bitten or injected the venom supply recently, and the reaction of the victim to the poison both mentally and physically. The treatment of snakebite has been the subject of much controversy. Some doctors recommend the "cut and suck" method, while others call for use of ice water. All agree that the victim should remain as calm as possible and get to a hospital immediately. The first thirty minutes are of utmost importance. A few minutes after a bite, only two small puncture wounds are visible, leading many victims into a false sense of security. They have been known to stop and eat on the way to the hospital. Obviously, this is not recommended.

These are but a few of the many critters that inhabit the Arizona country. For further practical study of the animals and reptiles, a visit to the Arizona-Sonora Desert Museum near Tucson is highly recommended. There they can be viewed and studied in their natural habitat.

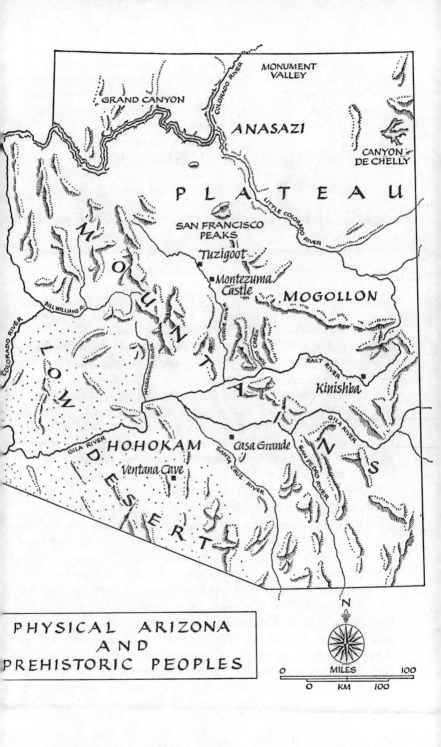

PHYSICAL ARIZONA
AND
PREHISTORIC PEOPLES

THE ONES WHO WERE
HERE BEFORE—
MOGOLLON, HOHOKAM, ANASAZI

PEOPLE WHO HAVE NOT developed a written method of recording events in their lives are referred to as prehistoric. In Arizona that would mean anything prior to the coming of the Spanish, or the years preceding 1540.

Recent discoveries have now placed man on the earth as far back as 3 to 5 million years ago. It is not known exactly when man first walked the land that is now Arizona. It might have been 25,000 or even 40,000 years ago. The science of archaeology is concerned with the study of prehistoric peoples, and we use the studies of the cultural anthropologists further to understand ancient peoples. The Southwest with its many prehistoric sites provides an excellent field laboratory for scientists. New discoveries are being made every year, many by amateurs rather than professionals. The famous Folsom discovery in New Mexico was made by a black cowboy named George McJunkin. Backyard gardeners in residential areas have uncovered ancient pottery intact, while entire villages have been discovered by construction workers building some new freeway. Scientists tell us that there is much more under the surface than has been uncovered to date. Unfortunately, many relic hunters have surreptitiously gone into an area and haphazardly removed many of these treasures to sell or use as a private collection. These amateur "collectors" too often destroy forever the knowledge that might be gained from the complex study that is required by scientists in the long process of determining the life-styles of these enigmatic prehistoric peoples. Recently groups of interested citizens have set up volunteer lookouts to keep watch over the ancient grounds in an effort to preserve them for the collection and study that will benefit all mankind in their quest for knowledge.

There are approximately twenty procedures available to archaeological research which can aid in the establishment of chronology. Carbon dating determines the age of prehistoric sites by measuring the radioactive carbon released from decomposed materials. This technique involves great skill and expensive labs to avoid contamination. Basically the process is to take an organic substance such as wood, charcoal, bones, or feathers and burn it in closed gas tubes with pure oxygen ignited by electric wires or arcs. The organic material is thus converted to carbon dioxide gas. The gas is then passed through a very sensitive scintillation-counter tube (similar in nature to a Geiger counter). Radiation given off by the disintegrating carbon atoms is measured and counted. This information is then computed with known data and a rough date is determined. It is possible to date material as far back as 1 million years by the carbon dating technique.

One of the more accurate methods used in determining the ages of these prehistoric peoples is tree ring dating or dendrochronology. Certain kinds of trees have rings, of varying width depending upon the amount of annual rainfall. Developed in Arizona by Dr. Andrew Douglass, dendrochronology is the science of comparing growth pattern rings on certain kinds of living trees with rings found in the beams of ancient dwellings to determine their age. Dr. Douglass began his work around the turn of the century while living in northern Arizona's timber country. By studying the rings on cut trees he was able to learn much about their history and the land that surrounds them. The size of a tree ring tells the scientist whether the weather that year was wet, normal, or dry. The rings chronicled the long droughts that sometimes plague the Southwest for years, as well as the wet cycles. Dr. Douglass compiled a "master time chart" of tree ring data dating back thousands of years to the time of Babylon. By comparing tree rings from beams of ancient dwellings, to the master time chart, scientists can determine the year those beams were cut down or stopped growing. Dendrochronology has accurately dated the archaeology of the past two thousand years in Arizona, allowing scientists to date an ancient ruin to within a year of construction. Visitors to the Arizona

State Museum on the University of Arizona campus may view the cross section of an ancient tree and by comparing the tree ring pattern on a log with an unknown date, such as one from an ancient dwelling, to the tree ring pattern of the ancient tree sample and the master time chart, one can determine when the log stopped growing. It is not always that simple as rings sometimes vary from one locale to another and many other statistical data are used to guarantee accuracy.

Archaeomagnetism is a recent development for dating ancient materials. This method uses the earth's magnetic dipoles and the magnetic clay minerals found in such artifacts as kilns, fire pits, and pottery to date prehistoric sites. Developed during the 1950s, archaeomagnetism is a common technique of dating today and has an error factor of plus or minus twenty-five years. Potassium argon dating is used on more ancient objects embedded in certain kinds of rocks. The degree of accuracy is plus or minus one hundred to two hundred thousand years.

Pottery, once fired, is almost as durable as plastic, and is another effective means of dating. Different designs, color, and style do much to provide the scientist with knowledge about the amount of cross-culturalization and cultural influence from neighboring peoples. The construction and decoration of the old Arizona pottery was all done without the aid of a potter's wheel or any other mechanical or measuring aid.

The earliest cultures in Arizona were the Paleo-Indian, dating back perhaps thirty thousand years. Essentially they were big-game hunters who disappeared about 10,000 B.C. Perhaps this occurred because of a change of climate which caused many species of animals to become extinct. Evidence of man-made weapons has been found near Bisbee dating back some twelve thousand years.

The Desert Culture of which the Cochise Culture is one phase began about five to nine thousand years ago and lasted until about 200 B.C. Originally food gatherers and hunters, these people eventually learned to use the grinding stone and became food producers, developing a primitive type of corn. For the first time in Arizona, man took a major step toward controlling his environment by becoming a food producer.

Dr. Emil Haury, dean of Arizona's archaeologists and former head of anthropology at the University of Arizona, led a study of prehistoric life in the vicinity of Ventana Cave, 100 miles west of

Tucson. Man by nature is the dirtiest of all animals, and one who prefers to live in his own accumulated litter. Archaeologists find this character trait helpful in their research, and with all this talk of litter today, the scientist would be hard pressed for information had it not been for those ancient litterbugs. The prehistoric garbage dumps are a most valuable source of information. Litter and graffiti, once they reach a certain age, have a way of accumulating value. The more recent prehistoric peoples left their debris on top of that of early cultures, creating a series of layers. At the bottom of the debris in Ventana Cave, the scientists found remnants of the earlier Folsom Culture; located above that was evidence of the Cochise Culture. The top layer contained refuse of the modern Papago Indians, who used the cave as a refuge during the food-gathering seasons.

Anthropologists have divided the prehistoric peoples in Arizona into three major cultural divisions. These pre-Columbian peoples all shared common problems. Water was scarce and what little there was had to be used judiciously. Food gathering and producing were chief concerns. Their lives were somewhat organized and some found time for athletic games. The three groups are: the Mogollon or mountain people; the Hohokam or desert and river people; and the Anasazi or plateau people.

The Mogollon Culture evolved from the Cochise Culture after the latter had learned pottery-making during the years preceding the Christian era. Their pottery was characterized by the colors brown or red. The Mogollon people, named for the early Spanish governor of New Mexico, were located in the east-central part of the state, extending over into the mountains of New Mexico. They were a combination of dry farmers, hunters, and food gatherers. Physically they were short and stocky, with round heads, the skulls flattened at the back resulting from prolonged periods in the cradleboard during infancy. Not much is known about their religion although it may have been somewhat complex. The dead were buried rather than cremated.

There was a great deal of cross-culturalization between the three groups, with each influencing the other. Eventually the other two more dominating cultures caused a diminishing of the Mogollon. One of the earliest dated Mogollon sites is Bear Ruin, circa A.D. 600–800. This ruin is located at Forestdale, 8 miles south of Show Low. Kinishba Ruins, near Fort Apache, is perhaps the best-known

Mogollon site in Arizona. It is also an important site because the architectural design exemplifies the merging of the Anasazi and Hohokam peoples with the Mogollon. Some believe the Mogollon migrated to Casas Grandes in Mexico around A.D. 900 and merged with other cultural groups. Other scientists theorize that they were absorbed by the Anasazi.

The largest of the three groups was the Hohokam. Hohokam is a Pima word meaning "the ancient ones" or "those who have gone." The communities of two distinct groups of these prehistorics were scattered in an area of some 49,000 square miles. The River group lived along the Gila, Salt, and Verde rivers, while the Desert Hohokam inhabited the regions south of the Gila. The latter subsisted on hunting and gathering and the former became the master farmers of the Southwest. Originating some three hundred years before Christ, some of the canals they engineered for irrigation are still in use in the Salt River Valley today. There may have been as many as 250 miles of canals in use throughout the valley. During the peak years, A.D. 1000 to 1200, there were as many as fifty thousand people living in the Salt River Valley. The Pueblo Grande Ruin, on East Washington Street in Phoenix, was a large community during this period and has thus far resisted the onslaught of modern civilization. Much to the displeasure of anthropologists, the Hohokam usually cremated their dead. Unfortunately this destroys much of the evidence needed to piece the cultural puzzle together.

Their main crops were maize, corn, cotton, beans, squash, and tobacco. The extensive canal systems enabled them to move into areas away from the river, thus granting them much more affluence and mobility. The fact that they were relatively affluent is evidenced by some of their structures, which included ball courts. Any society with time enough on its hands to participate in or watch athletic contests didn't spend all its time fighting for survival against the elements.

The cultural influence of the Salado peoples brought the Hohokam out of the traditional pit houses and into pueblo-type compounds sometime around A.D. 1100. The most famous of these was the Casa Grande Ruins near Coolidge. During its heyday, Arizona's first "skyscraper" was four stories high and had sixteen rooms. The walls were 4 feet thick at the base, tapering off to 18 inches at the top. The building also had a calendar, or at least that is what is generally believed. In the east and center walls, two holes 1.5

inches (3.5 cm.) in diameter were driven through. A beam of sunlight will penetrate through the east wall and enter the hole in the center wall in early March and again in early October. It is not known for certain, but it could be that this beam was to signify the time for planting and harvesting. There are other markings that twentieth-century man has been unable, as yet, to explain. Like the enigmatic Hohokam themselves, these things, for the time being, remain a mystery.

Sometime around A.D. 1400 the Hohokam disappeared. Where they went, if they went at all, has never been determined for certain. Possibly they drifted southward into Mexico, or, as others insist, they were the progenitors of the Pima and Papago tribes. It is generally believed the soil in the Salt River Valley became waterlogged and full of alkaline. Rather than face the threat of famine they withdrew. Ironically there might have been too much water rather than too little to sustain a culture in the valley.

The best-known and the most studied culture in the Southwest is the Anasazi, a Navajo word meaning "ancient ones." Located in the Four Corners area, this group built a society and sustained a lifestyle for several hundred years on some of the most arid, unproductive soil in America. The culture has been divided into two stages, called Basketmaker and Pueblo. Period I of the Basketmaker Period has been lost in history; however, Period II, from A.D. 200 to 500, saw the people adopting an agrarian society. Their homes were circular, one-room structures with clay floors and a fireplace in the center. Period III, from A.D. 500 to 700, brought with it the use of the bow and arrow instead of the primitive spear. Beans were added to the diet, the dog was domesticated, and the people learned to make music on a primitive flute. Following this period the Anasazi moved into more protective surroundings, perhaps because of the danger presented by more warlike tribes. The building of masonry-walled houses marked the beginning of the Pueblo stage. During this period, their pottery became more polished than the dull finish of former times. Around A.D. 1100 numerous pueblos were constructed, signifying an increase in population, including an urban center where more people could live in a small area. This was America's first attempt at condominium living. The largest apartment house in the United States prior to 1880 was a complex consisting of eight hundred rooms and thirty-two kivas (religious ceremonial rooms) at Pueblo Bonita in Chaco Canyon. Many of the old ruins such as Keet Seel, the largest and best-preserved in Arizona, and Betatakin, so remote that it was not seen by a white man until 1909, can be visited today.

Physically, the Anasazi were a tall people, some standing over 6 feet tall, with a relatively heavy bone structure. Their heads were rather long. Flat places found on the back of some skulls were the result of prolonged periods when they were strapped into a cradleboard during infancy. Study of fecal samples show they ate everything from chokecherries to yucca fibers. In one sample, a 3-inch cactus spine was found. One would hope they did soften these somewhat before eating. These studies are quite helpful to scientists in determining how these people subsisted and what were the driving forces in their lives. Recent discoveries in Anasazi ruins have lent evidence to the fact that these ancient people made a practice of cannibalism. Unusually large numbers of broken or crushed bones such as femurs indicate that the marrow contained within was a source of food and nourishment. These unfortunate souls could have been captives or deceased comrades. Food was stored as a guard against lean years. Dendrochronological dates have shown evidence of a great drought from 1276 to 1296 which caused a major shift in their living patterns. Areas such as Mesa Verde in southwestern Colorado were abandoned and the population shifted to the Zuñi, Hopi, and Rio Grande pueblos.

The Anasazi buried their dead in refuse heaps, not because they cared less for the deceased, but rather, it was simply an easy place to dig.

The years prior to A.D. 1500 were the final and greatest for the Anasazi; they were at the height of their glory. They migrated north into Utah, west to California, south to the Mogollon Rim, and east to the Pecos River. Subcultures developed and split away from the mainstream of Anasazi life.

An important subcultural group was the Sinagua. The Spanish translation of the word is "without water." These people settled mainly along the Verde River in central Arizona. Today evidence of the Sinagua culture is found at Montezuma Castle and Tuzigoot in the Verde Valley, the Walnut Canyon southeast of Flagstaff, and Wupatki near the Sunset Crater. It is believed that the Sinagua broke away from the mainstream of the Anasazi around A.D. 900. When Sunset Crater erupted in A.D. 1064 the resulting lava ashes left a thick layer of black mulch in the region east of Flagstaff. This water-conserving mulch gave much impetus to agricultural ventures by the Sinagua and for some two hundred years supported a population of more than four thousand farming families.

Another subcultural group, the Salado, are believed to be a blending of the three major cultures. They settled along the Salt and Gila river valleys around A.D. 1100. They had some influence upon the Hohokam, especially in architectural designs. The Salado influence is seen in Casa Grande on the Gila River. Unlike the Hohokam, the Salado buried their dead. This burial custom did have its effect on the Hohokam, as they ceased the practice of cremating their dead in the latter stages of their culture.

Along the Colorado river drainage system, a culture existed which is known as the Patayan, established about 5,000 years ago. This is evidenced by various stone tools and projectile points. The people gathered vegetable foods and hunted. By A.D. 500 it is noted that they were planting crops along the rivers' fertile flood plain. This was sometimes hazardous to farming due to the ever present chance of flooding and course variation of the great river. Such course alteration has also removed much of the archaeological records for the area.

Sometime after A.D. 1200 the Patayan Culture declined. However, it is suggested that they may still live on as the present native occupants of the Colorado River canyons.

One of the great enigmas of the Southwest is the lack of conclusive evidence as to what became of these peoples. From the time of their disappearance in the 1400s to the early accounts by historians in the 1700s there is a great vacuum. It is believed by many that their descendants are the Pueblo Indians of the Rio Grande, Zuñi, and Hopi villages. There is evidence in the Indian legends to support this. Their living patterns might have changed from other causes. It is known there were extreme droughts from time to time, and raids from nomadic Ute, Navajo, and Apache. These and other causes such as internal conflicts could have effected a change in their life-styles and habitats. Perhaps the answer lies in some undiscovered site. Evidently there was some great upheaval, for when the Spanish came, they noted signs of a great change which had occurred only recently, and they were not able to do much more than speculate as to what had transpired. The Anasazi, Hohokam, and Mogollon had all come and gone—disappearing like some wisp of smoke from a distant campfire. No one knows for sure where they went or why.

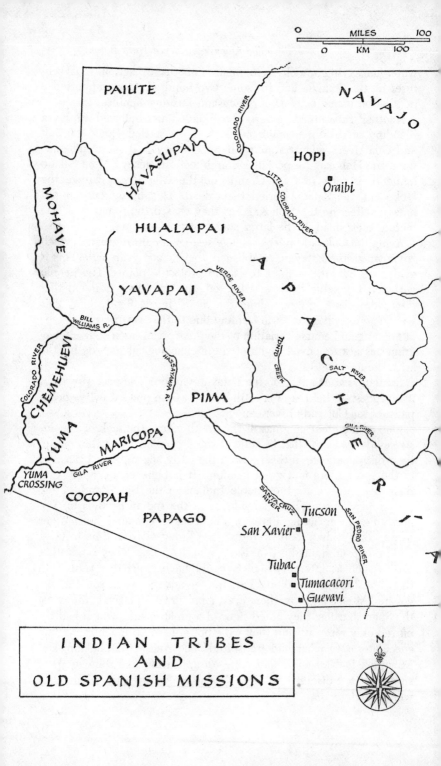

**INDIAN TRIBES
AND
OLD SPANISH MISSIONS**

THE PEOPLE

MAN ARRIVED LATE on the scene on the North American continent. Some scientists believe a land bridge perhaps 1,000 to 2,000 miles wide linking Alaska to Asia existed periodically during the past forty thousand years, the last time being some ten thousand years ago. It is believed that hunters in search of game followed this pathway, called Beringia, to the New World. Their descendants became what we know today as the native American Indians.

By and large these Indians were nomadic, drifting ever southward down the continent, never staying long in one place as they followed their prey. Their cyclic lives revolved around environment, religion, and nature's inhabitants upon which they subsisted. Thousands of years later the descendants of these prehistoric cultures battled each other in a series of raids and counterraids over such things as women, hunting grounds, and horses on the Great Plains of the American West. The strong tribes inhabited the more suitable locations and the weaker ones either moved on to less desirable areas, were exterminated, or were enslaved and eventually assimilated into the dominant groups.

Ironically, some of the tribes arrived in the geographical areas that they are identified with today after white men had already claimed the land for some European monarchy, though in reality neither race had made any permanent attempts to settle it.

Equally ironic is the fact that the Indian, especially on the Plains, owed his greatest glory to two essential items supplied by the white man. They were steel, from which he obtained traps, knives, axes, other weaponry, and cookware; and the horse.

When the white man arrived the Indians were still living in the stone age. This may be attributed to the fact that they didn't feel compelled to seek that evolutionary step into the steel age as malleable native metals such as gold and silver were available to be hammered into fine jewelry. Flint, chert, and obsidian were chiseled into suitable tools that satisfied their needs for hunting, warfare, and farming.

The significance of the horse in the culture, especially on the Plains, cannot be underestimated. The small ponies, refugees from Spanish stock, arrived on the Plains in the 1700s and gave the Indians far-reaching mobility for both warfare and hunting. As a pack animal the horse could pull several times the amount of baggage on a travois as his predecessor, the dog. With the horse there was less waste in the hunting of the buffalo as they could kill only what they needed. The old way of trying to cajole a herd toward some distant cliff was, at best, wasteful and not always successful. There was less hunger after the arrival of the horse because the hunters could meet their prey on more equal terms. Next to some act of bravery in the face of the enemy there was no greater opportunity for glory and excitement than the buffalo hunt. Although these traditions were already in existence prior to the horse, the arrival of the four-legged "God-dog" or "medicine-dog" intensified them greatly.

Another irony of history is that the horse originally existed on and about those same plains thousands of years before. They eventually drifted northward, crossing the Asian land bridge and winding up in Europe. Perhaps they even passed man traveling in the opposite direction as the hunters wandered southward into North America.

Some tribes in Arizona came from Mexico. Evidence of this is found in their language and customs. Other tribes such as the Apache and Navajo were wanderers, coming down to the Great Plains from Canada. These two nomadic tribes would be driven to the Southern Plains and eventually westward by the stronger tribes during periods of great cultural transition by the western Indians during the 1500s.

The Indian tribes in Arizona are as vastly different as is the terrain which they occupy. Many of the tribes still maintain their ancient, time-honored customs, living much the same as their ancestors. Others such as the Navajo and Apache have adjusted their way of life, economically speaking, to take advantage of vast natural resources of the land and convert them into a means of creating wealth for the tribe.

Arizona maintains the largest Indian population in the United States. There are nineteen reservations in the state. Various legislation down through the years has set aside large portions of land for Indian use. Sometimes the boundaries of these lands have been a matter for dispute between the tribes, and between the tribes and the government.

In 1887, the Dawes Act separated the land into 160-acre parcels to be divided and distributed among the Indians. The land was to be turned over to individuals after being kept in trust for a period of twenty-five years. Between the land swindlers and the population growth, the program failed for the obvious reasons. The program did provide many jobs for bureaucrats in Washington but provided little for the red man. In 1924, the Indian was granted full citizenship by his benevolent grandfather in the nation's capital. Ironically, the first Americans were not recognized as American citizens by the government until that late date. The 1934 Wheeler-Howard Act restored the tribal system and the reservations became as they once were in terms of governing. However, it was not until 1948 that the Arizona Supreme Court allowed the Indian to vote if he lived on a reservation!

The Indians, like the land, have many similar features and to the casual observer may tend to look and act alike. The land in Arizona changes dramatically from desert and plateau to forest and mountain. The differences between Indian tribes in the state are no less dramatic. Closer examination reveals a diversity of physical features as well as great differences in culture.

There are many different languages spoken by Indians in Arizona. A number of these are similar and perhaps spring from a common source. To lessen the confusion, etymologists divide the tribes into three major linguistic groups: the Athapascan, Ute-Aztecan, and Yuman. A small group of Shoshonean-speaking people inhabit northwestern Arizona. Although the languages might be similar, many other facets of the cultures are quite different.

The first Indians encountered by the white man in what is today

Arizona were the Papago. The Spanish called them Bean Eaters but like most tribes they had a word in their own language for themselves, *Taw-haw-no-aw-o-tahm,* which means "the desert people." Living on the second largest reservation in the United States, the Papago are now economically the poorest people in the Southwest. Their reservation runs south from below the Gila River all the way to the Mexican border. During times of drought, the arid land will hardly sustain the livestock on which much of the Papago economy is based. In the past they grew crops by "flash flood" farming. During the summer rain season they would move their homes to low-lying areas that were subject to flooding. When the rains came they planted their crops. Harvesting took place in the fall. Today there is still some "flash flood" farming but more modern methods of irrigation are gradually improving their life-style. The land is still devastated by droughts periodically. When the Spaniards arrived they found the Papago raising beans, corn, and squash. The newcomers introduced many new crops and taught the natives the rudiments of farming and cattle ranching. During the winter they maintain "quarters" in the higher elevations of the Baboquivari Mountains, where water is more plentiful. When the saguaro cactus comes into bloom they harvest its fruit. The pulp is made into a sweet jam and the juice is fermented and used as a ceremonial drink.

They are a communal people and their moral and religious leader was the Keeper of the Smoke, who presided over nightly meetings of the council. In early days he wielded a great deal of authority. Today, many Papago are of the Roman Catholic faith. The mission San Xavier del Bac, near Tucson, accommodates the Papago who live in the area as well as providing a school for the youth. The only communal activity they participate in today is the annual tribal cattle roundup.

The Papago have a fairly strong family unit; the sons and their families as well as the unmarried daughters remain with the family. Today the tribe is governed by a council of elected representatives. The tribal headquarters is at Sells. They are closely related to the Pima and possibly are descendants of the ancient Desert Hohokam.

Living in the valleys of the Salt and Gila are the Pima, or as they call themselves, the Akimoel Awatam, or "river people." Like their cousins to the south, the Papago, they speak the Ute-Aztecan language. When the Spaniards first encountered these river people and tried to interrogate them, the natives kept answering, "Pim," which meant "No," or "Don't understand." This resulted in the Spaniards naming them Pima.

Since their traditional land bordered Apachería the Pima served as the first line of defense against the hostile Apache during the Spanish colonial period. Later, as American immigrants moved west to California during the gold rush, the friendly Pima villages served as a supply base for the Argonauts prior to the long trek across the hostile deserts that lay ahead. Many Pima served in the United States Army as scouts during the Apache campaigns in later years. During this same period, there was cause for hard feelings among the Pima toward the white man over the giving of bribes and other appeasements to the Apache. The Pima, by being friendly to the white man, received nothing for his favors, while the Apache was being supplied with food and given large grants of land. It has been suggested that the Pima should have declared a small war upon the Americans. No doubt they would have lost; however, they might have gained a rich government contract or two, along with a sizable beef herd and other benefits.

The first white men noted the commune-type societies of the people living along the Gila River. The Pima government rested with a hereditary chief and a council. The youth of the Pima married "early and often." The young people were allowed to select their own mate. When a youth selected a bride he visited her home in the company of a young married friend who pleaded his cause for him. The suitor waited hopefully in the background, saying nothing. After several nights of this wooing by proxy, the prospective husband was either accepted or rejected without further ceremony. If she accepted, gifts were given to the bride after the informal ceremony but no gifts were made to the bride's parents as was the case in many other tribes. It was the custom for a widower to wed the sister of his deceased wife. If at any time a couple was dissatisfied with the union, they were allowed to swap partners with another, agreeable twosome.

Separation was lightly regarded and easily effected. The woman just went home to her parents or went off with another man, while the husband made similar arrangements.

Male children were preferred because they grew up to fight the Apache, the traditional enemy of the Pima. Deformed children were destroyed with the consent of the parents. Babies were sometimes nursed until they were six or seven years old.

Adultery was punished by turning the woman away from the home. The illegitimate daughters of prostitutes were destroyed in fear that they might grow up like their mothers. Because of the mild weather in the river valleys, neither sex wore much in the way of clothing from the waist up.

Upon returning from battle with their traditional enemy, the Apache, custom was that if a Pima had shed blood, the returning warriors would paint their faces black and seclude themselves from their women. However, if no blood had been shed by any Pima, their faces were painted white and the celebration was enjoyed by all. They were proud and able warriors, contrary to myth which always pictures them as peaceful, subservient farmers. According to tribal legend the Pima came away from battle with the Apache more often victorious than not.

The Pima were and are highly skilled in such handworks as earthenware, basketry, horsehair, and weaving. A Crafts Center near Sacaton along Interstate 10 serves as a museum and commercial outlet for the river people today.

The first Arizonan killed in World War I was a young Pima from Sacaton, Mathew Juan. Major Urban Giff of the U. S. Marines is thought to be the first Pima ever commissioned by the leathernecks. Giff, who received his commission in 1960, is from the Salt River Valley. Perhaps the most famous Pima of them all was a young man who had the fortune, or misfortune, of posing for the famous photograph of the flag-raising at Iwo Jima. The tragic story of Ira Hays and his struggle with notoriety has been dramatized both in song and by Hollywood.

Another tribe related linguistically to the Pima and Papago is the Yaqui. Originally from Mexico, they are not considered native U.S. Indians. The Yaqui stubbornly resisted Spanish and Mexican encroachment upon their land and were considered the most fierce warriors in all Mexico. Their history of resisting the white man in Mexico closely parallels that of the Apache and his epic struggle with the American government in the last half of the nineteenth century. During the times of political upheaval in Mexico, the Yaqui sought refuge in the United States after choosing the losing side in the struggles. There were attempts by Mexico to have them returned, but the United States refused to have them extradited.

Today they live mainly in three communities, one in Scottsdale, another south of Tempe, and the third in Tucson.

The fourth tribe from the Ute-Aztecan linguistic family in Arizona is the Hopi. Although related linguistically, they are otherwise quite different from the Pima, Papago, and Yaqui. Some Hopi also speak Tewan, a language derived from the Pueblo peoples along the Rio Grande. Calling themselves the Hopitu, or the "peaceful people," the Hopi are the only Pueblo people native to Arizona. Oraibi, a pueblo on Third Mesa, has been occupied since about A.D. 1100 and is said to be the longest continuously inhabited settlement in the United States. Once the Hopi occupied large areas of land. Following the Pueblo rebellion in 1680 against the Spanish the Hopi retreated to the high defensible plateau and its three mesas, where they still remain. Today some six thousand Hopi live on this land in north-central Arizona surrounded on all four sides by the Navajo reservation.

Much of the history of the Hopitu has been lost over the years. They have no written language, so the culture and ritual must be passed down by word of mouth, generation after generation.

When Hopi people marry, it must be to a person outside the mother's and father's clans. They rarely marry a non-Hopi; and although years ago there was some intermarriage between the Hopi and the Navajo, today these marriages are virtually non-existent.

The Hopi are a matriarchal society, and the clan is a family unit consisting of a group of people descended from a common maternal ancestor. Property such as the home, furnishings, seeds, and the garden are owned by the eldest woman in the clan. From the Spanish they borrowed the concept of community property. The man retains ownership of such things as the livestock, tools, ceremonial regalia, and the family automobile. In case of a divorce the man must leave the household. He may not take along any of the fruits of his labor for they belong to the clan, although he may keep those items mentioned above. In courtship customs it is the woman who makes the proposal. Traditionally, she does this by leaving a bag of sweets by her prospective mate's door.

The governing body of the Hopi is the Council of Elders, a body made up of clan and religious leaders. The land is held in trust by the tribe and it is apportioned to the clans. Discipline in the clan is usually handled by the eldest uncle. During the many ceremonies of the Hopi, a group calling themselves "the whippers" circulates among the children, swatting those who aren't paying strict attention.

A conservative, deeply religious people, their lives center around the kiva, an underground ceremonial chamber frequented mostly by the men. Each clan in the village has its own kiva where the men go for meditation, meetings, rituals, and seclusion. A ceremonial entrance is located in the roof, although there are side doors for practical use.

The strongest characteristics of the Hopi are the deep feeling for ceremony and an indomitable religious spirit. The two most important rituals are the bringing of rain and the curing of illness. The rituals have been dutifully explained by numerous writers; however, it should be noted that the highly complex, esoteric functions and meanings will probably never be fully understood by outsiders. The high point of the year is August, when the nine-day snake dance ritual is performed. Until recently outsiders were not welcome to these ceremonies except by invitation. There are strict rules which the visitors abide by. Cameras are not allowed during the ceremony.

Each of the nine days is spent in some specific ceremony; the culmination comes on the ninth day with the snake dance. Rattlesnakes are gathered from the rocky mesas and the desert land for use in the ceremony. Dancers carry these venomous rattlers in their mouths, and are accompanied by so-called huggars, whose job it is to distract the snake's attention away from the dancer's face with a feather. Occasionally dancers are bitten but apparently suffer no serious ill effects from these bites. The author had the opportunity to discuss this with a dancer who had been bitten on the cheek during his first dance. The only visible marks were two small dimple-like punctures that appeared when he smiled. When asked what medical care he received the man would only reply that the medicine man made him well. He would not discuss what treatment he received, saying only that it was part of the ritual. Following the ceremony, the gatherers take up the rattlers and release them so that they might return underground to inform the gods of the need for rain. The San Francisco Peaks, to the west of the Hopi land, are the homes of the Kachinas, the spirits of the ancestors. Each summer these Kachinas return with the clouds to bring water to the thirsty land.

The Hopi have become famous for their art and crafts throughout the world. The women are especially noted for their beautiful pottery and basketry, while the men have gained fame for their weaving, silver and turquoise jewelry, and in recent years painting and sculpture. Originally the Hopi imitated the Navajo in silversmithing. In 1938 the Museum of Northern Arizona encouraged them to develop a style of their own, which they have done to the enjoyment of all who respect and admire their creative genius.

Much to their dismay, the Hopi are completely surrounded by the Navajo. They have been at odds with their neighbors since 1600. The uneasy feelings the Pueblo people have about their larger neighbors are not without justification. Early writers referred to them as the Moqui, a Navajo word meaning "people already dead," which does seem to indicate adverse feelings.

However, the Hopi and the Navajo have also been an unusual variation of the term "friendly" enemies. In the early days when a Navajo was hungry, he would go to a Hopi village and ask for a meal. The Hopi would treat him to their finest cuisine, and when the guest was satiated, they would throw him off the mesa. Navajo relatives, not to be outdone, would organize a party for revenge, kill a Hopi man or steal some Hopi women and children, and when this was done the uneasy truce would go into effect once again. That is, until another unsuspecting Navajo stopped in for lunch and started the whole thing all over again.

Lewis Tewanima, a distance runner at the famous Carlisle Indian School, is one of the best-known Hopi outside Arizona. A classmate of the immortal Jim Thorpe, Tewanima performed in both the 1908 and 1912 Olympics.

There are seven tribes speaking the Yuman language in Arizona today. Located along the Arizona-California border and the high plateau country of western Arizona, they are a predominantly agrarian people. The tribes are the Mohave, Cocopah, Havasupai, Hualapai, Yuma, Maricopa, and Yavapai.

Historically the Mohave Indians were one of the most fierce tribes along the Colorado River. Their ability in hand-to-hand combat was unrivaled, a trait that caused smaller tribes to give them plenty of elbow room. They achieved some notoriety with the Americans in the 1860s by attacking prospectors and freighters along the road from Hardyville on the Colorado to Prescott. The Colorado River Indian Reservation was created for them in 1876 following a brief period of warfare against the U. S. Army. The majority today live on two reservations, Fort Mohave and the Colorado River Indian Reservation.

Fewer than a hundred persons make up the Cocopah tribe. Living on a small reservation south of Yuma, the majority work as farm laborers.

Living in one of the most remote yet beautiful regions of Arizona are the Havasupai Indians. This small tribe makes its home in Havasu Canyon, a branch of the Grand Canyon. The only way into the village is by helicopter or via the long, winding 7-mile trail down. It is not known for certain whether this tribe is an offshoot of the Hualapai Indians living above the rim or if they originally entered the canyon from the Colorado River to the west. Some historians say they came from the Little Colorado River Valley to the east. A peace-loving people, it is believed they were driven into the red-rock chasm by more warlike tribes. Today the Havasupai make their living by farming. Their income is supplemented by hikers and other tourists who are energetic enough to make the trip down into the canyon.

The Hualapai Indians originally lived along the Colorado River before altercations with the Mohave caused them to move eastward. Today they make their home in the high plateau country east of Kingman. Most are employed as cattlemen or lumbermen.

The tribe for which the language is named is really known as the Quechan people. When the Spanish first met the Quechan they requested a meeting with the native leader. A young man stepped forward and indicated he was "yuma," a word which meant "son of the chief." The Spanish misunderstood his oration, believing he was identifying the name of his tribe. From that time forward they were called Yuma. For years this fierce tribe controlled the strategic river crossing on the Colorado, and with it, the land route to California from Mexico and Santa Fe.

The Maricopa Indians had for years been at odds with their language kin along the lower Colorado. In the 1800s, this Yuman group moved up the Gila River, settling peacefully with the Pima where they reside today.

The traditional land of the Yavapai Indians was, unfortunately for them, the site of rich gold discoveries in the 1860s. The early settlers around Prescott waged a savage war against these nomadic peoples, who were mistakenly referred to as Apache. They were moved onto a reservation at Camp Verde in 1875 and shortly after-

ward to San Carlos. This proved unsuccessful and many moved to
Fort McDowell in the early 1900s. If plans for the building of Orme
Dam are implemented a lake will cover their lands and the Yavapai
will again have to pack up and move. The tribe is scattered today,
some living near Payson, some near Prescott and Camp Verde, and
others at Fort McDowell.

North of the Grand Canyon, in the strip country, lives a small
group of Paiute. They and the Chemehuevi Indians belong to the
Shoshonean language group. The Paiute are a part of the southern
Paiute tribe that traditionally inhabited the Great Basin, where
they were known as the "diggers." They were given this un-
complimentary sobriquet by other tribes because they subsisted
mostly on roots. During the ghost dance craze that swept through
the tribes in the late 1880s, the Paiute introduced the new religion
to some of the Arizona Indians along the Colorado.

The Chemehuevi Indians were originally from the Mohave Desert. They settled along the Colorado near the confluence of the Bill
Williams River. Today most of them live on the California side of
the Colorado River Indian Reservation.

The third major language group in Arizona is the Athapascan,
spoken by the Navajo and Apache. These nomadic people haven't
occupied the state much longer than have the white man. Originally from Canada (one must remember that the word "originally"
is a relative term), near Lake Athabasca, they drifted down on the
plains in eastern Colorado, where they were eventually driven into
the mountains by the fierce Kiowa and Comanche. Following the
usual social pattern, they moved in and weaker tribes were forced
to move on to some less desirable location.

With a population of over 125,000 and the wealthiest of all tribes,
as well as the largest, the Navajo occupy the largest reservation in
the United States. Originally called the "Apaches de Nabahu" or
"Apache of the Cultivated Fields," they carried on a war for generations with the Ute to the north, the Hopi to the south, and the
Spanish along the Rio Grande. Raiders by trade, they made many a
slave-hunting expedition on their neighbors, and were one of the
most dreaded tribes in the Southwest until 1863, when Colonel
Christopher (Kit) Carson and his troops cornered them at Canyon
de Chelly and Canyon del Muerto. Following their Long Walk
both to and from Fort Sumner, New Mexico, the Navajo have lived
in relative peace.

The family is the center of all activity among the Navajo and the home of the eldest woman or grandmother is the clan meeting place. All members of the clan are responsible for the behavior of one another. When one misbehaves, others might look at him and say, "He acts as if he had no relatives." Traditionally the Navajo are a matriarchal society and the property is retained by the woman's clan. When a man marries, he leaves his clan and joins that of his wife. Divorce was quite simple. If a man came home one day and found his saddle lying outside the hogan, there was no mistaking the message. It was time to move on.

Many of the old customs and traditions are still practiced by the elderly. When visiting an older person it is proper to let him be the first to speak. It is considered impolite simply to walk up and begin conversing. One must sit quietly for as long as it takes and in time the older person will speak. Only then is it courteous to begin speaking. When a Navajo visits another hogan he will not walk up to the door and knock. On the contrary, he will stand around outside the home quietly awaiting an invitation to enter. When it is extended he will come in; if it is not soon forthcoming he will go away.

There are many local customs and taboos among the Navajo, especially concerning the home and the land immediately surrounding them. Since the reservation is so large, many of these local taboos and customs are not always known throughout it. Following are examples of some well-known taboos: the door of the hogan must always face the east; a Navajo must never kill a snake or a coyote; they must never eat bear steak; a man must never look at his mother-in-law and must observe this taboo even though he lives in close proximity. This last is a matter of respect rather than rudeness and the family co-operates in the keeping of this ritual. Usually she would cover her face with a blanket when he approached and that would suffice.

The dead are not mentioned and when a person dies his clothes are sometimes put on backward and the moccasins are placed on opposite feet. This is to confuse the evil spirits who might want to follow the deceased. When a person dies inside the hogan, the body is removed through a hole cut in the north wall, and the hogan isn't used any more. It is possible to avoid this inconvenience by taking the person outside when death is inevitable. Since the spirits of the dead live in the north, there are no windows in the north wall of the hogan, thus prohibiting these spirits from observing the activities going on inside.

Living among the Navajo are individuals sensitive to non-physical forces. These psychics or, as they are called among the people, "hand tremblers" are known for their ability to locate missing items ranging from stolen property to downed aircraft on the remote reservation wilderness. Some of these abilities can be attributed to a vast network of informers at the disposal of the hand tremblers, but there are times when their psychic predictions defy either scientific or logical explanation.

When a Navajo is ill or disturbed, there are several options available. There is the diagnostician who can locate the ailment through ESP, knowledge, or intuition. The herbalist, who might also be a diagnostician, is adroit in the use of herbs to cure most common ailments. The serious cases go to the singer or chanter, who performs healing ceremonies which may last for as many as nine days and nights.

The medicine man is an important person to the Navajo and his hogan is constructed with great care and ceremony. The Navajo believe that bodily disorders are induced by mental or emotional disturbances, and therefore illness is the result of man being out of harmony with the universe. When this happens, the medicine man will organize a "sing," which could last from ten to fourteen days, depending usually on the wealth of the patient. Many friends will come to the "sing" in support of the patient for the gods to observe. The Navajo also believe that disease comes through the violation of a taboo. To cure the ill, sand paintings are used. The sand painting may take two to four hours to make and must follow a precise formula since mistakes are dangerous to all. However, if an outsider is watching, the medicine man will not make a perfect one but will make an intentional mistake somewhere on the painting. The sand painting is not a ceremony itself, but is related to several others, and it must be destroyed before dark.

The Navajo sweat bath is related to the preservation of health. The participants will gather hot stones and place them in the hogan. Prior to entry, each calls to the gods four times and is then allowed to enter. Following the steam bath, all take an abrasive sand bath.

The Navajo have historically been great borrowers from other cultures. They learned sheep raising and silverwork from the

Spanish; pottery and weaving from the Hopi; hell raising, it is said, came to them naturally.

The Navajo tribal government is made up of a council of elected leaders headed by a tribal chairman. They have operated under this system since 1924 when they came under the skillful leadership of their great tribal chairman Henry Chee Dodge. Navajo enjoy rodeos both as participants and spectators. Many of the young people have taken up the arts and crafts for which the tribe is known throughout the world. There is a modern college on the reservation, and although the residences near the campus are of modern structure, they are designed with traditional Navajo architecture in mind. Young people wear clothing that ranges from cowboy boots and hat to California mod. They are caught up in the same activities and customs that characterize the youth of any culture. The generation gap is not at all unlike that found in other cultures.

Today the Navajo is caught up in the beginnings of an industrial revolution. The coal mining and oil leases have been lucrative, and factories are being built. Some things never change as old people still cling to the traditional ways, thereby keeping the culture alive. A trip through the vast reservation in the Four Corners will reveal to the observer many of the old customs still being followed—the lonely sheepherder on a hillside gazing off into the distance; a silversmith practicing his skills; a weaver making her fine woven rugs; and the people in their bright traditional clothing. Time seems to stand still in this changeless land of beautiful wind-sculptured red rock, shifting sands, and peaceful serenity.

Most ethnologists believe that at one time the Apache and Navajo were much more closely related than they are today. They both speak the same Athapascan tongue, and have many other similar characteristics. They both drifted down originally from Canada. It is said that a split came and the more warlike Apache went off on his own. Like the Navajo they refer to themselves as the "Dine" ("Dineh"), or "the people." The name Apache is said to be a Spanish corruption of an old Zuñi word meaning "enemy." Another version of the etymology claims that it is a combination of the Yuman "apa" (man) and "ahwa" (war, fight, battle). Historically, the Apache has been a nomad. His life centered around the cult of the warrior. Before the coming of the Anglo-American, his traditional foe, the Mexican, provided him with a place to plunder. From west Texas to western Arizona, the Apache made his forays into the land south of the border, bringing back everything from livestock to women as plunder. He was next to impossible to pursue, for the band would split up like a covey of quail only to rendezvous at another point miles away. Worse yet, they might wait in ambush and the hunters would end up being the hunted. The Apache was a guerrilla fighter extraordinary, fighting on horseback as well as on foot. The warrior could and would travel as much as 90 miles in a single day. He knew every remote watering hole and could live indefinitely off the land. In the days before the widespread use of rifles, his weapons consisted of a lance and the bow and arrow. He would attach the arrowhead to the shaft with deer sinew. When dry, it held fast. However, when it penetrated the body, the sinew would moisten and loosen its hold on the arrowhead. When the shaft was removed, the point would remain in the wound. He would also poison his arrow points in various ways. Sometimes they would be dipped into some poisonous plant or a dead animal such as a skunk. Most pernicious, perhaps, was his technique of taking the fresh liver of an animal such as a deer and allowing it to be bitten by rattlesnakes collected for such an occasion. He would then allow the meat to putrefy for a few days. Prior to going off to battle, he would ceremoniously dip his arrow points into the rotten substance. It was said that the person on the receiving end of such a projectile suffered a most agonizing death.

The Spanish and Mexicans never came close to conquering the Apache, and the Americans did only after years of all-out campaigning.

The Apache never considered themselves a single nation. Because of the harsh conditions in which they lived, small bands were the rule. Their allegiance ran from family, to clan, to band, to group, and finally and rarely, to tribe. There were no hereditary chiefs as in some tribes. However, a chief's son could rise to a leadership role by proving himself in battle or raid. A man became a headman or leader on merit. If he failed, he was quickly dropped or ignored. If a band or clan encroached on another's rights, they would fight each other as quickly as they would fight Mexicans or Americans.

To get himself killed in a show of bravado was the last thing on the Apache's mind. To him, the real art was stealth and cunning. Women captured on a raid were always prized, not necessarily by the wives at home but certainly by the men. A woman captive could expect a harsh life, not only from the elements, but from the jealous spouses—especially if she was attractive. If captives were too young to travel, they were usually destroyed on the spot. Otherwise, the Apache raised them as their own. Many captives rose to positions of influence in the band. For an adult male captive, only the worst could be expected. The Apache, perhaps taking some lessons from his enemies, had many interesting ways of making death a long and loathsome ordeal.

The Apache had several great trails usually through the river valleys leading into Mexico, where he went in search of plunder that ranged from women and children to livestock. In the years prior to the coming of the Anglo-American, Taos, New Mexico, was the market place for the selling of captives and booty. When a woman was captured on a raid, she became the property of that warrior who captured her. However, it was most unfortunate if she was captured by two warriors, since it was a rule among the Apache to get rid of anything that caused animosities between the warriors of the band. Articles could be burned, horses killed, and a woman in the same position often met the same fate.

The Apache were endowed with many fine leaders and men of exceptional prowess over the years—men like Cochise, Juh, Geronimo, Chatto, Nana, Alchisay, Chihuahua, Victorio, and Mangas Coloradas. More will be said of these men in a later chapter.

Like the Navajo, the Apache family customs are matriarchal. The son is lost to his family by marriage, and he now belongs to the clan of his wife. Should his wife die, he would mourn for perhaps a year and then usually would marry one of his wife's sisters or cousins. In marriage, the consent of the girl's parents was necessary. During courtship, one of the suitor's relatives usually did the honors of negotiating. The usual dole to be paid to the prospective bride's father was horses. The suitor might leave several horses outside her father's wickiup and leave. If, when he returned the next day, the horses were taken and placed in the family corral, it meant his offer had been accepted. If, on the other hand, they were still standing where he had left them, it meant they were still considering his offer. If nothing was done by the second day, the prospective bride might be considered a bit stuffy. If, by the fourth day, nothing had been done to care for the horses, he was considered rejected. This was cause for great humiliation as there were probably several of his contemporaries watching the whole proceeding as he came and retrieved his dowry. He might have lost face, but was probably better off than his horses, which had gone unattended during the brief "courting" period. If the proposal was accepted, this was cause for three days of feasting. Following a week or two of honeymooning, the couple returned and moved into a wickiup near the wife's family. Like the Navajo, an Apache was never supposed to look at his mother-in-law, nor to speak directly to her. When she entered the wickiup or dwelling, he had to leave at once. In traveling together in a wagon or automobile, a curtain was hung between them so as not to violate the custom. The Apache is a very sociable person, the emphasis being placed on good character and cheerfulness, although an outsider might have to live among them for some time before becoming aware of this side of these seemingly stoic people.

The Apache are also a deeply religious people. They believe in a supreme being called Usen, who is the giver of all life. Usen is of no sex or place and the Apache cannot approach this god directly, but must go through some medium. This medium is revealed to the Apache through dreams and visions and may come in many forms, such as animals, insects, or elements of weather. Each Apache has his own medium, and when it is revealed to him, it becomes his guardian spirit or medicine.

Spirits, ghosts, and monsters are a vital part of life. The Apache believe that life for them began with the coming of the White Painted Woman of the world. She is the mother of all people. According to Apache lore, one day she was lying nude in the rain. When the water entered her body, a child was conceived and he was called Child of the Water. The child grew up and made things as they now are. He conquered the monsters and made the world safe for the people (Apache). When this was done, Child of the Water and White Painted Woman instructed the people on what was good and bad in the world. This being done, the two went to their home in the sky.

An important part of Apache tradition is the crown dancers. These dancers, who represent anonymous beings, with their ceremonial crowns and black face masks perform in most of the religious festivities, especially those dedicated to girls' puberty rites.

The medicine man is a powerful influence among the Apache even today. He is always paid for his work—the richer the client, the longer the ritual. Many Apache place more trust in the medicine man than in the Indian tribal leaders, who they feel have been influenced by the white man's bureaucratic system.

Whenever possible, the Apache preferred several wives. When one was unfaithful he might cut off her nose or ear, and when she displeased him or he felt in the mood, he might commence to beat her up. These two offenses, along with his fondness for a drink made of fermented corn juice called tiswin, were the cause of much consternation during the latter part of the nineteenth century when the Army had confined them to the reservation and was responsible for their behavior. It should be pointed out that the Apache were noted for their fidelity. Matrimonial misconduct was the exception rather than the rule. The Apache loved to gamble, even in a crooked game where he had no chance: like the old saying, "He knew it was crooked, but it was the only game in town."

When a woman was about to give birth, or as soon as labor pain set in, she was sometimes tied to a tree, hands above the head, and left in this position until the child was born. Apache women were known to give birth along the trail and be back, riding horseback, a few hours later.

Many young women today still participate in the sunrise ceremony, a sort of debutante celebration to commemorate a girl's entering womanhood. The ceremony lasts four days and requires the young lady to perform certain rituals. Older people will observe her conduct during this ordeal as it is believed that if she behaves well under this duress it is a sign that she will be able to cope with the difficulties of life.

Mule meat, horse meat, beef, and venison were relished by the Apache, but his staple diet, especially when he was on the trail, was mescal, a baked mush taken from the core of the century plant. He also carried pinole, a ground corn meal mixed with sugar, to supplement his diet. He would not eat turkey, fish, or bear meat, as they were taboo. The owl is considered to be a bad omen as are snakes. The hummingbird is considered a good omen.

The Apache, like the Navajo, had a great horror of death. The dead were buried immediately and the wickiup burned. The dead were not discussed.

He also had an aversion to crazy people. In early days, if an old prospector could convince the local bands that he was "touched," they might avoid his camp altogether. Since the nighttime was considered sacred to his ancestral dead, the Apache rarely fought after dark, preferring instead to attack just before dawn. He was not a great horseman as the Indians on the Plains were, but because of the rough terrain, he was much more skillful on foot and simply used the horse to transport him from one place to another. When hungry, he had no second thoughts when it came to eating his horse, for he could easily steal another.

The Apache practiced true democracy when it came to the choosing of leaders, and other decisions. If an individual or family was unhappy with existing conditions, they were free to move on. If they didn't approve of the leader, they were free to follow the leader of their choice. Therefore, they never felt bound by any treaty that they, as individuals, were opposed to.

Old family grudges still crop up from time to time. Some clans still bear hostile feelings as in days gone by. A fracas might start between individuals of different clans over some encroachment that occurred generations ago. Stranger still, the combatants don't even know what that encroachment was. During these disturbances the tribal police usually follow a policy of non-interference.

Today the Apache tribe occupies some of the most beautiful land in Arizona. The recreational facilities in the White Mountains are of the finest quality. There is a large ski resort and the fishing and hunting are some of the best in the state. Along with this, the tribe owns large numbers of beef cattle, while other lands are leased to the whites. In an ironic twist, the Apache has become quite a cowboy with his ranching and addiction to rodeos. They are known as America's Indian cowboys. Like the Navajo, many of the old still prefer to live in the traditional way, not that of raid and pillage, but by following other old customs.

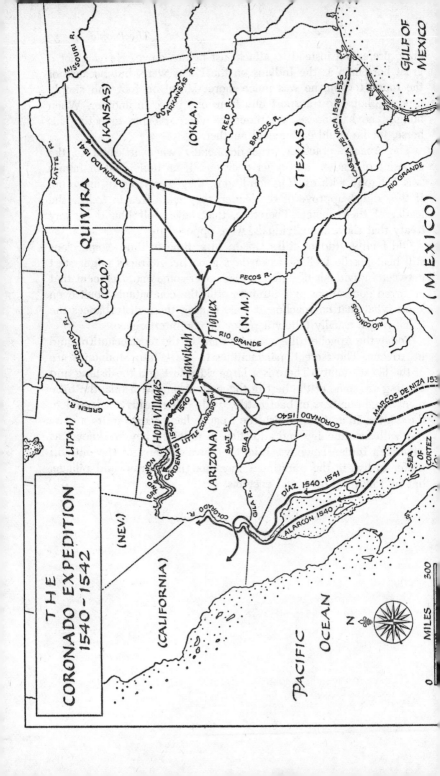

THE
CORONADO EXPEDITION
1540-1542

(UTAH)   (COLO.)

(NEV.)

(CALIFORNIA)   (ARIZONA)   (N.M.)

QUIVIRA

(KANSAS)   (OKLA.)

(TEXAS)

(MEXICO)

PACIFIC
OCEAN

GULF OF
MEXICO

SEA
OF
CORTEZ

MISSOURI R.
PLATTE R.
ARKANSAS R.
RED R.
BRAZOS R.
RIO GRANDE
PECOS R.
RIO CONCHOS
COLORADO R.
GREEN R.
LITTLE COLORADO R.
SALT R.
GILA R.
GILA R.
COLORADO R.

CORONADO 1541
Tiguex
Hawikuh
Hopi Villages
TOVAR 1540
CARDENAS 1540
GRAND CANYON
CORONADO 1540
MARCOS DE NIZA 1539
DÍAZ 1540-1541
ALARCON 1540
CABEZA DE VACA 1528-1536

N

MILES
0   300

THE SPANISH EXPLORATIONS—
GLORY, GOD, AND GOLD

THE MYTHS AND LEGENDS of golden cities and fabulous wealth in the New World in the 1500s ran rampant throughout the Old. Any story was believable as long as it reflected riches. Maps as widely different as they were inaccurate were being circulated and accepted as truth. Somewhere out there was a tribe of beautiful Amazon women who protected their virtue and their treasure with fierce determination. They were such warriors that they had their right breasts removed so as not to interfere with the bowstring as it sent the arrow flying. Another legend persisted of a gilded man who was so wealthy that each morning upon awakening his servants would oil his body, then cover him with a coat of gold dust. At the end of the day the dust would be discarded and not worn again. For some reason the number seven kept popping up. The Aztec myths told of "seven caves to the north" where there were great riches, while still another Spanish and Portuguese legend told of the exodus of Christians fleeing from the Arabs in 734. They founded the Seven Cities of Antilla, full of gold and other treasures. Where was Antilla? It was anywhere on the map one chose it to be.

Perhaps the greatest glory rested in the discovery of the fabled Strait of Anian, the northwest passage to the Orient. This all-water route to the Indies had been long sought after by the Europeans. It most assuredly had to exist, didn't it?

The year 1492 marked a turning point in man's history on this earth. Ferdinand and Isabella had united Spain into one country, the Moors had been driven out of Spain after hundreds of years of warfare, and an old, experienced seaman named Christopher Columbus was granted permission to explore the possibilities of an all-water route to the Orient.

Columbus found no riches in the New World he stumbled into, but the ones who followed uncovered riches beyond their wildest dreams. With just a few men and horses, Hernán Cortés took Mexico and the fabulous Aztec empire. Pizarro did the same with the Incas in Peru. These ventures lent no small amount of credibility to the possibilities of even greater riches to the north of Mexico City.

Into Mexico City rode one of the most formidable groups of fighting men the world has ever seen. The Spanish conquistador was bred to be a warrior. At war with the Moors for generation after generation, he knew no other life-style but that of a fighter. He was *mucho hombre* on his stallion and knew no such thing as fear. Most of the leaders coming to the New World were second and third sons of wealthy families in Spain. The laws of primogeniture whereby the oldest son inherited all sent them off to seek their fortunes by other means. They were also a romantic lot. Next to war the conquistador loved nothing more than the conquest of a fair damsel, and apparently they all must have been fair in his eyes, for Mexico City was never under such a siege as it was in the 1530s when the city was crawling with hot-blooded young Spaniards in search of wealth and fame.

The coming of the first white men to Arizona had its beginnings off the Florida coast in 1528. The Spanish Crown had awarded Panfilo de Narvaez a grant to settle in Florida. With six hundred men he set sail up the Florida coast. Charles V had been very gracious in giving these grants. Some aristocrat or wealthy person would make a sizable loan to the Crown and in return the king would grant the contributor a piece of the New World to go out and pacify. There were usually some strings attached, such as one half of the wealth found had to be given to the Crown, along with the 20 per cent tax on any treasure that might be discovered. So in 1528 Narvaez, with visions of wealth and possibly even of a fountain of youth, sailed into the Gulf of Mexico. A storm came up and the ship went down. There were a few survivors and these drifted for a time along the Gulf coast, finally beaching in the vicinity of Galveston Island. Struggling ashore, they were picked up by Indians, and thus began the epic eight-year journey back to civilization. The original group of survivors had been narrowed down to four: Alonzo Maldonado, Andrés Dorantes, Dorantes' slave Esteban, and Alvar Nuñez Cabeza de Vaca. Traded from tribe to tribe, the men enjoyed success with some and endured hardships with others. De Vaca set himself up as a medicine man and seemed to have great success treating the unfortunate along the way, thus earning extra privileges for the itinerants. While they moved slowly westward they heard tales of large humpbacked cows that grazed on the plains to the north, but more important, they heard stories of great cities up there also. The Indian concept of a great city versus the Spaniard left much room for debate, for when the Indian mentioned great cities, the Spaniard naturally thought of Paris and Madrid.

In 1536, the long odyssey ended with the discovery of the wanderers by a group of slave hunters from New Galacia, a province on the west coast of Mexico. They were taken to the viceroy of New Spain, Antonio de Mendoza, where they unraveled a story that launched gold fever throughout the New World and the Old.

Mendoza listened intently to the tales. Not only was there a possibility of great wealth, but there was also immortal fame to the man responsible for the discovery of the Strait of Anian. Mendoza was also a humane man, genuinely concerned for the welfare of the Indian. There were, no doubt, many lost souls to save in the land to the north. He decided first to reconnoiter the area before sending a large expedition. A guide was needed; somebody who had been there before. Dorantes, Maldonado, and de Vaca weren't interested. Esteban was a slave, so the viceroy purchased him from Dorantes and the black man prepared for another trip north. He and a friar named Marcos de Niza were to go north and check out the story of the great cities. Primarily they were to explore the opportunities for bringing Christianity to the heathen, but, and with a sly wink, the viceroy would also appreciate any knowledge of the existence of gold and silver. De Niza, who had been with Pizarro during the rape and pillage of Peru, was told to report his findings to the viceroy and no one else. Little did Mendoza know what a loquacious man he had picked for the job. If it was secrecy he wanted it would have been better to have sent the town crier.

In 1539 the journey began. Esteban and the friar apparently didn't agree with each other, either spiritually or morally. The

Moor, having watched de Vaca practice his hocus-pocus medicine during the odyssey, decided to pick up where his former maestro left off. Dressing himself in a wild assortment of feathers and bells and carrying a rattle, he conned the local villagers into believing he was some kind of great medicine man-magician. A lustful man, he never failed to request the services of several young women. The peaceful Indians always obliged. This behavior was a little more than de Niza could tolerate so he suggested that they split up. Esteban could go on ahead and the priest would follow, at a slower pace. The Moor would keep up lines of communication by sending a small wooden cross from time to time. The larger the cross, the closer they were to the Seven Cities. This agreed upon, Esteban left, obviously feeling a new sense of freedom.

Crossing into southeastern Arizona and along today's Arizona-New Mexico border, Esteban finally came to a village near what is now Gallup, New Mexico. Before entering, he sent back to the friar a cross the size of a man, a signal that he had found the place. Calling for a council, the Moor performed his usual rites, such as shaking his rattle in their faces. He then informed them that he was a representative of the great white race to the south. This chore being done, he asked if now he could have some women brought to him. Esteban didn't know it at the time but he was dealing with a different kind of Indian than the peaceful types to the south. These were Pueblo and they had already heard of what the great white race did to Indians in the south. Besides that, what, thought the logical-minded Indians, was a black man doing representing white men? That didn't make sense. Last of all, Pueblo women were chaste and this outsider had just audaciously requested the services of not just one, but several. To show that he was not invincible, they cut him up into little pieces right there and sent the survivors of his party scurrying back to the friar, who was by this time moving up at a rapid pace.

At this point the story takes on two versions. De Niza claimed that he traveled northward and viewed the golden city. He described it as a "land rich in gold, silver and other wealth, and great cities." He guessed the first city to have about 300,000 persons. The village he saw, if he saw it, was Hawikuh, a city built not of stone but mud and wattles. The other version of the story was that he gave his personal belongings to the surviving relatives of the deceased and hustled back to New Spain on the double. Whatever the case, the farther de Niza got from the Pueblo, the more courage he gained, and the closer to Mexico City, the more grandiose the stories of wealth became. Rumors were persistent throughout the city. The viceroy had all he could do to keep the would-be Argonauts of the city from going on their own search for the cities of gold. Each time de Niza told his story the fabled cities grew in wealth and size. It must be stated, in fairness to the friar, that he was really more interested in saving souls than golden cities, and, being a realist, he knew that if there was no wealth there would be no reason to send out the conquistadors and therefore no need to send the missionaries.

The viceroy was too busy to lead an expedition himself. He needed a front man, and he found that man in the person of the young governor of New Galacia, Francisco Vásquez de Coronado. Coronado, a handsome, dashing young man with a beautiful, wealthy wife, seemed to be the perfect choice.

The expedition was primarily sponsored by Mendoza and Coronado. The cost figures to roughly $2 million in today's terms. Prior to sending Coronado northward, Mendoza ordered Melchior Díaz with a small force to check out the friar's story. However, his patience would allow no further delay and when he received no word from Díaz the expedition went ahead. Quite possibly there would have been no expedition had they waited for Díaz, for when he did join the expedition he reported finding no great cities, no wealth, not even a turquoise stone.

The expedition left New Galacia in grand style. There were two hundred horsemen, one hundred infantry, two white women, one thousand Indian servants, and the leader clad in a suit of golden armor. Coronado would make certain that if he did meet that mythical gilded man of El Dorado, the Spanish leader would look just as impressive.

Fray Marcos de Niza and his fellow friars, traveling in the apostolic manner, that is, on foot and wearing sandals, had gone ahead of the expedition but it wasn't long before they were overtaken. Shortly thereafter when Díaz and his men joined the expedition and word began to trickle down through the ranks of what he had seen, or failed to see, the adventurers, footsore and weary from the monotonous journey, turned their wrath upon the friar.

Another factor that lowered morale was the new rule of behavior imposed on the Spaniards by the viceroy. Except in areas already "pacified," there was to be no harsh treatment of the natives. Goods taken were to be paid for and the women were to be left alone. These were orders completely alien to the nature of the conquistador; nevertheless, Coronado enforced them as best he could.

The expedition seemed born to bad luck from the start. Once while traveling through pacified country, which meant the soldiers could help themselves to anything they wanted, Lope de Samaniego led a group of foragers through the countryside. Apparently the natives weren't as pacified as Lope thought, for when he lifted the eyeguard on his helmet for a closer look, one of them shot an arrow right into the opening. It was the expedition's first fatality and Coronado decided to set a good example. He rounded up all the local natives in the area and hanged them.

While in Culiacán, they suffered another bad omen. A young man in the expedition named Trujillo had a dream which he graciously shared with his leader. In his dream, he killed Coronado and took his wife. This doesn't seem too shocking unless one considers the superstitious times in which they lived. Fray Marcos interpreted the dream as a sign that the devil himself had decided to do all that was in his power to hinder the expedition. It was up to all concerned to resist Lucifer and let nothing stop the Christians from going forth and saving the lost souls of the north. After all, that foul fiend was only jealous of the good that was going to be accomplished.

An auxiliary fleet of three ships under Hernando de Alarcón had been sent up the Sea of Cortez to rendezvous with Coronado. Unfortunately the ships had to sail in a northwesterly direction and Coronado moved more northeasterly. Alarcón did reach the vicinity of where Yuma is today. He left some notes under a tree and proclaimed that California was not an island, but a peninsula. This would have to be proven again, about 150 years later by Father Eusebio Kino. Other than that, Alarcón's fleet was of no use to the expedition.

As previously mentioned, next to war the conquistador preferred to make love. Though the rules forbade cavorting with the dusky maidens, Cupid or lust found a way. When the priests pointed out this unsavory behavior on the part of the soldiers to Coronado, he called the guilty parties together and had them mass-married, feeling that if they were to satisfy their lust, they might just as well satisfy it in the sanctity of the Church.

The Spanish were a very legalistic-minded people. Along with the priests on the journey traveled a lawyer. It was his responsibility to inform the natives that they were now under the protection of the Spanish Crown. These orders were usually read in Latin and since the natives could understand neither Latin nor Spanish, it really didn't seem to matter in which language these orders were read. Once the orders were read, the area was considered pacified and its residents citizens of the Crown. Now any violation of a rule could be punishable in the most severe way. Any practice of the old religion was heresy and punishable by death. In all fairness to the Church, one must consider the times. It was firmly believed that anyone not Christianized was doomed to hell for eternity. Therefore, the Church felt that it was solely responsible to see to it that all were saved. Little did it matter if it put one through a little hell on earth if he was guaranteed a trip to heaven upon dying.

Usually, just before an execution took place, a priest would save the soul of the doomed men, and thus with a clear conscience the executioners would send the Indians off into eternity, to everlasting heaven. There was a time several years later in New Mexico when a headman was told just before his execution that a priest would save his soul and send him to heaven. The doomed man's reply was that he would just as soon not go to heaven, as he was afraid he would find too many Spaniards there anyway.

Religious misunderstanding also had its lighter moments. One of the priests on the journey, Father Juan Padilla, placed a large cross in the ground before a group of natives. Interpreting the symbol in their own way, they began removing their garments and hanging them on the crossarms, at the same time engaging in a paganistic dance around it.

The expedition, still moving in a northeasterly direction, crossed into Arizona in the vicinity of where Bisbee is today. In the weeks that followed they crossed the Gila River and moved into the mountainous Mogollon country. It became increasingly apparent that Fray Marcos had never traveled this far north, and Melchior Díaz, who had, became the guide. Finally someone saw the city in the distance. The conquistadors could only stare in disbelief, for instead of a city larger than Mexico City, there was a village of some 150 poor natives, living in huts of mud and wattles.

The Spaniards, too hungry at the moment to think of anything but eating, made peaceful overtures, but the Indians were not in the least bit friendly; in fact, they told the soldiers to leave as they didn't feel they needed to be protected from anybody, except perhaps their new "protectors." After traditional sprinkling of corn meal in front of the Spaniards, they began firing their arrows and hurling stones at the conquistadors. His patience reaching the breaking point, Coronado sounded the charge. A conspicuous figure in his gilded armor, Coronado became a likely target. His head was rattled more than once by a boulder and he finally had to be carried from the field by his men. The battle lasted for only an hour. The Pueblo, no match for the Spaniards, called for a truce and left the village and its food supply to the hungry soldiers. The battle was fought on July 7, 1540, and though seldom mentioned in American history books, it was the first formal clash between white men and Indians in what is today's United States.

It came time for Coronado to reassess the whole operation, which so far had been a miserable failure. However, there was still a chance to salvage something. There was a lot of territory to explore and claim for Spain, and also another valuable commodity, the Indians themselves as a labor market. Spain was using the encomienda system extensively, in which natives performed the labor for the landowners. In the Spanish system, large estates were divided up and given to chief conquistadors for services rendered to the Crown. The encomienderos, as they were called, were in reality supposed to be benevolent fathers to their Indian children, teaching them the rudiments of civilization and Christendom. However, in most cases the difference between theory and practice was startling. In their greed for wealth the encomienderos drove the Indians relentlessly. Thousands died in the encomienda system, which was in reality slavery.

Coronado dispatched his most loyal lieutenant, Melchior Díaz, back to the Sea of Cortez to try to establish contact with the supply ships under Alarcón. This turned out to be a fateful trip for Díaz. When he arrived in the land of the Yuma Indians he found the message from Alarcón saying that he had been there and returned to Mexico. Díaz also found the local natives to be of a most inhospitable nature. Primitive giants, some stood well over 6 feet tall, with great strength to match. While preparing to cross the Colorado Díaz suspected foul play on the part of his hosts. Seizing one of them and "interrogating" him, the Spaniards learned that the Indians had planned to wait until Díaz's forces were split, then attack them. The captive was then killed and secretly submerged in the river. When the attack came the soldiers were ready. The hapless natives were no match for the conquistadors and the battle was over in short order. Crossing the river and into the area known today as the Imperial Valley, Díaz suffered an accident that cost him his life. The party had with them a greyhound dog belonging to one of the soldiers. The dog was chasing the sheep that the party had brought along for food. Díaz rode after the dog and heaved his lance at it. The lance missed the dog but stuck in the ground in front of him. Díaz couldn't stop his horse in time, and by some freak accident was thrown onto the lance. The spear entered his groin and ruptured his bladder. He lived for twenty days in great pain before dying in the desert near the Colorado. Coronado received the news of his lieutenant's death with great sorrow. His men reported that it would be fruitless to search for gold in that vast desert west of the Colorado. It seems almost comic-opera bad luck that Coronado, in his quest for gold and silver, had come so close. First, he had traveled within rock-throwing distance of the great silver deposits in the San Pedro Valley around Tombstone, and second, he passed up the opportunity to go to California, and the grestest gold strike of them all.

Coronado had also dispatched Pedro de Tovar westward from Hawikuh to the land of the Hopi. Friar Padilla, a former soldier, accompanied him. The Hopi, living in structures similar to the Zuñi already encountered, were no more friendly than their counterparts to the east. When the Spaniards approached the village, the Hopi, as was their custom, spread corn meal on a line and challenged the visitors to cross over. When they did, one of the Hopi ran up and clubbed a horse. With that the Spaniard followed his basic instincts and charged. The battle lasted for only a short time, and though there were only twenty soldiers in the force they weren't long in dispensing of the Pueblo people. So peace was made and another Indian tribe was pacified. Before Tovar returned to the main force he was given an important piece of information. To the west was a great river. When he presented this bit of information to his leader, another foray was quickly planned. The whole expedition could be salvaged if, by some chance, that river might be the one leading to the sea. García López de Cárdenas and twenty-five men were dispatched to check out the story. The trip took twenty days but the river was never reached, for the party arrived at the edge of the

Grand Canyon. The thoughts of the men as they gazed upon that wonder have not been recorded, though they were probably no different from those of a person today standing there looking at it for the first time.

The Spaniards did try to climb down to the river far below, but to no avail. At this point, Coronado seems to have given up completely on anything in a westward direction.

More visitors came, this time from over on the Pecos River. They were led by two chiefs; the most impressive was a tall man the Spaniards named Bigotes, "whiskers." He was the spokesman. Bigotes told them many stories of his land and the animals that inhabited it, one of them being the humpbacked cows, or as we know them today, the bison. Once again the dying flame of hope was kindled in the conquistadors. Perhaps El Dorado was not lost after all. Another group of men, this time led by Hernando de Alvarado, was sent to investigate. On their journey they passed the "city in the sky," Acoma, built upon a high mesa, surely one of the ancient wonders of the world. However, the Spaniards were not duly impressed except to observe that it appeared invulnerable. Others would learn just how strong it was, in the years to come.

Alvarado and his men, guided by Bigotes, visited the pueblo of Taos and finally, in the great pass through the Sangre de Cristo Mountains, they came to the home of their guide. It was called Pecos, or Cicuyne.

When Alvarado was ready to move again Bigotes decided to stay with his pueblo, and provided instead two guides for the Spaniards. These guides were actually captives from tribes farther east. One was a Wichita, and the other, a Turkish-looking man the Spaniards named El Turco, was a Pawnee. There was, no doubt, a method in the madness of the hosts as they pointed their visitors in the direction of the endless, desolate land to the east.

El Turco did lead them out on the Plains, where they encountered the bison. They feasted on the meat and pronounced it to be as good as the cattle of Spain, though they did find that the hunt could be precarious at times. It was the first time the horse was used to hunt the buffalo. Little did they realize that a whole Indian culture would eventually be built around the horse. El Turco, knowing what was foremost in the minds and hearts of a conquistador by this time, told them of a great city of gold to the northeast called Quivira. Going even further in his imaginative tale he told the anxious Spaniards that he owned a gold bracelet from Quivira but it had been taken from him by Bigotes.

No doubt the natives' desire to return to their homeland promoted these tales, but Alvarado chose instead to return to Pecos and check the story further. El Turco was somewhat perplexed but had no choice but to return also. When confronted with the story of the gold bracelet Bigotes was genuinely astonished. Relations between the Spanish and the Pueblo people had been friendly up until then, but Alvarado's patience was wearing thin. He had them all locked up until such time that the truth was really known. This breach of faith aroused the usually peaceful Pueblo to great hostility. Once again the lust for gold had destroyed any hope of friendship between the two peoples.

When Coronado arrived at Tiguex with the main force to set up winter quarters, El Turco was brought before him to unravel his story. Like the friar Marcos de Niza, his story got bigger with each telling. Even more amazing, the Spaniards, in their blind greed, believed him. Maybe it was just that they wanted to believe him so much that it became easy to swallow stories of great sailing ships and eating with utensils made of silver and gold. El Turco was hailed as having supernatural powers and the two Pecos chiefs, Bigotes and the Cacique, were accused of lying. Unable to wring a confession out of them Alvarado had dogs turned loose on the two. Still they maintained their innocence. Finally they were locked up for the winter. Another incident which stirred up a furor among the natives occurred just before the arrival of Coronado. Juan de Villegas, a hot-blooded young grandee in Cárdenas' group, gazed upon a pretty young woman on one of the upper floors of a pueblo one day and lusted for her. Calling her husband down to hold his horse, he climbed up the ladder and raped the woman. It was the apex of audacity when a man would ask you to hold his horse while he ravished your wife, but such was the attitude of the guests toward their Indian hosts. These incidents did much to arouse the hostile feelings of the natives to a fighting pitch and there were other instances also where the Spaniards commandeered food and clothing at their every whim. The Indians were smoldering and open conflict was imminent.

It started when a horse herd was driven off by the Indians and the herder was killed. The Spaniards went in pursuit only to find a number of the animals shot full of arrows along the road near the pueblo of Arenal, where the woman had been raped. To kill a half-breed herdsman was one thing, but to kill a Spaniard's horse was still another. A council of war was called and Cárdenas was given the responsibility of punishing the "rebels." The men of Arenal fought desperately and it was only when Cárdenas and his men broke into a lower room and built a few large smudge fires that the defenders were driven to surrender. Having gathered some two hundred prisoners in the melee, Cárdenas had the same number of stakes driven into the ground. All were to be executed as an example to the others. When the prisoners saw the wood being gathered for their cremation they made a break for freedom. When the gunfire slaughter that ensued was over there were still some thirty survivors and these were put to the torch. Moho, another pueblo in Tiguex, was next. Refusing the usual requests for surrender, the warriors prepared themselves for a long siege. Once again the Spaniards tried to drive the defenders out by building a fire in the bottom room. However, Moho, unlike Arenal, was much better fortified, with interwoven logs inside its outside layer of adobe. Frustrated in these attempts and suffering many casualties from boulders and poisoned arrows, the conquistadors attacked again and again. Finally, after fifty days of siege the Indians made a break for freedom. Only a few escaped by swimming across the Rio Grande. The rest were cut down. All twelve pueblos of Tiguex were now completely pacified.

Meanwhile at Coronado's headquarters, plans were being made to move on in search of Quivira. Firmly convinced that El Turco could lead the way, Bigotes and the Cacique were released. Refusing to let bygones be bygones, the chiefs informed El Turco that it would be wise to lead the Spaniards out into the Llano Estacado or Staked Plain and let them perish. It wasn't difficult for a man with the storytelling ability of El Turco to have the entire 1,500-man force follow him into no man's land. Only the good fortune of spring rains kept them from perishing from thirst. It is said the area received its name when the conquistadors marked their trail with stakes so as not to lose their way.

Finally the true story came to light. El Turco broke down and confessed that the whole thing had been a ruse, a plot to lead the expedition out onto the vast, endless plains where they would perish. There was no Quivira, at least there was no city of gold, no ships pulled by golden oars, no wagons filled with the precious yellow metal, nothing. El Turco was put in irons while his fate was pondered.

Coronado decided to send the bulk of his army back to Tiguex and he would lead a small force northward. Apparently he still held out some hope for finding the golden city. Under the guidance of Isopete, the Wichita captive, Coronado moved northeast, crossing the Arkansas River and into where Kansas is today. At last Quivira was found and much to the dismay of all, it was no richer than Hawikuh.

El Turco had one more card to play. He attempted to get the Wichita to overpower Coronado's small force. However, this ploy was found out and Coronado decided that it was time to deal with this troublesome culprit once and for all. After his final confession was wrung (incidentally, not his church confession), El Turco was bound and garroted to death. The first great liar, Marcos de Niza, had returned to Mexico City in disgrace. The second was unceremoniously choked to death on the plains of Kansas.

It had seemed so long ago in early 1540, when, full of hopes and dreams, Coronado had ridden north. Now, in the cold light of dawn, he had to face the reality of a return to Mexico City, the mission and himself a failure. For a proud man it was a hard pill to swallow.

It is ironic that while Coronado was camped on the Arkansas, another conquistador approaching from the other side of the continent had established a base farther down that same river. Hernando de Soto was also chasing a golden dream, a dream that for him ended even more tragically than for his counterpart from the west.

In the spring of 1542, all the Spaniards, with the exception of three priests who chose to remain, returned to New Spain. A few months before, Coronado had fallen from his horse during a race. He had received severe head injuries and for a time it was thought he would not live. He did survive but never fully recovered.

There were charges brought against him by some disgruntled members of the expedition, ranging from cruelty to the natives to gambling; however, these were all dismissed.

Coronado's career was at an end, and as if things weren't bad enough, according to legend, his beautiful wife Beatrice had fallen in love with another man during his absence. Maybe there was some ominous sign in the dream of Trujillo so many months and so many long miles before.

When death took Coronado at the youthful age of forty-four, he had no way of knowing that his fateful expedition had claimed for Spain all of what is today's American Southwest. The states of Arizona, New Mexico, Texas, Oklahoma, Colorado, and Kansas had felt the resounding hoofbeats of the stallions they rode. They had also been the first white men to gaze upon the Grand Canyon and to feast upon the great American bison. The gold and silver was there all right, but in their rush to find it, the conquistadors ran right by it.

Another problem that had come forth in the past and would plague the Spanish in the future was the constant bickering between the priest and the soldier. Each had his own method for subjugating and civilizing the Indian and they were much too different to be compatible.

In the meantime, Philip II had risen to power in Spain, replacing Charles V in 1556 when the latter abdicated. Although she did not know it, Spain was on the decline. The great discoveries in the New World had made her the richest and most powerful nation in Europe but the squandering of her wealth and the Inquisition had taken their toll. Her empire was declining, never to reach those pinnacles again.

It was during this same period that Sir Francis Drake sailed his *Golden Hind* up along the California coast and claimed it for his queen. After refitting his ship off the coast of California he daringly set sail across the Pacific. When Drake arrived triumphantly in England, Spanish spies surmised that he had located the Northwest Passage, never dreaming that his treasure-laden ship could have successfully navigated the globe. When news of Drake's mythical "discovery" reached New Spain the viceroy was determined to move north and establish Spanish control of the Passage. England and Spain were not alone in this quest for empire; Russia and France joined in also. Nearly too late, Spain realized the importance of establishing her claim to the northern frontier. More than just establishing a claim, she must find a way of holding it.

It was forty years after Coronado's unceremonious return to Mexico City before another serious expedition was made into what is today's United States. Three priests had gone north to the land of the Pueblo and hadn't been heard from. A party under the leadership of Antonio de Espejo went up the Rio Grande in search of

1. Apache family in the 1800s. *Arizona State Lib.*

2. Old Apache woman, age 106. *Arizona State Lib.*

3. Apache woman in typical camp dress. *Arizona State Lib.*

4. Apache woman with nose cut off as a punishment for adultery. *Arizona State Lib.*

5. A scene in Geronimo's camp, 1886; the white captive boy is Jimmy McKinn (note the Negro captive on the far left). *Arizona State Lib.*

6. Father Tomás Garcés, Franciscan priest who accompanied de Anza to California. He was martyred by the Yuma Indians in 1781. *Sharlot Hall Museum.*

7. Father Eusebio Kino, Jesuit priest in the Pimería Alta for twenty-four years. He was also a cattle rancher, farmer, mathematician, cartographer, and Arizona's first promoter. This photo is a composite likeness of Kino. His statue is in Statuary Hall, Washington, D.C. *Arizona State Lib.*

8. John Slaughter, cattleman from Texas who settled on the old San Bernardino Land Grant and later became sheriff of Cochise County. Armed with a shotgun and a short temper, he did much to rid Cochise County of the rustler element. *Arizona Historical Foundation, Brandes Collection.*

9. Pete Kitchen, pioneer rancher near Nogales; famous for his hogs and for the havoc he raised with the Apache near his ranch. *Arizona State Lib.*

10. Uncle Billy Fourr at a pioneers' reunion in 1925. In the 1880s he defended his ranch in the Dragoon Mountains against both rustlers and Apache. *Arizona Historical Foundation.*

11. King S. Woolsey, pioneer rancher in Yavapai County and well-known Apache fighter. *Sharlot Hall Museum.*

12. Hi Jolly monument, honoring the drivers in the Camel Corps, located near Quartzsite, Arizona. *Arizona Historical Foundation.*

them. He was also looking for a legendary lost lake of gold, somewhere west of the Rio Grande. After learning that the priests had been killed, Espejo left most of his party at Acoma. Traveling westward to the area around the Verde Valley, he found evidence of rich mineral deposits. Americans working the region in the 1860s found many signs of the old Spanish Argonauts. Espejo would have liked to have returned to work the mines; however, he lacked the proper connections with the viceroy. Others with more influence would be aroused by Espejo's glowing reports and would pick up the license to explore and claim the land. Others still would make illegal exploration trips into the area.

The first great colonization attempt up the Rio Grande came in 1595 and was led by Juan de Oñate. His father was one of the richest men in America. His wife was the granddaughter of Cortés and the great-granddaughter of Montezuma. He was at this time about forty-seven years old and had established quite a reputation on his own as a warrior, miner, and colonizer. Oñate drove a hard bargain with the Crown over particular legal matters concerning the expedition and the colonization that would follow, but in the end he seems to have generally prevailed. The Crown was usually pretty lenient when it came to granting titles and land grants, particularly when it didn't cost anything to do so. It wasn't until 1598 that the expedition did finally get under way. Near present-day El Paso, Oñate claimed all land and the adjoining provinces for God, for Spain, and for himself. They had all been claimed many times before, but this time it was different. The Spaniard had come to stay. With him Oñate brought some four hundred colonists and the first permanent herds of cattle, some seven thousand head. He also gave the land its official name, New Mexico. The wild, roving band of plunderers who ravaged the colonists along the Rio Grande were first referred to as Apache, from the Zuñi word meaning "enemy," in Oñate's journals. Oñate's party brought the first wheeled vehicles into the American Southwest. These were two-wheeled carts called *caretas*. To Oñate fell the difficult task of pacifying the Indians who occupied the land.

At first there was little trouble between the two peoples, especially in the pueblos along the Rio Grande. However, to the west, the people of Acoma were being stirred up by one of the caciques who was all too familiar with Spanish treatment of the natives. A small Spanish force led by Juan de Zaldivar, a nephew of Oñate's, was ambushed while visiting the village and though the Spanish fought bravely the rout was complete. Zaldivar was among the dead. During the fight five Spaniards leaped over the cliffs, falling some 350 feet to the plain below. Four of the five survived and lived to fight another day. For the people of Acoma that day was not far away. Vincente de Zaldivar, brother of the slain leader, was picked by Oñate to avenge the dead Spaniards. In the fierce fight that followed, and against overwhelming odds, the Spaniards scaled the cliffs and destroyed Acoma. Only six hundred of the three thousand villagers were alive at the end. These were brought back to the Rio Grande for trial. The men over twenty-five years of age were sentenced to the loss of one foot and twenty years' enslavement. The women and children over age twelve were also given twenty years, while the children under twelve were turned over to the priests. Two Hopi who had witnessed the melee while visiting Acoma were sent home with their right hands removed as a warning to the others. Things quieted down in the Pueblo country for a time.

Juan de Oñate had many successes in his venture into New Mexico. With Captain Marcos Farfán he traveled west over today's Arizona in 1605–6. They did more to reveal Arizona's mineral wealth than any others up to that time. Traveling west to the Colorado, then down to the Gila, Oñate declared California to be an island, a rumor that persisted for a hundred years, or until Father Eusebio Kino came along and found out otherwise. Oñate's travels took him far eastward into Kansas, where he lost what is probably the first significant battle for the whites against the Indians in the West. However, he did give to Spain a legitimate claim to an immense region including Arizona, Colorado, Nevada, New Mexico, Texas, Oklahoma, and Kansas. Oñate had put the Spanish stamp on the Southwest permanently. No small achievement, for in their own way the Spanish were great colonizers.

Oñate did have his failures. He failed in his endeavor to domesticate the buffalo and he didn't find the fabled Northwest Passage. California was not an island, at least not yet, but most important the flare-ups between soldiers and the priests would, in the end, lead to his downfall. He resigned in 1607 but wasn't replaced until Pedro de Peralta arrived two years later. In 1610 the city of Santa Fe was founded.

The exit of Oñate from New Mexico signaled the end of an era in the history of the white men in the Southwest. It was the last failure of the conquistador. Spain now turned to the missionary.

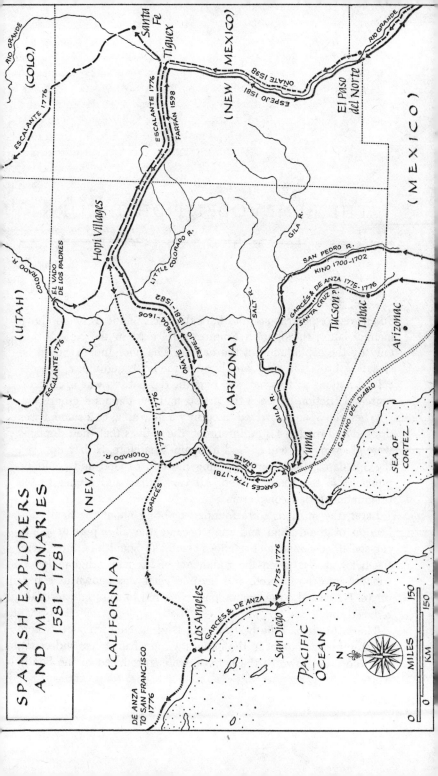

SPANISH EXPLORERS AND MISSIONARIES 1581–1781

(UTAH)

(NEV.)

(CALIFORNIA)

(ARIZONA)

(NEW MEXICO)

(COLO.)

(MEXICO)

RIO GRANDE

Santa Fe

Tiguex

EL PASO del Norte

RIO GRANDE

ONATE 1598

ESPEJO 1581

ESCALANTE 1776

FARFAN 1598

ESCALANTE 1776

Hopi Villages

EL VADO DE LOS PADRES

COLORADO R.

ESCALANTE 1776

LITTLE COLORADO R.

ESPEJO 1581–1582

OÑATE 1604–1606

SALT R.

SAN PEDRO R.

KINO 1700–1702

GARCÉS & DE ANZA 1775–1776

SANTA CRUZ R.

Tucson

Tubac

Arizonac

GILA R.

GILA R.

OÑATE

GARCES 1775–1776

GARCES 1774–1781

OÑATE

Yuma

CAMINO DEL DIABLO

SEA OF CORTEZ

COLORADO R.

Los Angeles

GARCES & DE ANZA 1775–1776

San Diego

DE ANZA TO SAN FRANCISCO 1776

PACIFIC OCEAN

N

MILES   0   150

KM   0   150

THE BENEVOLENT DICTATORS

SINCE THE CONQUISTADORS, and later the encomienderos, were above manual labor, the Spanish Empire could exist in the New World only by the exploitation of the natives. The poor Indian would be enslaved, broken in spirit and body in the fields and mines. Preconceived notions as to what was best for the natives was a constant source of friction between the priests and the temporal groups.

When the Spanish arrived to occupy a new area, a document was drafted and read in Latin, informing the natives that their domains were given by the will of God to Spain. Therefore, if they opposed the Spaniards, they were opposing the will of God and could be punished in the name of God. All very fitting and proper to the pragmatic-minded conquerors.

Later, the missions were founded to bring about the final pacification of the Indian and they became the all-important political, social, economic, and religious centers of Spanish culture. Here, the heathen was given the rudiments of his new religion, indoctrinated into the Church, and became what was known as a neophyte. He was also unceremoniously referred to as a *reducido,* "the reduced one."

The missions had the best farming land, usually irrigated, where agriculture was taught to the natives. Crops, fruit trees, and cattle, heretofore unknown to the natives, were introduced to the Southwest.

Religious dogma was not just confined to the Catholic Church. Most religious groups during that period of history had the feeling that theirs was the only true religion, and one who didn't believe in that particular sect was guilty of heresy, an offense punishable by death. During this enlightened age, one was even forbidden to speak out against the Church for fear of a charge of blasphemy.

Spain was the bastion of the Roman Catholic Church. Nowhere else in the world was the Catholic religion followed more dogmatically than in the Spanish Empire, yet nowhere did the Pope have less authority than in Spain. The Church was Spain's most important institution and its activities were intertwined with all aspects of the workings of Spain and her New World colonies. Religious orthodoxy was always demanded within the system, yet there was also a great fusion of temporal and spiritual power. One of the outstanding characteristics of the Spanish administrative system was that no one trusted anyone else. The Church officials kept a constant watch on the activities of the viceroy, military, and governors. The secular agencies, in turn, carefully scrutinized the functions of the Church. The complicated Spanish bureaucracy did much to add to the confusion and brought about much internal conflict.

The priests and the civil officials disagreed most often on the handling of the natives. To the temporal groups, the Indian was a means to an end. He was made to work in the fields or the mines for the enrichment of the landowners. Although there were cases of extreme cruelty on the part of some priests, for the most part they hoped to Christianize the heathen one way or another. Any punishment around the mission was usually doled out by the Spanish soldiers rather than the priests, although it might have been ordered by the latter. The priests, understandably, didn't want to be cast into the role of barbarous villains.

The construction of the missions and presidios was done by Indian labor, under the supervision of the Spanish. The Indian's time schedule was divided into periods and strictly followed. This daily schedule consisted of work, study, and prayer. At night they were locked up in compounds, lest they might desire to give up their new religion and seek the old heathenistic ways. The unmarried males and females were kept in separate dormitories to ensure against unions not sanctioned by the Church.

For all their incorrigible ways, especially during a time of rebellion, the Pueblo peoples were the easiest to keep tabs on for they were, by nature, an easygoing, tractable people. More important, they were a sedentary group rather than nomadic. Living in their permanent structures, confinement was unnecessary. The Church merely moved in with them. With the nomads it was much more difficult, for they had to be gathered in like little chicks and kept under constant surveillance by the padres.

In the conflicts between the priests and the civil officials, the priests usually had the advantage. Who in his right mind could dispute the word of a man of God during this time of the Inquisition? Charges brought against a priest were charges against the Church and whosoever should testify against the Church would surely be going against God himself. No man desired to find himself in that unenviable position.

The Inquisition was the infamous period of religious intolerance that lasted in Spain for several hundred years. During this time thousands of dissidents were put to death by devious means while hundreds of thousands were condemned to prisons and impoverished. Many were burned at the stake while others were tried and found guilty in absentia. Not allowed to appear in their own defense, and sometimes jailed for several years without a trial, these Spaniards were at the mercy of the sinister group of men dedicated to the preservation of absolute Catholicism. The diabolical means of punishment, including the rack, the iron boot, the red-hot iron, were still being used as late as 1834 when the Inquisition was abolished in Spain. By this time, most of the intelligentsia had exited from that nation, one way or another.

Three religious orders, the Franciscans, the Dominicans, and the Jesuits, were instrumental in the colonizing of the Southwest and California.

The first missionaries came to Arizona some twenty years after Oñate's visit. They were Franciscans from the missions along the Rio Grande and they worked among the Hopi. The latter were living in permanent homes and villages, making them easily accessible to the white men. The missions built on Hopi land were the first permanent structures built for use by whites in Arizona. Not much is known about the five missions, as the old records were destroyed, but it is known that they caused much hard feeling among the Hopi, who never did welcome the newcomers.

The Pueblo revolt in 1680 was the most devastating of all the Indian rebellions in the Southwest and though it occurred in New

Mexico, its effects were far-reaching. Its leader had the ironically unlikely name of Popé.

When the Spanish had come, they promised, in return for tribute and other services from the natives, protection from the predator bands of Apache and Navajo. This proved to be an impossible task as the Spaniards, for all their bravery and prowess on the battlefield, could not cope with the guerrilla tactics of the nomads. The priests had driven the Pueblo medicine men underground by declaring any deviation from the Catholic religion would bring about the death penalty. Rather than stamping out the native rituals, they had made them even more enticing. The medicine man, surreptitiously practicing his religion, became a hero and sometimes a martyr, making his followers more devout. The forbidden fruit was something to relish. As taxes increased and protection decreased, Popé began to lay plans to drive the Spaniards out once and for all. The revolt was probably one of the best-kept secrets of all time in Indian warfare. Even the women weren't told. Anyone letting the secret slip to the priests would be put to death. The word did reach the Spaniards just prior to the revolt but not in time to avert disaster. Hundreds of Spanish were killed as they were driven all the way to El Paso del Norte. It was twelve years before they were able to return, and during that time, all traces of the Spanish and the Catholic religion were wiped out in New Mexico. Even the names Jesus and Mary were forbidden.

Interestingly enough, all the wrongs committed by the Spanish during their occupation of New Mexico were perpetrated even more blatantly by Popé during his reign. His absolute power seemed to have corrupted him absolutely. The Apache and Navajo were still a menace, taxes were high, and Popé had himself carried around in a most elegant manner. Nothing was too good for His Majesty. Popé was able to maintain his hold on the people, however, and it wasn't until his death several years later that the Spanish under Diego de Vargas were able to gain a new foothold in New Mexico—this time to stay.

The man destined to become the greatest missionary in the history of the Southwest arrived here through a twisted chain of events. Born in Italy and educated in Germany, Eusebio Francisco Kino so distinguished himself in his studies that he might have become a famous European scholar. However, after being given up for dead during a serious illness, miraculously his life was spared.

He attributed this miracle to his patron saint, Francis Xavier. In gratitude, he dedicated his life to missionary work, and joined the Jesuit Order. Kino had hoped to be assigned to the Orient, but when the orders were issued he found himself on his way to Mexico. His first six years were spent in Lower California, or the Baja, but in 1687 he was ordered to Pimería Alta, a region extending from the Altar River in Sonora to the Gila watershed in the north. It was here that for the next twenty-four years Kino would gain immortality not only as a missionary, but also as a cartographer, explorer, cattleman, farmer, and Arizona's first genuine promoter.

No actual portrait of Kino exists. A composite likeness of the "padre on horseback" was created from descriptive accounts by his contemporaries. His successor at the Mission Dolores, Padre Luis Velarde, wrote reverently of him: "In saying his breviary he always wept. . . . He was merciful to others but cruel to himself. . . . He died as he had lived, with extreme humility and poverty." A kind, humble, sensitive man, Kino never lost his temper except in dealing with sinners. He bittered his food with herbs to make it distasteful and subjected himself to whippings as penance. He was addicted to none of the vices such as snuff, wine, or tobacco and he never slept in a bed, preferring instead to sleep on the ground with his horse blankets for bedcovers.

The natives, in their childlike way, worshiped him and he returned those feelings with kindness and devotion. There was a time when he rode 62 miles in one day to rescue an Indian who had been sentenced to death by Spanish officials.

Kino was a tireless wanderer. He explored more of Arizona's vast regions than any man since Oñate. It has been estimated that in the twenty-four years of missionary work he traveled some 75,000 miles in Arizona. When he was fifty-one, he made a 1,500-mile trip to Mexico City on horseback in just fifty-three days. On another exploring mission the zealous Black Robe rode an average of 40 miles a day for twenty-six consecutive days. He was about fifty-five years old at the time. It was during this journey that the famous story of the "blue shells" was born. He had noticed some Pima Indians with some blue shells which he had also seen before on the Pacific coast of Lower California. He deduced from this evidence the logical conclusion that there must be an overland route to California, and contrary to popular belief, California was not an island. He persisted in this until his dying day, but Spanish officials paid little attention.

Kino established his first mission at Dolores, Sonora, in March 1687. It was to remain his favorite to the end. He entered Arizona in 1691 and went as far north as the *ranchería* of Bac, just south of Tucson. He came again in 1694. This time he journeyed down to the Gila, where he visited the Casa Grande ruins. In 1697 he was back, this time with livestock for the natives.

The first mission in Arizona was at Guevavi, near present-day Nogales, in 1692, followed by Tumacacori in 1696. In 1700 Kino laid the cornerstone for the beautiful San Xavier del Bac, a short distance from where the present structure stands. Kino never got to see the missions in the finished state that we see them today, as the construction was a long and tedious task. Both San Xavier and Tumacacori took one hundred years to complete, thanks to frequent visits from the Apache and periods of disinterest or inability on the part of the Church.

Kino spent a great deal of time on his own in the Pimería Alta and he never had more than ten churchmen at one time to assist him. In a land where the white man was universally hated, the natives had genuine love and respect for the padre on horseback who lived among them and shared their lives. When the Pima in the Altar Valley revolted in 1695 and martyred Father Francisco Saeta, Kino refused to flee and waited alone to be executed. The Indians refused to harm him and when the revolt was ended, he went on with his work as before, bearing no malice toward the revolting band.

Perhaps Kino's greatest legacy to the natives was the bringing of fruit trees, crops, vegetables, sheep, mules, and cattle into Arizona. The padre was the area's first farmer-cattle baron. Believing that Indians could best be converted to Christianity when they were shown that the new ways brought about a more abundant life, Kino set about educating the natives on the rudiments of farming and ranching.

Kino died in 1711 at Magdalena while dedicating a new mission. He was buried at the site and his grave was not rediscovered until 1966. The intrepid old missionary, so genuine and long-suffering, founded twenty-nine missions and seventy-three visitas (small mission stations) during his brilliant career in Pimería Alta.

In the National Statuary Hall in Washington, D.C., each state is allowed two statues. One of them from Arizona is General John Greenway, a twentieth-century miner-soldier. The other is Padre Eusebio Francisco Kino, a man of God. The diverse characters of the two seem incongruous at first glance yet they are the epitome of the kinds of people who came to Arizona and founded a place in the wilderness.

The Kino years were the pinnacle of success for the Jesuit Order in Pimería Alta. Operating under a philosophy that Christianity was easier to swallow on a full stomach, Kino provided the natives with the benefits of a more abundant materialistic life. He taught them how to plant, cultivate the new fruits and vegetables he introduced. Furthermore he brought into the Pimería Alta the first cattle and sheep herds.

There were other padres on the northern frontier who had the integrity of Father Kino, but none had his inexhaustible physical strength. Men with such un-Spanish-sounding names as Keller, Mittendorf, Sedelmayr, and Pfefferkon, along with Father Augustín de Campos and Father Luis Velarde, would carry the cross to the natives with some success. In 1743, Padre Ignacio Keller attempted to go north to the Gila but was attacked by Apache and driven back. He never again ventured north of San Xavier. Later in 1743, another priest, Jacob Sedelmayr, journeyed to the Gila and foresaw the building of visitas all along that river to the Colorado. Kino had been gone too long. The new generation of Pima greeted Sedelmayr with disinterest, and the Apache with noticeable hostility. For eleven years Father Ignacio Pfefferkon tried, but he also met with limited success. Unhappy with his station on the frontier and perhaps desiring something more comfortable, like an office in Mexico City, Pfefferkon later wrote an interesting but critical narrative of his experiences. The Jesuits' control of Pimería Alta was on the decline. Not one Apache was ever converted. The only time one would enter the chapel was to sack it, and they did that whenever they got the chance. The land was so controlled by the Apache that many called it Apachería rather than Pimería Alta.

Because some of their best farm lands had been taken over by the Spaniards, because of the rivalry between native leaders and the priests, and because of their anger at the Spaniards for harsh punishments, the Pima and Papago grew increasingly hostile. Finally in 1751 they revolted, and for a short time not one white man inhabited Arizona. Guevavi, Tumacacori, and San Xavier were plundered. In the aftermath, the Jesuits blamed the governor for bestowing too many gifts on the native leaders, giving them grandiose ideas concerning their own self-importance. The governor in turn accused the padres of cruelty to the Indians, a charge which was never proved. In any case, the next year the Spanish came back and established a presidio at Tubac. This time they brought with them the first white women to enter Arizona. Apparently they had come to stay.

The Christian world received a severe jolt in 1767 when, with the stroke of a pen, the impetuous Carlos III of Spain, fearful of their influence, expelled the Jesuits from the Americas. Throughout the Western Hemisphere Jesuit priests were arrested and unceremoniously taken away. Many had spent the greater part of their lives on the truculent frontier. Some died while awaiting the ships to come for them. The great and glorious period of the Society of Jesus had come to a disappointing end and through no fault of the frontier padres. In Europe the Jesuits were becoming all too powerful and feared. Writers of great influence such as Voltaire and Diderot united in an attempt to extirpate the Society and they almost succeeded. There was no appeal to the king's expulsion decree so the padres packed their few worldly possessions and withdrew. They had hardly vacated San Xavier when the Apache swooped down and destroyed it.

The following year saw the men of St. Francis in their brown robes come into the Pimería Alta. The Franciscans had characteristically kept a barrier between the padre and the native. They had at times been accused of cruelty, and discouraged the use of the native tongue among the natives. However, they did achieve notable success in working with the natives, especially men like Father Junípero Serra, the "Gentle Conquistador," who successfully explored and settled California, and Francisco Tomás Garcés, who next to Kino was Arizona's greatest missionary.

When the Jesuits left, their place was taken by fourteen Franciscans, Garcés among them. Only thirty years old at the time, he was affectionately called "Old Man" by the natives, who grew to love him. A man of simple tastes, he lived and ate as the Indians did.

Garcés made his headquarters at San Xavier from 1768 to 1776, but much of his time was spent on the road. The zealous priest made three journeys to the Gila. On his third trip Garcés followed the river down to another great river which he named the Colorado because of the reddish sand that colored the waters. Continuing westward, he met some Indians who told him of seeing white men farther west. He saw two openings in the Sierra and reported his findings to Juan Bautista de Anza, the commander at Tubac.

De Anza, whose father was killed in battle with the Apache, was born in the Pimería Alta and came from a famous family of soldiers. He asked for and received permission to explore the land to the west of the Colorado River. On January 1, 1774, de Anza, Garcés, and thirty-four soldiers left Tubac. Avoiding Apachería, they made their way west along the Camino del Diablo, which runs along the present-day international border toward Yuma. Arriving in the village of the Yuma Indians, they struck up a fast friendship with the local natives and their leader, Chief Palma. From the Colorado, the expedition made its way west to the mission at San Gabriel, near present-day Los Angeles. De Anza and the soldiers traveled up the California coast to Monterey, while Garcés returned home again. The new viceroy, Antonio Bucareli, was well pleased with the expedition and ordered another to follow the same route, this time bringing along settlers. Bucareli had also sent an inspector named Hugo O'Conor into Pimería Alta in 1775. O'Conor, a long-time Irish mercenary fighting for Spain, recommended that a garrison be built at the rendezvous point of the Apache where they gathered for their forays up the Santa Cruz Valley. The gathering place was some 9 miles north of San Xavier. O'Conor's plan was implemented, and in 1776 a walled city was born on the banks of the Santa Cruz River. Customarily the Papago named their villages after prominent landmarks. Near the site of the new presidio was an old Papago *ranchería* called Chuk Shon, which meant "dark color at the base of the mountain." The name referred to nearby Sentinel Mountain. The Spanish pronunciation of Chuk Shon sounded more like Tuqui Son and was eventually corrupted into Tucson. For the next 150 years Tucson would be Arizona's largest city.

Bucareli was most anxious to gain solid control of California by an overland road from Mexico City to the San Francisco Bay via Tucson. De Anza left Tubac in October 1775 with 240 soldiers and settlers, among them three priests, Garcés, Tomás Eixarch, and the official chaplain, Pedro Font. Approximately 40 of the settlers were women. The only fatality of the journey was the death of a woman while giving birth. Two other women also brought forth into this world new lives on the trip. The redoubtable de Anza acted as midwife. The expedition also had with them some 1,000 head of livestock.

Garcés and Eixarch remained at the Yuma villages, and after suffering many hardships crossing the desert de Anza finally reached San Gabriel on January 1, 1776. From San Gabriel it was a relatively easy trip up the El Camino Real to Monterey, and thence up the peninsula to where in 1776 a small village was born and called Yerba Buena. The name was later changed to San Francisco.

When de Anza returned to the Yuma villages on the Colorado he found his nomadic priest had gone exploring. However, de Anza did pick up a hitchhiker. Chief Palma had decided he would like to go to Mexico City and meet the viceroy. While in the capital Palma was baptized in the cathedral and given stately treatment. Many promises were made to the chief and gifts were bestowed. More was to come. This bit of gift-giving and promise-making would result in dire consequences for Father Garcés and the others in the years to come.

Meanwhile Garcés had gone up the Colorado some fifteen days' journey to about where Needles, California, is located today. From there he went west to San Gabriel. Returning to the Colorado he became the first white man to enter the Grand Canyon from the west. Entering the land of the Hopi he found them not at all receptive. During his brief visit he discussed the future of the country, mentioning the fact that someday the land would be widely settled by the white man and that the Hopi must learn to accept the white man's ways, or at least tolerate them. The Hopi responded to the priest's prophetic words with ridicule and sent him on his way. That evening the sagacious Garcés recorded these events in his journal. Upon finishing he also recorded in his notes the date, July 4, 1776. He did send a letter to Father Silvestre Valez de Escalante at the Zuñi pueblos to the east suggesting a road to link Santa Fe to California. Garcés then returned to the Yuma villages and thence back home to San Xavier. He had traveled 2,000 miles with only the natives for companions.

Escalante thought the idea of a road to California was a good one and he secured permission to go exploring. With seven soldiers and another priest, Father Atanasio Dominguez, he journeyed into southwestern Colorado and over to the Great Salt Lake. Growing discouraged, they finally gave up and returned to Santa Fe. On the way home they crossed the Colorado River where Lake Powell is today. The spot is still known as El Vado de los Padres—the Crossing of the Fathers.

The long, slow disintegration of Spain as a world power was beginning to take noticeable effect in the northern frontier. Missions that had been promised were never built. The gifts promised for Chief Palma and his people never arrived. It was the lack of gifts that hurt more than anything else. Palma was losing face with his people when the Spaniards didn't deliver the goods. In the belief that the natives might be better assimilated into Spanish culture, the settlers, soldiers, and priests were all put in close proximity to one another. No doubt this was also an economy move to cut costs. Mistreatment of natives became more flagrant with the influx of civilians and soldiers. The Spanish settlers took the choice land away from the Indians for farming, and morale was low on both sides. It needed only a spark to set off a revolt, and that spark arrived in the person of Lieutenant Governor Fernando de Rivera y Moncada of California and some forty soldiers. Rivera and his men were returning to California from Sonora and while camped in the area turned their horses and cattle loose to feed on the Indian crops. Then they audaciously helped themselves to the horses belonging to the natives to replenish their own herd. When the Yuma came to retrieve their steeds, the Spaniards impudently accused them of horse-stealing and had them horsewhipped.

On Tuesday, July 17, 1781, the Indians struck. They had planned well and took the Spaniards by surprise. Only three soldiers escaped with their lives, along with four settlers. The two pueblos were put to the torch and all of Rivera's men were hacked and clubbed to death. Interestingly, all women and children were spared. None of the women were molested in any way, a rare if not unparalleled act in Indian massacres. Garcés was spared for two days, but on the nineteenth he was beaten to death.

The glory that had been hers was gone. Spanish culture was on the decline. First had come the conquistador with his dreams of glory and gold. In his footsteps and traveling in the apostolic manner came the missionaries. They too had dreams of glory, the glory of God, and the rescuing of the heathen from the fires of hell. But now, far off in the most remote area of the northern frontier on a hot summer day, these dreams all came to an end. Here two civilizations met on a virgin land and decided an issue as ancient as history itself. Those bodies lying in the sun gave limp testimony to an era that was past, never to return again.

Garcés perhaps summed it all up when he observed, "We have failed. It is not because we have not tried. It is because we have not understood."

With the closing of the land route to California, the hopes of colonizing Upper California were seriously curtailed. The only route open would be by sea, and that was precarious at best.

The missionary, like the conquistador and the encomiendero, had failed in the Northern Provinces. However, there were successes. The indefatigable religious work of the priests goes without saying, but equally important to the livelihood of the natives were the skills that the priests brought with them. The Indians were introduced to the raising of their own fruits and vegetables along with cattle-raising. For the industrious natives, at least, starvation and hand-to-mouth existence would be a thing of the past. Because the priests had come among them life would be better, and perhaps therein lies the missions' greatest legacy.

THE LAST DAYS OF THE
SPANISH EMPIRE

THERE WERE MANY REASONS why the missionaries, like the conquistadors, failed in their attempts to hold the Pimería Alta for the Crown. The natives couldn't or wouldn't give up their nomadic ways. They disliked the work forced upon them by the Spaniards. They liked even less the punishment dealt out by their white guardians. The language problem caused a gap between the two peoples, as did the racial superiority feelings. Probably the most difficult problem facing the Spanish in subjugating the Indian was the fact that they could never effectively defeat the red man because the Indians weren't organized and therefore there was no leader to surrender for them; they had no capital city or home base to hand over. The Indian lived in a kind of "do your own thing" society. When he adapted himself to the horse, which he borrowed from the Spaniard, the added mobility rendered the Spanish strategy completely useless. This is especially true when one considers that the mother country was up to her neck in world problems and lacked both the money and the manpower to hold the northern frontier any longer.

In the late seventeenth century Spain tried a peace-at-any-price program relying principally upon bribery, especially with the troublesome Apache and Comanche. The other alternative, extermination, had failed miserably for the reasons mentioned above. The tools used in the bribery were liquor and guns. The liquor would debauch the Indian, and the guns of inferior quality would make him less dependent on his trusty lance and bow and arrow. It was thought that between the two, the Apache would become weakened and thus easier to manage.

Bernardo de Gálvez, a cousin to José de Gálvez, the author of the Spanish expansion program into Upper California in the 1770s, became viceroy in 1785. Like his cousin he was a visionary and a mover. He had already established a reputation as an Indian fighter. The Gálvez plan, entitled *Instructions for Governing the Interior Provinces*, called for all-out war on all Indians not at peace with Spain. Once the Indians asked for peace they would be relocated near the presidios in settlements known as *establecimientos de paz* (establishments of peace). Here they would be debauched on alcoholic beverages supplied by the Spanish. The Apache would also be given old surplus firearms for hunting purposes. The Indians placed great importance on the guns even though they were not nearly as suitable for warfare as the traditional bow, arrow, and lance. Of course the Spanish would control the market on alcohol, powder, shot, and replacement parts. If the bands were too large to be moved or controlled, Gálvez proposed that traders open posts among them, doubling as spies and keeping the Spanish advised on their nefarious activities. The plan also called for keeping the various tribes at war with each other, yet keeping them all friendly toward Spain. This called for considerable adroitness, and amazingly enough it worked. The hostiles became dependent upon the handouts for survival, accomplishing what neither cross nor sword had been able to. For the next twenty-five years, there was relative quiet in the Northern Provinces.

Spain's troubles with her provinces on the northern frontier were small compared with the problems confronting her in Mexico City. It had started with Father Hidalgo in 1810, and at first it seemed that the revolution was lost when the priest was executed. But the revolution spread and by 1821 the harness of Mother Spain was thrown off and a new nation was born. She was no longer the workhorse colony, she was a frisky young revolutionary colt calling herself Mexico.

For a short time Augustín Iturbide, one of the leaders of the revolution, was at the helm, but he likened himself to an emperor rather than implementing the republican-type government favored by most. Iturbide was soon forced to flee. He, like some thirteen other leaders during those bloody times, died violently. Poor Mexico! In the twenty-five-year period between 1821 and 1846, the young republic suffered through no fewer than seventeen revolutions.

Besieged with troubles of her own, Mexico City was forced to let her remote outposts shift pretty much for themselves. There were no funds for supporting an army to protect the settlers, nor was the program of bribery able to continue. In 1827 following a period of controversy between the large landowners and the Church, Mexico expelled the Franciscans, and the missionary program was laid to rest. The once stately missions fell to ruin. Their appeasement program ended, the Apache once more took to the plunder trail. It has been estimated that from 1821 to 1835 some five thousand people died from hostile action in Pimería Alta, while another four thousand were driven out. More than one hundred mines, settlements, and ranches were wiped out during this same period. Most of these disasters took place after 1830.

The new Mexican Republic had been opposed by churchmen from the start, a fact which led, no doubt, to their eventual expulsion. The ruling classes and rich landowners seeking to strip the Church of its powers gave the government its staunchest support.

At this time Old Sonora extended vaguely up to the Gila River, but in 1825 a new state called Occidente was created from the states of Sonora and Sinaloa, including what is today's Arizona. Sonora had opposed this consolidation violently until 1825 when the Yaqui Indians revolted. Sinaloa, much richer and with more manpower, made the marriage more palatable for the Sonorans. However, when the two were not fighting the Yaqui much time and effort was spent in trying to regain separate status. Finally in 1830 the two were divorced, to the relief of both, and the short-lived state of Occidente was no more.

All these events had little effect on the remote outposts of Tubac and Tucson. In all likelihood they were probably about as uninterested in the regained separate status of Sonora as they had been in the achievement of Mexican independence a few years before.

In 1824 New Mexico had broken away from the states of Chihuahua and Durango, and claimed all of Arizona north of the Gila, as did also the state of California. However, neither concerned themselves with the region except as something to be dreaded when crossing.

In 1776 the hub of culture in the Great Southwest was Santa Fe, a thriving community and trade center on the Rio Grande. Santa Fe was soon destined to become the link with an area on the eastern coast of North America that was just now beginning to flex its youthful muscles in protest against an oppressive and overprotective parent, just as New Spain would do in the years that followed. The trade route that would be established between the cities of St. Louis and Santa Fe would play a significant role in the future destiny of both Mexico and the United States.

Before the Americans came, Spain's most serious threat on her northern frontier had been France. Both had used the natives in their respective struggle for empire. Spain had used the mission and France had used trade items. Naturally France had been the more successful of the two, forcing the Spanish to establish presidios on the Texas frontier to protect her interests. Armed with French guns, the Comanche played no small part in keeping the life-style of the settlers in a state of constant turmoil.

The French had never been a serious colonial threat in the Southwest, or at least not to the extent as the next sole occupant of the Mississippi Valley. In 1803 Thomas Jefferson acquired from France that vast, unknown region across the wide Missouri in what is called the Louisiana Purchase. No one knew for sure where the nebulous boundaries were located. In 1806, Lieutenant Zebulon Pike was sent on a dubious exploration odyssey which took him west into Colorado and south to the vicinity where the headwaters of the Rio Grande began their long journey south to the Gulf of Mexico. High in the Sangre de Cristo Mountains, Pike was picked up by Spanish soldiers after spending a near disastrous winter in the Colorado Rockies. He and his party were taken to Santa Fe, where he was questioned by authorities. Pike maintained that he was merely "lost" and had wandered into Spanish territory by accident. Eventually the Americans were politely returned to their home country.

Over the next few years there were many more incursions by those "human grizzly bears" from over on the Mississippi, mostly on horse-hunting expeditions into Texas. When the Mexican revolution came many Americans joined in the fighting, siding with the revolutionaries against Spain. Those hell-bent-for-leather frontiersmen were a welcome addition. Most of them were raised on the frontier and fighting came to them naturally. Ironically, many of these same Americans would meet again on the same battlefields against their former allies in yet another quest for independence in the not too distant future. Apparently those intractable rebels back in Boston just didn't know what they started that night when they brewed British tea in Boston Harbor, igniting a series of revolutions that continues to this day throughout the world.

With Mexican independence in 1821 came a whole new philosophy in foreign commerce. No longer restricted to trading only with the mother country, Mexico immediately opened her previously closed doors to American traders and colonists.

Her reasons for opening up colonization to the Americans were mostly selfish. The rampaging Comanche were a constant threat, not only to Texas, but to the interior of Mexico as well. The first of the Plains Indians to acquire the horse, they had built their entire culture around it. As a Cossack-type warrior, none could match the Comanche in riding skill and deadliness in battle. Some of the brain trusts in Mexico City thought that as the Americans and Comanche loved to fight so much, why not bring the two together?

A land giveaway program was initiated in Texas, attracting the land-hungry Americans in droves. In the *empresario* program, a man was given 640 acres of land, his wife an additional 320, while 100 acres was awarded for each child and 80 for each slave. In 1825 this amount was increased to grant a man 1 square league (4,428 acres) of ranch land plus 1 labor (177 acres) of farm land. All one had to do was bring a note of good citizenship from home, swear allegiance to Mexico, and become a Catholic. The Mexicans for their part hoped to form an American buffer zone against the Comanche and their Kiowa cohorts. If the Indians had someone nearer home to harass, so much the better for the interior of Mexico. The strategy did work; the Mexicans and Americans who staked a claim in Texas had their work cut out for them. The Texas frontier was alive with raid and counterraid over the next few years as both sides struggled for dominance. Evidently the program worked well, for in 1821 the population of Texas was some 3,500 and by 1830 it had reached almost 20,000. But the Mexicans had been too successful in their real estate giveaway, for when General Manuel de Mier y Terán visited the place in 1828 and witnessed the "Americanization" of the province, he hurried back to the capital and gave warning to the government either to occupy Texas now or forget it. Heeding his warnings, Mexico toughened up her immigration restrictions for Americans, sent Mexican colonists into the area, encouraged Catholic European countries to send immigrants, and established more garrisons in Texas to maintain control. But it was too late. There were too many cultural differences between the two, their laws and customs were incompatible, and mutual distrust eventually led to open conflict. At first the Americans wanted only a public education system and separate statehood for Texas, away from the influence of the state of Coahuila, nevertheless remaining citizens of Mexico. But the government turned a deaf ear to the requests and soon president-dictator Antonio López de Santa Anna found himself with a full-scale revolt on his hands.

The action started for real when the Americans refused to surrender a cannon to the Mexicans at Gonzales, just east of San Antonio. From there the Americans captured the city of San Antonio, paroling the Mexican soldiers to leave Texas and never return. When the news of this humiliating defeat reached Santa Anna he was infuriated. The Americans, secure in their minds that the revolution was over and separate status acquired, went about their business as usual. Meanwhile the presidente, having assumed command of a large army, recrossed the Rio Grande with a mind to put the upstart revolutionaries to the sword, thus ending this protest business once and for all.

A force of Americans consisting of some of the most colorful names in the annals of American history were surrounded and killed after an epic thirteen-day struggle against insurmountable odds. Travis, Crockett, Bowie, Dickinson, and Bonham were only a few of the 187 brave men who made their final stand in an old mission located on a plain one half mile east of San Antonio de Bexar. Strategically speaking, the Alamo served no useful purpose to either side. Santa Anna didn't need to attack, he could have easily starved the Texans out. He chose instead to fight, suffering some sixteen hundred casualties needlessly. The core of his army was destroyed. The Americans who lost gained the most in the end. Precious time was given Sam Houston, who was desperately trying to keep both a government and an army together. But perhaps most important, the terrible defeat at the Alamo strengthened the moral cause and gave the Texans a vengeful battle cry. A few weeks later at San Jacinto, Houston gave the men their final instructions: "Victory is certain, trust in God and fear not." While the makeshift band merrily played "Will You Come to the Bower I Have Shaded

For You" and the resounding cries of "Remember the Alamo" echoed in the air, the destiny of Texas and eventually the whole American Southwest was settled. It was the most devastating defeat ever inflicted upon an opponent by an American army. Lasting only a few minutes, Santa Anna's entire army, some fifteen hundred strong, were either killed, captured, or wounded. On the American side there were six killed and twenty-five wounded. Marquis James, in his Pulitzer Prize-winning biography of Houston, described the epic event poignantly: "On an obscure meadow of bright grass, nursed by a water course named hardly on any map, wet steel would decide which civilization should prevail on these shores and which submit in the clash of men and symbols impending—the conquistador and the frontiersman, the Inquisition and the Magna Charta, the rosary and the rifle." The new Republic of Texas would suffer many hardships and trials in the next few years. But her citizens, both Mexican and American, were of frontier stock, a unique breed of self-sufficient people who had hacked out a living on the inhospitable frontier. They weren't going to let a little thing like organizing a workable government slow them down.

THE ROAD TO SANTA FE

THE MEXICAN REVOLUTION brought about a major change in foreign policy toward the giant to the north. The city of Santa Fe, long neglected by her capital far to the south, expressed a strong desire to exchange trade goods with her neighbor. This was a complete reversal of the old Spanish mercantile system, which required the colony to trade only with the mother country.

The first efforts to establish a trade were made in 1804 by one William Morrison, who trusted a French Creole named Baptiste le Land with his goods. Le Land took the trade items to Santa Fe, sold them, pocketed the money, and remained in Santa Fe. International commerce between the two thriving cites of St. Louis and Santa Fe didn't exactly get off to a flying start. Zebulon Pike returned from New Spain in 1807 and reported to the merchants the many opportunities for trade in Santa Fe; however, most of the enterprising merchants who braved the trip between 1812 and 1821 were forced to endure the hospitality and culinary delights of the Santa Fe jail.

In 1821 two trappers, Jacob Fowler and Hugh Glenn, drifted down through Raton Pass and into Santa Fe. That same year, William Becknell journeyed into the city after a trading expedition into the Indian country to the north. Becknell's party returned to St. Louis heavily laden with Mexican blankets, silver, and mules. In 1822 he led another party, this time taking along the first three wagons over the trail. One of the men accompanying Becknell on this trip was Ewing Young, destined to be known as the greatest trapper in the Southwest.

At this time St. Louis was a boisterous city of some 4,600. It was raw and crude, and Edward Kern described the place as a "dirty place filled with Indians, Spaniards, and Jews." Actually the starting place was Franklin, but high waters soon washed the little burg away. Other cities like Westport and Independence also rose to prominence during this period as jumping-off places to that vast Unknown west of the Missouri.

In 1824 Becknell again led a party of 25 wagons, $30,000 worth of goods, and 150 mules and horses. It was the first great caravan to make the trek over the Santa Fe Trail. The party returned with over $180,000 in silver coin and $10,000 in fur.

From this time on the trade business was in full swing, the wagons usually going on west to a point some 150 miles west of Independence called Council Groves where the traders rendezvoused. The Pittsburg and Murphy wagons used in carrying the goods could carry up to 4 tons. Horses, mules, or oxen served as teams and a man could expect to make about 15 to 20 miles a day depending on conditions along the way. Josiah Gregg, in his classic *Commerce of the Prairies,* described some of the action as he remembered it:

> We now moved on slowly and leisurely, for all anxiety on the subject of water had been happily set at rest by frequent falls of rain. But imagine our consternation and dismay when, upon descending into the valley of the Cimarron on the morning of the 19th of June, a band of Indian warriors on horse-back suddenly appeared before us from behind the ravines—an imposing array of death dealing savages! It was a genuine alarm—a tangible reality! These warriors, however, as we soon discovered, were only the vanguard of a countless host, who were by this time pouring over the opposite ridge, and galloping directly towards us.
>
> The wagons were soon irregularly formed upon the hill-side; but in accordance with the habitual carelessness of caravan traders a great portion of the men were unprepared for the emergency. Scores of guns were empty, and as many more had been wetted by the recent showers and would not go off. Here was one calling for balls—another for powder—a third for flints. Exclamations such as "I've broke my ramrod"—"I've split my caps"—"I've rammed down a ball without powder"—"My gun is choked; give me yours"—were heard from

different quarters; while a timorous green-horn would perhaps cry out, "Here, take my gun, you can out-shoot me!"

It wasn't only the Indians who made life precarious for the travelers. The country was literally crawling with rattlesnakes, the critters slithering through the grass trying to keep out of the way of both animals and men. Worse yet was to wake up in the morning to find one of them had crawled into your blankets. Thirst caused by long stretches without water was always a problem on the journey. Gregg described how the desperate, thirst-crazed men in Captain Becknell's expedition shot a buffalo out near the Cimarron and knowing that the animal would have had knowledge of some remote watering place, cut into the beast and an "invigorating draught" was "procured from its stomach," which the men drank with "exquisite delight." Accidental gunshot wounds were not uncommon. Kit Carson made his first trip west over the Santa Fe Trail, and in his autobiography described an amputation from a gunshot wound done in rather primitive fashion. A knife, a saw, and a hot iron to sear the wound were the necessary instruments. It might be added that several assistants were needed to hold the patient down while the operation was in progress.

Another who made his first trip west during the heyday of the Santa Fe trade was Charles Trumbull Hayden, a man destined to have a tremendous impact on the history of territorial Arizona.

Both governments made strong efforts to protect the traders going both ways. American military units gave escort to the Mexican border, where the caravans were picked up by Mexican units who took them the rest of the way. The procedure was reversed when going in the opposite direction.

Upon arrival in Santa Fe the wagons were taken to the local customhouse, where they were inspected and taxed by local authorities. Whatever the tax might be, and it fluctuated depending on the greed of the officials, it didn't seem to matter much to the traders, for they simply increased their prices and passed the cost on to the consumer.

Some of the traders went on to California over the Old Spanish and Gila trails while many took their goods south to Chihuahua City, where they always did a brisk business.

All in all, the business was advantageous to both sides. The Americans had a great need for the fine Mexican mules and silver. The Mexicans, far from the industrial centers of their homeland, were always short of essential items for day-to-day living. A commercial link had been established for the first time on a large scale. Many of the traders never returned to their homeland to stay but rather chose to remain in the Southwest. Some married Mexican girls and raised families, becoming prominent businessmen, forming a fine blending of cultures that is characteristic of the Southwest today. Still others went off into the mountains on some other adventure. For better or for worse, from the Mexican point of view, the American was here to stay, a permanent fixture in the great Southwest.

THE RECKLESS BREED

LONG BEFORE ORDINARY WHITE MEN braved the arduous task of cross-ing into the great American desert and beyond, long before latter-day explorers "discovered" the mountain passes to California and Oregon, and long before the cattlemen drove the herds north or the miners went west to dig for the riches that the mountains held, a fearless, intractable, reckless breed of men challenged the moun-tains for another type of treasure.

The market for beaver furs in the first half of the nineteenth cen-tury provided the incentive to businessmen in search of wealth and young men in search of adventure. From the now famous adver-tisement run by William Ashley in 1822 when he sent out a call that attracted such names in the annals of trapping as Jim Bridger, David Jackson, Jim Beckwourth, and Jedidiah Smith, to all "en-terprising young men . . ." to its demise in the 1840s, the fur trade was one of the vanguards of American industry. John Jacob Astor of the American Fur Company was comparable to such latter-day magnates as John D. Rockefeller and William Andrews Clark in their respective fields. Every man wore a hat, and every hat was beaver, generally speaking.

The men who took part in the fur trade left an impact on the West that is immeasurable. Not many were literate, so the details of their adventures are scarce and few records were kept. The West at this time was a vast social outlet and some of the trappers, ostracized from their former societies, went native in the new land. Some never went home again. Bill Williams, Edward Rose, and Jim Beckwourth were among a few who became respected Indian chiefs. Rose was described once as having led a most bloodthirsty attack on another Indian tribe, taking part also in the macabre mutilation celebrations that followed.

Not a few lost their lives in the mountains. In 1856 Antoine Robidoux could account for only 3 out of 300 who went into the Rockies some thirty years earlier. James O. Pattie recalled only 16 survivors out of 160 in only one year on the Gila. Darwin's theory of survival of the fittest was never more pragmatically proved than during the trapping period. If the Indians didn't remove his top-knot, or worse, there were many other hazards that could cause a trapper to "go under." Grizzly bears were numerous, and at that time had no fear of man. Trappers reported seeing as many as 220 in a day, sometimes in bunches of 50 or 60. Weighing 1,000 pounds or so, able to run up to speeds of 35 miles per hour, and with a bad disposition to match, the grizzly was as big a threat as the most hostile band of Indians. There were also many other ways of shortening the life expectancy of the trappers. Fatal quarrels with friends, thirst, hunger, storm, accident, and disease also took their toll.

Others crossed that line which separates a man living a savage-like life from a man who is actually a savage. One such man was Charley Gardner, nicknamed Phil in honor of his home town of Philadelphia. He once went into the mountains with an Indian companion. There was a violent storm and the two were given up as lost by the others. A few days later Phil rode into camp alone, pulled a piece of human leg out of his pack, and tossed it on the ground exclaiming, "There, damn you, I won't have to gnaw on you any more." Thereafter his friends referred to him as Cannibal Phil. It was said that sometime later he spent another rugged winter in the mountains; this time the object of his culinary work was his Indian wife.

The quest for food was an obsession in a land where one would suppose that game would always be plentiful. A hungry trapper might sit down and eat 4 or 5 pounds of meat at a sitting, not knowing when his next meal might come, or if he would even get a chance to eat again before some hostile Indian did him in. The crossing of a desert might reduce him to eating ants or crickets. Some reported making stew with the ears of their mules or soaking their moccasins until they were soft enough to eat. It's not surprising that when he did find game plentiful, a feast was held and he ate until his "meatbag," or stomach, was filled. When it was available, he used the dried dung of the buffalo for fuel, called buffalo chips, which he insisted imparted a peppery flavor to the meat. Otherwise he used dried aspen, which made a good fire without much smoke, or pitch pine, the most flammable. Visitors to the mountains must have been aghast while witnessing the ritual of feasting, for the trappers put on quite a show. If the menu for the evening was to be buffalo, the hump ribs would be placed over the coals to broil. While waiting for the main course to cook they would break open a thighbone and dig out the marrow. Then they scooped blood out of the cavity and added to that a little water, enough to make a soupy substance, adding to the brew the bone marrow and sprinkling on some salt and pepper. The mountain cocktail was ready to drink. This no doubt satisfied some physiological need, but it also sickened the curious observer who might happen to be visiting the mountains. It has been reported that the favorite meat of some of the trappers was panther or cat, although most seemed to have favored the buffalo meat.

The trapper's clothes were homemade and usually buckskin. When riding in wet weather it was necessary to remove the clothing lest it shrink. During meals he rubbed his greasy hands over the leather. This served to waterproof the clothing. He also attached a fringe along the seams. This not only looked fancy but it caused water to run off rather than soak in during wet weather when it wasn't possible to remove his clothes. In hostile Indian country some designed a coat of mail by hardening the leather of a buckskin overshirt, thus increasing the chances of survival in case of attack.

Kit Carson once told of an experience suffered in his younger days when, traveling to Bent's Fort, he chanced to run into a rainstorm. He found shelter in an abandoned tepee where he spent the night. The next morning he noticed a terrible itch. Riding on to the fort, he explained his dilemma to William Bent, who told him to remove his clothes. Bent took the clothes and deposited them on the nearest anthill, where, in no time at all, all the lice were devoured. After a thorough scrubbing in some solution Carson was pronounced fit, a much wiser lad for his experience.

The trapper's skin weathered with the elements until it was much the same as the clothes he wore. His hair grew long and only his beard distinguished him from the red man. Around his neck in a small leather bag he carried his "possibles," mostly personal articles such as a pipe, tobacco, bullet mold, bullet pouch, and awl. Strapped over his shoulder was a powder horn and from the belt around his waist hung a pistol, hatchet, and knife. Like the Indian he chose moccasins for footwear rather than boots, and for a cover he wore a low crown felt or a cap made of skins. His favorite rifle was one made especially for the mountain trade by the Hawken brothers of St. Louis. The Hawken rifle was a .40 to .69 caliber with a short 36-inch barrel and a range of only 200 yards, but that seemed enough in the mountains, where long-range firing was not the rule. He preferred the Green River knife to others for both fighting and skinning. The knife was manufactured by the John Russell Works in Green River, Massachusetts. Stamped on the blade of this revered knife were the words: "J. Russell and Company Green River Works." Many accounts of hand-to-hand fighting were accentuated with the words, "I ran him up to the Green River," meaning he drove the blade up to the words "Green River." If he had been lucky enough to run the knife in all the way he simply said, "I gave him the Works."

Basically there were only two types of trappers, the engagé, or lowly company employee, and the aristocrat of the trade, the free trapper. It is the latter with whom we will be concerned. He went where he pleased, trapped wherever and whenever he wanted, and sold his furs to the highest bidder. However, if the situation warranted it he would band up with other free trappers voluntarily. His equipment usually consisted of a rifle, a hundred flints, 25 pounds of powder, 100 pounds of lead, a horn, a knife, a hatchet, shot bag, and four to six traps weighing 5 pounds and costing anywhere from $12 to $16 apiece. A party of trappers would pick an open area called a hole for a base camp. Here they would find plenty of game and water. After establishing the camp they would go out in small groups in search of beaver "sign." The beaver, being the cagey critter that he was, made trapping extremely difficult. When finding sign the trapper would have to wade in the icy water quite a distance to escape detection by his wary adversary. The trapper would then set his trap and bait it. The trap was secured by a 5-foot chain attached to a pole driven into the stream bed. For bait he used the castor of a male or female musk gland which he always carried. This bait would be placed on a float about 4 inches above the trap so that when the beaver approached the bait, he would place his paw in the trap and spring it. When he tried to swim away toward deeper water, the beaver would find himself held fast by the chain attached to the pole. When this happened the beaver would usually drown, though it was common enough for one to gnaw his entrapped member off and escape.

Like gold dust on the mining frontier, beaver fur was the medium of exchange in the mountains. Unique to the American industry was the rendezvous system, dreamed and schemed by William Ashley in 1825. The procedure was simple: the trader would buy his supplies in St. Louis and transport them out to the trappers in the field. Like the modern-day shopping centers, the merchants took the goods out to the people instead of vice versa. The advantages of these ventures were that they were extremely profitable to the merchants and convenient to the trappers. The prices charged the trappers were exorbitant, as much as a 2,000 per cent markup, but trapper and Indian had only two choices, buy or go without. Alcohol bought in St. Louis for $.15 a gallon was sold in a diluted form for $5.00 a pint. Coffee went for $.15 a pound in St. Louis and $2.00 a pound in the mountains. Flour, $.02 a pound in St. Louis, was $2.00 a pound trapper's price. Tobacco was $3.00 a pound and blankets sold for $15 to $20 apiece. Neither the risk of loss nor the high cost of transportation warranted these outrageous prices.

The trappers gathered at their annual rendezvous, a location predesignated the year before, and proceeded to barter and sell. In exchange for pelts, necessities for the coming year were obtained, plus various geegaws which they purchased for their Indian wives or girl friends. The trappers vied with one another to see who could adorn his woman with the finest assortment of threads and ornaments. When the trading was finished, out came the whiskey and the fun and frolic began. For the next several days they drank, held shooting matches, fought, wrestled, made love to Indian girls, ran races, and indulged in other such forms of recreation until it was time to head back again to the mountains for the fall hunt. Arizona, because of its remoteness and relatively minor role in the over-all trade, never hosted a rendezvous. However, the wild escapades in Taos and Santa Fe were every bit as eventful as any mountain rendezvous. Also, during the heyday of trapping Arizona was still a part of Mexico, and American trappers were not exactly welcomed by the locals.

The species of beaver inhabiting the Gila, Colorado, and their tributaries was the Sonoran, slightly lighter in color and slightly inferior to the pelts collected in regions farther north. They ranged in weight from 30 to 60 pounds, some weighing as much as 100 pounds. The pelt weighed from 1½ to 20 pounds, and the price ran from $4.00 to $6.00 apiece. However, during the peak year 1832, the price went up to $9.00, and dropped to about $1.00 by the end of the era in 1840. A mule could carry about two hundred pelts and one man could handle three or four mules. The interested mathematician might calculate the dollar worth of a successful season using these figures as a guideline.

The trapping seasons were the spring and fall, although in the Southwest the season lasted year round.

The first American trappers to enter Arizona, according to best records, arrived in 1826. The party listed among its members three men destined to become legendary in the annals of trapping along the Gila. One, Bill Williams, is considered among some historians as the best example of the free trapper. More will be said of him later. Ewing Young, mentor of Kit Carson and others, is considered the greatest of the Southwest's trappers. The third, James Ohio Pattie, is best remembered for a narrative written several years later of his experiences in the Southwest. Pattie, the hero of the adventure, was a larger-than-life figure. His story is historically accurate in most parts, although he seems to have exaggerated his role and assumed many others in the narration. The title of the book is a story in itself:

> The personal Narrative of James Ohio Pattie of Kentucky, during an Expedition from St. Louis, through the vast regions between that place and the Pacific Ocean and thence back through the City of Mexico to Vera Cruz, during journeying of six years, in which he and his father, who accompanied him suffered unheard of hardships and dangers, had various conflicts with the Indians and were made captives in which captivity his father died; together with a description of the country, and various nations through which they passed, edited by Timothy Flint.

Relations between the Mexicans and the Americans were not usually cordial. But that wasn't the case the day James O. Pattie and his friends arrived to find that a Comanche war party had made a raid on the city and stolen several young women. The trappers, a gallant breed to the last man, were off to the rescue. The Comanche, not realizing they were being followed, had relaxed their guard. The girls, stripped of their clothing, were forced to walk ahead of the band. The trappers set up an ambush and when the shooting started James leaped out to rescue one of the prisoners. Pulling her up onto his horse he gallantly covered her with his own buckskin shirt and delivered her safely back to her father's doorstep. It turned out that the girl's father was the former governor. The gracious man offered James a place to stay and apparently the young lady was most obliging. From that time forth, James always received a friendly welcome upon his arrival in Santa Fe.

There were many other hair-raising adventures in the narrative, from hand-to-hand combat with a grizzly bear to Indian massacres. Our hero always prevailed. His father Sylvester didn't do quite so well. He was managing a mining operation at Santa Rita del Cobre when another man swindled him out of his savings. Joining his son, they journeyed to California, where the interlopers were thrown into jail, their Santa Fe trapping license not being valid in California. While in captivity Sylvester died, but James once again turned misfortune into success when an outbreak of smallpox struck and our hero rose to the occasion. It seems that among his many talents Pattie was somewhat knowledgeable in the practice of medicine. Charges against him were dropped when he inoculated some 22,000 Californians against the dreaded disease, or at least so he claimed.

It is known that many of these events happened just as Pattie recalled; however, just what his personal role was is subject for debate.

Perhaps Timothy Flint, in his desire to sell more copies, did the exaggerating rather than Pattie. It's not known what happened to Pattie, as he disappeared from the pages of history shortly after the narrative was written. It is believed that he went to California again and perished in a raging snowstorm in the Sierra Nevada. If Pattie was not the hero he claimed to be along the Gila, he was the first American to write about these events, thus earning for himself a significant role in its history.

Of all the men who trapped the rivers and streams from the Canadian border to the Gila River, the truest aristocrat of the trade was the intractable, intrepid Old Bill Williams. Not much was known about Old Bill until just a few years ago when Alpheus H. Favour, a Prescott attorney, published a book on the mountain man after years of exhaustive research.

A stubborn, eccentric man obligated to nobody but himself, Bill Williams survived many years in a truculent environment that did in many of his contemporaries. In a land where no one went in alone to trap, Bill did, and he always returned with his mules loaded down with pelts. He always knew when to make a stand and when to run for it, no doubt the reason he lived so long.

He is known today as the number-one horse thief in the Old West for his trips to California, where he relieved the locals of many of their splendid horses. He drove them back into the mountains, where they always brought a good price.

Old Bill went West the first time as a Methodist missionary to work among the Osage Indians. Interestingly enough they converted him to paganism instead of the other way around, although he is supposed to have delivered many a sermon to his contemporaries around the campfires during those nights in the mountains. The sermons were highlighted with spicings of profanity, which the trappers no doubt took as a matter of course.

In a society where eccentricity was a way of life, Bill was considered a bit strange. The others thought him dirty and greasy, and he was even accused of being a cannibal. Most of the time Old Bill just trapped alone, his only companions being his rifle and his mule, with whom he engaged in unilateral conversation.

He got along well with the Indians; in fact, he married two Indian girls and was made a chief in the Ute tribe. Contrary to popular belief he never spent much time in the vicinity of the mountain and town named in his honor. Years later another mountain man, Antoine Leroux, while leading a surveying expedition mentioned that Old Bill had once spent the night on that tall mountain over "yonder," and so the mountain now had a name. Bill Williams Mountain stands alone miles away from any others of its stature. Somehow it seems rather fitting.

When free trappers banded together for self-preservation they usually elected a partisan, or captain, to act as leader. The partisan had nearly as much authority as did the captain of a ship. The greatest of these in the Southwest was Ewing Young. Young had made that trek over the Santa Fe Trail in 1822 with Becknell. He later led several trapping expeditions down along the Gila and its tributaries. He also led the first American group that viewed the Grand Canyon. Young served as mentor for a lad who had run away from home at the age of sixteen and had also come down the Santa Fe Trail in search of adventure. A reward of one penny had been offered for the return of the boy to the saddlery shop where he had been indentured. Trapper, scout, Indian agent, and general, Kit Carson would prove to be worth a lot more to his government in many ways before he was through.

Another mountain man who left a permanent mark on the state was Paulino Weaver. Half Indian, though he acted whole, Weaver later served as one of the guides for the Mormon Battalion when it built the first wagon road from Santa Fe to California. In 1862, he took part in the fabulous gold discovery at La Paz on the Colorado River, and a year later participated in another while leading the A. H. Peeples party up the Hassayampa River. The Rich Hill find was reputed to be the richest placer gold discovery in the history of Arizona. Weaver spent the next few years in and around Prescott, where he worked as a scout for the government. He died in 1866 at Camp Lincoln (Verde), and was later reburied at Prescott's Sharlot Hall Museum, and is today considered that city's "first citizen."

These trappers and their contemporaries were the embodiment of free spirit and independence. They were rebels against the restraints of society and chose to live their lives in the vast unknown where death could come at any moment in a variety of ways. Many returned to society, only partially, to serve as guides for the immigrant trains that came west in the 1840s and 1850s. Today's superhighways cross deserts and mountains over their trails. It seems ironic that men who sought sanctuary in the West would, in the final analysis, be the ones who led the society they despised into their final refuge.

The mountain men left a rich legacy, for the wilderness is still out there beckoning to some adventuresome soul. There exists in the West today a hardy breed of men who periodically forsake the modern conveniences and challenge the wilderness and nature for high adventure, reliving those times when man survived in the mountains on wits and courage.

Jeff Hengesbaugh of Scottsdale is one of these twentieth-century mountain men. In 1973 he led a small expedition overland from Phoenix through the backcountry to Calgary, Alberta. Using the tools and trappings of the mountain men of old and surviving on their own resourcefulness, they traded for essential goods along the way. The party covered some three thousand miles in a little more than six months. Two years later the intrepid Hengesbaugh, following many of the old trails of the mountain men, rode horseback from Arizona to the Green river country of Wyoming for the 150th anniversary of the first rendezvous. The spirits of that reckless breed of old still ride the backcountry with the likes of Jeff Hengesbaugh and his friends.

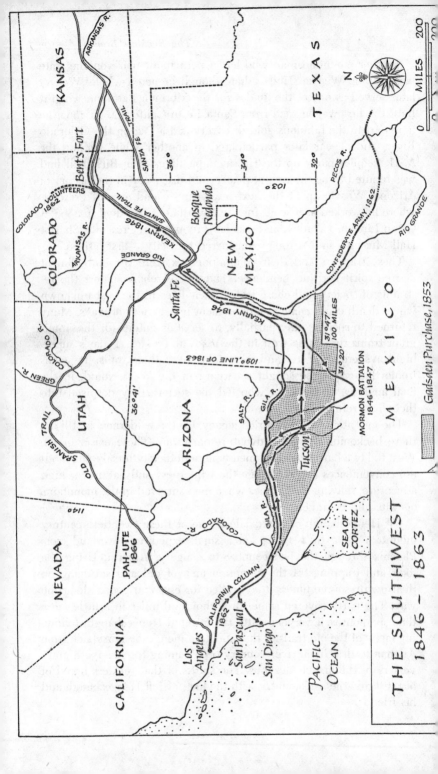

THE SOUTHWEST
1846 - 1863

Gadsden Purchase, 1853

WAR WITH MEXICO

In the years following her break with Spain, Mexico was beset with many internal problems. Leaders came and went with a great deal of violence and regularity. Many died by the gun in the turmoil. During one twenty-four-hour period, no less than three different men became president. One only lasted forty-five minutes. However, one man survived the tragedies that befell the others. Antonio López de Santa Anna was his name. This redoubtable miscreant with a voracious appetite for power would, in his tenure as president-dictator of Mexico, manage to lose a little less than half her entire nation. The states of California, Arizona, New Mexico, and Texas and parts of several others were all lost forever to the young republic. Most of the money received in the settlements never reached the Mexican people but was intercepted by the vainglorious leader. His career had many vicissitudes. He was president-dictator of Mexico eleven times. Santa Anna, being the actor he was, always followed his cue. Like a performer waiting in the wings, this perfidious martinet always seemed to know when to emerge and when to exit from the stage of Mexican politics. No less than sixteen other Mexican leaders of note met death in the turmoil that overwhelmed the country in those early years. Not Santa Anna, who was destined to die peacefully in bed at a ripe old age.

A story is told that when the Mexican army was grouping around San Antonio in 1836, el presidente gazed upon a beautiful young maiden who was doing her laundry on the banks of the river. He desired her company for some amorous adventure; however, her mother insisted that a marriage must take place first. This seemed to be no major problem to the resourceful dictator, for he merely had one of his officers dress up as a priest and the two were "married." After a few days of "honeymooning" the bride was put on board a stage and sent to Mexico City and the groom made preparation for his infamous siege of the Alamo. They had forgotten to tell the young lady and her mother that el presidente already had a first lady living in the capital. Nothing was ever heard from the new bride as she probably was unceremoniously dropped off somewhere in Mexico. An incident took place in 1838 that depicts another side of Santa Anna. The incident went down in history as the Pastry War. In the city of Vera Cruz, a pastry shop owned by a Frenchman was visited one night by a group of Mexican officers. Following a brief altercation, the officers locked the chef in the back room and commenced eating all his pastries. The Frenchman sued for damages but the Mexican government ignored the claims. Eventually the French fleet blockaded Vera Cruz in an attempt to settle the claims; before our hero could lead a valiant charge, the Mexican fortress surrendered. Once again Mexico called on Santa Anna to restore Mexican pride. Meanwhile, the French having proved their point, prepared to retreat. However, before they left, a landing party went ashore, causing rumors of another invasion. Santa Anna was awakened in the middle of the night, thought a full-scale attack was at hand, and clad only in his nightshirt, mounted his steed and rode off in the opposite direction. When informed of the circumstances he very sheepishly returned. Once again fate was kind, for the French were at that moment pulling away. Santa Anna jumped on his white horse and charged. The bored French admiral fired a random shot in the general direction of the figure on horseback who was gesturing madly on shore. The shot landed near, so near in fact that Santa Anna found himself minus a leg. Like the opera star singing out his lifeblood, Santa Anna dictated no less than fifteen "deathbed messages" to the Mexican people. Soon he was up and around, spry as ever, sporting a new wooden leg. He saw to it that his lost leg was given a full military burial with honors on a hill overlooking Vera Cruz. It is said that whenever the climate of politics got a little too hot, Santa Anna would develop a terrible limp. He would reacquaint the people with the unfortunate circumstances surrounding the loss of his leg while defending his beloved Mexico from those hated foreign invaders. To climax the whole ludicrous episode, in 1842 he had the leg dug up and brought to the capital to lie in state. It is not overly surprising that there are no statues to honor this man in Mexico today.

Santa Anna became president-dictator of Mexico in 1833 and immediately began putting down revolts all over Mexico in the most brutal manner. In southern Mexico there was not much trouble from the revolutionaries for they were mostly armed with rakes and pitchforks. However, in the north the situation was different. The American colonists were armed with rifles and years of Comanche warfare had trained them well.

Following the Texas revolution in 1836 were years of uneasy feelings between the United States and Mexico. Realists in Mexico knew that she would never regain her lost colony but the hotheads pressed for war. In the United States the slavery question and the threat of trouble with her southern neighbor kept the proposed statehood of Texas just that, in a proposed state. By the 1840s the wave of Manifest Destiny had begun to sweep the nation. "Annex Texas and California," the expansionists declared. Finally John Slidell was sent to offer Mexico the "fair price" of $25 million for the land between the Rio Grande and the Pacific. A basic philosophical dispute over land now came into focus. To the land-hungry American, land was something to accumulate and sell at a profit. To the Mexican it was something to hand down to your children for generation after generation. Slidell was flatly refused and other means would have to be developed if the young American nation was going to flex her muscles and grow.

In the meantime, the great "pathfinder" John C. Frémont was on another of his famous mapping expeditions in the Far West. This time he was for some unexplainable reason in California, where the Californios politely asked him to leave. He did for a time, but when word arrived that war had broken out between the United States and Mexico, he gathered his truculent army of mountain men and took California by storm. This "Bear Flag revolt" was over almost before it started and with California now securely in the hands of the Americans, Frémont sent his "pathfinder" Kit Carson east with dispatches to inform Washington of the victory in California.

The over-all strategy for fighting the war with Mexico consisted of three armies. The first, led by "Old Rough and Ready" Zachary Taylor, would invade the northern part of Mexico, while Winfield Scott would attack Vera Cruz from the sea and go for the capital city. The third army is the one with which this chronicle is going to be concerned.

The Indians called him the "Horse-chief of the Long Knives," and the whites have called him the "Father of the U. S. Cavalry," but for Stephen Watts Kearny in this age of historical enlightenment, his name still goes misspelled on plaques and monuments. Several towns have been named either for him or his famous nephew Phil Kearny of Civil War fame. For some reason folks continue to spell it incorrectly, preferring instead the spelling "Kearney."

The primary mission of Kearny's Army of the West was the golden prize, California. Shortly after the hostilities with Mexico began, Kearny, then a colonel in the dragoons, was given an appointment to organize and lead an expedition down the Santa Fe Trail to Santa Fe, thence across Arizona and on to California.

Leaving Fort Leavenworth on June 28, 1846, with some eighteen hundred men, including Colonel Alexander Doniphan with his famed Missouri Volunteers and a large contingent of Mormons, the Army of the West advanced to Bent's Fort on the Arkansas River. From this bastion that represented the American jumping-off point into Mexican territory, Kearny's army entered Mexico and took Santa Fe, New Mexico, without firing a single shot. This was done with the considerable help of a Santa Fe trader named James Magoffin and Captain Phillip St. George Cooke of Kearny's command, who rode into Santa Fe ahead of the army and enticed Governor Manuel Armijo to take exit. The bribe attempt was successful and the unscrupulous governor left in such a hurry that he forgot to take his wife along. By and large Santa Fe was left undefended and the Army of the West entered unopposed.

While in Santa Fe Kearny proclaimed himself governor, during which time he pledged to the natives protection from the hostile Indians, a code of law, and a bill of rights. He ordered Colonel Doniphan to postpone his planned expedition into Chihuahua and deal with the recalcitrant Navajo first.

On September 25, 1846, Kearny's army of three hundred dragoons, led by mountain men Tom Fitzpatrick and Antoine Robidoux, started down the Rio Grande en route for California.

It was a most fateful meeting that September day just outside of Socorro when Kearny met Kit Carson traveling east with dispatches proclaiming victory in California. "How can this be?" Kearny must have asked himself. California was supposed to have been taken by his Army of the West. One thing was certain, Kearny had orders to take California and assume control. One way or another that was just what he meant to do. Ordering two hundred of his dragoons to return to Santa Fe, Kearny took the remaining one hundred and proceeded on a rapid march to the Pacific. The reluctant Carson was ordered to turn around and serve as guide, the dispatches given to Tom "Broken Hand" Fitzpatrick, who in turn delivered them to the President. Carson no doubt was unhappy with his new assignment. Not only did he not get to deliver the dispatches to Washington, but his family, whom he hadn't seen for some time, were just a few miles up the Rio Grande at Taos. However, duty called and Carson led the dragoons down the Gila Trail toward California.

When Kearny reached the vicinity of the Santa Rita del Cobre mines he chanced to encounter Apache chieftain Mangas Coloradas, who offered to aid the Americans in their war against his traditional adversaries, the Mexicans. Kearny politely refused and the army continued on into Arizona. Accompanying the Army of the West on the historic trek was Lieutenant William Emory, whose *Notes of a Military Reconnaissance* is by far the most accurate historic account of the journey. Not only did the West Pointer give informational accounts of military actions and events, but his remarkable descriptions of the land with its fauna and flora provided a wonderful introduction to the studies of archaeology, anthropology, and ethnology in the Southwest.

When the Army of the West reached the Yuma Crossing word of their coming had already been passed on to the Mexicans or Californios by the local natives in the area. As the army pushed ever westward, signs began to indicate that maybe the Americans weren't in control of California after all. Prior to reaching Warner's Ranch, about 60 miles from San Diego, Kearny was informed that the Californios held all the land and the Americans were in control of the seaports. This sudden turn of events caused the general to send to San Diego for aid. By the time the dragoons arrived at Stokes Ranch, Captain Archibald Gillespie of the U. S. Marines, Lieutenant Edward F. "Ned" Beale of the Navy, and a contingent of troops had arrived to reinforce them.

When informed of the presence of Californios nearby, General Kearny sent a patrol out to investigate. The patrol crept up on the enemy troops and found them, of all things, taking a siesta. At that moment, the dragoons could have rounded up all the Californios' horses and captured the entire 180 men without a struggle. Instead they rustled around, making a lot of noise, even to the point of leaving some equipment behind in their rush to rejoin the main force. Even the leader of the Californios, Andrés Pico, wasn't convinced of the presence of American troops until his men brought to him a dragoon jacket and a blanket with U.S. stamped on it. The comic-opera events preceding the battle and the tragic contest that followed will never be considered one of our nation's proudest moments. We have our Bunker Hill, New Orleans, San Juan Hill, and Bastogne. Luckily there was only one San Pascual.

San Pascual is a hilly, rugged area about 35 miles out of San Diego. It was a rainy morning that December 6 when the two opposing forces faced each other across an open plain. Pico's lancers, among the best horsemen in the world, watched anxiously as the dragoons, on their worn-out service mules, prepared to advance on that cold, wet plain. Kearny had given the signal to advance at a trot, but this order was misunderstood by Lieutenant Abraham R. Johnston and his twelve men. With still over three quarters of a mile to go they charged full speed ahead. Captain Benjamin D. Moore took off in pursuit in an attempt to stop them. By this time twenty-eight out of Kearny's forty-man force were charging toward the still waiting lancers. The Americans, mounted on their worn-out mules, much of their powder wet from the rain, were now strung out across the plain. Pico wisely began to retreat and by the time the Americans caught up to him they had been charging full speed for over a mile and a half. Now it was Pico's time to charge and Captain Moore fell, mortally wounded by no fewer than sixteen lances. When the dragoons tried to fire, they found that their weapons, wet from the weather, were of no use. The lancers now took their *reatas,* or ropes, and pulled the dragoons from their mules and lanced them. During the charge, Carson's horse was shot out from under him and his rifle was broken in the fall. The intrepid little trapper ran on foot to join the melee. Even General Kearny was not spared, as he suffered a humiliating lance wound in the worst possible place a horseman could: it would be a long time before the general would sit comfortably again. Quick action by

Lieutenant Emory was all that saved Kearny's life. As if to rub a little more salt in the wounds, Pico's men roped and dragged off one of the two howitzers that the dragoons had lugged all the way from Fort Leavenworth. Only two of the twenty-two killed in Kearny's force died by gunfire; the rest were dispatched by the adroit lancers.

When the Californios broke off the battle, Kearny dispatched Beale, Carson, and an Indian to sneak through the enemy lines and run to San Diego for help. All three men made it safely through the lines, although all lost their shoes in the process and had to hoof it to San Diego barefoot.

When the rescue party arrived at the scene they found the Army of the West in poor condition. From its glorious beginning to this unhappy ending, the dragoons marched unceremoniously into the city of San Diego.

There would be other battles fought in the rolling hills of California but the most memorable one would be the struggle for power between John C. Frémont, who considered himself governor of California, and Stephen Watts Kearny, who had orders from the President awarding him the governorship. However, that classic struggle is beyond the scope of this chronicle. Frémont did suffer a severe setback in his career but not for long as he shortly got into politics and became the first senator from the new state of California and later the first Republican candidate for President. Kearny did not get another chance at the war; while in Vera Cruz he contracted typhoid fever and died shortly after.

The controversy over the battles of San Pasqual and Kearny vs. Frémont is still present today. The twentieth-century Army historians, in re-creating the San Pascual fiasco, have decreed that since Pico and his lancers left the field victory belonged to the dragoons. However, for those who were there that day in December 1846, there was no doubt as to who got the best of whom.

Another part of Kearny's army, and one that played a more significant role, was the so-called Mormon Battalion. This group, made up of Latter-day Saints under the leadership of military officers, would carve a road through the Arizona wilderness, much of which is still used today.

Brigham Young and the President of the United States James K. Polk never had much fondness for each other but each was smart enough to recognize a good deal when he saw it. Brigham needed three things badly—money for his struggling Church, the desire to show the government that the Mormons could be good citizens, and a way west for his people. Polk needed warm bodies to serve the country in time of war.

The man Kearny picked to lead the Mormons on this historic trek was Captain Phillip St. George Cooke, and a more unlikely candidate could not be found. Cooke was a professional soldier, a cavalryman's cavalryman who wanted nothing better than to lead the thrust into Mexico at the head of his troops. He found his new assignment extremely distasteful and the Mormons reciprocated. It was mutual dislike from the start. Cooke's first chore was to cull out the old and the weak, including the children, that the Saints had brought along for the trip. Finally with some 397 men and 5 women, the journey began. Following a more southerly route than Kearny because of the wagons, the Mormons slowly but surely cut a wagon road west. The only battle they fought was near today's Benson when they were attacked by wild bulls. Humorous as it might seem today, it was no laughing matter as the longhorns charged time and again at the soldiers. These were the same animals that were hunted for trophy just like any other wild animal by European big-game hunters of the period. Finally the bulls were driven away, ending what is known tongue-in-cheek in southern Arizona as the first battle of "Bull Run."

Cooke also complained about his three guides, Baptiste Charbonneau, Paulino Weaver, and Antoine Leroux, but in justice to them it was probably the first time these mountain men had cause for locating a passageway wide enough for a wagon road.

On December 17, 1846, the Mormon Battalion came within sight of Tucson. After some discussion the Mexican commander decided to evacuate the Old Pueblo, allowing the Americans to enter and spend their money. Old Glory was raised over the tiny community of some five hundred people. Shortly afterward the Americans moved on.

The Mormon Battalion finally reached the end of their journey in January 1847. They had traveled over 1,000 miles in 102 days and before they parted company, Cooke and his Mormon soldiers had developed the greatest respect for each other. The experiences they shared along the trail throughout the arduous trip no doubt caused them to develop a new sensitivity to each other's viewpoint. No doubt many a young man named his first son in honor of that famed cavalryman. Cooke never did get the opportunity to lead a gallant charge into the enemy. Not in this war anyway. However, his contribution was much more than if he had ridden into mere battle. His road across Arizona would become the favorite all-season route for thousands of immigrants over the next several years. As for the Mormons, they were mustered out of the Army in California. Most of them returned to the new Promised Land at the Great Salt Lake. Many remembered the fertile valleys they passed through on their trek and years later when the call came for settlers to go off into the Territory of Arizona, they returned again, this time to stay.

War with Mexico finally ended with the Treaty of Guadalupe Hidalgo, signed on February 2, 1848. Mexico lost nearly half her land in the transaction, a bitter pill to swallow. Gone was Upper California, Arizona north of the Gila, Nevada, Utah, most of New Mexico, and parts of Colorado and Wyoming.

As for the new United States-Mexico boundary, Article V of the treaty stipulated that a line would commence three marine leagues from land in the Gulf of Mexico, up the deepest channel of the Rio Grande to the southern boundary of the New Mexico territorial line. From there it would follow a westerly course to the west boundary line of the Territory, somewhere near the Continental Divide; thence north to the first branch of the Gila River, then down the deepest channel to where that river meets the Colorado. From a distance of one marine league south of the bay of San Diego, a line would run directly to the junction of the Gila and the Colorado.

Mexico lost something else too, something she was not sad to see depart: the responsibility for the 120,000 Indians within the new boundary lines was now a problem for the United States to cope with. Mexico even persuaded the naïve American treaty makers to agree to assume all claims against the Indians, amounting to some $3 million, and pay indemnity for any further depredations. The United States also agreed to police the international border, a nigh impossible task at the time. Lastly, Mexico, or perhaps Señor Santa Anna and his cronies, received some $15 million as compensation for the lost lands.

BOUND FOR THE PROMISED LAND

THE HISTORY OF THE Mormons in Arizona is a volume in itself and will be only summarized in this chronicle. The religion was founded in 1830, in western New York, through revelations of the prophet Joseph Smith. Smith and his followers had successive locations in Ohio, Missouri, and Illinois. Industrious and clannish, they oftentimes incurred the wrath of their neighbors. In 1844, Smith was murdered by a mob in Carthage, Illinois, touching off widespread violence. The new leader, forty-three-year-old Brigham Young, decided to take his people to some location so undesirable and inhospitable that no outsider would ever dare to try to settle there and the Saints could worship their God and live their lives as they pleased. In 1847, Young led his people to the "Promised Land" of Deseret, or as it became known later, Utah. There, a great city was born on the shores of the Great Salt Lake. The story of the early Mormons in Utah is an epic account of man's indomitable will to survive in the face of almost insurmountable odds. They might well never have made it had it not been for the intrepid leadership of the sagacious Brigham Young, who prodded, cajoled, and directed his people through the formative years. Young was no doubt a great spiritual leader; however, he was also one of the most capable executives this country ever produced. Had he never been associated with the Saints, it is likely he would still have gained fame in whatever his chosen field.

The Mormon settlement in Utah became the prototype for future agrarian development of the arid Southwest. Theirs was the first large-scale irrigation program used in the West.

In the 1850s, following the war with Mexico, the whole West was opened for settlement. Gold had been discovered in California, and the rich agricultural areas of Oregon lured immigrants by the thousands. In order to reach their new "Promised Land" they had to cross the empire of the Mormons. Ironically, the anti-Mormon element from Missouri that Young had led his people away from was also a part of this westward movement. By and large, the immigrant parties were important for economic reasons: as they passed through the Mormon communities they purchased produce and merchandise.

However, there were still hostile feelings between the two factions, which culminated with the Mountain Meadows Massacre in 1857. The disaster occurred when a band of Indians, reputedly led by Mormons, wiped out an entire wagon train in southwestern Utah. The result was the so-called Mormon War of 1857. After a short occupation by the United States Army, an uneasy peace prevailed for the next several years.

The trail blazer for the Mormons into Arizona was a kindly frontiersman named Jacob Hamblin, who first entered the land of the Hopi in 1858. Six years later, he opened a road that crossed the Colorado River near the "El Vado de los Padres" (The Crossing of the Fathers), the path taken by Franciscan padres Escalante and Dominguez in 1776.

John D. Lee began operating a ferryboat at the crossing in 1872. Five years later, Lee was executed by a firing squad for his part in the Mountain Meadows Massacre some twenty years earlier. He was standing in his own coffin protesting his innocence at the time of his execution. Over the next several years, the Hamblin Trail was the main pathway for the Mormon settlers into Arizona. The industrious Saints settled in small communities stretching from Littlefield in the northwest corner of the Arizona Strip to Springerville near the far end of the trail. Farmers and ranchers, they also did much missionary work among the Indians. Eventually, they would push farther south into the Gila and Salt river valleys, where their descendants remain solidly planted in the state's history and culture today. Mesa, the capital of Mormonism in Arizona, began with the first settlers in 1878, and is today one of the largest cities in the state.

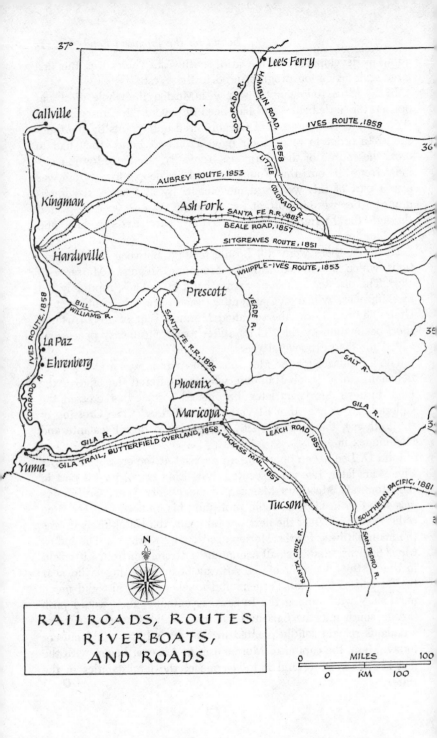

37°

Lee's Ferry

Callville

COLORADO R.

HAMBLIN ROAD, 1858

IVES ROUTE, 1858

36°

Kingman

AUBREY ROUTE, 1853

LITTLE COLORADO R.

Ash Fork

SANTA FE R.R. 1883

BEALE ROAD, 1857

SITGREAVES ROUTE, 1851

Hardyville

WHIPPLE-IVES ROUTE, 1853

Prescott

VERDE R.

35°

IVES ROUTE, 1858

BILL WILLIAMS R.

SANTA FE R.R., 1895

La Paz

Ehrenberg

SALT R.

COLORADO R.

Phoenix

Maricopa

GILA R.

GILA R.

LEACH ROAD, 1857

Yuma

GILA TRAIL; BUTTERFIELD OVERLAND, 1858; JACKASS MAIL, 1857

SOUTHERN PACIFIC, 1881

Tucson

SANTA CRUZ R.

SAN PEDRO R.

N

RAILROADS, ROUTES
RIVERBOATS,
AND ROADS

0   MILES   100

0   KM   100

RAILS, ROUTES, RIVERBOATS,
AND ROADS

HAVING SECURED THE RIGHT to a back seat in the overland coach as far as Tucson, I looked forward, with comparatively little dread, to sixteen days and nights of continuous travel. But the arrival of a woman and her brother, dashed, at the very outset, my hopes of an easy journey, and obliged me to take the front seat, where, with my back to the horses, I began to foresee the coming discomfort. The coach was fitted with three seats, and these were occupied by nine passengers. As the occupants of the front and middle seats faced each other, it was necessary for these six people to interlock their knees; and there being room inside for only ten of the twelve legs, each side of the coach was graced by a foot, now dangling near the wheel, now trying in vain to find a place of support. An unusually heavy mail in the boot, by weighing down the rear, kept those of us who were on the front seat constantly bent forward, thus, by taking away all support from our backs, rendering rest at all times out of the question.

My immediate neighbors were a tall Missourian, with his wife and two young daughters; and from this family arose a large part of the discomfort of the journey. The man was a border bully, armed with revolver, knife, and rifle; the woman, a very hag, ever following the disgusting habit of dipping—filling the air, and covering her clothes with snuff; the girls, for several days overcome by seasickness, and in this having no regard for the clothes of their neighbors;—these were circumstances which offered slight promise of comfort on a journey which, at the best, could only be tedious and difficult. (Excerpt from *Pumpelly's Arizona*, Raphael Pumpelly, 1860)

Historically the trails leading north and south in Arizona were trails of failure, frustration, and violence for the white man. These were the original Apache plunder trails following the river valleys into Mexico. Coming in the opposite direction were the trails of the conquistadors and the padres. By and large the east-west trails were roads of promise. Following the Gila River to the Yuma Crossing, early Spanish traders and missionaries traveled between Santa Fe and California. When gold was discovered in California, this same route, along with a northern crossing along what is today's Interstate 40, carried the Argonauts to the gold fields. Later, when rich mineral deposits were discovered in Arizona, there was an eastward flow of traffic from California. Both the Civil War and the "backwash of the gold rush" brought a steady stream of immigrants to the territory.

The first wagon road into what is today's Arizona was built by the famous Mormon Battalion during the war with Mexico in 1846. The indefatigable Mormons completed the monumental task of building a road from Santa Fe to San Diego in 102 days. The road entered Arizona in the extreme southeast corner of the state and went north to about where Benson is today. From there it went to Tucson, thence north to the Gila River and west to the Yuma Crossing. Another trail called the Leach Road entered Arizona thence turned north at the San Pedro River and followed that stream down to the Gila. It was 47 miles shorter, but missed Tucson and because of this was doomed to failure.

The so-called public works agency for the Southwest was the Army Corps of Topographical Engineers. Though not considered to be quite as colorful as their "predecessors," the mountain men, nonetheless these engineers did outstanding work in surveying and mapping the West. They were a peculiar American institution. This small, elite force of professionals performed an invaluable service to the entire West. A combination of romance and science, these men were the forerunners of today's astronauts.

The first great task undertaken by the Corps of Engineers was to establish a new boundary line across the Southwest. Since the Boundary Commission was under the State Department and had civilian employees, there was the usual friction between the civilian and military personnel. That was but one of many difficulties the men were to encounter. Article V of the Treaty of Guadalupe Hidalgo had specified certain boundaries or lines which the surveyors were to follow. Some of the information was taken from an inaccurate map drawn in 1847 by James Disturnell. Eventually the problems were worked out, but not before some bitter disputes between the American boundary officials and their Mexican counterparts. Of primary concern to the United States Government was a suitable route for a railroad. Interestingly, when all was said and done there was still not a desirable location within the new boundaries to lay track and more land had to be purchased later.

John Weller was first chosen to lead the boundary team, but a political change in Washington ended his tenure before it actually started. The "old pathfinder" John C. Frémont was the next pick. He chose instead to run for the office of senator from the new state of California. Third choice was the less than competent John Russell Bartlett. However, Bartlett was ably assisted by Andrew B. Gray and, most important, Major William Emory, a brilliant cartographer and one of the most accomplished men in the boundary business. Emory had crossed Arizona during the late war with General Kearny and his Army of the West, chronicling his experiences and observations for future scientists. Antoine Leroux, a guide for the Mormon Battalion in their historic trek, served the Boundary Commission in the same capacity. In spite of many problems such as faulty maps, troublesome Apache, disputes with Mexicans, and Bartlett's general ineptness, the Boundary Commission finally completed its less than successful mission. More diplomacy and land purchase would be necessary before the long-needed railroad route could be established.

In 1851 Captain Lorenzo Sitgreaves with Lieutenant J. G. Parke and the redoubtable Leroux surveyed a route across northern Arizona to the Colorado River and thence to Yuma. The route along the 35th parallel became the route of the Santa Fe Railroad some thirty years later. In 1853 explorer Francis X. Aubrey led a party heading east from California, crossing northern Arizona a little to the north of the Sitgreaves route. He later reported encountering Indians who were using golden bullets to shoot rabbits. For one broken-down old mule, Aubrey reported he received a lump of gold that weighed a pound and a half. He also mentioned getting $1,500 worth of the yellow metal for some old garments. Aubrey was killed in a knife fight a short time later in Santa Fe over a newspaper story about his remarkable journey which might have suggested that his tales were something less than the truth.

In 1853 Jefferson Davis, then Secretary of War, sent Lieutenant Amiel W. Whipple with Lieutenant Joseph C. Ives as chief assistant and Leroux as guide to survey another railroad route. This survey was just south of the Sitgreaves route and located several passes through the mountains. About this same time Lieutenant Parke and Lieutenant George Stoneman traced a southern route along the old Cooke wagon road for a route across Arizona near the 32nd parallel.

There were some civilian surveyors on the job during these years also. The Texas and Pacific Railroad hired Andrew B. Gray and Peter Brady to survey a southern route along the Cooke wagon road. Brady, who was elected captain of the party, would later play a major role in the history of the territory as a businessman, sheriff, and legislator.

Routes were established and the immigrants began to pour into Arizona—not to stay, though: they were merely passing through on their way to the Promised Land and many probably thought they were passing through hell itself to get there. Throughout the history of the westward movement, naïveté probably more than anything else sustained the immigrants. Had they known ahead of time the terrible vicissitudes that they would encounter along the way, from snow-packed mountain passes to burning deserts and the various bands of hostile Indians, they might never have left their green sanctuary east of the Mississippi. But naïve they were and West they came.

One such family was that of Royce Oatman. The Oatman family arrived in Tucson in 1851 with a large party of immigrants bound for California. Their wagon train voted to stay awhile in the Old Pueblo to rest up before making the trip across the desert. Oatman was impatient to get moving so he packed up his family and set out on his own.

Rarely did bands of hostile Indians bother a large party of wagons, although small parties were always fair game. The Oatmans stopped to camp near today's Gila Bend and before long several wild-looking natives, probably Yavapai, made an appearance. Oatman decided it best to give them anything they demanded in hopes that they would go away. However, this was not to be as the natives whipped out clubs and attacked the family. The parents and two children were killed outright. Sixteen-year-old Lorenzo was pitched into a gulch and left for dead. Two girls, Olive and

Mary Ann, were carried off. When Lorenzo regained consciousness and saw the slaughter, he headed back down the trail, where he chanced to encounter another party of immigrants.

For the next several years he searched in vain for his sisters. Mary Ann, only ten years old and weakened by the terrible ordeal, died in captivity. Finally some six years later, Henry Grinnell of Yuma was able to ransom Olive from a band of Mohave living along the Colorado River. That same year Royal Stratton, an eastern minister, wrote a wild, hair-raising book on Olive's experiences while a captive. Most of these tales had been conjured up in the devious mind of Mr. Stratton himself. A story was later told of how poor Olive finally died in an insane asylum in California as a result of her ordeal. Actually, Olive lived a long and industrious life. In 1865 she married a lawyer named John Fairchild; she raised a family and died in Sherman, Texas, in 1903.

It wasn't long before the United States Government realized some of the errors it had made in the Treaty of Guadalupe Hidalgo. The treaty stipulated that the United States was to keep watch over the 120,000 Indians they had just inherited and to pay for any damage they did on Mexican soil. There was also the problem of a railroad right of way. To solve this, James Gadsden from South Carolina was appointed American Minister to Mexico. Gadsden, a railroad man, was instructed to secure from Mexico a suitable railroad route to the Pacific. In 1853 an agreement was reached whereby the United States was excused from paying indemnities to Mexican citizens for the nefarious acts of their wards and most important, the Mexican government agreed to sell the United States a large parcel of land south of the Gila River. There were 29,670 acres in all and Gadsden paid $10 million for them. This time part of the money, $3 million, was to be withheld until completion of the survey so as to speed up the process. The man chosen commissioner of the survey was Major William Emory. Emory, who had played a key role in other surveys, was a most capable choice for the task. It's been often questioned as to why the line didn't run a little farther south, thereby giving Arizona access to the Sea of Cortez. The idea of a seaport for Arizona was commendable; however, it wasn't American shortsightedness that caused this deletion, but reluctance on the part of Mexico to part with so much land. After all, she had just lost nearly half of her land in the recent war and the citizenry wouldn't stand for much more. Besides, Mexico wanted a land route to the Baja as well as control of the mouth of the Colorado; also, she didn't want to give up the rich Altar Valley. Perhaps there might have been a slim chance of gaining this seaport, short of war, through diplomacy, but Congress was not in the mood to press for more land at the time and Mexico was not in the mood to part with any more.

The new boundary would settle once and for all the disputed area around El Paso and the Mesilla Valley which had brought the United States and Mexico to the brink of another war. Also the Cooke wagon road, a popular all-weather road with the forty-niners which had traversed Mexican territory, was now with one small exception within American boundaries. Lastly, the way was paved to implement the construction of a southern, all-weather railroad route to the Pacific. The sectional conflict that was now developing in the eastern part of the United States would delay this for nearly thirty years. The new boundary line commenced in the middle of the Rio Grande at 31° 47′ North latitude, west from there for 100 miles, then south to 31° 20′ North latitude, west from there to the 111th meridian, then in a straight line to a point in the middle of the Colorado River 20 miles south of the junction of the Gila and the Colorado. From there it went upstream until it joined the earlier treaty line separating Upper or Alta California from Baja California.

According to historian T. E. Farish there were actually three proposals for the location of the boundary line. One would follow a point from the center of the Rio Grande along the 30th parallel to the Gulf of California for the sum of $25 million. The second proposal was to proceed from a point some 8 miles above El Paso, west 100 miles, thence south to North latitude 31°, thence west to the Gulf of California. The third proposal was the one previously described, which Congress approved, thanks in part to the slavery and slave territory questions. The Northern Congress did not want a large territorial acquisition, fearing it would become populated by slaveholding Southerners. Another significant contributing factor as to why Congress selected number three was the skilled lobbying of the Mexican minister in Washington, Juan Alamonte. Juan Alamonte did not want to see Mexico lose the land route to Lower California. Without it, he reasoned, the entire peninsula would soon be occupied by the United States. At that time the United States was primarily interested in a southern railroad route, and that's what it got.

There was much controversy in the U. S. Congress over the new acquisition. There were enough derogatory remarks to fill a small volume. Even Kit Carson contributed to the declamation when he declared that the territory was so worthless "it wouldn't feed a wolf."

The purchase of land south of the Gila did eventually become one of the southern railroad routes to the Pacific. An even more important factor was the mineral wealth of the land. The whole area was a veritable shelf of copper, silver, and gold, which up to this day makes Arizona the leading producer of copper in the United States. She also produces more of the red metal than any single nation in the free world.

The task of transporting goods across the great southwestern deserts was never an easy one in those early days. The terrain was rough enough to tear up the feet of horses and mules in a short time. Water was always scarce and suitable forage for the animals was unavailable, so feed had to be carried by the pack animals, taking up valuable space. Secretary of War Jefferson Davis was convinced that the solution to this transportation problem would be the use of camels. Why not? They worked in other parts of the world with similar terrain. So Congress appropriated the money and representatives were sent to Asia Minor to purchase the beasts of burden.

The camels arrived in Texas in the spring of 1856 and were an immediate success. They could carry 800 pounds, live off the local forage, and go for long periods without water. Besides that, they could travel 35 to 75 miles a day. Homely beasts with terrible breath, they were known to be extremely temperamental. Coupled with a spirit of intractable independence, this made them difficult to handle. The mule skinners hated them, packers and teamsters cursed them unmercifully, and horses and mules shied when they ambled by. The language barrier also presented no small problem. The Americans couldn't speak Arabic and the camels wouldn't learn English. Following the old adage it takes a camel driver to drive a camel, the government imported several Arabic drivers to come to this country and see to the task. They were a colorful bunch with names like Long Tom, Short Tom, and Greek George. The most famous of them all was a young man named Hadji Ali. In typical southwestern vernacular he became known as Hi Jolly. Hi Jolly never returned to his native land but remained to his dying day in the Southwest. He is buried at Quartzsite, near the Colorado River. By rights Hi Jolly should have been retired on a nice government pension for all the duties he performed in the service of his adopted country. He died in 1902, like many other legendary figures in the Southwest, broke. But unlike many others, he will never be forgotten, for in the cemetery at Quartzsite there stands a monument in the shape of a pyramid with the figure of a camel on top. The inscription reads, "The Last Campground of Hi Jolly." Where else in the world is such an honor bestowed on a camel driver?

The American who was to implement the camel program, Lieutenant Edward F. "Ned" Beale, was completely sold on the camels and championed their attributes. He knew them better than any American. Beale even referred to them as lovable and docile. Even so, Beale had a hard time convincing others, especially when whole pack trains were known to stampede at the mere sight of the camels.

The beasts passed the supreme test when Beale was challenged to pit his camels against packers' mules on a 60-mile trek. Using six camels against twelve mules, a 2.5-ton load was divided among the camels and a likewise amount was loaded on two Army wagons, each drawn by six mules. The camels finished the trip in two and one half days while the mules took four. However, the camel experiment was doomed from the start. There was political opposition from the mule market in St. Louis and war in the East was imminent, thus postponing any further experiments in the Southwest.

When the Civil War broke out the camel experiment was all but forgotten. Some were sold at auction in California, others went to work in the mining operations in Nevada, and many were turned loose in the desert, where they became the subject of legend and lore, thereby lending another colorful facet to the history of Arizona. One Nevada town still has an ordinance prohibiting camels from using the main street. Old-timers along the Colorado told of a group of drunken miners who tied a dead body onto the back of a camel as a prank. The camel ran off into the desert, where it eventually went insane, becoming known as the "Red Ghost." The "Red Ghost" did terrorize a number of people and was known to have killed at least one person before it was finally shot.

No doubt many an old prospector sat down to relax after a long day spent looking for some lost bonanza, fed his burro, and cooked his dinner over a lonely campfire. Then after taking several pulls on his bottle of favorite sour mash, he looked up and saw the silhouette of some wandering camel over on yonder hillside. If he was not all too familiar with the story of Hi Jolly, Ned Beale, and their humpbacked friends, he was likely to have blamed the whole thing on the hallucinogenic effects of the spirits.

Even if there were camels to haul the freight there was still a need for something or someone to haul the passengers, and at a much faster pace. In California the citizens grew so impatient that 75,000 of them petitioned Congress for some immediate solution to the problem. Congress debated and reacted, and the "Jackass Mail" was born.

In 1857 James Birch began his famous San Antonio to San Diego run. The line was so named because riding muleback was the only way the passengers could cross the desert west of Yuma. Passengers were charged $200 apiece to take advantage of the opportunity of riding from San Diego to Tucson, including the 180 miles to be ridden muleback. It cost another $150 to go on to San Antonio. Each person was allowed 30 pounds of baggage, excluding blankets and arms. That same year the government subsidized John Butterfield's Overland Mail to the tune of $600,000 a year to run a line from Tipton, Missouri, near St. Louis, to San Francisco via El Paso, Tucson, and Los Angeles. Butterfield was a genius when it came to clockwork scheduling and implementation of the operation. Stations were placed approximately 18 miles apart over the 2,800-mile journey. Managers, mechanics, drivers, and guards had to be hired. More than fifteen hundred horses and mules were purchased. Stations were constructed. Miraculously, the task was completed in less than one year and by the middle of September 1858 Butterfield was ready to go. "Remember, boys, nothing on God's earth must stop the United States Mail," Butterfield had admonished his employees, and nothing did. Only once, at Apache Pass in 1861, was the U. S. Mail halted temporarily by Indian attack. The trip took anywhere from twenty-two to twenty-six days, depending on circumstances along the way. Some of the horses and mules were so wild they had to be blindfolded before they could be hitched up. The cost of a trip from St. Louis to San Francisco was $200 plus meals, which usually consisted of jerky, beans, venison, mule meat, salt pork, and coffee. A large supply of mustard was always kept on hand for the gourmet who didn't like the taste of the food and desired a change. The stage could usually make about 120 miles in a twenty-four hour period. On steep grades the men were required to get out and walk or help push. The trip was long and the roads were rough. In the West, the open, lighter Celerity Wagons were the most popular. The seats could fold back into a bed with as many as ten people trying to sleep at the same time. Coaches could hold nine people inside, providing the passengers locked knees. When necessary several more could ride on the roof. It's difficult to imagine one of those trips today. Hollywood hasn't helped. Hundreds of times we have seen a beautifully dressed lady disembark from the stage after a thousand-mile journey. Not a hair is out of place, nor is her makeup mussed, and she looks like Cinderella on her way to the ball. When one considers the sleepless nights, the lack of shock absorbers, the non-existence of body deodorant, and the riding with eight other people for twenty-two days, it's no wonder that Hollywood hasn't attempted to duplicate the reality. There were recorded cases of people going insane on the trip. It was reported that during one trip across southern Arizona, a passenger suddenly leaped from the moving stage and ran off screaming into the desert, never to be seen again.

The first Overland stage that arrived in Tucson had on board a man destined to become one of Arizona's most illustrious citizens, Charles T. Hayden. Hayden had been a merchant and freighter along the Sante Fe Trail since 1848. In 1871, he moved to the Salt River Valley, where he established a ferryboat business transporting passengers and goods across the Salt River. Hayden was widely known throughout the Southwest as a miller, freighter, merchant, and farmer. He also served many civic interests including chairman of the first Board of Trustees of the Territorial Normal School at Tempe, now Arizona State University. His son Carl later served in the U. S. Congress from 1912 to 1969, longer than anybody else in the nation's history.

The Civil War brought a temporary end to stagecoach travel along the Butterfield line since most of the route crossed through Confederate territory. With the soldiers being called back East to join the fighting, Indian problems began to mount and the safety of the passengers could not be guaranteed. For the next few years there was no stagecoach traffic in Arizona.

In the 1870s companies such as the Southern Overland U. S. Mail and the Tucson, Arizona City and San Diego reopened the transcontinental line, carrying both passengers and freight up until the coming of the railroad in 1881. Even then stagecoaches still carried passengers and freight to outlying areas, some operating into the 1930s.

Overlooked many times by historians was a much traveled north-south road into Arizona from Utah. Jacob Hamblin's Mormon Road began transporting settlers into the territory around 1860. They crossed at Lee's Ferry and then over to the Mormon settlement at Joseph City. From there the Saints spread out into settlements all across northern and eastern Arizona.

One of the most unlikely modes of transportation in Arizona was the steamboats on the Colorado River. The high cost of freighting goods across the desert brought about the business in the 1850s. The price per ton to ship goods from San Diego by wagon ran as high as $800. In search of a cheaper means of transportation, primarily to supply the new military post at Fort Yuma, the government began making attempts to determine the navigability of the Colorado. The man who opened the door to steam navigation on the Colorado but who is not usually credited for it was Lieutenant George Derby, a Topographical Engineer. Derby made a study in 1852, taking his 120-ton schooner, the *Invincible*, some 30 miles above the mouth of the Colorado. He and his crew then paddled a small boat another 60 miles to Yuma. Derby reported that flat-bottomed, shallow-draft boats could navigate the shallow waters of the Colorado.

In 1852, Captain George Johnson was given the first contract to supply Fort Yuma. He used barges at first and was unsuccessful. The next to try was Captain James Turnbull. He brought in the *Uncle Sam*, the first steamer to navigate the river. This underpowered craft was somewhat successful but eventually foundered on Pilot Knob. Johnson returned in 1854 with another vessel which met all the requirements of horsepower and low draft. This steamer, called the *General Jessup*, had a 70 horsepower engine, and was 104 feet long. It was the first really successful steamboat on the river. In 1858, it went all the way to El Dorado Canyon. In one of the more unusual encounters in Arizona history, the steamboat and its crew met Lieutenant Edward Beale and his camel corps in the vicinity of today's Needles, California.

Shortly after the *General Jessup* made her run the U. S. Army got into the steamship business. Growing concern over the independence of the Mormons in Utah caused Congress to appropriate some $75,000 to explore the possibilities of navigating far up the river. Captain Johnson offered to make the trip in his own craft for only $3,000, but the Army refused, preferring instead to spend the appropriation on a little iron-hulled boat called the *Explorer*. The boat was built in Philadelphia and tested on the Delaware River, where it was learned that the hull bent amidships like a bow. Still, the *Explorer* was dismantled and sent in sections from New York to Panama, hauled overland to the Pacific and then by ship to San Francisco. The itinerant little iron-hull was then shipped by schooner to the mouth of the Colorado, where it was to be reassembled. The man picked for this task was Lieutenant Joseph C. Ives of the Army Corps of Topographical Engineers. Lieutenant Ives and his men, after facing many discomforts such as having their tent blow away in a storm and being constantly sprayed by ocean water, finally finished the job on Christmas Day, 1857. Progress up the river to Fort Yuma was slow as the sand bars and snags impeded progress. Ten days later the weary crew arrived at the military post. Ives then took the *Explorer* up the Colorado to the entrance of Black Canyon where Boulder Dam stands today.

When the War Department read Ives's report and estimated cost projections, they promptly sold the *Explorer* to Captain Johnson's newly organized Colorado Steam Navigation Company. Johnson soon put her to work hauling firewood on the Gila River. Not one to suffer such indignities, the little iron-hull, perhaps in a last show of independence, broke free and drifted some 9 miles down the Colorado where she plunged deep into a slough. Then a flash flood on the Colorado washed her out onto the desert, where drifting sands soon covered her. There she lay like some unwanted pariah for more than fifty years. She was discovered when a party of surveyors saw a rusty iron plate protruding out of the sand. Further investigation revealed the strange object to be the long-lost steamship.

The steamboats on the Colorado weren't the floating palaces that Mark Twain wrote about. They were built to be strictly functional. They were unusually wide so they could carry heavy loads in the shallow water. Most of the boats had two decks and a wheelhouse although some of the later models were larger. Stern-wheelers were preferred to the side-wheelers. Shifting sand bars were a constant hazard, and oftentimes the water was so shallow that the pilots had to navigate in less than 2 feet. At times the pilots had to reverse the boat and use the paddle wheel literally to chew their way through a sand bar. As commerce increased, bigger and better steamers came into use. Some carried up to 120 tons of cargo and had three decks.

Going up the Colorado obviously took more time than coming down. In some areas farther up the river winches were used to pull the steamers through the rapids. One pilot reported a trip upstream from El Dorado to Rioville took him seventeen hours, while the same trip down took less than three.

Passenger fares from California to Arizona in the 1870s ranged from $40 to $90 one way. The trip began in San Francisco, and prior to 1870 went by sail down around the tip of Baja California and up to the mouth of the Colorado, where the passengers and freight were shifted to tiny steamers. After 1870 steamships were used for the ocean voyage. Martha Summerhays, a young Army wife, painted a rather vivid picture of travel on the Colorado in August 1874. "The temperature was 122 degrees in the shade, the drinking water was 86 degrees, and the butter poured like oil. The spoiled food caused the refrigerator to stink indescribably, the meat turned green, and it was too hot to nap." A "quick trip" up the Colorado to Fort Mohave took eighteen days.

Major ports along the Colorado were Yuma, Ehrenberg, and Hardyville. There were river ports as far up the river as Rioville, where the Virgin River meets the Colorado. For a time the Mormons in Utah used the port of Callville as a base to bring in supplies from California. Both of these ports are now covered by the waters of Lake Mead.

The steamboat business lasted for over fifty years on the Colorado. For half that time it was the most important means of transporting goods in and out of Arizona. Pilots like Johnson, Jack Mellon, and Isaac Polhamus were legendary figures on the river.

Captain George Johnson ran the Colorado Steam Navigation Company until 1878, when he sold out to the Southern Pacific Railroad. The east-west route of the railroad followed a more natural flow of traffic, though, for a time, the steamers continued to act as feeder lines for the railroad. With the construction of Laguna Dam in 1908, the colorful era of the steamboats on the Colorado was ended.

While steamboats were navigating the Colorado, camels were traversing what is today's Interstate 40, and John Butterfield's coaches were crossing over the Gila Trail, another group of individuals were carving out a legend for themselves hauling ore, freight, and express between the mines and small communities of Arizona. "The freighter was a very important personage in the days before the railroad came," wrote Colonel James H. McClintock. "As a rule he was a professional, closely allied to the stage driver, who cursed him for cutting up the road and for raising too much dust. Some of the freighting outfits of those days were awe-inspiring affairs. The team might be anything up to twenty-four mules driven by a jerk-line and handled with a skill marvelous to the uninitiated. The mule, without doubt, was the greatest traction factor in the up-building of the Southwest. Oxen, at first, were tried but for them the country was too hot and too dry. Horses, except in the Mexican 'rawhide' outfit, suffered much from the same disadvantages."

The freighting wagons were built in Yuma, Phoenix, Tucson, and Prescott, especially for the rough country in the mining regions. The wheels in the lead wagon were 8 feet high. Behind each team of mules were three or four wagons, each diminishing in size to the last one, which was used for feed for the animals and personal items for the freighter and his "swamper," or helper. The freighters usually traveled in groups whenever possible, especially in dangerous country.

California was booming and the natural east-west flow of traffic was being hindered by the lack of a southern railroad route. The Civil War was over, ending also the major resistance to a southern transcontinental line. In 1866, the Atlantic and Pacific Railroad made plans to build a line from Springfield, Missouri, across Arizona to San Diego along the 35th parallel. However, during the Panic of '73 the A and P went broke. The Atchison, Topeka & Santa Fe Railroad officials saw an opportunity to pick up the lucrative land grants that had been awarded to the A and P. Congress had appropriated a grant of twenty sections for every mile of track laid in the territories of Arizona and New Mexico. The Santa Fe took over the A and P in 1876 and picked up the grants. Operating under the name A and P, for a time, the line became officially the AT&SF in 1879. In May 1880 the construction crews left Albuquerque. By November 1881 they were in Winslow. In August 1883 the line had reached Needles, California, just across the Colorado River. Towns such as Holbrook, Winslow, Seligman, and Kingman were all named for people associated with the railroad in one form or another.

Congress had also commissioned another railroad, the Texas and Pacific, to build a line from Marshall, Texas, to San Diego along the 32nd parallel. By 1873 it had built as far west as Fort Worth, Texas. But it too met financial disaster in the Panic of '73. The Southern Pacific out in California was now faced with a dilemma, for they had already built a line to Fort Yuma on the Colorado and were interested in moving eastward, picking up the lucrative land grants and federal loans along the way. These land grants and loans were given to the railroads crossing federal lands, not state land. As an inducement to the railroads to build lines across unpopulated areas the government awarded twenty sections of land for every mile of track laid, free right of way, free use of timber and mineral to build the line, and a loan of $16,000 if the track were laid across flat land, $32,000 if laid across foothills, and $48,000 if laid in mountainous country. Building a railroad line under these conditions could be a profitable venture, and in most cases it was. After some wheeling and dealing the SP was finally able to secure from the Arizona and New Mexico legislatures a right of way to El Paso.

The Southern Pacific arrived at the west bank of the Colorado River in the spring of 1877, and spent the summer constructing a bridge to the other side. The bridge was built with the permission and blessing of the federal government. When it was completed the railroad was refused permission by the Secretary of War to cross over a federal stream or across the military reservation on the other side.

There are two versions as to what transpired next. One story says that the Southern Pacific engineers, unable to resist the temptation, drove an engine quietly across the bridge in the dead of night while the fort was fast asleep. As soon as they were safely on the other side "the engineer tied down the whistle valve and used all the steam he had in celebrating the advent of the iron horse into new territory." Awaking from their slumber, the aroused soldiers chased the would-be interlopers back to California.

A slightly modified version of that story says that the entire military force at Yuma consisted of five people: Major Thomas Dunn, the commanding officer; Leonard Loring, the assistant surgeon; a sergeant; an enlisted man; and one prisoner.

To avoid any confrontation with the military authorities over the order preventing the railroad from crossing the federal stream, the company decided surreptitiously to lay the tracks to the bridge at night. The suspicious Major Dunn countered this move by placing a guard at the end of the tracks until eleven o'clock each night. The railroaders waited until the sentry went off duty and then went to work laying track toward the bridge. Apparently, everything went without a hitch until somebody dropped a rail on the bridge, its resounding noise awakening the garrison. The troopers, all four of them, rushed to the scene of the crime, where they prevented any further construction, temporarily at least. The soldiers standing on the tracks with fixed bayonets were no match for what happened next. Somebody started a rail car full of material down the tracks toward the startled troopers. Deciding that discretion was the better part of valor, they cleared off the tracks. Major Dunn, realizing he had done all within his power to carry out the Secretary of War's ludicrous orders, gathered his "force" and retreated to the environs of the fort.

By morning, work was completed and the Southern Pacific rolled triumphantly into Yuma.

In time, franchises were granted and the railroad extended its ribbon of steel across the Arizona desert, creating temporary boomtowns along the way, the most notable being Maricopa, some 35 miles south of Phoenix.

On March 20, 1880, there was great cause for celebration in Tucson, for the railroad had at long last arrived. Richard Gird of Tombstone presented the city with a silver spike from the Tombstone mines in honor of the occasion. After a great deal of speechmaking, ballyhoo, and spirits, telegrams were sent all over the country. The "Old Pueblo" had arrived and in her eagerness to boast, telegrams were sent to various dignitaries throughout the United States. This being done, some of her more inebriated citizens decided to send a telegram to Pope Leo XIII at the Vatican, which ran as follows:

> To His Holiness, the Pope of Rome, Italy:
> The mayor of Tucson begs the honor of reminding Your Holiness that this ancient and honorable pueblo was founded by the Spaniards under the sanction of the Church more than three centuries ago, and to in-

form Your Holiness that a railroad from San Francisco, California now connects us with the entire Christian World.

R. N. LEATHERWOOD, Mayor

But before the telegrapher could send the announcement, some of the more discreet locals advised him to reconsider. It is said that they slipped him a few bucks to "can" the telegram and forget the whole thing. Perhaps suffering from guilt feelings over having not sent the telegram as ethics required, the conscientious telegrapher finally decided that if he didn't send it, the least he could do for the city fathers was to give them a reply even if it wasn't genuine. After all, that's how legends are born, and besides, who was he to cast a sour note over the gala celebration by having the Pope ignore Tucson's coming-out party. The telegrapher sat down and penned a reply suitable for the occasion and finishing, he carried the message over to the assemblage, where Mayor Leatherwood received the paper and without bothering to preview the "reply," read aloud:

His Holiness the Pope acknowledges with appreciation receipt of your telegram informing him that the ancient city of Tucson at last has been connected by rail with the outside world and sends his benediction, but for his own satisfaction would ask, where the hell is Tucson?

"ANTONELLI"

Still, there were lines to be built. In 1887 the Maricopa, Phoenix & Salt River Railroad was built from Phoenix to Maricopa, where it joined the Southern Pacific. In 1926 that line was moved from Maricopa, going just south of Tempe and thence to Picacho, and that is the route of the SP today.

On January 22, 1892, work was begun on a line from Ash Fork to Phoenix. Called the Peavine, it reached Prescott in 1893, and Phoenix in 1895. Many historians consider this linkage to be the end of frontier days for Arizona, for now there were northern and southern transcontinental lines with the capital city joined to both by rail.

There were dozens of other railroads throughout the territory, mostly in the mining regions. Some of these are still in operation today.

The railroads were not without their promotional schemes. In 1885 Tom Bullock began construction of a standard-gauge line from Seligman to Prescott. Bullock sold bonds to the local citizens to finance the 75-mile line. When the Peavine was built on higher ground farther east, Bullock's Prescott and Central Arizona Railroad went out of business. Bullock promptly tore up the track and moved his goods to California, leaving the locals high and dry. Before the bonds were made good to the taxpayers, the Bullock Road had cost the people of Arizona several million dollars.

Perhaps the most superhuman effort by the railroad entrepreneurs occurred in the 1880s when the Mineral Belt Railroad went broke while attempting to tunnel through the Mogollon Rim. The plan was to build a line from Globe up to the Santa Fe main line by drilling through the great precipice that runs diagonally across the central part of the state.

Recent energy problems have brought about a renaissance of railroad travel everywhere. People are rediscovering the rails. There is something nostalgic and relaxing about getting on a train and riding up to Prescott to spend a leisurely weekend. Perhaps those days will come again.

No history of railroad transportation in the Southwest would be complete without a brief discourse on one of the most revolutionary periods in passenger traffic.

Before the days of the railroad dining cars, passengers were forced to eat in the local hash houses wherever the train happened to stop. The food was terrible and the service was even worse. The passengers would rush in, place an order, and just about the time the food arrived, the conductor would shout, "All aboard." Meal tickets were sold to the passengers by the trainmen prior to stopping and it is not unlikely that they received a kickback on meal tickets when the meal was not eaten. It is conceivable that the same meal could be sold more than once and probably was.

Not only were conditions deplorable for train passengers but they were even worse for single men in the cities and towns. They had to endure these conditions on a permanent basis. Travelers were at the mercy of the local restaurants and hotels while residents cooked their food under primitive conditions at home. The basic tool was the frying pan and it was cause for much dyspepsia among the Southwesterners.

It took a gentleman from England named Fred Harvey to bring real cuisine to the American Southwest. After experiencing some of the eating conditions along the rail lines, Harvey approached the Santa Fe Railroad in the early 1870s with the sagacious idea of providing the passengers with attractive surroundings, superior service, and above all, good food. The railroad company accepted his proposals enthusiastically, for food services had been one of the most serious problems plaguing all the railroads at this time. The Santa Fe agreed to supply the buildings along with the transporting of food, furnishings, and personnel, free of charge. In addition, Harvey was to receive all the profits from this venture. Evidently the Englishman was not only a good restaurant man, but a shrewd bargainer as well.

The first Harvey House opened for business at Topeka, Kansas, in the spring of 1876, and was an immediate success. French chefs were hired away from prominent restaurants in the East and paid handsome salaries. In at least one instance the Harvey House chef was making more money than the president of a local bank. Foods were purchased from local farmers.

During the next twenty years, Harvey opened his Spanish-style restaurant-hotels at hundred-mile intervals throughout the Southwest. It was said that they were spaced that distance so they would keep "western traffic from settling in one place where Harvey served his meals."

Arizona had five Harvey Houses along the main line in the early days. These were located at Winslow, Williams, Ash Fork, Seligman, and Kingman.

It wasn't just the excellent food that attracted the Southwesterners to his establishments in droves. Harvey added one more ingredient, the feminine touch. In a land where women were scarce, Harvey provided the Southwest with as wholesome a group of young women as had yet been seen in that region. The old adage about there being "No ladies west of Dodge City and no women west of Albuquerque" no longer held true.

The Harvey Girls were recruited in the eastern part of the country through newspaper advertisements which read: "Young women 18 to 30 years of age, of good character, attractive and intelligent, as waitresses in Harvey Eating Houses in the West. Good wages with room and meals furnished."

For a young lady hoping to escape from the hometown doldrums or one with hopes of acting out some romantic role and adventure, the ad sounded like a dream come true. For many it was, for they were a welcome sight to the lonely cattlemen, miners, and railroaders. Few of them stayed single long. Cowboy humorist Will

Rogers once said, "Fred Harvey kept the West in food and wives." The turnover of help was never a problem as there was always a long waiting list of applicants anxious to go West and work as a Harvey Girl.

The pay was only $17.50 a month and the girls were required to live in dormitories similar to that of a very conservative college sorority house. They had to be in by 10:30 P.M. on weekdays and 11:30 P.M. on Saturdays. A matronly housemother saw to it that the ladies always obeyed Mr. Harvey's strict rules of conduct.

Not all of Harvey's girls were comely. One old-timer noted that "though rapid and efficient and the girls were all neatly dressed in good health, there were no beauties among them." It was said that Harvey made a practice of hiring the more common-looking girls because the pretty ones always got themselves married shortly after arriving. "The plain ones seemed to get in less trouble," another old-timer observed. Whatever the case, the wholesome Harvey Girls, affectionately called "biscuit shooters" by the locals, represented the finest type of young American womanhood.

The Harvey system was the amalgamation of efficiency, cuisine, service, and feminine charm. Prior to reaching the station, a brakeman would take orders and then wire the information ahead. When the train was a mile away from the meal stop it would blow its whistle. Upon hearing the whistle scream, a uniformed employee would ring a gong which signaled the waitresses to set up the first course. By the time the train arrived and the hungry passengers were ushered in, the meal was ready to serve. Waitresses were not allowed to serve men without a coat in the dining room; however, any man who didn't have one was given a "loaner" by the establishment, compliments of Fred Harvey.

Everything on the table had to be set in a prescribed manner. The water glasses, silverware, salt and pepper shakers all had their proper place. Conversation between the girls was forbidden while the train was in the station. However, they quickly learned to communicate through the use of signals and codes. The "drink girl," or the one who poured the drinks, knew that if the customer's cup was turned upside down it meant he had ordered tea. When the cup was upright in the saucer, coffee was desired, and if the cup was taken away, the customer wanted milk. Usually the girls learned to talk to each other through the sides of their mouths to escape detection from the watchful eyes of the company inspectors who were constantly passing through. A frequent inspector was Fred Harvey himself. The boss man loved surprise visits to his establishments and was known to fire a manager on the spot if all wasn't up to Fred Harvey standards.

Around the turn of the century one could be served a breakfast consisting of cereal or fruit, eggs riding atop a steak, hash browns, and a stack of six large hotcakes with butter and maple syrup, topped off with apple pie and coffee, all for only $.50. Dinners went for a quarter more and always included a fancy gourmet dish or wild game.

The railroads have played an important role in the history of the state both in passenger traffic and freight. They've also come a long way since the enterprising Del Potter registered his mule-powered Clifton and Northern Railroad as a common carrier thus enabling him to exchange free passes for travel with most of the major railroads across the country.

There were still many people in Arizona who had not yet seen a train when Dr. Hiram W. Fenner of Tucson unloaded the first automobile at the Southern Pacific depot in Tucson around the turn of the century. While a curious crowd gathered round, Dr. Fenner fired up the contraption, and for Arizona the age of the horseless carriage had begun.

Arizona had been late on the scene in accepting the motorcar and one of the reasons was the poor condition of its roads. But this didn't keep her from being the scene of many exciting road races. It wasn't much different until after World War I, when public pressure was such that the road-building program was begun in earnest.

One of the most unusual highways in the country was the famed Plank Road west of Yuma. Built in 1916, out of wooden planks, it crossed the White Sand Hills between Yuma and Holtville, California. The road was only 8 feet wide and was held together by three strands of cable. It was also portable and laid out in 12-foot sections which could be moved whenever necessary. The speed limit was 10 miles per hour, though it was said that the passengers complained of seeing double when speeds of over 7 miles per hour were reached on the bumpy thoroughfare. Service stations sold not only gas and oil, but shovels as well. Desert travelers would deflate the tires on their Model T's from 65 lbs. to about 15 lbs., then using canvas or fire hose, they would make several wraps around the wheels, thus giving them better traction.

It was said that the constantly shifting sands would cause the road to shift or be buried, halting traffic for as much as a week while a team of mules attached to a grader would be driven out to repair the damage.

Passing sidings were located every quarter of a mile and marked by old tires placed on posts. If two vehicles met in between the sidings one would hopefully extend the courtesy of reversing his direction, allowing the other to pass. However, it is known that on at least one occasion when two drivers couldn't agree on who was to back up one pulled a pistol on the other and "backed him" to the siding.

THE EARLY DAYS OF APACHE WARFARE

THE LENGTHY CONQUEST of Apachería was not a continuous war, but an armed truce at best. The first recorded conflict between Anglo-Americans and Apache was with the James O. Pattie party of trappers in the 1820s. According to his narrative they encountered hostiles on numerous occasions. These skirmishes between trappers and Apache were mostly concerned with the Apache desire to possess the trapper's mules and other accessories. Rights of prior possession and other real estate problems didn't arise at this early date.

In the late 1830s, the Mexican government's *Proyectos de Guerra* policy of paying a bounty for the scalps of Apache led to an encounter sometimes referred to as the "Picnic Massacre." The story actually begins several years earlier with a rather unusual Indian named Juan José. Juan had been raised in one of the missions and therefore had an adequate grasp of the Spanish language. When a band of Mexicans killed his father, Juan turned on them with vengeance. He was not only adept as a warrior, but he also turned out to be a thorn in the Mexican side in other ways. Juan's people would intercept Mexican couriers and bring the messages to the young Mimbreño chief to interpret. This gave the Apache an advantage over their adversaries as Juan and his people always had advance warnings of Mexican stratagems.

By agreement with the local authorities, meaning bribery, Juan had agreed to let the Mexicans work in the Apache-controlled

Santa Rita del Cobre mines under certain conditions. No one was to leave the town without the consent of the Mimbreño. In due time business at the mines was moving along briskly. There was also a population explosion of sorts. This truce did not by any means keep the Mimbreño from continuing their habit of murder and pillage in other areas. Needless to say, the Mexicans were much chagrined and set out to find an ultimate solution to the problem.

There lived in the neighborhood a man of questionable integrity named James Johnson. Johnson and Juan José had met on occasion and were on friendly terms. The Mexicans knew this and took the opportunity to offer Johnson a substantial fee if he would remove Juan José's topknot. Johnson, being a true and loyal friend but at the same time a subscriber to the scalphunter code, immediately agreed. There are varying accounts as to what actually transpired, but the one most generally accepted was given by Ben Wilson, who later became the first Anglo mayor of Los Angeles. At this time, Wilson was operating a trading post in Sonora and was acquainted with Juan José. He was camped nearby when the incident occurred and received his story from eyewitnesses.

Johnson, a man named Charlie Gleason, and a group of Missouri interlopers or mountain men had enticed Juan and his band to join them in some festivities. Juan was aware that his friend had been approached by the Mexican authorities, but he seemingly felt assured that Johnson would never betray him. To brighten the occasion Johnson had brought along some pinole or treats. Pinole is a ground corn meal mixed with sugar and was a favorite of the Apache, or any Southwesterner, for that matter. Among the saddles and blankets Johnson had also carefully concealed a small howitzer loaded with scrap iron and nails. At a prearranged signal, Johnson lit the fuse and the gun, pointed at the pinole-munching Apache, exploded in their midst. According to prearranged plan, Gleason was supposed to have made sure Juan José did not survive the attack. The chief was led off to one side by Gleason for conversation and when the howitzer went off he shot the Apache, though not fatally.

Juan José, although wounded, fought furiously and quickly gained the advantage over his adversary. At this moment the Apache hesitated and looked questioningly at Johnson, who was a short distance away. Johnson came toward him, aimed his weapon, and fired, killing the once friendly chief.

When the affair was ended, Juan José and several others lay dead or dying. But one young man didn't die in the massacre, and the Mexicans and Americans alike would long regret it. He crawled away from the mess, a man with vengeance in his heart. They would pay dearly. He would see to that. For the next twenty-six years the mere mention of his name would strike terror from the lonely mining camps to the cities alike. He rose to become the greatest Apache chief of them all. He was Mangas Coloradas, "Red Sleeves."

Sonora had first offered the bounty for scalps in 1835, and Chihuahua had followed suit with a bounty of their own two years later. There was little co-ordination between the two governments. One would be at peace with the Apache, usually through bribery, while the other was at war. If Sonora was at war, the Apache would plunder there and always find a ready market for their booty in Chihuahua. About the time Sonora would make peace, Chihuahua would go to war and the situation would reverse itself. The government in Mexico City left the problems of defense to the states and the states left it to the people themselves. Finally, out of frustration and fear, the Mexicans began offering bounties: $100 for an adult male, $50 for a woman, and $25 for a young child. Pesos and American dollars had the same monetary value at that time.

James Kirker had been a mountain man with that first historic Ashley-Henry expedition to the Rockies in 1822. Later he drifted down to New Mexico and eventually wound up in the employ of the Mexican government as a scalphunter. He formed a company consisting of border riffraff and called it, appropriately, the Apache Company. Many of them were Shawnee, Delaware, and Creek Indians, together with a number of unemployed trappers from up around Bent's Fort. The Mexican governor of Chihuahua offered Kirker a dollar a day, plus one half the booty. In 1839 his company was reported to have made over $100,000.

It didn't take long for friction to develop between employer and employee. On one side, Mexican politics, where turbulence was the rule rather than the exception, governors changed as often as did the seasons. A new governor usually didn't feel duty-bound to honor any agreement made by his predecessor. The hunters might return with their packs full of scalps only to be told that there was no money to pay for the service. On the other side, how was one to tell which scalp was a peaceful Indian or Mexican, for that matter, and which was an Apache? Most assuredly, it didn't take the hunters long to discover that it was a lot easier to remove the scalp from a peaceful Opata Indian or a Mexican farmer than from the elusive Apache. Only blonds and Blacks were safe from those unruly, hair-raising bounty collectors on the Mexican frontier.

There was also some professional jealousy involved between the Mexican Army and the scalphunters. Not bound by bureaucratic red tape and with pesos as an incentive, the scalphunters could and did go into the Apache stronghold seeking bounty. Poor pay and low morale hindered the incentives of the Mexicans. Consequently, the Nortéamericanos were regarded by the local populace as saviors of the frontier while the Army seethed in frustration.

Kirker's career had many vicissitudes during his tenure with the Mexicans. As the result of a squabble with them over non-payment for services, he went to work doing the same ghastly work for the Apache against the Mexicans. Not that the Apache needed any help from Don Santiago Kirker: it was probably more the principle of the matter that counted. Whatever the case, the Mexicans found no humor in the caper, especially when they learned that Kirker was made a chief and along with his crew was being paid a bounty for any Mexican scalps they happened on. In exasperation, the Mexicans rehired the redheaded erstwhile fur trapper. The honeymoon didn't last long, and Don Santiago soon found himself on the most wanted list again, this time for several reasons. The United States and Mexico had gone to war and no American knew the northern Mexican frontier like James Kirker. The Americans knew it and so did Mexico. The Mexicans offered to make him a colonel in their Army, but he suspected this was merely a ruse to get their hands on him. In 1846 he joined Colonel Alexander Doniphan's colorful ragtag army of Missouri Volunteers. He must have felt right at home. Most likely it was a case of mutual admiration. The Volunteers pronounced him absolutely fearless. Mounted on a fine horse, armed with a silver-inlayed Hawken rifle, and wearing a large sombrero, Don Santiago must have cut a fine figure riding full speed, leaning over the side of his horse, and letting his long hair sweep along the ground.

Kirker knew all the watering places and all the trails. He gave to Doniphan a complete plan of the fortifications in the city of Sacramento. He played a major role in the American conquest, although he is remembered today by most as the "King of the Scalphunters."

James Kirker has been judged rather harshly by some modern historians. One must always take into account the times and conditions in which a man lives. To those Mexicans in the tiny frontier settlements living in constant fear of Apache attack, Don Santiago and his gang were avenging angels sent by the Almighty to deliver them from the evil that surrounded them.

Another "scalphunter extraordinaire" on the Mexican frontier was John Joel Glanton. He was born in Edgefield County, South Carolina, the same county that produced those two intrepid heroes of the Texas revolution, James Bonham and William Barret Travis. Like Bonham and Travis, Glanton went to Texas for adventure and fortune. He got plenty of the former while serving as a free scout in and around the vicinity of San Antonio. He just barely escaped the terrible massacre of Colonel James Fannin and his three hundred men at Goliad, shortly after the Alamo fell.

According to a story told some years later by Sam Chamberlain, who rode with Glanton's gang, John developed a deep and lasting hatred for the Indians after they murdered his beautiful fiancée. The girl had been stolen at Gonzales prior to the wedding. Glanton and some other settlers went in pursuit. They overtook and defeated the band but to no avail. The girl had been beaten to death and scalped.

When gold was discovered in California, Glanton joined up with a group of adventurers and headed for the gold fields. Their first stop was Chihuahua City, where they found the Mexicans in a desperate situation, as the local militia had been unable to quell the Apache raids. The governor offered Glanton and his friends the astronomical price of $250 for male captives, $200 for the scalp of an adult male, and $150 for the scalp of a female or child under twelve years of age. Proof of work had to include the right ear of the victim with each trophy. Before long, the gang was doing such a fine job that they were creating a shortage of prey. To meet this crisis, the hunters did what Kirker and others before them had done. They simply began to remove the hair from the peaceful agricultural Indians or the local Mexicans in the nearby villages. This became all too obvious when Mexicans began turning up in alleys with their scalp and right ear missing. The governor now offered a reward of $8,000 for a single scalp—Glanton's.

It was "ho for California" once again. On the way they stopped at Piños Altos, a small village near the foot of the Sierra Madre.

Once again Glanton enhanced his claim as one of the original ugly Americans by pulling down the Mexican flag and attaching it to a mule's tail. To make matters worse, he leaped upon the animal's back and rode through town dragging the Mexican national colors in the dust. That was more than the usually tranquil villagers could take. They drove the rascals out of town. Next stop was Tucson, a near-deserted city under siege from the Apache. Most of the able-bodied men had gone off to California.Those remaining were living in constant fear of attack. The gang took charge, met with the Apache leaders, introduced "six-shooter" diplomacy, and soon peace was at hand. Tucson was grateful, but the peaceful life in the Old Pueblo was without excitement and profits, so Glanton dropped down into Sonora and engaged once again in the business he knew best. It was here that he met Sam Chamberlain, the man who chronicled the expedition for historians.

In time, the market began to play out. This, coupled with a defeat at the hands of the Apache, influenced Glanton's decision to head for California once more.

At the confluence of the Gila and Colorado rivers, there was a prosperous little venture run by a Dr. Able Lincoln. Dr. Lincoln was in the lucrative business of transporting Argonauts and settlers across the river at so much per head or vehicle. Business must have been brisk as he had written his parents that the ferry had grossed over $60,000. The only competitor was a group of Yuma Indians operating a small ferry farther downstream.

Glanton took one look at the place and decided to muscle in. Once he had done this, he advised Dr. Lincoln of his decision. Not content just to have a thriving business of transporting people, the gang began relieving the travelers of some of their extra accessories.

Meantime the Yuma Indians had hired a white man named Callaghan to run their ferry for them. Glanton thought it rather nervy of those impertinent Indians to go into direct competition with his boat on his river. The next day Callaghan was found shot to death, and the boat had been cut loose. Nobody seemed to know "who done it."

The Yuma were biding their time, planning. They would use the same strategy as their ancient ancestors had attempted against the Spaniards some three hundred years previously. This time there would be no Melchior Díaz to "smell a rat." They would divide and conquer. The plan worked perfectly. Some of Glanton's men were caught on one side of the river, the rest on the other. Eleven ferrymen were dead without firing a shot. Even the unfortunate Dr. Lincoln did not escape the slaughter. When the melee was finished, the bodies were taken out and burned. There were some survivors. A few escaped and made their way overland to Los Angeles. One of these survivors, Sam Chamberlain, wrote of the whole episode in an autobiography appropriately titled *My Confession*. His confession may not be altogether accurate as to time, dates, and events; nevertheless, it is still an important work.

It is known that the Glanton gang buried some $15,000 in sacks under a tree near the crossing. As far as is known the money is still there, adding another page to the numerous lost treasure stories that abound in the Southwest.

The Indians evidently divided up another gold cache found at the shack. Travelers reported for months afterward of being paid enormous amounts of gold for menial items they carried.

When the surviving members of the Glanton gang straggled into Los Angeles and told their story, little sympathy was generated. The local populace was well aware of the activities going on at the crossing the past few months. It was the season for the spring flood of immigrants and sensing that a small taste of American blood might tempt the Yuma to commit more inhospitable acts of butchery, it was decided to send an army to punish the Indians. This nefarious group of rascals became known to history as the Gila Expedition.

Never before or since has there been an army like the Gila Expedition. It was the most overpaid, inept, inglorious gathering of bureaucratic bunglers and thieves that ever rode the West.

The governor of California authorized the raising of one hundred men to comprise the group. General Joshua Bean of the militia ordered Quartermaster Joseph C. Morehead to raise, equip, and get the army into the field. Nothing had been said about money, so Bean told Morehead to take what he needed and issue drafts. The state would later take care of the bill. This carte blanche system allowed Morehead plenty of leeway to wheel and deal as he pleased. He purchased teams of horses at exorbitant prices from the local farmers. The merchants, obviously knowing of the crisis at hand and being of a patriotic nature, set their prices accordingly. There followed a short period of runaway inflation unparalleled in the state's history. Morehead recruited soldiers by offering wages of $5.00 a day. Most of the volunteers didn't make that much in a week working at their civilian jobs; even Regular Army pay wasn't much more than that for an entire month's toil. The 100-man roster grew to 142. Morehead's liberal monetary enticements were even greater for lieutenants; they got $10 a day.

The crisis had arisen during the spring season, but it was late August before the army was sworn in. Incidentally, there had been no record of mistreatment to travelers on the part of the Yuma. On the contrary, the Indians with their new-found wealth got along quite well with the California-bound tourists.

A party of Californians led by L. J. F. Jaeger had already gone to the Yuma Crossing and were busy reconstructing the ferry when Morehead's army arrived. All was peaceful, but with the arrival of the expedition any semblance of peace and tranquillity came to an end abruptly. Morehead called for a conference with the old chief and informed him that he, Morehead, would call his soldiers off if the Yuma could cough up the $60,000 taken during the massacre. No one is quite sure where Morehead got that figure. Apparently it was the result of hearsay. No doubt it was cached treasure that motivated the Gila Expedition rather than a moral desire to avenge the deaths of Glanton's gang or protection of the emigrants on the Gila Trail.

"Give up the money or prepare yourselves for a severe beating," said Morehead, with a countenance that was nothing short of sheer audacity.

The Yuma chose to fight it out. The glorious Gila Expedition was immediately driven from the field in a most inglorious manner. That was the first and last battle Morehead's band of rogues ever engaged in. The remainder of their sojourn was spent in general mischief around the crossing, creating one nuisance after another even to the extent of relieving homeward-bound Mexicans of whatever gold they might have picked up in California.

Governor Burnett eventually called his wayward knights home, much to the relief of all concerned, especially the citizens along the Colorado River. However, Morehead and his troops were not eager to return with their mission unaccomplished. It took a second order to get the band moving.

It must have created a mild tremor along the San Andreas Fault when the tabs started rolling in. It seems that none of the parties responsible kept records of expenditures. There were charges and countercharges of incompetence. When the bill was tabulated, the young state of California found she owed $113,482.25 for services from an army that was an unnecessary liability to start with. It had won no victories in the field, and for sure had done nothing to promote public relations along the Colorado River.

THE CAMPAIGNERS

THERE WERE STRETCHES of country picturesque to look upon and capable of cultivation, especially with irrigation; and other expanses not a bit more fertile than so many brick-yards, where all was desolation, the home of the cactus and the coyote. Arizona was in those days separated from "God's country" by a space of more than fifteen hundred miles, without a railroad, and the officer or soldier who once got out there rarely returned for years.

Our battalion slowly crawled from camp to camp, with no incident to break the dull monotony beyond the ever-recurring signal smokes of the Apache, to show that our progress was duly watched from the peaks on each flank; or the occasional breaking down of some of the wagons and the accompanying despair of the quartermaster, with whose afflictions I sympathized sincerely, as that quartermaster was myself. . . .

During this campaign we were often obliged to leave the warm valleys in the morning and climb to the higher altitudes and go into bivouac upon summits where the snow was hip deep, as on the Matitzal, the Mogollon plateau, and the Sierra Ancha. To add to the discomfort, the pine was so thoroughly soaked through with snow and rain that it would not burn, and unless cedar could be found, the command was in bad luck.

John Gregory Bourke, *On the Border with Crook*, 1891.

One of the most thankless tasks on the western frontier was the mission assigned the U. S. Army. The federal government in Washington couldn't seem to make up its mind regarding the Indian. In essence they ordered the Army to "be a friend to the Indian but when he makes trouble, go in and destroy him." This difficult assignment was compounded even further when the Interior Department and War Department were involved in a power struggle as to who would have final jurisdiction in the so-called "Indian question."

Out West the soldiers found themselves caught in the middle once again. When they attacked the hostiles, the eastern papers called them murderers. When they were showing a benevolent attitude the Westerners accused them of coddling, or other words too fierce to print. Moreover, there were times when they found themselves in the role of peacemaker between two or more tribes. In view of twentieth-century political events, we all know the peacemaker is never really very popular. One can only hope that history will, in the final analysis, serve as vindicator.

Long before the white man came, warfare between tribes was much more fierce than some modern-day historians would like to believe. The struggle between tribes for land, women, and hunting grounds was of epic proportions, especially on the Plains, where the strong, warlike tribes prevailed and the weaker ones moved to less desirable locations. Those who didn't move were either enslaved or exterminated.

When the Army first came West in the early 1830s, the Indians were so busy fighting each other that they hardly noticed or paid much attention to the blue-coated warriors and their mammoth, grain-fed ponies. The first military intrusions in the West were made up of infantry units who trudged alongside the trade wagons on the Santa Fe Trail. These caravans had been coming under steady harassment from roving bands of Comanche, described by early witnesses as creatures with six legs, two of their own and four of their pony's. Others called them the finest light cavalry in the world. These Cossacks of the Plains were more than slightly amused when the government sent foot soldiers out to "protect" the traders. Later, in 1833, when Congress did authorize a U. S. Cavalry, government regulations called for so much equipment to be carried that it proved impossible for the larger, grain-fed cavalry mounts ever to catch up with the little grass-fed mustangs.

Years later, fighting a completely different kind of war in Arizona, the horse would, at times, be a hindrance. The wily Apache, guided by the terrain in which he lived, preferred to fight on foot.

A horse was a necessary tool to take him out of danger, but once in the rugged mountains he would stop, butcher and eat the horse, and take out the entrails and make himself a water container. Once filled, the bag was slung over his shoulders and he would be on his way again. He could travel 90 miles without stopping and was a formidable foe for the horse soldier. It took twenty-five years to subdue him.

Men joined the Army for various reasons. Almost all the officers came from West Point, with the exception of the Civil War period. The menagerie of officers the Indian was attracting ranged from glory-seekers and politically ambitious men like Custer and Nelson Miles, to unshowy, rough country campaigners like George Crook. All were volunteers in the frontier Army. About one half of the enlisted men were native-born Americans. The others came primarily from Ireland. However, Germany, England, France, and Switzerland contributed more than a few.

By and large boys joined the Army for about the same reasons they do today. Either jobs were scarce on the outside or joining gave them a chance to leave the old homestead and "see the elephant." Some were escaping from the law or acting out some glorious role. Still others were merely trying to get a free trip West to the gold fields. The Army didn't photograph or fingerprint soldiers at that time, and on the posts it was considered "impolite" to inquire into a man's past. He might have been a colonel in the Confederate Army a few years earlier, but now, under a new name and wearing a blue uniform bearing the chevrons of a sergeant, he was just another common soldier.

Desertion was high, with the exception of the Black units, where it was held to a minimum. About one third of the frontier Army deserted for one reason or another. Suicide and alcohol, especially alcohol, were cause for giving the Army many severe headaches. Drunkenness was usually tolerated when an officer was the offender, but let some poor enlisted man get caught and there was always hell to pay. One punishment dealt out to a man caught carrying a bottle was to make him finish it and then bury the now "dead soldier" in a hole 10 feet long, by 10 feet wide, by 10 feet deep. Another was to tie a heavy log on his shoulders and let him spend the next day in repentance, walking off his hang-over in the hot sun.

When a man deserted and was unfortunate enough to get caught, the Army saw to it that a good example was set for the others who might have had some propensity for taking exit from the confines of the post. Until the period following the Civil War he could be branded with the letter "D" on the left cheek of his posterior region. The culprit was then given lashes, followed by a trip to the infirmary, where his wounds were washed out with salt water. Afterward he might be unceremoniously dismissed from the Army and turned loose on the inhospitable frontier, afoot.

By and large, rules forbidding these types of punishments were passed between the years 1861 to 1917.

Most of the time spent in the Army was spent waiting for something to happen. Rank came slowly. Sometimes there was a ten-year wait between promotions. Figuring the averages, a man might expect to be in only one Indian fight during his entire five-year enlistment. This was not usually the case in Arizona: statistics didn't count for much in Apachería during those years.

Typical meals on the posts consisted of such culinary delights as beef hash, dry bread, and coffee for breakfast, followed by a lunch of sliced beef, dry bread, and coffee. Evening meals were just simply bread and coffee.

Spartan living conditons, fatigue, poor rations, and little appreciation from his fellow countrymen were the grim prospects the soldiers faced. In 1868 there were approximately 200,000 Indians living on the Great Plains. The population of the Army stationed in the West at this same time was 2,600 men. Some posts had fewer than 50 men. When asked why he did not set up a stronger line of defense, one exasperated officer replied, "Sir, I have no troop, only three men." Incidentally, a troop numbered from 40 to 60 men at that time.

The pay had dropped in 1871 from $16 a month to $13. Corporals received $15 and sergeants $21. They were usually paid with paper money, which in turn was discounted 50 per cent by the local merchants. The soldier could buy his necessities at the post commissary. If he had any money left after the loan sharks collected their dues, he could go to a nearby "hog ranch" where cheap liquor and girls could be had. The liquor was so strong you could burn it in your lantern and the girls were so bad that the prospectors and cowboys wouldn't go near them.

A dashing young cavalry officer on leave in Washington might catch the eye and the heart of some fair damsel. He might even win her hand in marriage. But horrors, what foreboding thoughts must have raced through the young socialite's mind when she accompanied her young lieutenant to his new duty assignment in the Arizona Territory. From nineteenth-century brownstone architecture to Fort McDowell adobe (a quick transition from modern to prehistoric); one had always to remember to shake out a shoe before putting it on to ensure that a scorpion had not taken up residence the night before. A silent, slithering rattlesnake would have no reservations about crawling into her living room to escape the afternoon rays of the sun. The nights were so hot that the residents had to carry their beds out onto the parade field for cooler slumber. It was also necessary to place tomato cans filled with water under the legs of the bed to keep the ants from climbing up and crawling in. When it did rain, the showers came down in such torrents as to flood the entire area.

Life on the post was, at best, boring. The infantry drilled and performed menial tasks while the cavalryman drilled and cared for his mount. There was more status in being a cavalryman and he was never hesitant to let the foot soldier know it. One of the few pleasures the infantryman could delight in was to see the gallant knight, dressed in a white coverall jacket, unceremoniously sweeping out his horse's stall twice a day.

Army mounts were always well treated and cared for. With the exception of combat, when horse casualties were high, the chargers could expect a long life. It was not uncommon for one still to be in service when he was past twenty-five years old.

Army regulations stated that the soldiers take one bath a week. As might be expected, some posts had no bathhouse. One soldier dryly noted that it "wasn't so bad, everybody smelled the same." Regulations also called for certain rules regarding uniforms, but the soldiers had other ideas, especially in the hot, arid land of the Apache. As a rule they wore whatever was comfortable. On the return from the long, arduous campaign into the Sierra Madre in the 1880s, the troopers looked more like Mexican irregulars than the blue-uniformed, yellow-bandana-wearing Hollywood stereotype.

Little time was spent in rifle practice. The budget-minded government wouldn't spend the necessary funds to purchase ammunition. As one officer later recorded, "I wanted to have target practice but I was told I would have to pay for the ammunition myself." In the 1880s the Army was finally allowed to practice marksmanship on a regular basis. Each man was allotted twenty rounds a month for practice.

As might be expected in such a Spartan existence, women were scarce and always in demand. A pretty girl out West on a visit might expect several immediate proposals of marriage. For a plain-looking one it might take a week or two longer. Employment agencies would send young girls out from eastern cities to work as domestics for the officers' wives. They were usually taken as brides shortly thereafter by the bachelor officers. In at least one instance the agency was requested to seek out the ugliest girls they could possibly find. This was done in hopes that the employer would not lose the employee to matrimony so rapidly. The agency complied with the request. The homeliest girls that could be located were hired and sent West. In the short span of two months they were all married.

Another integral part of post life was the laundresses. Most were married to enlisted men. If a soldier wanted to get married, he had first to secure permission from his commanding officer. This was usually granted depending on the current need for laundresses at the post. Using a logic that only the bureaucratic mind of the Army could understand, regulations stipulated a quota of one laundress to every nineteen and one half men. If there was no opening for a laundress at the post, the marriage would have to be postponed until an opening occurred.

Bureaucracy and red tape plagued the military constantly. The Army's most successful Indian fighter, George Crook, stated there was "no red tape when Indian fighting." During one period, an order came out of Washington requiring that the Indians must shoot first before the soldiers could open fire. Colonel Edwin Sumner circumvented this regulation with such finesse that it deserves mentioning. His troop chanced to encounter a band of known hostiles still some distance away. The colonel called for one of his Indian scouts to ride to the front of the column and fire at the antagonists. This being done, Sumner shouted, "Let it be noted that an Indian fired first." Hesitating momentarily, he turned toward his troops and shouted with great alacrity, "Charge!"

THE BASCOM AFFAIR

THE 1850s SAW RELATIVELY LITTLE warfare between red man and white in Old Arizona. The principal reason was that with the exception of a few mining ventures in the vicinity of Tubac and some small ranches along the Santa Cruz Valley, there just weren't enough whites around to raid. However, a few Anglo-American and Mexican ranchers and miners in the vicinity died at the hands of the Apache. To alleviate some of the problems, Washington established four military posts located at strategic positions inside or along the boundaries of present-day Arizona. In 1851 a post was built at Fort Defiance in the Four Corners area, to keep an eye on the Navajo. Fort Buchanan, between the Santa Cruz and San Pedro rivers, was constructed in 1856 for the protection of miners and ranchers in the southern and southeastern sections. Fort Yuma, on the California side of the river, was built in 1849. This post was established about the time of the Glanton massacre and was designed to offer protection to thirsty immigrants on their way to California. The fourth was located up the Colorado along the northern route across Arizona. Lieutenant Edward F. Beale of camel-train fame suggested a fort there as a shelter for California-bound tourists. The post was named Fort Mohave and was also used as a base of operations against hostile Indians in that region.

By and large, nearly all of the atrocities committed in central and southern Arizona were attributed to the Apache. This was not always accurate, although it was customary to blame them or simply to refer to any band of plunderers, no matter what tribe, as Apache. This, of course, tends to generate a greater emotional response from the listeners than if, for example, you were to say, "I was attacked by a band of Cocopah." If you were going to be raided, why not have the job done by the very best in the business?

Trouble on a large scale wasn't long in coming. With the eventual influx of whites in the late 1850s, the inevitable clash of cultures was imminent. John Ward had come to Arizona in the late 1850s from California. One version says he left on invitation from the vigilantes of San Francisco. In 1860 he was working a small ranch on Sonoita Creek, where he and his Mexican mistress Jesusa were running a few head of cattle. He also worked part time at nearby Fort Buchanan as a government beef contractor. Jesusa had a young son living with them named Felix. At this point the story varies with different historians. One version has it that she had been captured by Pinal Apache and during her incarceration had conceived and given birth to a son. The other, a more probable version, was that she had married a light-haired man named Tellez. She had borne him a daughter and a son, and after her husband died, she met and took up residence with Ward. Ward has been painted both as a drunkard who constantly whipped the boy, causing him to run away on several occasions, and as a kind stepfather who was genuinely fond of the lad. The reader must be aware that history is like interviewing witnesses to an auto accident or a street fight. There are many versions and alterations depending on the observer's frame of reference. History is many times merely the rumor we choose to believe, or a myth that we all agree upon.

One October day in 1860, Ward rode into Fort Buchanan and reported that his stepson and some cattle had been stolen. For some unexplained reason, it was not until January 29, 1861, some three months later, that Lieutenant George Bascom and a detail of fifty-four men were dispatched to locate the missing boy.

It is not surprising that Bascom headed for Apache Pass. It was known that Cochise and his people lived there and it was also known that Cochise and his band frequently made forays along Sonoita Creek. It was 150 miles to the Butterfield stage station at the pass. Bascom reached the station on February 3. After making camp near the station, the officer informed the manager that he would like to meet with Cochise.

The next day Cochise and some of his relatives walked into Bascom's camp. Using an interpreter, Bascom asked the Chiricahua about the missing boy. Cochise informed the officer that he had no knowledge of the incident but he would be glad to look into the matter and see what the possibilities were of getting the boy back. This was not exactly the response that Bascom wanted, so, following usual procedure, he informed the chief that he and his relatives would be held as hostages until the boy was returned. Cochise instantly made a break for freedom. He succeeded, but his relatives were not so lucky. The Army had three hostages. Now it was Cochise's turn to act.

The following day the warrior called for another parley. Culver, the station manager, Wallace, who spoke the Apache language, and another man named Welsh went out to talk. After a brief conversation Cochise gave the signal and several warriors pounced on the trio. Culver and Welsh, both huge men, broke away and made a dash for the station. Culver was struck by a bullet just as he reached the door. Welsh fared no better. He was accidentally shot by a soldier just as he reached safety. Wallace was caught and unceremoniously carried off. He reappeared as an Apache prisoner the next day to plead with Bascom to release the hostages. "Not without the Ward boy," Bascom replied. Once again Wallace was dragged away.

Meanwhile, the eastbound stagecoach from Tucson with eleven people on board was making its way through the west end of the pass. As the coach rambled down a steep grade several shots rang out. Two men were hit, as were the two lead mules. The two mules were cut loose and the coach raced desperately for the station. At the bottom of a hill approaching the station was a small wooden bridge. Prior to the attack, the Apache had removed the side planks over which the wheels would run in hopes of wrecking the coach at that point. However, they were to be denied, as a near-disaster was averted when the coach, traveling at great speed, bellied right across. At this juncture the Apache gave up the chase and the coach limped safely into the station yard.

A similar plan had been set up for the westbound stage at the other end of the pass. A commonly used method for stopping small trains by the bands was to pile up dried grass in some narrow passageway. When the wagons were far enough into the pass as to make turning impossible, the Apache would set fire to the grass.

Apparently one of the warriors was negligent in his duty as the stage rode right over the unlit heap and it reached the station unmolested.

Meanwhile, Cochise and his band had attacked a Mexican supply train destined for the stage station. The Mexican prisoners were chained to the wagon wheels and burned alive. Two Americans were taken prisoner in hopes of an exchange for Bascom's hostages. Again Wallace was sent down to present Cochise's demands and again the same impasse was reached.

A messenger had been sent to William S. Oury, a stage employee at Tucson, informing him of the dilemma. Oury immediately sent a messenger to Fort Breckinridge (Camp Grant) for help. Two companies of dragoons were dispatched east down Aravaipa Canyon to rendezvous with Oury at Ewells Station a few miles west of the beleaguered station at Apache Pass. From Fort Buchanan another group of mounted infantry under Assistant Surgeon B. J. D. Irwin set out on a rescue mission. In a raging snowstorm they covered 65 miles in one day, reaching Dragoon Springs, some 30 miles west of the pass.

The next day, Irwin's troops engaged in battle with a band of Coyotero who were returning from a raid with a large herd of cattle and ponies. In a running battle the soldiers succeeded in capturing three warriors and some seventy head of livestock.

By a miraculous stroke of luck, Irwin's force reached Apache Pass without further incident. They probably would have run into an ambush by Apache lurking near the entrance to the pass, but the warriors, noticing some soldiers marching across the valley to the north, and suspecting that some new threat was advancing around to attack from the east side of the pass, immediately gathered their forces and rushed to the opposite end. This bit of unwitting luck allowed Irwin's forces to enter from the west side unopposed. Actually, these soldiers marching to the north were a completely different group on their way to Fort Bliss, Texas, and completely unaware of the drama taking place a few miles to the south.

On that same day, February 14, the two companies of dragoons under the command of Lieutenant Isaiah Moore arrived from Fort Breckinridge, along with Oury and a party of volunteers from Tucson.

Activity around the pass was relatively quiet for the next two or three days. On the seventeenth, the bodies of the American hostages were discovered by a patrol about a mile and a half from the station. They were mutilated beyond recognition. Oury was able to identify the body of Wallace by the gold in his teeth. The others were assumed to be from the ambushed supply train.

It was decided that the Apache hostages must hang in retaliation. Bascom protested the action, but was informed by Dr. Irwin that the three Coyotero prisoners would hang anyway. Lieutenant Bascom relented when given assurance by Moore that the senior officers present would accept full responsibility. All six hostages were taken to a spot near the graves of the Americans and hanged. The bodies remained hanging limply in the trees for several months afterward, unclaimed by the relatives. The Apache, by custom, have a great horror of death and will not go near a dead body. Cochise later remarked that he could understand it better if the soldiers had tortured the prisoners to death. To the Apache, hanging seemed inhumane and cowardly.

The missing boy, Felix Tellez, was never recovered. It was later proved that Cochise and his band did not kidnap the boy. It's generally believed that Felix was taken by a band of Pinal. He reappeared in history some twenty years later as a one-eyed scout and interpreter for General Crook under the name of Mickey Free. When asked to recall the ordeal, he replied that he couldn't remember too much except that it was a long, hard ride for a small boy.

The wrath of Cochise and other chieftains was aroused, and within two months, 150 whites had been butchered in southern Arizona and southwestern New Mexico.

Some historians have fixed the blame on Lieutenant Bascom, calling him a "brash young man fresh out of West Point." Lieutenant Bascom was not "fresh out of West Point," nor was he necessarily brash. He was an able officer, who when he took Cochise hostage was following a procedure that was common on the frontier. Cochise, for his part, did have a working agreement with the Butterfield people. But this did not keep him and his band from the plunder and pillage of other Anglo-Americans and Mexicans.

Bascom emerged from the incident a scapegoat, and never got a chance to vindicate himself, if at the time it was really even necessary. He was killed a year later fighting the Confederates at Valverde, New Mexico. Cochise emerged from it all a hero to his people, a living martyr.

The ones who really suffered were the five thousand or so whites and Indians who would die in the next few years. The Bascom affair was the spark that set it off, although the war itself was inevitable. As one crusty old philosopher so aptly remarked, "The lion shall lie down with the lamb . . . so long as you keep adding a few fresh lambs from time to time."

The Butterfield stage line was back in business shortly thereafter. Activities between the North and South curtailed any more government spending on a southern route to the Pacific. On March 2, 1861, the stage contract was annulled and John Butterfield's four-wheeled chariots would rumble no more through the narrow, precipitous passes that embellish southeastern Arizona—at least not until the politicians in the East settled their differences on the battlefield.

THE CIVIL WAR IN THE
SOUTHWEST

THE GREAT WAR IN THE EAST completely overshadowed the savage fighting that took place between red man and white. A major reason, of course, was the great number of casualties suffered by both the Gray and the Blue; a less important one was the news media. Western warfare was strictly second-page copy. However, one of the most crucial battles of the war, a small skirmish by Civil War standards, was fought in the Southwest at Glorieta Pass, New Mexico, in 1862.

While serving the United States as Secretary of War, Jefferson Davis, a Southerner, had pushed hard for a southern route to California. The camel experiment and the early railroad surveys had all been with his blessing. Like most politicians, Davis was interested in seeing to it that the section of the nation he represented benefited from the economic advantages a southern route to the Pacific would bring. As the breach between the North and South widened it became increasingly important to Southerners in Washington to see to it that the military posts in the Southwest were kept well stocked with supplies. In the event of war these could be quickly confiscated by southern forces. The Southerners were also quick to realize the advantages that a transcontinental link with California would provide. The South was seeking recognition and aid from England; if California were attached to the Confederacy, the South would then be an ocean-to-ocean power, a claim that would add much prestige to the southern cause. By and large the citizens of Arizona and New Mexico were little concerned with the sectional conflict that was developing in the East. The Californians were embroiled in sectional differences of their own. The northern half leaned toward the Union while the agrarian southern half favored the South. A large number of federal troops remained in California throughout the war, thus ensuring the Golden State's allegiance to the Union. In 1861 a large number of citizens in both California and New Mexico were proposing to ignore both North and South, preferring instead to form a confederacy of Pacific states.

When war finally did break out, the North, more concerned with concentrating its forces along the Rio Grande, abandoned the posts in Arizona. The Apache interpreted the troop withdrawals as a sign of the white man's surrender. Seizing the opportunity, they went on a campaign of wholesale murder and pillage. Sonoran border bandits, not to be outdone, also took advantage of the helpless settlers and ranchers, who now found themselves suddenly without protection. Even the Mexican mineworkers got into the act, as on more than one occasion they murdered their American employers for plunder. There was a period when the settlement of Tubac was under siege from two sides. To the north was the Apache and on the south side lurking about like hungry coyotes were the bandits. Tucson once again became a walled-in city.

Many United States Army officers stationed in the Southwest chose to remain with the Confederacy for one reason or another. Robert E. Lee was in Texas when war broke out. Always a man of high principle, he traveled to Washington to tender his resignation. Even after President Lincoln offered him command of the Union armies, Lee still chose to return to his home state of Virginia and serve her in whatever capacity she might choose. Captain Richard S. Ewell, in command of Fort Buchanan, Arizona, at the outbreak of hostilities, an ardent Southerner, chose to fight with the Gray. He rose to the rank of general, serving with "Stonewall" Jackson and later with Lee at Gettysburg.

General David E. Twiggs of Georgia, an old war horse who had fought in all of America's wars since 1812, suffering mixed emotions, surrendered the entire Department of Texas along with her posts and supplies to the Confederates. An officer in his department, Captain George Stoneman of Mormon Battalion fame, refused to obey Twiggs' order and with part of his command managed to make it safely to Union territory. Before the war ended, Stoneman rose to the rank of general and later commanded the Department of Arizona.

That old intrepid Knight of the Plains, Phillip St. George Cooke, epitomized the way the war literally tore families apart. When Lincoln's first call for 75,000 volunteers brought a wave of resignations from the southern officers, Cooke learned that his son and two sons-in-law had chosen to leave the Army and espouse the Confederate cause. One son-in-law, General "Jeb" Stuart, became a famous cavalry officer with Lee's Army of Virginia. It is one of those ironic events of a war of this nature that General Cooke of the Union Army spent time in pursuit of his elusive, dashing son-in-law. Unfortunately Stuart was killed at Yellow Tavern. Cooke's son, John Rogers Cooke, did survive the war and bitter feelings prevailed between the two, who were not reconciled until 1887. The war had taken three of his four children. Only a nephew, John Esten Cooke, was willing to forgive an old soldier who unselfishly placed duty to country above duty to home state.

. When war broke out, southern strategy called for a quick seizure of New Mexico, Arizona, and southern California. On July 25, 1861, Colonel John Baylor and his Texas Mounted Rifles crossed into New Mexico. The conquest should have been an easy one. Public opinion in New Mexico was, by and large, one of apathy. In 1850, she had been pro-North, but during the next decade several changes had come about concerning her attitude toward the slavery question. There had even been some talk of joining neither North nor South, but forming a confederacy of Pacific states. If Jefferson Davis had sent in the Georgia Militia or the Tennessee Volunteers to occupy New Mexico, things might have gone differently. If anything could arouse those New Mexicans to fight, it was the thought of being invaded by those belligerent Texans. Memories of land-grabbing and filibustering expeditions were still too fresh in the minds of its citizens to be lethargic.

When Baylor crossed the line, the nearest Union troops were some 40 miles up the Rio Grande at Fort Fillmore, stationed there under the command of Major Isaac Lynde. Baylor had originally planned to take Fort Fillmore by surprise. But failing in this, he settled for the occupation of Mesilla instead.

Later that day, old Major Lynde, whose forces outnumbered the

Confederates by more than two to one, moved up to do battle. He sent couriers ahead, requesting Baylor and his men to surrender. "We will fight first and surrender afterwards," Baylor spitefully replied. After a short skirmish the Union troops retreated from the field.

The next day Major Lynde set fire to his post and began marching his men eastward toward Fort Stanton. On the way, by brilliant maneuvering, they "captured" a saloon and liberated its supplies. Colonel Baylor went in pursuit and when he caught up with the New Mexico force, the old major surrendered his entire group without firing a shot. He was later dismissed from the Army for "lack of zeal in fighting his country's enemies." The prisoners were soon paroled when it was learned there was only a short supply of liquor on hand. Presumably the victors feared that the insatiable vanquished might imbibe more than their fair share, leaving the victors with no spoils of which to partake.

A few days later, Colonel Baylor issued a proclamation announcing officially that he had taken possession of the Territory of Arizona for the Confederacy. Its boundary was set at the 34th parallel on the north and from the panhandle of Texas to the Colorado River on the west. Mesilla would be its capital and he, John Baylor, would be governor.

The new provisional government had two serious problems at the start. To the north, General E. R. S. Canby had some 2,500 troops poised and ready to attack and to the west the Apache had closed all roads to Tucson. In fact, one might say that the Apache actually occupied Confederate Arizona.

Baylor organized two groups of volunteers to fight Apache in Arizona. He designated them the Arizona Guards and the Arizona Rangers. Each force had approximately thirty men. Still, conditions continued to deteriorate and on March 20, 1862, Baylor issued his famous extermination order: "Use all means to persuade the Apaches of any tribe to come in for the purpose of making peace, and when you get them all together, kill all the grown Indians and take the children prisoners and sell them to defray the expense of killing the Indians."

President Davis was not pleased when he learned of the order. Selling the idea of slavery, the "peculiar institution," to Europeans was difficult enough without this added complication. Governor Baylor found himself out of a job and the order rescinded.

The Confederates decided to follow up Baylor's initial success with another larger force which would strike northward up the Rio Grande. This unsavory band of looters called themselves the Texas Brigade. Their leader, Henry Hopkins Sibley, was a gifted officer when sober, which wasn't often. Sibley graduated from West Point in 1838. He had fought in the Mexican war and the Indian campaigns of the fifties. His greatest contribution was the invention of military camp stoves and tents named in his honor. When the war broke out he was stationed in New Mexico, but, bitter over his failures to receive a promotion, he resigned his commission and hurried to Richmond. There he convinced President Davis of a strategy in which New Mexico could be taken. Sibley was given a command, and in December 1862 he led his Army of New Mexico into Mesilla, pausing only long enough to send a small detachment west, under Captain Sherrod Hunter, to occupy Tucson. Next, Sibley drove his army up the Rio Grande toward Fort Craig. The commander of that post was Colonel E. R. S. Canby. In another one of those ironies of war, he just also happened to be Sibley's brother-in-law. At this juncture Sibley made an all-out attempt to cajole Canby's men into deserting and joining the southern cause. One of his enticements was pay, which the Union troops hadn't been getting. To head off a full-scale exit by his troops, Canby raised some private funds. He also dug into his own pockets, and came up with the necessary monetary remunerations.

On February 21, the two forces met at Valverde. Canby had set his Union forces on the west bank of the Rio Grande. The men dug in on top of a long, steep mesa giving them command of two places the Confederates would likely cross.

After feinting in one direction, Sibley moved his men toward the Valverde crossing. Canby had guessed right and was waiting for him. When the two armies came together, the "Walking Whiskey Keg" was too drunk to stay in his saddle. Colonel Tom Green, hero of San Jacinto and the Mexican war, relieved his commander and no doubt saved the day for the Confederacy. Green's motto was "When in doubt, charge." He knew no other command. The Rebels, maddened and half-crazy with thirst, hammered the Union lines, mostly relying on revolvers and bowie knives. A suicidal saber charge by the Texans won the day. The Union lines folded and ran. One of the Union casualties that day was Captain George Bascom, a central figure in the Apache Pass incident. That intrepid old

13. Apache scouts around 1880. *Arizona State Lib.*

14. Captain Crawford's body arrives at Lang's Ranch, New Mexico, 1886, following his murder in Mexico. *Arizona State Lib.*

15. Lieutenant Charles B. Gatewood: "the man who captured Geronimo." *Arizona Historical Foundation, Sacks Collection.*

16. Major William Emory, soldier-scientist who led several boundary surveys in the 1850s. *Arizona Historical Foundation.*

17. Christopher "Kit" Carson, trapper, guide, and Civil War general. *Arizona State Lib.*

18. General George Crook, one of the few to win the trust and respect of the Indian. *Sharlot Hall Museum.*

19. Al Sieber, Civil War hero and later Chief of Scouts for General Crook during the Apache wars. *Sharlot Hall Museum.*

20. Nellie Cashman, "angel of the mining camps," Argonaut, philanthropist, and vagabond. According to the miners, her reputation was "unimpeachable." *Arizona State Lib.*

21. Olive Oatman, captive of the Colorado River Indians for several years. In the tradition of the tribe, her face was tattooed when she reached the marriage age. *Arizona State Lib.*

22. Martha Summerhays, Army wife who lived on several military posts in Arizona in the 1870s. Her writings on that period have become classics. *Arizona State Lib.*

23. Ed Schieffelin, discoverer of the rich Tombstone mining district. *Sharlot Hall Museum.*

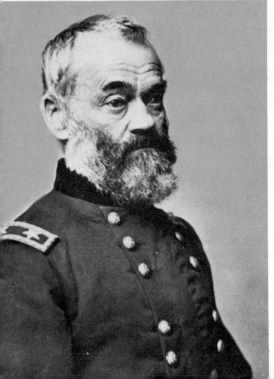

24. Sam Heintzelman, commanding officer at Fort Yuma, mining magnate, and a leader in the fight for territorial status. *Arizona Historical Foundation, Sacks Collection.*

mountain man Kit Carson, now Colonel Christopher Carson, leading a regiment of Union volunteers he had recruited, had the only unit that held firm. But it was not enough and Canby ordered his forces to fall back to Fort Craig, where he had taken logs and disguised them to look like cannons. The Texans, fooled completely by the ruse, decided to bypass the post. "My Quaker guns stopped Sibley," Canby later remarked.

Another person present from the Bascom affair was Captain James "Paddy" Graydon. Graydon had been a rancher in southern Arizona and when war broke out he joined the Union Army. He was given command of a company of scouts. Paddy's outfit was unique in the annals of war, or at least it so appeared. The record shows that he made it through the war without the loss of a single man either by death or desertion. When a man turned up missing he would simply "recruit" the next unfortunate lad who happened by, addressing him by the name of the missing person. Paddy's roster was always at full company strength.

The night before the main battle at Valverde, Paddy dreamed up a scheme that should qualify him as one of those pioneers in the tactical use of a guided missile. The technology was absent but the idea was the same. He suggested to his major that by taking two unserviceable old mules and loading them with high explosives, a few men could lead them across the river and point them in the direction of the Rebel camp. Once that was accomplished, the fuses would be lit and with a slap on the rump the "missiles" would be on their way.

It was promptly decided to implement the plan, and soon Paddy was surreptitiously leading the explosive-laden mules across the Rio Grande. When he was near enough to the camp, he lit the fuses, pointed the "missiles" toward the Rebels, slapped them on the rump, and turned to leave. As he was making his way back to the river, he chanced to look back. Horrors, the mules were right behind him. When he quickened his pace, they followed suit. The fuses were getting shorter and so was Paddy's time if he didn't do something in a hurry. He broke into a dead run followed with a headlong leap into the Rio Grande, just as the explosives blew sky-high. Paddy's adventure wasn't all for nought. He did succeed in waking up the Confederate camp and stampeding their cattle herd.

The Texas Brigade marched up the Rio Grande, meeting little opposition along the way. Soon they occupied Albuquerque and

Santa Fe. The real prize was farther up the old Santa Fe Trail at Fort Union, where a large store of supplies was cached. Perhaps more important, Fort Union was the gateway to the rich mineral area of Colorado.

Sibley anticipated no serious problems in his conquest. Unknown to him, a large relief force of Colorado hard-rock miners was on its way to New Mexico. One of the officers with the Colorado force was a fanatical, Bible-toting Methodist preacher-turned-warrior named John Chivington. Two years later Chivington would achieve infamy as the perpetrator of the massacre of Indians at Sand Creek, Colorado. But this time John Chivington would not only save the day for the Union Army, he would save the entire West from being cut off from her eastern allies.

The Colorado Volunteers were another of those groups of irregular, superb fighting men that appear on the pages of history from time to time. They worked hard, played hard, and most of all they loved a good fight. The Texans would soon learn that these were not the apathetic New Mexicans of previous battles. The Colorado brawlers had come to do battle.

The first clash occurred when Chivington's men encountered the advance troops of the Texan army. Cannons boomed and grapeshot fell around the undaunted preacher. He ordered his infantry forward. The Confederate commander ordered his men to fall back. In the midst of this, Chivington sent his cavalry into the battle. The Rebels went into a full retreat back down the canyon. Chivington did not pursue as he had no knowledge of where the Confederate reinforcements might be. He fell back and made camp.

The next day the two forces battled again. This time the Rebels took the advantage. Just when victory was within their grasp, they called for a truce to remove the wounded. The surprised Union officers agreed and the battle ended. The following day when the truce expired, the Coloradoans were even more surprised to find that the Texans had left the field.

The reason for this unexpected turn of events was that Chivington and his men, guided by Lieutenant Colonel Manuel Chaves, had followed a path over the mountains, dropping down behind the Confederate lines and hitting the Rebel supply train. After destroying the supplies, Chaves, a legendary figure in New Mexico history and a native of the area, brought the men back up the mountain again and returned to the Union lines. When word had reached the

Confederate front lines that the supplies were gone, a truce was called. Before the truce expired the Texans had hastened a retreat all the way back to Santa Fe. Victory was within their grasp that day at Glorieta Pass and they failed to seize it. They would not get another chance.

Sibley and his band of looters began the long retreat back to Texas. He had made two fatal errors and they were costly. First, he had not provided adequate supply lines for his troops, which as any commander knows is crucial. Perhaps more important, he had made no serious attempt to befriend the New Mexicans. The South had reached its high-water mark of conquest in the West. If she had succeeded at Glorieta Pass nothing could have prevented her from advancing on Denver. From there it would have been a relatively simple task to seal off the vast mineral riches from the Union. Those same riches would have made a prestigious difference in the eyes of the Europeans, whose favor the Confederacy so desperately needed. But Sibley failed and the South never posed a serious threat to New Mexico and the West again.

—Meanwhile in Tucson, the Texans who occupied that city were unaware of the turn of events in New Mexico. Captain Hunter and his men had encountered little trouble occupying the Old Pueblo, as the Apache-harassed residents were all too happy to see soldiers and they didn't care what color the uniform. The Texans did a little Indian fighting but spent most of their time confiscating the property of Union sympathizers. Most of the residents were not unwilling to swear an oath of allegiance to the Confederacy. Many of them were already Southerners. However, many residents preferred to leave rather than accept southern rule. Estevan Ochóa had been running a successful freighting company in Tucson for several years, and when asked to swear allegiance he replied that he owed all his success to the United States and he preferred to cast his lot with the Grand Old Republic. His property taken, he was given a horse and told to leave. Turned loose in the heart of Apache country, Ochóa rode east, eventually reaching the Rio Grande safely. When the Union forces reoccupied Tucson, Ochóa returned triumphantly. A man of high principle and character, he rebuilt his business. The firm of Tully and Ochóa was a legend in the freight business during territorial days. Estevan Ochóa remained a leading citizen in Tucson for years to come, serving as mayor of that city

and territorial legislator. He was instrumental in the early development of the public school system in that city.

The Confederates in occupation were aware of a large Union
force approaching Arizona from the west, though they didn't know
just where it was. Captain Hunter tried with some success to create
an illusion of having a much larger force by scattering his men and
raiding several places at the same time. But his small band was no
match for the California Column and he knew it. He led a patrol to
the Pima villages on the Gila River, where he captured a supply of
flour being stored for the Californians. Meantime, Colonel James
Carleton of the California Column dispatched Captain William
McCleave ahead with orders to destroy the pesky Hunter and his
men. Captain Hunter arrived at the mill first, and, upon learning of
McCleave's pending arrival, he posed as the owner of the mill. The
guise worked as McCleave unwittingly walked right into Hunter's
trap. McCleave, now a prisoner of war, was given escort to the Rio
Grande. His host on that trip was Lieutenant Jack Swilling, a man
who was destined to leave his mark on the history of the Territory
in many ways.

The chagrined Colonel Carleton now sent Lieutenant Colonel
Joseph R. West with a much larger force in pursuit of Hunter's
band. West, in turn, ordered Captain William P. Calloway to take
his 272 men ahead to try to make contact with the Rebels. A small
skirmish was fought at Stanwix Station near present-day Sentinel,
and one Union soldier was wounded.

When Captain Calloway arrived at the Pima villages he was informed that the Confederates were at Picacho, a tall peak on the
way to Tucson. He ordered Lieutenants Baldwin and Barrett to
take two detachments and go to the peak. The plan was for Lieutenant James Barrett to enter the pass from the east while Baldwin
would come in from the west. Their orders were to find the enemy
and wait for reinforcements.

Lieutenant Barrett, no doubt anxious to engage in combat after
the long trip from the coast, pushed several miles ahead of Baldwin.
On the morning of April 15, 1862, Barrett and his men charged the
small Rebel camp at Picacho Pass. There were only three Confederates there at the time and all were taken prisoner. Unaware that
his gunfire was attracting other Rebel troops nearby, and disregard-
ing words of caution from his scout, Barrett began tying up his captives. Another Confederate force arrived suddenly and opened fire

just as Barrett was mounting his horse. The Union officer was struck by a shot and was killed instantly. Before the melee was over two more Union soldiers lay dead and four were wounded. The others broke and ran, leaving some equipment and all three prisoners behind. When Captain Calloway learned of the skirmish he pulled his forces all the way back to the Pima villages to "regroup." William C. Tobin could thank the brass ornament on his hat for saving his life in the battle. The bullet was deflected, nevertheless causing a serious, but not fatal, head wound. For a period afterward the two dead troopers, Johnson and Leonard, were eulogized by their comrades each day at roll call. Each time their names were read at muster another soldier answered, "He died for his country." Barrett was posthumously congratulated and a fort was built at the Pima villages and named in his honor. The Battle of Picacho Pass, as it became known, is supposed to have been the westernmost battle of the Civil War.

When word arrived of Sibley's retreat from Mexico, coupled with the advance of a large Union force from the west, Hunter had no choice but to take his small force and return to Texas. On the return trip, the Apache made life even more miserable for the Texans. Having little regard for uniforms of any color and the men wearing them, Hunter's force was subjected to constant harassment as it crossed Apachería on its way home. At least one man stayed behind. It seems that Lieutenant Jack Swilling was wanted in Texas for some misdeed. Rather than go back, he deserted and remained in Arizona.

THE CALIFORNIA COLUMN

CALIFORNIA HAD SOLVED MOST of the sectional differences between the northern and southern groups that had been plaguing her for those past few years—at least enough so to group together an ill-disciplined group of some eighteen hundred miners, ranchers, and opportunists calling themselves the California Column.

They were under the command of Colonel James Carleton, a stern-looking Regular Army man with a mission of ridding the Southwest of both Confederates and Indians. He also seems to have been a man with strong political and financial ambitions.

After suffering the usual vicissitudes of crossing the southwestern deserts, the Column arrived at Fort Yuma early in 1862. One of the members giving an interesting account of the journey was George O. Hand, described as a forty-niner, carpenter, veterinarian, saloon-keeper, janitor, gambler, soldier, mail contractor, and patriot. Was there anything else? Yes, he also loved to quote Shakespeare and get drunk, or perhaps it was to get drunk and quote Shakespeare. Hand kept a diary which was reprinted years later on the editorial page of the *Arizona Daily Star*. He remained in Tucson after leaving the Army, becoming a local character. His diary is most interesting as it vividly reflects military life from the viewpoint of the enlisted man.

Most of the volunteers were of the rugged-individual type and resented discipline in any way, shape, or form. If they felt like getting drunk, they did. If the rigors of Spartan military life got to be too much, they deserted. While on the march, they took pot shots at various game along the trail, be it jack rabbit or quail. When they found liquor in the villages, they confiscated it. More than once, the Column was delayed several hours from breaking camp because the men were still hung over from the previous evening's gaiety. Hand's diary graphically describes, in part, the life:

> June 1st, No inspection, officers with the exception of Captain Greene and Thayer, too drunk to hold it.

> July 4th, One gill of patriotism was issued to each man in the garrison. Officers not being men got none. About half the men procured passes and crossed the river to Colorado City. The last heard of them they were drunk and fighting; on the whole this is the most miserably spend 4th within my recollection. . . . we had several fights during the eve, songs and occasional fighting. July 5th was also celebrated.

The following day records:

> The new steamer, Colorado No. 2, made her trial trip. Officers and Spanish women are the invited guests or passengers. She equals all expectations. They were a drunken party when they returned.

Eventually, the main force arrived at Tucson. The flag was raised and Carleton declared Arizona a territory of the Union. It was several months later before the bureaucratic assemblage in Washington got around to declaring the same.

East of Tucson, those two diabolical purveyors of evil, Cochise and Mangas Coloradas had already learned of this new threat from the west. Carleton had inadvertently given them the information via some scouts who were passing through on their way to the Rio Grande. The scouts, a Sergeant Wheeling, a Private John Jones, and a Mexican guide named Chavez were carrying dispatches for General Canby in New Mexico. In a running fight Chavez and Wheeling were killed. Jones barely escaped death only to be captured by Confederates at the Rio Grande.

Their curiosity aroused, the Apache leaders sent scouts of their own to the vicinity of Tucson, where they discovered Carleton's army. The two chieftains began making preparations to resist the Column at Apache Pass, a narrow defile near today's Arizona-New Mexico border.

In early June, Carleton sent another group, much larger this time, with more dispatches for Canby. Lieutenant Colonel E. E. Eyre and his men, numbering 140, met Cochise in the pass. With the exception of one incident where three men were cut off from the rest and killed, the Column passed through safely. Apparently Cochise was waiting for Mangas Coloradas and his Mimbreño to arrive before starting any full-scale action. By the time Carleton's main force arrived, the Apache were ready.

On July 8, 1862, Captain Tom Roberts and his men were ordered to move eastward to the old Butterfield stage station at San Simon. Their mission was to fortify the station and give protection to the supply trains for the main column.

Roberts, with 126 men in his command, divided his force to ensure there would be adequate water supplies at each camp. Captain John C. Cremony was left with a small detachment of men to follow up with the supply wagons.

On the afternoon of the fourteenth, Roberts, accompanied by sixty infantry soldiers and seven cavalrymen, plus a battery of two 12-pound prairie howitzers, set out for Apache Pass, some 40 miles away. He arrived at the entrance to the pass about noon the next day. When they were only a half mile from the old abandoned stage station, the Apache, who were concealed in the surrounding hills, opened fire on the rear of the Column. The soldiers returned the fire, killing four and losing one. Roberts withdrew to the summit of the pass and regrouped his men. He sent skirmishers out on both sides of the road and loaded his howitzers. The soldiers were desperate in the knowledge that unless they took the spring, some 600 yards beyond the station, they would surely perish, as the only water supply was 40 miles away. They literally bulled their way to the station walls. By now Roberts' men had undergone nineteen hours of marching and six hours of fighting on just one cup of coffee each.

On the two hills just east of the station the Apache had built a breastwork of rocks, giving them a commanding view of the spring below. They had the advantage of firing on the soldiers from a range of about 400 feet, thus thwarting any attempt to rush the spring. Roberts brought his howitzers up and placed them in a dry wash. He opened fire, killing several on the hilltop. The shock of the new weapon was too much for the Apache. They retreated from the field and Roberts and his men won the day. The Apache leaders later said that they could defeat the soldier but not the "wagon that shoots twice." They saw it first explode harmlessly down below, but then the thing exploded a second time, and right above their heads, scattering pieces of iron in all directions. The Army won that round and the thirsty troopers filled their canteens and drank heartily that night.

Later that evening Roberts dispatched six cavalrymen to the supply train with orders to park it and see to its protection. He would follow with part of the infantry. Meanwhile, Captain Cremony and the supply train had advanced to a point about 15 miles from the entrance to Apache Pass. As the six cavalrymen rode out into Sulphur Springs Valley to the west of the pass, they were jumped by a large number of well-armed Apache. In the opening fire one soldier was shot in the arm and two horses were wounded. Private John Teal fell behind and found himself cut off from the rest of the group. Realizing they could be of no help to Teal, the others rode on, and after a frantic chase reached the supply train safely. Teal, meanwhile, had turned his horse southward, heading down the valley in hopes of outdistancing the warriors. It was to no avail. The warriors closed in. A well-placed shot dropped the horse. Teal jumped free and secured a position behind the dying animal. His only chance of escape was to keep the Apache at a safe distance until darkness approached. The rapid firing of his breech-loading carbine confused the Apache, who up to now had not encountered such a weapon. They circled around cautiously. The standoff had lasted for about an hour when one unusually large Indian rode up close. Teal took careful aim and fired, sending the bullet into the huge midsection of the Apache. The others lost interest in Teal at this point. They took the wounded warrior and rode away hurriedly. Wasting little time, Teal took his saddle and bridle and began the 8-mile trek to the supply train. He arrived late that same evening, much to the surprise of his friends, who had given him up for dead, or worse.

It was later learned that the warrior Private Teal had shot was none other than Mangas Coloradas. Carrying their wounded chieftain southward, the Apache rode into the little settlement of Janos, woke up the local doctor, and told him: "Mangas hurt. You make Mangas well and Janos lives. If Mangas dies, Janos dies." No physician has ever operated under more trying conditions. Luckily the good doctor was aided by the rawhide constitution of his patient.

The bullet was extracted, the wound bound, and true to their word, the warriors left.

Old Mangas never recovered fully from his wound. He was murdered a year later near Silver City, New Mexico, while a prisoner of the same Colonel James R. West who crossed Arizona with the California Column.

Shortly after Teal came in from his ordeal, Captain Roberts and his infantry joined the supply train. After a brief pause, the Column set out for the pass. When they reached the stone station house they learned that the Apache were again in control of the spring and the high ground.

The next morning, Roberts, this time having an accurate knowledge of the terrain, placed his men accordingly. The wagons and mules were forted in the corral; the artillery and troopers were in place. To the tune of bugle, fife, and drum, which must have been something of an anomaly in the middle of Apachería, the soldiers advanced toward the spring. Once again the howitzers blasted the hilltop, filling the air with spherical case shot. When the Apache fled the artillery fire, they found themselves an easy target for the riflemen. Those who escaped were cut down by the cavalry. It was to be an oft-repeated story in the latter days of the Indian wars.

The Battle of Apache Pass was the largest gathering of Apache ever assembled in Arizona for battle against the Army. Some 700 warriors under the combined leadership of Cochise and Mangas Coloradas, the principal leaders, fought against 126 soldiers. Roberts reported losing 2 men in the battle, while the Apache loss was set at 63. The Apache blamed most of their losses on the "wagons that shoot twice." Never again would the Apache attempt to challenge the Americans on the battlefield. Future warfare would be strictly on Apache terms.

A few days later, Colonel, now General, Carleton, arrived at the pass. It was decided that a post was needed there for the protection of military and civilians alike, so Fort Bowie was officially established on July 28, 1862. Named for Colonel George Washington Bowie of the California Volunteers, Fort Bowie was destined to become one of the most crucial posts in the Apache wars.

With New Mexico rid of the Confederates, Carleton, no lover of Indians, turned his full attention to their destruction. He too issued an extermination order that must have brought shades of Colonel

Baylor to the minds of many. "Male Indians are to be slain wherever they can be found," he proclaimed.

General Carleton was fortunate to have in his command Colonel
Christopher Carson, a man known for his prowess in battle. The Indians, too, were fortunate in that Carson didn't follow the extermination order to the letter. In eastern New Mexico against the Mescalero, and in the Four Corners against the Navajo, the little
mountain man displayed a tenacious fighting ability as well as a degree of humanitarianism to his defeated and dispossessed foe. In
each case Carson took the hostile Indians prisoner rather than follow an extermination policy. At Canyon de Chelly and Canyon del
Muerto, in northern Arizona, Carson's volunteers battled the Navajo, who up to this time had been indomitable. Their refuge had
been the great unmapped canyons that abound in that part of the
country. Carson's steady harassment finally drove them out of the
heretofore impregnable bastion. The volunteers, sweeping through
the red-rock chasms, destroyed the Navajo's crops and ponies. Hunger and cold took their toll and by the spring of 1864 some eight
thousand Navajo surrendered.

To relocate the vanquished Indians, Carleton selected the most
desolate, useless piece of ground in eastern New Mexico and designated it as a reservation. It was located near the Pecos River and
called Bosque Redondo. To complicate matters further, he assigned
the Apache and their not too friendly cousins the Navajo occupation of the same area. The Apache soon departed for their beloved
mountains. Five years later, in 1868, the Navajo, broken in spirit,
concluded the second half of their Long Walk, 400 miles back to
the Four Corners, never to hit the plunder trail again.

Eventually, remnants of the California Volunteers would filter
back into Arizona, some by way of New Mexico, and others from
duty posts in various areas. They would build other forts and
camps to protect the miners and ranchers. Gold was discovered in
the Bradshaws, and Fort Whipple was built to offer protection. The
Verde Valley settlers had Camp Lincoln, later renamed Camp
Verde. Fort McDowell was constructed for the settlers in the Gila
and Salt river valleys, Fort Apache in the White Mountains, and
Fort Lowell just outside of Tucson became a supply base. These
and many more, some temporary and some permanent, would be
built by the soldiers in the next few years. By 1886, 20 per cent of
the entire U. S. Army would be stationed in the Territory.

CIVILIAN EXPEDITIONS OF
THE SIXTIES

———⌣———⌣———

WHEN THE FEDERAL TROOPS began burning their posts prior to abandonment early in the Civil War, signs were ominous to the white men who remained. For the time being, they would be on their own. Some, like Pete Kitchen, turned their ranches into veritable fortresses. Others hurried to cities like Tucson. Many packed up and left altogether.

Those who remained formed groups of volunteers. Most offensive Apache fighting was in the form of semi-military expeditions. Not having the discipline of regular soldiers, the practices of "honorable" warfare were not always followed. Once while raiding an Indian village, Sugarfoot Jack, a miscreant who had come to Arizona with the California Column but was discharged for thievery, incurred the wrath of his friends when he tossed a small child into a fire. Later, upon finding another toddler crying in the ruins, he reached down tenderly and picked it up. Seating himself upon a rock, he danced it upon his knee until it started to smile. Then, taking his revolver, he fired point-blank into the tot's face, scattering the remains upon himself. This enraged even the battle-hardened veterans. Sugarfoot Jack might have met his end right there if he hadn't scurried off into the woods, hiding until the others cooled down. A violent man, Sugarfoot Jack died a violent death on the Rio Grande sometime later at a fandango, when he wound up on the wrong end of a knife.

A tiny child taken by either side might be picked up by its feet and have its head dashed against a tree or rock. This may sound cruel, but it was considered by the fighters more merciful in the long run. Their theory was that the child would not be strong enough to withstand the rigors of the trip and would most likely perish along the trail anyway. It should be stated that there were numerous cases where hard-bitten fighters on both sides did adopt the orphaned children left over from some skirmish.

Pinole, a treat made of ground corn mixed with sugar, was a favorite of the Apache. Knowing this, the white men would mix little pieces of broken glass or strychnine into it. When eaten in this form, it was known to raise all kinds of havoc with the stomach and intestines.

Adult male prisoners were never taken by the Apache, or at least not kept alive for very long if they were. Travelers and lone prospectors were the most vulnerable. The Apache chose both time and location for the ambush. Early accounts in the Prescott newspapers tell of atrocities committed on a regular basis in that vicinity. One man captured near town was shot full of arrows, but not in the vital parts of his anatomy. He was carefully kept alive so that he could witness his final moments on earth. Another victim near Fort Bowie was found with his head tied into a large soapweed bush. The bush had been set afire, roasting the unfortunate traveler alive. These and many other atrocities were practiced on persons unlucky enough to let themselves be taken alive. Interestingly, some of the most accomplished of the torturers were said to be the Apache women.

One historian has stated that these mutilation practices may have been learned from the Anglo-Americans and Mexicans, as they were contrary to Apache custom. If this is true, one might surmise that the Apache had learned the trade well.

In the late 1860s a great deal more attention was focused on the Indian problem. The Civil War was over and the Army concentrated its efforts once again on bringing peace to the frontier. Casualty rates in Arizona ranked among the highest in the Army. Arizona was considered to be the most dangerous duty assignment in the entire Army. The small outposts and camps were located in remote mountainous regions susceptible to ambush within a few yards of the station. To move from one area to another necessitated passing through narrow canyons. Pursuit was always hazardous, as conditions could easily cause the hunter suddenly to become the hunted, and the soldiers would be lucky to escape with their lives. Unless one is familiar with the terrain, it is most difficult really to appreciate the kind of hard campaigning that was necessary to bring the Apache wars to a successful conclusion.

The latter part of the 1860s saw the military take to the field in northwestern Arizona against the Walapai Indians. This relatively quiet area turned troublesome following the senseless killing of a chief named Wauba Yuba by Sam Miller, a local citizen in the area. There was no apparent reason for the shooting. Nevertheless, a local jury excused Sam and even gave him a vote of thanks for his deed.

In the months that followed, the road from Hardyville, on the Colorado, to Prescott was the scene of many bloody depredations, as the aroused Walapai exacted revenge upon the travelers. The Grand Army of the Colorado, as it was dubbed by the local press, took to the campaign trail in the vicinity of today's Kingman. Following several weeks of toil and a few small skirmishes, the Walapai, for the most part, gave up their warlike ways and agreed to settle on a reservation of the government's choosing. A few years later, little by little, they returned to the cool, pleasant lands of their earlier days. In 1875, the government set this aside as a permanent reservation, where the Walapai remain today.

Notoriety has its price, and at times can become an albatross. Once the name of some scandalous rascal becomes a household word, he becomes the target of every sharpshooter.

Physical features can have the same effect. One such person was a Yavapai Indian named Big Rump. The anatomical feature which gave him his unflattering sobriquet also made him a most noteworthy villain in the Prescott area. Big Rump, because of this notoriety, received blame for most of the mischievous conduct that took place in those parts. The unfriendly press also did much to enhance his villainous image (one must presume that "Big Rump" was a euphemism created by the press in place of a more descriptive colloquialism used by the locals). Fame is, unfortunately, a fleeting thing. Big Rump's luck finally ran out during a skirmish with some traditional foes, the Pima.

Delshay, an Apache of some renown, gave the Army such fits that a price was put on his head. Sometime thereafter, two bands brought in different heads, each claiming theirs was the authentic cranium. With shades of Solomon, the officer pacified both bands by paying each the bounty money, trusting to chance that the sins of the other poor soul were more than just a case of strong resemblance.

There were many brave officers on the frontier but none braver than Lieutenant Howard Cushing. A member of a family of war heroes, Cushing's reputation as a relentless Indian fighter was well established long before he arrived in Arizona. He had that rare natural quality that made him a leader of men. His troopers idolized him and fellow officers had the highest regard for him. His ability was such that he was kept in the field constantly, pursuing wherever and whenever needed. For more than a year, Cushing led countless scouts through Apachería. His luck finally ran out in May of 1871, when, in the Whetstone Mountains near the San Pedro River, his troop was ambushed by a band thought to be under the leadership of a well-known Apache warrior named Juh.

There was much confusion within the military in governing and co-ordinating activities in Apachería, which included both Arizona and New Mexico. Arizona was in the Military Department of California until 1870, while New Mexico was in the Department of Missouri. Bureaucratic chaos usually prevailed when officers tried to carry out orders that conflicted with those from another department. Regimental jealousy no doubt caused many problems in addition. Combine these with the fighting between civil and military officials, plus the fact that it sometimes took three months to give or receive written orders within the department, and you have a general idea of some of the problems the Army faced. One tends to believe that it still would have been a long and difficult war even if there had been no Apache to fight!

Temperatures were rising in Tucson in the spring of 1871. Apache depredations were extending inside the city limits. The angry citizens were demanding action. Only the right incident or excuse for vigilante action was needed. It wasn't long in coming.

A few miles north and east of Tucson, at the junction of the Aravaipa and San Pedro rivers, was Camp Grant. It was described by Lieutenant John Bourke as "the most thoroughly God-forsaken post of all those supposed to be included in the annual congressional appropriations." In charge of the camp was a lieutenant named Royal Whitman. One day five old Apache women came into the camp and asked for food. Whitman supplied their needs and the women advised him that there were many other Apache in the vicinity who wished to come in peace and do some trading. Soon the officer found himself in charge of some five hundred Indians under the leadership of Eskiminzin, a man so controversial that even today historians can't decide whether he was an "honorable" leader or a rogue. Lacking the authority to make a treaty with the Apache, Whitman wrote to his department commander General George Stoneman for instructions. When he received no answer the officer then put his charges to work, with apparently good results. Still there was no reply from California. The depredations continued throughout southern Arizona. As was the case many times in the West, the nearest and most convenient Indians were blamed.

In Tucson, a vigilance committee was formed and led by two of her most well-known citizens, Jesus Elias and William S. Oury. Elias spoke for the Mexican populace and Oury for the Anglo-American. It was decided that the guilty Apache must be punished. "Evidence" indicated that the culprits were at Camp Grant.

The action was well planned. Selecting a time when the soldiers were away, and recruiting 94 Papago Indians to do the dirty work, the party headed toward the old fort. There were 48 Mexicans and only 6 Americans in the group, indicating that a lot of the "boys" around town were doing a lot of talking, but when it came time for action, not many had the stomach for it. It was one of the most sadistic attacks yet seen on the frontier. When the slaughter was over, 132 Apache were dead. Among the dead only 8 were men; the others were not in the camp at the time of the attack. Twenty-seven prisoners were taken and later sold in Sonora as slaves.

When word of the massacre reached the eastern states, there was outrage. President Grant called it "murder," and ordered Governor Safford to bring the guilty parties to trial. A trial was held and the case presented. The jury took nineteen minutes to call for acquittal of the defendants. No jury in Arizona would have ruled it any other way, considering the times and emotions. The furor didn't lessen. President Grant ordered the Secretary to the Commissioner of Indian Affairs, Vincent Colyer, and after him, General Oliver Howard, the famed "Christian General," to Arizona for purposes of promoting a peace policy. But more important, General Stoneman was relieved of his command. In his place came a man promoted over many senior officers and destined to become the most successful Indian-fighting general in history, George Crook.

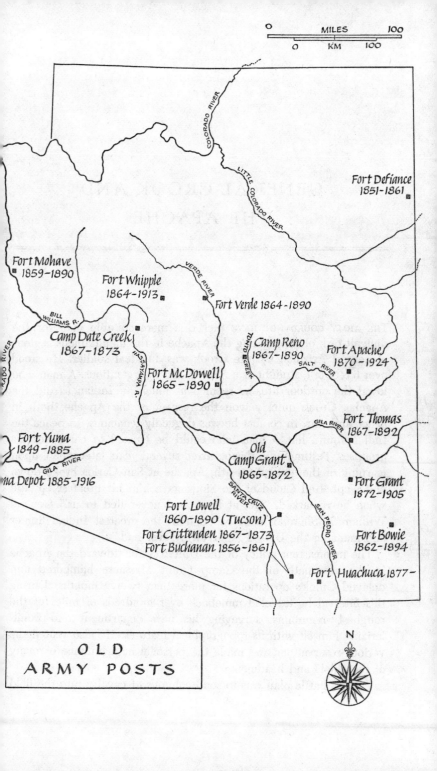

MILES 100

KM 100

COLORADO RIVER

LITTLE COLORADO RIVER

Fort Defiance
1851–1861

Fort Mohave
1859–1890

Fort Whipple
1864–1913

VERDE RIVER

Fort Verde 1864–1890

BILL WILLIAMS R.

Camp Date Creek
1867–1873

Camp Reno
1867–1890

TONTO CREEK

SALT RIVER

Fort Apache
1870–1924

COLORADO RIVER

HASSAYAMPA R.

Fort McDowell
1865–1890

Fort Thomas
1867–1892

GILA RIVER

Fort Yuma
1849–1885

GILA RIVER

Old
Camp Grant
1865–1872

na Depot 1885–1916

SANTA CRUZ RIVER

Fort Grant
1872–1905

Fort Lowell
1860–1890 (Tucson)

Fort Crittenden 1867–1873
Fort Buchanan 1856–1861

SAN PEDRO RIVER

Fort Bowie
1862–1894

Fort Huachuca 1877–

N

OLD
ARMY POSTS

GENERAL CROOK AND
THE APACHE

THE ARMY COULD NOT HAVE picked a more suitable man for the difficult task of subjugating the Apache in the mountainous regions of central Arizona. George Crook was an ideal soldier. He stood over 6 feet tall, straight as a ramrod and unpretentious. A man who loved the outdoor life, he seemed as much an Indian as did the Apache. Crook quickly won the respect of the Apache, both in peace and war. In combat he was doggedly tenacious. In peace the Indian found him a man who could be trusted to carry out his promises. Testimony to this occurred several years later when, upon learning of the general's death, Apache at San Carlos broke down and wept. Red Cloud of the Sioux gave him his greatest epitaph when he remarked, "He, at least, had never lied to us." General William T. Sherman once called him "the greatest Indian fighter and manager the United States Army ever had."

The inconsistent policy of the United States toward the Apache in the aftermath of the Camp Grant Massacre hampered and delayed Crook's operations for more than twelve months. During this interval he traveled muleback over hundreds of miles of the roughest mountains, surveying his new department and familiarizing himself with its topographical features. He also visited the various reservations and made the personal acquaintance of many of the chiefs and headmen.

Crook's battle plan was to send columns of cavalry into the field on seek-and-destroy missions, smashing those groups of hostiles who had refused to surrender to the soldiers, while stirring up and scattering the remainder. It was to be a winter campaign, for experience had shown that the mountain bands were much more vulnerable at this time of year.

The Tonto Basin country, in which the hostiles lived and roamed, comprised several hundred square miles and contained some of the roughest country in the United States. Much of it was still unexplored and known only to the Indians. It was from this immense stronghold that the hostiles made their forays against the settlements along the Gila and Salt river valleys.

Cavalry units dispatched from the various posts were to crisscross with each other in the field. These units would be highly mobile and guided by Apache scouts.

The scouts and soldiers were ordered to remain in the field, engaging the hostiles in combat whenever possible. If the horses played out they were to continue the chase on foot. Every effort would be made to induce the hostiles to surrender. Prisoners were to be treated well as Crook hoped to enlist these into his units as scouts. The wilder the Apache the more likely he was to know the whereabouts of others with the same propensities. Many of these Apache clans in the Tonto Basin had as great a dislike for each other as they did for the people they pillaged upon and Crook knew this.

Army pay and other privileges extended to the Apache who became scouts persuaded a large number to change sides. At the conclusion of the campaign many of the hostiles testified that they could have held out indefinitely against the soldiers but the presence of the Apache scouts convinced them that further resistance was futile.

The soldiers and scouts were to keep a constant pressure on the hostiles; if contact wasn't made at least they would be kept on the move and with luck even be driven into another unit. The total effect of this battle plan was to have a demoralizing result upon the hostiles and would soon lead to their demise in that region.

In December of 1872, Major William Brown with two companies of 5th Cavalry combed the Mescal, Pinal, Superstition, Sierra Ancha, and Mazatzal ranges. Most of the fighting was done by the Apache scouts. They traveled several hours ahead of the regular troops and would never forego a fight. Usually by the time the regulars arrived, the melee was over.

Climbing the Superstitions again, Major Brown's command encountered Captain James Burns from Fort McDowell on a similar mission. Burns's troop had just recently attacked a *ranchería* in the Four Peaks area. They had taken two prisoners, one a bright young lad of six or seven who was named "Mike Burns." The officers later saw to it that young Mike received some education, including a tenure at the famous Carlisle Indian School in Pennsylvania. Many years later, Mike Burns gave some interesting versions of the campaign from the Apache point of view.

The Apache scouts were invaluable on the campaign trail. Lieutenant John G. Bourke, who knew them well, wrote, "It grew increasingly apparent that the success of the troops depended on the scouts. Without the scouts the troops couldn't find the enemy; with the scouts they rarely missed. It was as simple as that." He added, "The longer we knew the scouts, the better we liked them." For one reason or another scouts from the other tribes usually fell short of expectations in the rugged campaign.

On the evening of December 27, 1872, the combined command of 220 men camped in a narrow canyon above the Salt River. One of Brown's scouts, an Apache named Nantaje, claimed he could lead the command into the high cliffs above the river. Nantaje had been raised in the cave and was now at odds with the band occupying it. A dangerous, narrow trail led to the cave and it was probably better that the soldiers moved at night, as daylight might have been cause for severe cases of acrophobia. Near sunrise the men saw the cave. The hostiles, celebrating a successful raid of the settlements below, didn't notice the soldiers moving around them. Heavy firing commenced, the soldiers and their allies firing into the ceiling of the cave, ricocheting bullets on the inhabitants. During a brief lull, Brown called upon the defenders to surrender or at least send out their women and children. His request was met with loud jeers and taunts from the warriors inside the shallow opening.

As the battle raged, another troop of cavalry led by Captain Burns approached from above. They had gone off earlier in the day following another trail, and returning, heard the cracking sounds of rifle fire below. Burns stopped his men, and looking over the crest of the precipice, caught a panorama of the dramatic events taking place below. After surveying the situation Burns had several of his men remove their suspenders. These were tied together, making a harness. He then tied two of his men in and lowered them over the edge. It must have come as quite a shock to the hostiles huddled below to look up and see two bodies swinging precariously overhead, raining pistol balls down among them. It was in all probability one of the earliest experiments in aerial warfare ever undertaken by our Army, though its practicality could be seriously debated. It didn't take long for the two "paraswingers" to expend all their ammunition, and caught up in the excitement of the event, throw their empty pistols at the enemy below. This type of warfare was far too expensive to an economy-minded Army, but it did suggest a novel way of ending the battle altogether. Boulders were gathered and tossed on the now helpless Apache. This turned out to be the fatal blow. Major Brown signaled a halt to the rock barrage. A final charge was made on the cave from below, but when the soldiers went over the parapet, there was no one left to fight. The battle had lasted for five hours, ending sometime around noon.

The command left the canyon with eighteen captives, all women and children. Many of these were badly wounded. Some of the others might have been saved except that the troops did not have any medical supplies. It was not standard operating procedure to have a medical officer accompany a scout in Arizona territory at this time.

Bourke, in his diary, reported seventy-six Apache killed, fifty-seven of whom were warriors. The results of the battle were far-reaching. It had wiped out the band of Nanni-Chaddi, a nefarious braggart who had made life miserable for inhabitants of the Gila and Salt river valleys for the last several years. Only a short time before, he had boasted that no troops had ever found his hideout and none ever would. Most of all, it demonstrated that U.S. troops could, when properly guided, follow the hostiles into the most remote canyons and beat them at their own game.

Significant as the fight was at the time, it was forgotten soon enough by all except its participants. Thirty-four years later the site was rediscovered by Jeff Adams, later sheriff of Maricopa County, while on a picnic with friends. The cave, or better yet, the opening, can still be seen by boating enthusiasts today. Perched high on the cliffs above the narrow channel at the far end of Canyon Lake, it overlooks Horse Mesa Dam.

Another major battle was fought a few weeks later by Captain

George Randall's troops at Turret Butte in the Bloody Basin. An Apache woman had been coerced into leading the soldiers to the hostile camp. It was reported that many Apache suicidally leaped over the cliff rather than surrender. However, this is unlikely, as the cliffs on the butte do not lend themselves to being the type from which a man could leap to his death. More likely they slipped down the hill and escaped into the night. The casualty reports also vary to the extent that one historian reports thirty-three killed while another said forty-seven.

With the Turret Butte battle, Apache resistance in the Tonto Basin was broken. In the spring of 1873, some 2,300 Apache-Mohave (Yavapai) arrived at Camp Verde seeking peace. Crook welcomed them and promised fair treatment if they would promise to live in peace.

The second offensive lasted through most of 1874, and was primarily a series of scouts against outlaw Apache who refused to give up the old way, or, in some cases, those who came and went as they pleased from the confines of the reservation.

The reservations, evolving from earlier visits by Colyer and Howard, were staffed by churches using surplus preachers and doctors. The two most successful converters, Catholics and Mormons, were excluded from this group. As usual, there was considerable overlapping of authority and bickering between the civil and military authorities. During periods of grave danger, co-operation was present. When all was quiet again, the infighting was frequent. The Apache were quick to notice this rivalry and take advantage of the situation whenever possible. Corruption on the part of the agents was not uncommon. The system was an open invitation to steal. General Crook reported one case where an agent on a $2,500 annual salary stayed a year and went home with $50,000.

By and large the Apache were happy on the reservation at Camp Verde, no doubt lending some support to the notion that they should be moved to a somewhat less suitable location. Some Washington official had decided that since the Apache groups had been classified as one tribe, why shouldn't they all live happily together on the same reservation? None more unsuitable for man or beast could be found than San Carlos. The bureau simply wished to group all the Apache together. Little if any consideration was given to climate, environment, or customs. General Crook objected, but to no avail. The Indians were unceremoniously told to pack up and move. During this period, a group led by Delshay, Chunz, Chan-Deisi, and Eskiminzin bolted. A bounty was offered for their heads and all were collected on with the exception of Eskiminzin.

It was to the benefit of the reservation Apache that, at this time, there should appear on the scene a brash young man named John Clum. Sent out by the Dutch Reformed Church and only twenty-three years old, Clum was not long in making his presence felt. Considered intractable by the military, whom he never missed an opportunity to criticize, Clum was no doubt cocky and arrogant. On the other hand he was thoroughly honest and hard-working. He trusted the Apache and was, in turn, trusted by his wards. He thought they were capable of self-government and of policing themselves and they proved him right. For a time anyway, the Apache at San Carlos were in good hands.

His first day on the job, Clum was greeted with a row of heads lined up on the parade field, compliments of the local bounty hunters. Some of these heads were over two weeks old. If the New York lad was feeling squeamish, he did not let on, but went about his work.

One of Clum's early tasks was the removal of the Army from the reservation. The military was not exactly eager to comply with Clum's request, but in the end he prevailed. Believing that the Indians would respond better if they were allowed to govern themselves, Clum organized a police force of Apache. Inspections were held, the villages were kept clean for health purposes, and a judicial system was established among the groups. A check-out system was used for firearms when game was needed, and last but not least, the making of the intoxicant tiswin was forbidden. All in all, this was no small deed for a young eastern dude. Clum's brief work and influence with the Apache was significant indeed, but in the end, the system would defeat him. Resigning in disgust, John Clum went to Tombstone, where he played a major part in the early, colorful history of that opulent mining camp.

The story of Tom Jeffords and Cochise is a classic on the relationship between the white man and the red man. It has been told and retold and consequently will only be summarized here. Jeffords was operating a mail route through Chiricahua country and, seeking to secure safe passage for his riders, he rode alone into the stronghold of Cochise. The old chieftain, impressed with the courage and honesty of the redheaded ex-soldier, agreed to let the mail riders pass through unmolested. Their friendship grew and when General Oliver O. Howard, the one-armed "Christian General," came to Arizona on a mission of peace in 1871, he sought out Jeffords to arrange a meeting with Cochise. The Chiricahua leader was also impressed with Howard and a settlement was reached, preventing a battlefield solution to the problems between whites and Apache in southeastern Arizona. Cochise and General Crook never got the chance to match tactics, as the old Chiricahua chieftain died not long after.

During the negotiations, Cochise asked for and received the land he already inhabited as a reservation. He also got his wish that Jeffords be named agent. Necessarily, there were problems. The reservation was an excellent sanctuary for bands raiding into Mexico and after Cochise's death in 1874, the government wasted little time in arranging the Chiricahua's transfer north to San Carlos on the Gila. This move has been called the Indian Bureau's "crowning folly." Clum was sent down to implement the order, but on the way back most of the warriors fled. It was here that Clum had his most memorable experience as an agent. In May 1877 he was ordered to Ojo Caliente, New Mexico, to bring in the last of the western Apache. They were to be transplanted to "hell's forty acres," as San Carlos was called. In a bold move, Clum and his Indian police captured both Geronimo and Victorio, the former being returned in chains.

It has been stated that Clum and the military didn't see eye to eye on matters concerning the Apache; however, Clum's relations with Crook seemed cordial enough. When the general was transferred in 1875, matters grew steadily worse, and finally in July 1877 Clum resigned. A tireless wanderer, John Clum would leave his mark in a number of places from the Mexican border to Alaska. But he never lost his warm admiration for his Apache. Just before his death in 1932, he returned once more to visit his friends and to relive some of those early adventures.

In September of 1877, Victorio, leader of the Warm Springs since the death of Mangas Coloradas, bolted from San Carlos with over three hundred men, women, and children. After a wild spree they surrendered at Fort Wingate near Gallup, New Mexico. They were sent back to their old home at Warm Springs, but shortly thereafter returned to San Carlos. Once again they fled, but returned. This time they were sent to Tularosa, but bolted again in September 1879, this time for good.

Though he spent little time in Arizona, Victorio gave the residents on both sides of the international border little peace and tranquillity in 1879–80. It is said he killed over one thousand people during this lengthy excursion. He met and defeated several Army units, displaying brilliant tactical maneuvers in the process. The drama and heroic deeds of both warring factions would be a Hollywood scriptwriter's dream. Lieutenant Charles Gatewood and his Company "A" Scouts from Fort Apache played a major role in much of the pursuit, which took place mostly in New Mexico. It was a tough, no-holds-barred campaign, filled with desperate chases and hardships. Even the hardy Apache scouts, traveling mostly on foot, found it hard to endure. Victorio's dirty tricks crew did much to discourage pursuit and encourage morale problems by fouling up the water supplies. One water hole had been left a thick pool of mudlike mortar. Another had the carcass of a disemboweled coyote tossed in.

In time the pursuit got to be too arduous on the U.S. side and Victorio headed south. In October 1880 the Mexicans trapped him, and either by treachery or lack of ammunition, most of his band was butchered by a large Mexican force under General Joaquín Terrazus. Victorio, perhaps the greatest of all Apache war generals, died a warrior's death. His followers would see to it that the Mexicans paid dearly in the months to come.

In the annals of campaigning, none surpasses old Nana and his epic trek through Apachería. A part of Victorio's band, Nana escaped the horrible affray at Tres Castillos. An old man, well past seventy and wearing a heavy gold watch chain in each ear, he cut quite a figure as he led the Army on a chase that lasted two months and covered over a thousand miles. With never more than forty warriors, he fought a dozen battles and won them all, losing only four men wounded. There were more than fourteen hundred soldiers chasing the artful dodger when he finally retreated into the Sierra Madre.

The story of the Wounded Knee Massacre has been told many times, yet few people are aware of a similar incident that occurred in Arizona some ten years earlier. It revolved around Nock-ay-del-klinne, a slight-built man with a mystical nature who was mixing some of the white man's religion with Apache. He was particularly interested in the resurrection of Jesus, and began teaching his followers the new religion and forecasting the return of two dead chiefs. Nock-ay-del-klinne may have been under the influence of Geronimo and others. It wasn't long until not only the reservation Indians were coming under his spell but the scouts stationed at nearby Fort Apache as well. It was reported that the dances were having a strange effect on the men. The religion was loosely styled enough so that each could interpret it in his or her own manner. The militants saw it as warlike and the peaceful ones saw the so-called "mad medicine man" as a man of peace. Whatever the case, the Apache were becoming unruly and the Army uneasy.

Finally General Eugene A. Carr with 117 men from Fort Apache set out for Cibicue, a few miles west of the post, to bring Nock-ay-del-klinne in. As might be expected, his disciples rallied to the cause and a shoot-out followed. The medicine man was killed, as were several soldiers. It was the only time the Apache scouts ever rebelled, for several went over to the other side during the skirmish. Religion most assuredly had a profound effect on their decision. Later, two would be sent to Alcatraz, at that time a military prison, and three more were hanged at Fort Apache.

On the return trip to the fort, General Carr and his men were nearly annihilated by vengeful braves. Stories were actually circulated, erroneously, in eastern newspapers that the entire group had been wiped out. It was believable, as Custer had ridden into the valley of the Little Big Horn only a few short years before.

Fort Apache was under siege for a short time, a fact mentioned because of the infrequency of such an occurrence in western history. It was during this affair that Will C. Barnes, destined to become a well-known Arizona cattleman, historian, and statesman, won the Congressional Medal of Honor for bravery. Barnes volunteered to serve as a lookout some distance from the post during the action, keeping the military informed as to the movements of the hostile bands of Apache who were scouring the nearby countryside. During the brief period the fort at the confluence of the White and Black rivers was under siege some buildings were set afire and several soldiers and civilians were killed in the vicinity of the post. The affray marked the only time a military post was to come under attack in Arizona history.

In the weeks following the clash at Cibicue, the rebels became more hostile. Some of the wilder Apache rallied around Na-ti-o-tish, a warrior of some renown, and went on a wild spree into an old familiar haunt, the Tonto Basin.

From the town of Globe sprang another of those irrepressible volunteer groups, the Globe Rangers. They only numbered a dozen men, all well heeled and loaded with some of the local spirits. Upon reaching the Middleton Ranch, they stopped to take a siesta. No guards were posted, and with the stillness broken only by the steady drone of deep snoring, the hostiles crept in and stole all the horses, leaving the slightly tarnished volunteers afoot.

The citizens of Tucson had also been unhappy with the accomplishments of the military. Consequently they enlisted the services of some civilian irregulars to pursue the hostiles into Mexico. The group was headed by William Ross, a former officer in Crook's command and now a resident of Tucson. A man of considerable ability and ingenuity, Ross had played a significant role in the Battle of the Salt River Caves several years earlier.

While south of the international line, Ross and his men found themselves surrounded, not by hostile Apache, but by the somewhat less hostile but equally dangerous Mexican troops. The Mexicans didn't look kindly upon armed brigands on their side of the border. The outdated records in possession of the Mexican commander revealed that William Ross was an officer in the U. S. Army. What, the Mexicans wondered aloud, was he doing in Mexico posing as a civilian?

They were all very nearly executed as filibusterers before the fast-talking Ross was finally able to convince the Mexicans that his was a civil action and that he and his men had been duly appointed to pursue the fugitives by civilian authorities in Tucson. Still, the Mexicans disarmed the men and sent them home several hundred miles through the heart of Apachería. Ross cleverly had his men carry short poles to simulate rifles. The guise worked, as the "militia" returned home without further incident. At least they bore no visible scars from their ordeal.

On July 17, 1882, the last major battle was fought in Arizona. Called the Battle of Big Dry Wash, it was fought near General Springs or East Clear Creek on the Mogollon Rim. Some of the rebels from Cibicue had tried to set up an ambush, but Al Sieber and his scouts "smelled a rat." When the smoke cleared, about twenty Apache lay dead, including Na-ti-o-tish. The hostiles were no match for the concentrated efforts of the Army, who lost only two men in the fight. It has been called the end of an era in Apache affairs. However, there was still a lot of action yet to come. The situation was getting desperate. Once again, General Crook was called to command. He immediately sought out the headmen of the various bands for council. The old campaigner found things had not gone well for the reservation Apache since his departure several years earlier.

The Indian Ring consisted of a group of opportunists who operated at both the local and national level. These government contractors were getting rich by supplying both the military and the Apache. The Apache chiefs complained that the Ring was sabotaging efforts to make the Indians self-sufficient. Let the Indian become self-supporting and peaceful, then what would the avaricious Ring do for a livelihood? Without marauding Apache terrorizing the frontier there would be no need for the many regiments of troops or the posts to purchase the millions of dollars' worth of goods these people had for sale. This time Crook would be fighting a war on two fronts: the still hostile Chiricahua and the Indian Ring of civilians. He was destined to win the former but lose the latter.

The civilian agents incurred the wrath of the Apache also. Incidents were cited where agents had sold clothing and supplies in Globe that had been intended for the Indians. Fields of melons and other crops were destroyed so that Indians would have to depend solely on the agents for their supplies. The food rations were so meager that the people were starving on the small amounts issued. The scandal reached all the way to Washington and some high-ranking heads rolled.

Most of the Apache seemed satisfied with the results of Crook's efforts. Yet the Chiricahua continued to display a propensity for the periodical excursions south of the border, both for plunder and to visit relatives still living there. Since they were wards of the United States, the government was compelled to prevent these trips; however, certain rules of international etiquette had to be followed with Mexico and the Apache knew it. On July 29, 1882, the United States and Mexico agreed on a "hot pursuit" policy whereby either side could cross the international line when in hot pursuit of the hostiles. This treaty dealt a severe blow to the forays of the Chiricahua.

Crook placed Captain Emmett Crawford in military control of the affairs on the reservations. Lieutenant Charles Gatewood was assigned to Fort Apache and Lieutenant Britton Davis to San Carlos.

These young officers would play a leading role in the arduous campaign that followed. A Hollywood image of the dashing cavalry officer could not be created that would depict any better the high quality of these men. They were placed on detached duty from regular military service, answering only to General Crook.

The redoubtable Al Sieber was named chief of scouts while Archie McIntosh, an extremely gifted man, especially when sober, and veteran scout Sam Bowman, a black man, were picked as his assistants. Sieber was perhaps the most capable of all General Crook's white scouts. A veteran soldier and civilian scout spent weeks in the field with his Apache scouts in pursuit of hostile bands.

Never before in the history of the Indian wars was such a group of battle-tested, dedicated, and experienced men placed under one command. The task ahead would be a supreme test of courage and tenacity. The country itself would be every bit as hostile as the Apache. The Sierra Madre was an inhospitable, temperamental, and vacillating old woman. She would not relinquish her wayward children from their heretofore secure sanctuary without a fight.

In the meantime the raids continued. Led by such able men as Bonito, Juh, Ulzana, Chihuahua, and Chatto, the Apache cut a wide swath through Arizona and Mexico. The situation got so tense that certain newspapers suggested the government remove all military personnel and establish local ranger companies. Apparently the recent comic-opera adventures of the Tucson and Globe Rangers had done little to dispel the enthusiasm wrought up in locals or their desire to ride off in glory to the applause of hero-worshiping throngs.

In March of 1883, the bands of Chihuahua and Chatto attacked the family of Judge and Mrs. H. C. McComas near Silver City, New Mexico. The body of their six-year-old son Charlie was never found. The raiders covered some 800 miles, killed twenty-six whites while losing only two of their own. Although the raid was a success, fate dealt the Apache a severe blow, though they didn't realize it at the time. One of the young warriors on the raid, remorseful over the death of a comrade, grew discouraged and chose to leave the band. He was destined to become the key to Crook's Sierra Madre campaign. The general had the men and the mule pack trains ready. This discouraged warrior added the last indispensable ingredient. He was a man who knew all the hiding places, a man who could take the Army right into the heart of the Sierra Madre. To the Apache his name was Tso-ay. Because of his fair complexion, the soldiers called him Peaches.

On the home front, Crook was still having distractions. Another ranger company was formed, this time in Tombstone. Satisfied that the problem could best be handled by civilians and that the crux of the matter was not in Mexico (for none wanted to chase Indians in that inhospitable place) but in San Carlos, they boldly set out to teach the Apache a lesson they wouldn't soon forget. Upon reaching the southern edge of the reservation they encountered an old man gathering mescal. Britton Davis later wrote: "They fired at him, but fortunately missed. He fled north and they fled south. That ended the massacre." Enthusiasm for the adventure abated as the whiskey supply diminished. Bourke concluded dryly that the Tombstone toughs had "expired of thirst." Bourke also mentioned that the town of Tombstone had never known such peace and tranquillity as when the "rum-poisoned bummers" were on the trail. No doubt the good citizens of the city encouraged them to stay out on the campaign trail as long as possible.

On May 1, 1883, the campaigners departed from their base camp at San Bernardino, near the international border in Cochise County. Outside contact would be lost for weeks and rumors of annihilation and failure were sure to persist.

With the Apache scout Peaches acting as guide, the command turned into the Sierra Madre, entering a land Bourke described as "grand to look at, but hell to travel." Pack mules slipped and fell over the precipice several hundred feet below. Rocks and boulders fell from above. The days were scorching hot and the nights frigid. Even in this inhospitable existence, some of the men were able to forsake the arduous campaign life, temporarily at least. In Bacerac, Al Sieber and some of his packers uncovered a cache of several gallons of fresh mescal and decided to have a *baile*, or dance. Every passer-by was "drafted" into participating in the joyous event. The women wisely made a hasty retreat to the sanctuary of their homes. A band consisting of two squeaky fiddlers, a bass drum, a snare drum, and one saxhorn with several keys missing served as entertainment. Apparently, from the inharmonious cacophony pouring forth, it would be safe to assume that not one member of the band could read a single note of music. Regardless, a good time was had by all, hosts and draftees alike. The dance finally broke up when the supply of mescal ran out and some poor soul fell through the bass drum.

Deeper into the mountains the troopers rode. The days turned into weeks and still the elusive Apache remained hidden in his mountain strongholds. Finally, Crook dispatched Captain Crawford with the scouts and shortly thereafter contact was established with the hostiles. Following a skirmish in which several Apache were killed or captured, several of the leaders came in to talk with the Nantan, or chief, as the Apache called Crook. Though he was not the most notorious of the leaders, Geronimo was considered the key. He was the most cunning and suspicious. If Crook could convince him to surrender, the others would follow suit. If Geronimo bolted, the campaigners would have to start all over again.

Finally Geronimo, Ka-ya-ten-nay (said to be the principal leader), Nana, Chihuahua, and the others agreed to return to San Carlos. Crook released Geronimo and Chatto on their own recognizance to gather up their bands and return later to the reservation. Months went by and it seemed that Crook had been duped by the chieftains, but finally in February 1884 they both returned. An interesting sideline to the return trip was told by Britton Davis, who was sent to the border to await the hostiles. While crossing the Sulphur Springs Valley, they were intercepted by two white men from Tucson. After a short period of casual conversation, the men informed Davis that they were on official business, one being a marshal and the other being a customs agent. They were taking Geronimo and his stolen cattle to Tucson, where the hostile would be brought to trial. There was no way out, or so it seemed to Davis. His orders were to bring Geronimo to San Carlos. He, Crawford, and Gatewood had all been placed on detached service and assigned to Crook's staff. They took orders only from him. All other officers in the department were to keep "hands off" regardless of rank. But this was a civil matter. To defy the marshal and his posse would mean a fight.

A solution to the dilemma arrived in the person of an old buddy of Davis' who happened to ride over from nearby Fort Bowie. Bo Blake was cheerful, full of personality and disarming charm, and most important of all, brought a bottle of good scotch and a willingness to share it. Before the night was through, the marshal and his customs agent were in deep slumber while Blake guided the band safely to San Carlos without further incident. The next morning the "bewildered" Lieutenant Davis explained his "loss" to the marshal, but to no avail. The civilian officers did accept the explanation somewhat reluctantly, and with nothing more to accomplish they mounted their horses and rode back to Tucson empty-handed.

In the aftermath, the stolen cattle, some five hundred head, were taken from Geronimo and sold. The money was given as compensation to the Mexican owners. Geronimo was not pleased with the loss. This was a constant source of irritation until a year later when he made his last whirlwind foray into Mexico.

In the months that followed there were many instances where progress was shown in the assimilation of the Apache. Other times there were severe reversals. The making of tiswin was forbidden by Crook, as was the beating of wives. Both of these were cause for disgruntlement among the Apache. They felt that the agreement that they had made with the government was to live at peace with the whites. Drinking tiswin and wife-beating were personal matters of no concern to anyone but themselves. After all, didn't the whites like their toddy and didn't they feel compelled to strike their wives occasionally?

Some of the men like Chatto rose to high rank in the scouts and became "good Indians," while others such as Ka-ya-ten-nay were surly and hard to manage. Eventually he attempted to assassinate Davis and ended up in Alcatraz. During this tenure he was given a chance to view life in San Francisco in hopes that the experience might have some positive effect on him. Apparently it did, for upon his release he performed numerous services for Crook on later campaigns.

The three "bad Indians" at San Carlos, and the ones most suspected as troublemakers, were Mangas, Chihuahua, and Geronimo. Mangas, the son of the great Mangas Coloradas, was never the leader his father was. He had a wife who hated the Americans and goaded him constantly. She was also well known for her prowess as a maker of the finest tiswin around. Her product was constantly in demand. Chihuahua, who liked his tiswin, was an able leader but probably didn't want to bolt again, preferring only to talk about it. Sardonic and intractable, Geronimo took advantage of the situation to stir up trouble. The situation at San Carlos was getting more tense by the day.

The outbreak occurred on May 18, 1885. The trouble had actually started a few days earlier when some of the leaders, drunk on tiswin, called for a council meeting with Davis. During the session that followed, the Apache confessed to drinking tiswin and beating their women. What did he, the "stout Nantan" as they called the muscular lieutenant, plan to do about it?

Davis informed them he was wiring General Crook for instructions and an answer would be forthcoming. Here is where there occurred one of those seemingly insignificant events in the chain of historical events that would be cause for trouble of the highest magnitude. Frustrated by civilian bureaucrats in his attempts to deal with the Indians, Captain Crawford had asked for and received a transfer back to his regiment in Texas. His replacement was Captain Francis Pierce, a man not nearly so skilled in dealing with the Apache as was Crawford. A "fatal" mistake, Davis later labeled it.

The ill-fated wire reached Captain Pierce at San Carlos. He in turn woke up the sleeping Al Sieber and asked what should be done. Sieber, sleeping off a wild night of alcohol and cards, replied that Davis could "handle it." Thus the telegram was pigeonholed. It was four months before Crook read it. Meantime Geronimo and Mangas were well on their way to Mexico. They were soon followed by Chihuahua, old Nana, and Nachez, a son of Cochise. The Apache, wise to the white man's talking wires, cut the telegraph lines down on their way out. They had also taken the extra time to tie the ends of the wire back together with rawhide. This way the circuit was broken and it was most difficult to find the break, especially if it was done where the line ran through a tree.

The next several months of campaigning brought little success and much frustration. In the fall of 1885, Britton Davis resigned from the Army to go into the family business. Young, energetic, with a sincere liking and respect for the Apache, he was one of Crook's most dependable lieutenants.

The following January, Crook suffered an even greater loss. Captain Emmett Crawford was treacherously shot and killed by Mexican mercenaries. He had just made contact with the hostiles deep in Mexico, and in a skirmish, defeated them. Talks were in progress when the Mexicans appeared. Wearing his Army uniform, Crawford stepped forward and informed the new arrivals of the nature of his business. A few seconds later shots rang out and Crawford fell with a severe head wound. He lived for four days but never regained consciousness. In this episode, ironically, the hostile Apache appeared as curious bystanders while the Mexicans and Americans debated the issue. Geronimo did, however, offer to exterminate the Mexicans. Protests were later made to Mexico over the killing of Crawford but to no avail. It was a solemn group of soldiers who carried their captain back across the line in a wooden box. No other officer had given so much of himself during those troubled, frustrating years. Captain Emmett Crawford, an embodiment of the gallant knights of old, the ideal cavalryman, was dead.

Following the death of Crawford, Geronimo agreed to meet with General Crook at Cañon de los Embudos (Canyon of the Tricksters). With patience Crook listened while Geronimo spoke. His oratory usually took hours and it took a man with the patience of Job to tolerate it. An agreement to surrender was finally reached. During the night John Tribollet, probably in the employ of the Ring, entered Geronimo's camp and dispensed liquor freely among the Apache. He then informed the hostiles that Crook planned to kill them once they crossed the American border. During the night Geronimo bolted again, perhaps understandably breaking his word once more.

Correspondence between Washington and Crook began to indicate a serious breach over opposing philosophies in dealing with the Apache. General Phil Sheridan, commander of the Army, suggested that too much trust was being placed in the scouts and that perhaps the Army should set up strictly defensive positions to stop the murder and pillage of ranches and settlements. Crook's reply was that he had spent the better part of his career on the campaign trail and was, perhaps, too wedded to his own methods. If Washington didn't like what he was doing, he would respectfully ask to be relieved of his assignment. Sheridan promptly replaced him with a successful but vainglorious, politically ambitious officer named Nelson Miles.

Miles was all too happy to wrap up the campaign and assume the credit. Who knows where recognition like that could lead? Possibly as far as the White House. He began his operations by dismissing most of the scouts and installing heliograph units at various strategic points all the way to the Mexican border. They were impressive, but played no significant role in the events to come.

There were now five thousand troops, or roughly 20 per cent of the entire U. S. Army, in Arizona, in pursuit of fewer than forty hostile Apache, only sixteen of them warriors. The end was near in August 1886, when it was learned that the warriors were restless and tired of running. With Crawford and Davis gone, the responsibility fell upon the shoulders of Lieutenant Charles Gatewood to carry out the terse surrender proposal. Accompanied by two Apache scouts named Kayitah and Martine, Gatewood, who was known to Geronimo, went to the Chiricahua camp and after some haggling the hostiles agreed to come in.

On September 3, 1886, Geronimo met with General Miles at Skeleton Canyon and the final agreements were reached, or so the Apache thought. They were to go to Florida for a period of two years. Their families would be allowed to return to their homes. Twenty-seven years later, the Chiricahua were still in exile and still considered prisoners of war. That case is unparalleled in our history, but even greater was the crime against the scouts. Technically, they were soldiers in the U. S. Army; however, since the government was undecided as to what to do with them, it was decided to send them to Florida also. Even the two scouts who went into Geronimo's camp with Gatewood were shipped out on the same train. Years later, the former hostiles would recall how the only bright spot in their long internment was that the scouts, despite their loyalty, had to serve time alongside the "bad Injuns." Their only crime was that they were Chiricahua Apache.

Chatto, whom Britton Davis described as "one of the finest men, red or white, I have ever met," was living quietly on a farm when General Miles talked him into going to Washington as part of a peace delegation. There he was entertained by various dignitaries including President Cleveland, who presented him with a peace medal. On the return trip they were detained for no apparent reason at Carlisle, Pennsylvania. Later they were stopped at Fort Leavenworth. Again the reasons were not explained. In time the direction of Chatto's train ride was reversed and he wound up in Florida as a prisoner of war, or at least in the same confinement.

The question of what to do with the Apache brought forth all kinds of suggestions. One of the more interesting was that of Senator James Fair, the Comstock millionaire, who suggested giving the Apache a useless piece of land off the California coast to have "as long as the grass shall grow." The piece of real estate he was referring to was Santa Catalina Island.

The aftermath of the Geronimo campaign was a menagerie of paradoxes and ironies. The losers, and some of the winners, were sent to Florida, thence to Alabama, and finally to Fort Sill, Oklahoma. All of these climates were alien to their natural habitat. Eventually a few returned to New Mexico. Nachez passed away in 1921, and Chatto was killed in an auto accident in 1934. The inimitable Geronimo became a showman, performing in wild West shows and posing for photographs. It was said that when he, Quanah Parker, American Horse, and other warriors rode in Teddy Roosevelt's inaugural parade in 1905, they caused even a greater spectacle than the old Roughrider himself. Geronimo, though, was bitter to the end. He once saw General Miles sitting in the grandstand during a performance. The old warrior went into the audience and tried to kill his former adversary. Geronimo finally died in 1909 at Fort Sill. He never did make it home. That old unreconstructed rebel considered by most the "brains of the whole outfit," Nana, summed it up best for all when he remarked just before his death at the age of ninety-six, "I feel I have no country."

Even the winning side didn't fare too well. Crook died in 1890, frustrated in his attempts to gain freedom for the Apache, and bitter over the way Miles handled the whole situation. The real hero, Charles Gatewood, was shelved by Miles so that he and Captain Henry Lawton could assume the greater part of the glory. Both Miles and Lawton gained promotions and recognition. Lawton, who rose to the rank of general, was later killed in the Philippines, reportedly by one of his own men. Gatewood had nothing but bad luck following his ordeal. He was finally transferred out of Arizona and was injured in the performance of duty while stationed in Wyoming. He was retired on the half pay of a lieutenant. He died, bitter and unrecognized by his country.

Nelson Miles' star was rising and he seized every opportunity to promote himself. The citizens of Tucson wanted to honor him as the "man who captured Geronimo," but when they took up a collection for money to purchase an engraved silver sword, they found themselves embarrassingly short of funds. Miles very graciously consented to pay the cost of the trophy out of his own pocket. He did finally rise to the rank of commanding general of the Army, a post he held when the United States went to war with Spain in 1898. The war was so badly bungled that Miles' career suffered a severe jolt. More soldiers died from eating meat preserved in form-aldehyde than from bullets. Chaos was the rule rather than the exception. For uniforms, the troops wore the same type as was worn in the winter campaigns of Montana. Summer tropical uniforms didn't arrive until the war was over and the boys had returned to chilly New York. Even the landings didn't go right for Miles. Volunteers under Teddy Roosevelt invaded Cuba while Miles stormed ashore with another force at Puerto Rico. Where all the glory went on that one goes without saying. Miles' presidential hopes were dashed once more, while Teddy rode up San Juan Hill charging all the way to the White House. Roosevelt was no admirer of Miles and finally the old general was retired unceremoniously, his ego shattered by an ego greater than his own.

The Indian or Tucson Ring also lost out. When the Apache and the Army were gone, so were the lucrative government contracts with which they had so long embellished themselves. They did make some attempts at creating periodical "Indian scares" in hopes of recalling troops to the Territory.

The year 1886 was by no means the end of Apache hostilities in Arizona, but it did mark the end of an era. Other men not mentioned previously won their spurs on the campaigns. John J. Pershing was then a young lieutenant, fresh from West Point. Drs. Walter Reed and Leonard Wood first gained prominence in Arizona, the latter winning the Congressional Medal of Honor for bravery in the latter stages of the Geronimo campaign. Frederic Remington first became widely known from his sketches of military life during this time. Black troops of the 9th and 10th Cavalry did much to gain acceptance both inside and outside the Army by their brave exploits and deeds along the Mexican border.

This work wouldn't be complete without mentioning Masai's Long Walk, as neither side had an exclusive claim to bravery and fortitude. Masai was riding one of the trains bound for Florida. Just east of St. Louis he saw an opportunity to escape and he took it. Leaping from the train, he made his way West. Living off the land and using his instincts for survival, Masai crossed through an alien and hostile land to reach his home again. The incredible journey took him a whole year to complete.

There would be more campaigns before the frontier was closed for good. But none matched the dogged tenacity, dedication to duty, or the Herculean effort in the maintaining of a way of life as was faced by both Indian and white during those truculent years.

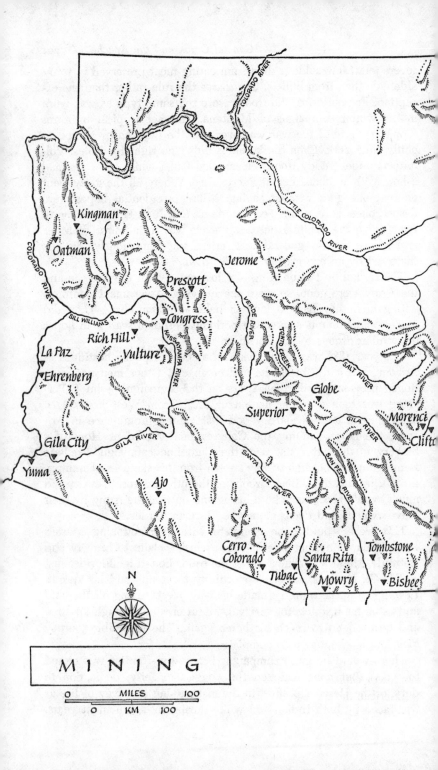

COLORADO RIVER

LITTLE COLORADO RIVER

Kingman

Oatman

COLORADO RIVER

BILL WILLIAMS R.

Jerome

Prescott

Congress

Rich Hill

VERDE RIVER

TONTO CREEK

SALT RIVER

Vulture

HASSAYAMPA RIVER

La Paz

Ehrenberg

Globe

Superior

GILA RIVER

Morenci

Clifton

Gila City

GILA RIVER

Yuma

Ajo

SANTA CRUZ RIVER

SAN PEDRO RIVER

Cerro
Colorado

Santa Rita

Tombstone

Tubac

Mowry

Bisbee

N

MINING

0	MILES	100
0	KM	100

BOOMTOWNS AND
MINERAL MANIA

No SINGLE ADVENTURER IN THE HISTORY of the westward movement had a greater impact on the land than did the early-day jackass prospector. It was he who opened up the country to the large mining concerns, merchants, ranchers, soldiers, and settlers who followed in his footsteps. Tent towns sprang up almost overnight in the remote regions where the mineral deposits appeared. Many of these became permanent cities, learning to recycle or rechannel their resources once the minerals were gone. Others, like San Francisco, became wealthy financial centers for the rich mining districts in the Comstock and Mother Lode located in the mountains to the east. For some, boomtown became ghost town. They're still out there, some of them or parts of them. Vandals have done much to despoil their picturesque beauty over the years.

The rocky wilderness of the American West turned out to be the richest treasure of natural resources in the history of the civilized world, and any man had the right, providing he staked a claim, to pack out as much of it as his mules could carry.

Placer gold, the kind you could pan out of a stream or mine with the toe of your boot, became scarce after the early years, leaving the real mining to the big companies. There was still plenty of gold, but it was cooked into the rock and few prospectors had the resources or capital to get it out.

American mining was no longer the domain of the washbowl-on-my-knee prospector as engineers, technicians, wealthy speculators, political nabobs, and heavy equipment moved in. They hollowed out the mountains and removed the mineral, leaving the unsightly, sterile entrails scattered about for future generations. Local smelters roasted the ore using sulfuric chemicals which gave off fumes so corrosive, it was said, that they would peel the hair off a jackass. Forests were stripped of their timber to make charcoal for the smelters and provide square-set rigging for the tunnels and shafts.

Mining was big business now, in the hands of Cornish, Welsh, and Irish professionals. These were real hard-rock bindle stiffs, skilled in the workings of deep underground mining. They gouged out the drifts and stopes under the most hazardous conditions. The pressure and heat were unbearable as the men labored in constant peril. They were lowered some 3,000 feet into the earth, where the temperature was 120 degrees and the air was so foul that a man suffered from constant nausea and could only work for a few minutes at a time. A man never knew when he came on shift where or when he would come face to face with death. Some were scalded to death by underground hot springs, while others were drowned in water-filled sumps.

At the Comstock, a break in a clay seam at the 400-foot level brought such a stream that it created a steaming lake 100 feet long, 30 feet wide, and 120 feet deep.

A man could be blown sky-high by misfired dynamite or asphyxiated by noxious gas. Fires and cave-ins menaced the underground mines constantly. If the natural elements weren't enough, there was the chance of faulty equipment such as the time when the cables controlling a cage snapped and nine miners fell 1,000 feet to their death. The advent of the steam drills seemingly made life easier for the single and double jackers. However, drills kicked up clouds of rock dust which the miners breathed. The drills were nicknamed "widowmakers" in honor of the deaths that resulted from the dreaded silicosis of the lungs.

Companies more interested in profits than the welfare of the men were casually indifferent to the deplorable conditions. "Men are cheaper than timber" seemed to be the prevailing attitude. The only restitution a widow and her family might expect after an accident was whatever the local citizenry might collect. Nineteenth-century bindle stiffs voluntarily went into the bowels of the earth, working a ten-hour shift six days a week, and earning $3.00 a day.

It was called the era of the ten-day miner, as that was about as long as one lasted. It was said that the mines worked in three shifts—"those coming down the road looking for a job, those on the job, and those that were fed up and moving on." Part of the price of the rich mineral taken from the mountains was paid for in advance by the men who worked inside them.

(Although many of the underground mines are closing down their operations these days, the diminishing breed of men, the wandering elite of the trade, the "tramp miner," still travels the 2,000-mile circuit from Morenci, Arizona, to Butte, Montana. They are keeping alive the traditions of the legions of men who preceded them in braving the dark depths of the western mountains.)

On payday, which usually came once a month, a miner could pursue whatever dreams might have been conjured up in the tunnels, including the dubious pleasures of the parlor houses and saloons that had sprung up around the mining camps. Recreational activities usually consisted of playing cards, drinking, and wenching. The "soiled doves" or shady ladies flocked to the towns and went into business either as "hostesses" in the saloons or in the bawdyhouses on the "row." At times, citizens of the communities bragged with civic pride that their local girls surpassed any other mining camp when it came to charity, manners, and honesty. During hard times, however, local citizens, especially avaricious merchants, were quick to pressure the gamblers and notorious women to leave town by one means or another—the thought being that any money the miners did have should not be expended on such vices but instead should be in the hands of the "reputable" businesses. One such roundup netted in a town of fifteen thousand a total of three tinhorn gamblers and two notorious women, thereby "saving" the economic life of the community.

The technicalities of staking claims and the controversy over boundaries and mineral rights brought about the need for lawyers and they, too, flocked into the camps. There was enough litigation going on to keep an army of attorneys busy at all times.

The easy path to wealth in the camps was not to indulge in the art of mining itself but rather instead to supply some need that the Argonauts could not get along without. Sagacious men reaped vast fortunes in this manner. Lumber was always in demand as were nails and other such essentials. During the early days of the gold rush in California, a man named Philip Armour opened a butcher shop in the Mother Lode. Mark Hopkins got his grubstake running a grocery store in Placerville, while a chap named J. M. Studebaker was building and selling wheelbarrows to the prospectors. A young immigrant named Levi Strauss decided that the regular pants the men wore couldn't hold up under the strenuous work at the diggings, so he took canvas from the wagons and tents, creating a hardy pair of trousers.

Others found small amounts of wealth by subscribing to the age-old policy of "mining the miner." Tinhorn gamblers, card sharks, and prostitutes did their best to see that the miners returned to the diggings with empty pockets.

Those early California gold camps with their boardwalks, muddy streets, false-front buildings, and tent houses were as vivacious as their names implied. Towns like Whiskey Bar, Hangtown, Devil's Retreat, Flapjack Canyon, Red Dog, You Bet, Gouge Eye, Gomorrah, and Rough and Ready beckoned hopeful Argonauts who were always eager to pack up and move on to some more desirable bonanza rumored to be just over the next canyon.

In the days before the mints began turning out coins for currency, purchases for such things as drinks were made by the "pinch" method whereby the bartender simply reached into a miner's "poke" sack with his thumb and forefinger and took out as much dust as he could squeeze between the two. The amount taken was usually worth somewhere between $.75 and $1.00 depending on the size of the bartender's fingers. It goes without saying that saloon owners used to observe the hands of prospective employees carefully, hiring only the ham-handed ones whenever possible. A story is told of one enterprising bartender in California who used accidentally to spill small amounts of his "pinch" on the barroom floor during the course of transferring the dust from the poke sack to the money box. Several times during his shift he would step outside the back door, where he had conveniently situated a mudhole. After muddying his boots, he would re-enter the bar and walk back and forth over the spilled dust. This being accomplished, he would walk over to a bucket and scrape the mud off his boots. It may seem a bit tedious to the observer, although it was said on weekends alone the resourceful bartender would take his bucket home and pan out a hundred dollars' worth of dust.

The women who followed the strikes brought a touch of class to a male-dominated society. In some of the more remote camps the men sometimes went for months without seeing a so-called "respectable woman." Once, a miner came in to one of the larger towns and chanced to see a man escorting his wife along the sidewalk just in front of him. The lady was well dressed and over her face was a veil. The miner approached the two rather awkwardly and asked the man if it would be considered impolite if he might just for a moment look upon the woman's face. The man said he didn't mind and the woman gently lifted her veil, whereupon the miner gazed into her face, and apparently satisfied that women did indeed still exist, he gratefully thanked the couple and the two parties went their separate ways.

Another time, a group of miners were returning to their cabin after a long day's work when they chanced to see women's lingerie hanging from a line outside a miner's shack. Not used to such fineries, they rushed over to the cabin and demanded to meet the woman who inhabited the place. Much to their disappointment, the shack had no female occupants and the lingerie hanging on the line was just somebody's idea of a crude joke. However, one enterprising miner did pick up some women's underwear while in San Francisco and carried it with him high into the Mother Lode, where he charged the miners admission to see the lacy garments. For an extra charge, the men were even allowed to touch them.

The shady ladies who set up business in the mining camps sometimes came from cities as far away as Berlin, Paris, and London. Many of the madams acquired great wealth, some becoming the richest and most successful businesswomen in their respective states. Many others were doomed to die lonely deaths in the camps from such disorders as pneumonia and alcoholism. Still others married and moved to a new area and started life over again on a new plane.

Some of the "parlor houses" were quite elegant, importing their furniture all the way from Europe. Guns and vulgarity were not allowed in these establishments. Also, in order to be allowed to enter, it was necessary to bathe first. It might be concluded that if the houses did nothing else, they cajoled the men of the West into taking an occasional bath and in the process they also learned something about etiquette.

Not all the entertainment in the mining towns was in the saloons. Many towns boasted both legitimate and "illegitimate" theater. Shakespearean plays were always popular. One night in Virginia

City's Maguires Theater, actress Adah Isaacs Menken, clad only in a flesh-colored maillot, or body stocking, rode horseback across the stage during the play *Mazeppa*. The ecstatic miners cheered her performance enthusiastically. Applause was not enough. They lavished the stage with silver coins. When the money was counted, it was said that the great Menken pocketed over $100,000. Not bad for one night's performance, even in the mining West.

One night in Tombstone, during a performance of *Uncle Tom's Cabin*, just as Eliza made her dramatic crossing of the river, a drunken spectator, acting out some part of his own, stood up and shot the bloodhound that was pursuing her. Fortunately for all involved, it was a real dog and not an actor in a dog's costume.

The old Bird Cage Theater in Tombstone was more low-brow. Here the waitresses doubled as performers and the show was usually made up of leg shows and black-outs. There were private loge rooms in the balcony where the curtains could be drawn for greater privacy. A stairway from backstage led up to these rooms, thus giving prospective customers an opportunity to solicit without ever leaving their booths.

Other forms of recreation took up what little free time the miner did have. Baseball and boxing were always popular. The miners' insatiable urge to gamble could be satisfied by wagering on the outcome of some sporting event. For the hard-rock miners, the most popular contest of all was single-jack and double-jack drilling. Every mining town worth its salt had a July Fourth drilling contest. Men competed from all over the West for prestige and prize money.

In single-jack drilling, one man armed with drills and a 4-pound hammer would drill into a block of granite for fifteen minutes. At the end of the period his drill hole would be measured. The man with the deepest hole would be declared the winner. Double-jack drilling was a two-man operation. Several drills and a 9-pound hammer were the tools. A judge would stand nearby and pour water into the hole. A good team could make eighty-five strokes a minute, one man swinging, the other rotating the drill. They could switch places every sixty seconds without missing a stroke. It was common for a good team to make 42 inches or more. The record, so far as is known, is 50 inches.

The teams followed a code whereby under no circumstances would they stop until their fifteen minutes were up. A story is told of one contest where a hammer hit the side of the drill, and glancing off, struck the head of a contestant. The event continued uninterrupted. Each time the hammer struck the drill, blood mixed with water splashed both team-mates and the judge. Undaunted, they completed the contest, setting a new drilling record in the process.

When the Argonauts first came to California and established mining camps, there were no laws to speak of. It was truly a "lawless society." Killings, robberies, and other peccancies were commonplace occurrences. Towns bragged with some credibility of "having a man" each morning before breakfast. It was not a compatible situation to say the least, so the moralistic citizenry did what Americans have been doing from the time they first set foot on Plymouth Rock—they held meetings. Laws were established regulating everything from claims to social behavior. Violation of these miners' laws could mean anything from banishment to the hangman's noose, depending on the seriousness of the crime. For the most part, any resemblance between conduct at these meetings and Robert's Rules of Order was purely coincidental. Whatever justice could be carried out with great expendiency, and seemed logical to the group, was usually the procedure followed. Lawyers with a propensity toward technicalities of the law were sometimes given escort out of town by the irascible miners.

The legal code established during these formative years would serve the entire mining West, including Alaska, in the years to come.

A miner from early-day strikes in Georgia, Isaac Humphrey, is credited with inventing a couple of contraptions that revolutionized early-day mining techniques. However, contraptions similar to his were used by Mexican placer miners and before them, the Spanish. The first was the rocker or cradle. With this, the miner could double the amount of dirt he could mine with a pan and thus double his take of gold. Following this, Humphrey designed the sluice box where the miner could now move five hundred shovel loads of dirt over the previous fifty that the pan could do. These tools also changed the style of the operation. Now prospectors worked as partners or in small groups and divided up the take. Other variations of Humphrey's implements were used in dry climates such as Arizona's deserts provided. Modern-day prospectors are having success using dredging equipment, a vacuum-like machine that with scuba gear allows the miner to go where the early-day prospector couldn't—right to the river bottom.

Basically the miners encountered the gold in two forms. The easiest to obtain was placer. Placer gold is that which is broken off from the Mother Lode and through erosion from weather has washed down into the streams and lower areas. There the prospector could pick it up off the ground, pry it out with a pocketknife, or pan it out of a stream. The largest nugget ever found in the United States was at Calaveras, California. It weighed 195 troy pounds and was worth over $40,000 at the time. The world record holder is Australia, where miners uncovered a nugget of 630 pounds, of which 472 pounds were pure gold.

Gold is unique in that it remains fairly pure in its natural state. It attaches itself physically to the ore, but not chemically. Silver and other metals are more difficult to mine because they will mix chemically with the ore.

The second type, and more difficult to mine, was the lode gold. In lode mining, the gold must be separated from the ore. Ore is defined as rock containing enough mineral value to warrant the expense of mining it. To do this, the miner would have to crush the ore and separate the gold from the rock. Mercury or quicksilver will attach itself to gold, but will reject the rock. The combination of gold and mercury creates an amalgam and would have to be separated. The expensive mercury was reclaimed to be used again. To salvage the mercury, the miner would use a retort of some kind to evaporate it. When this was done, the rich mineral was all that remained. One way of separating the amalgam was to use tubing somewhat similar to a whiskey still. The amalgam would be placed in a pot and heated. The mercury would evaporate through the tubing, leaving the gold. The mercury could be reclaimed by collecting the drippings from the tubing.

One of the more ingenious salvage techniques used by the miners was to take a potato and remove the insides of one half. The miner would then insert his amalgam into the empty half, wire the potato back together, and roast it. When the roasting was finished, the empty half of the potato would contain a gold button and the vaporized mercury was absorbed into the other half of the potato.

By and large, the early American mining techniques used in the Far West were learned from the Mexicans or their Spanish predecessors. Mexico City had a school for miners seventy-five years before the United States did, graduating some of the world's top mining engineers. The Mexican *gambusino* (miner) had a "nose for ore" and was considered a first-class mining man by his contemporaries. The patio method and the arrastra were but a couple of the many extraction and separation techniques adopted from Mexico.

There is an old saying that a prospector must possess "an eye like an artist and be able to dig like a gopher." The successful prospector had to have a great deal of knowledge in basic geology. If he didn't, he could waste weeks or even months in barren areas and find no "color" at all. The good prospector seldom had trouble finding someone to grubstake him. When he did find a promising area, he would stake a claim both for himself and for his "sponsor." Then, by custom, he would give his partner the choice of which claim he wanted and the prospector would take the other. Granted, business didn't always operate this smoothly.

Water is a most essential ingredient to the prospector. Without it, other methods have to be found to wash out the yellow metal. Gold is approximately nineteen times heavier than water and three to four times heavier than sand. The miner would look in places where the water had slowed down, such as the bend of a stream. He would then dig down to the cracks and crevices in the bedrock. The metal is still there. The old-timers say that for every dime taken out, there is still a dollar's worth waiting to be found. Every prospector, amateur or professional, knows gold is where you find it. However, one exasperated gold-seeker spoke for the great majority of would-be Argonauts when he exclaimed, "Gold is where I can't find it."

High-grading was simply shoplifting ore from one's employer. A miner might take a few choice pieces of ore home with him at the end of a shift, set up his own little smelter at home, and in a small way go into business for himself. It was said that a lot of the bow-legged people in the West got that way not from riding horses, but from carrying their ore-laden lunch buckets home from work. To circumvent this, the mines would hold inspections after each shift. The men would shed clothes and stand while various personal and not so personal areas of their bodies were checked. A man caught high-grading was fired and hard pressed to find another job in the district.

In at least one case, two would-be high-graders didn't fare too well in their nefarious scheme. It seems they had set up a small smelter in the confines of their home. The breathing of the dangerous fumes of mercury caused the men to lose not only their hair, but their teeth as well. The company felt that justice had been served and didn't press charges against the hapless pair.

When P. T. Barnum said, "There's a sucker born every minute," he could easily have been talking about the sale of mining claims. The name Clark on a stock certificate, even if it wasn't Senator William Andrews Clark, was good enough reason for some unsuspecting investor to sink his life savings into western mining stocks. Stock peddlers and swindlers ran rampant. They could print, issue, sell, and be on the next train out of town, all in the same day. Stock certificates from non-existent mines could be sold even in the very communities where the non-existent mines didn't exist. The list of stock swindlers in the mining West is long and was all a part in the financial wheelings and dealings that in many cases attached a stigma to an area that it might never shed. *Caveat emptor* was the rule in the financial dealings on mining properties.

A peccancy used in unloading a useless claim or mine on some naïve buyer was called "salting." The seller would take ore from a productive mine and carefully scatter it about his non-productive claim in hopes of closing a sale on the property. Others might take a shotgun, load the charge with gold dust, and blast the walls of the shaft. The gold, being malleable, would imbed itself into the rock, giving the worthless claim a highly mineralized façade.

The game of selling a worthless mine could conceivably become a matter of who could outwit whom. The seller might impregnate the walls with gold but the wise buyer might ask to have the walls blasted to see what was inside the rock. The seller might install salted gold into the headsticks of his dynamite and when the charge went off, the interior would be salted. To circumvent this, the buyer would suggest that they use the dynamite sticks he had brought along for just such an occasion. It should go without saying that an experienced buyer always brought along his own geologist. Many times an entire community would plot against the buyer, since the economic stability of a region might hinge on the successful sale.

Gold is soluble in aqua regia, forming a gold chloride. This gold chloride is soluble in water. Using a syringe, one could inject gold into a crevice or even a sack of ore samples. Bichloride of gold was

25. Charles D. Poston, promoter, entrepreneur, leader in the fight for territorial status, and known today as the "father of Arizona." *Sharlot Hall Museum.*

26. Dr. James Douglas, mining engineer; pioneered many mining techniques; the town of Douglas is named for him. *Arizona State Lib.*

27. William Andrews Clark, multi-millionaire mining magnate, senator from Montana, and developer of the United Verde mines in Jerome. *Sharlot Hall Museum.*

28. Jack Swilling, adventurer, Confederate officer, Union scout, Argonaut, and "father of irrigation in the Salt River Valley." *Arizona Historical Foundation.*

29. Captain James H. McClintock, Arizona Roughrider, writer, and state historian. He was photographed here following serious wounds at Las Guásimas. *Arizona State Lib.*

30. Ira Hays, Pima Indian, hero of famous flag-raising photograph on Iwo Jima in World War II. *Arizona State Lib.*

31. Lieutenant Frank
Luke, the "balloon
buster" in World War
I. He was the first
aviator to win the Con-
gressional Medal of
Honor. *Arizona State
Lib.*

32. Colonel Alexander
O. Brodie, commander
of Arizona Volunteers
in the Roughrider Regi-
ment, 1898. Later a
territorial governor.
Sharlot Hall Museum.

33. Dr. John Handy, Tucson physician who worked toward the required licensing of physicians to practice in Arizona. He was shot to death in Tucson over an argument with his estranged wife's lawyer. *Arizona Historical Foundation.*

34. Dr. and Mrs. John L. Gregg. Gregg, Tempe's first physician, amputated his own leg after an accidental gunshot wound. *Arizona Historical Foundation.*

35. Dr. C. E. Yount, early Prescott physician; he brought the first microscope into Arizona around the turn of the century. He was a pioneer in the study of humans and the screwworm fly. *Arizona Historical Foundation.*

36. Walter Reed, who first became interested in the study of yellow fever while stationed in Arizona. *Arizona Historical Foundation.*

37. Dr. Carlos Montezuma, Apache who later became one of Chicago's most famous physicians and an early advocate of Indian rights. *Arizona State Lib.*

38. Dr. George Good-
fellow, Tombstone
physician during its
heyday. He was known
nationally for his pub-
lished articles on the
treatment of gunshot
wounds. *Arizona State
Library.*

39. Dr. Lewis Owings,
of Mesilla, New Mexico,
the "first" territorial
governor of Arizona.
*Arizona Historical
Foundation.*

used for medicinal purposes during the 1900s for such things as alcoholism and kidney ailments. When taken internally, the bichloride of gold will pass through the body, exiting with high assay value. The knowledgeable salter could load himself on the auferous substance and "salt" any crack, crevice, or ore sample as nature or the spirit moved him.

A story is told of an early-day miner in Arizona who did such a convincing job of salting his mine that when the buyer did make an offer, the old miner couldn't bring himself to sell the claim, having convinced himself that his claim really was a rich one. Such was the indomitable faith of the prospector.

Mining in Arizona began in earnest after the Gadsden Purchase was completed in 1854. There had been some exploratory work done by the Spaniards Espejo and Oñate, but there was really no practical way to get the ore out. The missions had also done some mining on a small scale, but it would be left to the enterprising Americans to tap Arizona's great mineral resources extensively. There was no Crown to share the wealth, no Church demanding a share, only the miners themselves, and they would prove quite resourceful at lavishing their new-found wealth.

Charles Poston, a first-rate promoter, was not going to wait for the United States officially to take control of the Gadsden Purchase before checking out its mineral wealth. In Oklahoma land rush days he would have been referred to as a "sooner." He and Herman Ehrenberg, a German mining engineer, set sail from San Francisco. However, an unexpected shipwreck left the two ashore near the Mexican port of Guaymas. It was suspected for a time that they might be filibusterers, and the two would-be Argonauts were detained temporarily. Fortunately for them, Poston's gift of loquacity carried the day.

Heading first to Tubac and then over to the country around Ajo, they collected a few ore samples and commenced their journey back to San Francisco. When the two arrived at the Yuma Crossing on the Colorado River, which was about a half mile across at that point, they found that there were not any funds available to pay for their passage. The ferryman, an enterprising German named L. J. F. Jaeger, wanted no less than $25 to transport men and equipment, about $25 more than Poston was carrying. Never one to let small obstacles hinder his progress, Poston's next move displayed a knack for improvisation that is essential for one to be successful in the field of mining promotions.

Seemingly not caring whether he ever crossed that torrent, Poston set about the business of surveying the location for a townsite. Curiosity finally got the best of the old ferryman.

"What do you think you're doing here?" he inquired.

"Planning a city of the future," replied Poston.

"Here?"

"Look over there!" Poston said, gesturing toward the junction of the Gila River and the Colorado. "Wherever two great rivers meet, a great city always arises. Why, there's Pittsburgh, St. Louis, and now . . ." He paused for a reflective moment and then cried with great alacrity, "Colorado City!"

It didn't take any more salesmanship on the part of the surveyors. Jaeger was convinced. Would it be possible for him to get in on the ground floor of this wonderful opportunity, he queried. Indeed it would. Passage across the river for some choice city lots. The entrepreneurs went merrily on their way to California. On arriving in San Diego, Poston did register Colorado City as a community and in San Francisco he sold the plans and acreage for $10,000. There was no doubt that Poston would be able to hold his own with those astute financiers with whom he would be dealing soon.

Before leaving Fort Yuma, Charlie Poston had established a working relationship with the post commander, Captain Sam Heintzelman. Heintzelman, like many military men stationed on the frontier, was more interested in assuming the role of a mining magnate than playing nursemaid to immigrants along the Gila Trail or chasing hostile Indians across the desert. That the financial rewards were most assuredly greater goes without saying. (Charlie and Sam would play major roles in the establishment of Arizona as a territory a few years later.)

Poston went to New York City in hopes of raising money to finance a mining company. He had trouble obtaining necessary capital for the venture. When his friend Heintzelman, who had been transferred to a military post near Cincinnati, heard of Poston's dilemma he invited him to meet some friends who might be interested in financing the operation. Poston was off to Cincinnati, where the capital was raised and a company calling itself the Sonora Exploring and Mining Company was formed. The next stop for the itinerant promoter was San Antonio, Texas, where he recruited a group of men "armed with Sharps rifles, Colt revolvers and the recklessness of youth." Mining operations near the abandoned presidio at Tubac began soon after, and the community began to take on the atmosphere of a primitive utopia.

We had "no laws but love," Poston later wrote. A man of his importance must have a title befitting his new role as alcalde over the community, so thenceforth he became known as "Colonel" Poston. As "El Cadí" over some eight hundred people, mostly Mexican, he baptized babies and he married couples, not necessarily in that order. He even divorced them. Had there been anybody in the area to declare war on, Colonel Poston could even have done that.

War was almost declared on the colonel. Father Joseph Machebeuf arrived on the scene from Santa Fe and declared all marriages null and void, excommunicating the whole sinful bunch. Some of the menfolk might not have minded the edict that much, but there were a lot of highly emotional young mothers and bawling children to contend with. Something had to be done in a hurry to rectify the shameful situation. Even the priest was in agreement on that point.

Displaying wisdom that behooved a man of his position, Colonel Poston adroitly solved the dilemma. Following a short deliberation with Machebeuf, Poston agreed to contribute $500 to the Church and the priest agreed to remarry all the young couples. The colonel then threw a grand holiday and dance in honor of the happy brides and grooms. The children were also in attendance at their parents' wedding celebration.

Except for raiding Apache, life in Tubac must have been relatively carefree. Poston spent much of his leisure time sitting in one of the natural pools of water in the Santa Cruz River, reading newspapers, smoking Mexican cigars, and pondering the imponderables.

There was little government, if any, and no taxes or laws. Poston even had a solution for the monetary problems. He merely printed his own money. Each *boleta*, as they were called, had a picture of a certain animal and each animal represented a certain value. For example, the image of a pig was pictured on the twelve-and-one-half-cent or one-bit piece; a calf was on the twenty-five-cent or two-bit piece; a rooster was worth fifty cents or four bits; one dollar was represented by a horse; five dollars by a bull; and ten dollars by a lion. It was truly an economic masterpiece. After all, the Mexicans couldn't read English but they could easily determine what a lion on a piece of cardboard was worth. Food and other basic necessities came down from Sonora, while the nearby mission orchards at Tumacacori supplied the community with fresh fruit.

Goods were hauled into Tubac by wagon. One of the freighters doing business with Poston during those years was Charles Trumbull Hayden, who later operated a ferryboat business and mill on the Salt River.

The mining business was good, doing $3,000 a day in silver. There were always plenty of Apache in the vicinity to keep the local residents from becoming too complacent. Business boomed until 1861, when the federal troops were removed and the Apache finally had things their own way, at least temporarily. Poston was busy with other schemes by this time anyway. In 1862, he was in Washington promoting again—this time it was an attempt to achieve territorial status for Arizona.

Another man important in the early development and promotion of Arizona was Sylvester Mowry. Mowry, like Heintzelman, was a soldier. He was also a flamboyant person of sorts, evidenced by the fact that he was originally transferred to Fort Yuma from Salt Lake in 1855 as punishment for alleged "romantic indiscretions" with another man's wife. Like Poston, Mowry was a first-rate promoter and like most promoters he had a propensity toward being ostentatious and made a few enemies along the way. One unadmiring critic described him as being "conspicuous as a peacock." His exuberance in promoting various schemes caused more than one fracas.

In 1859 he fought a famous duel with Tubac newspaper editor Ed Cross. Mowry was promoting territorial status for Arizona and while doing so was also inflating population figures and committing other such minor transgressions associated with salesmanship. Cross, who was a large stockholder in a mining operation that was at odds with Mowry's firm, took exception to some statements made by the promoter. Although he did not attack Mowry personally, and he signed the editorial using the pen name Gila, there was no mistaking the author or his intentions. Mowry soon found out and a duel was suggested. They chose the eighth day of July for the occasion. Using two Burnside rifles and standing at forty paces, they fired several ineffective shots and then decided to drop the whole matter. It should be recorded that the day was not a total loss. Both sides descended on the local store and took possession of a 42-gallon barrel of prime whiskey, and according to contemporary accounts, a good time was had by all.

Mowry got himself elected as delegate to Congress merely by suggesting that he was available for the position. It should be pointed out that no one else wanted the job. Apparently no one in Washington wanted a delegate from Arizona either, as he was denied a seat by that great assemblage of lawmakers. After the procedure was repeated with the same end results, Mowry withdrew from public service and threw himself back into his mining ventures. The Mowry Mine, just south of today's Patagonia, was one of the richest producers of silver in the country at that time.

When the Civil War came and the federal troops left, Mowry defended his mine from Apache harassment and kept on producing silver. The Confederates occupied the territory for a few weeks before being driven out by General James Carleton and the California Column. Carleton immediately placed Mowry under arrest and confiscated his mining property. Following his arrest as a "Confederate sympathizer, spy, and traitor," Mowry was ordered to his old duty station at Yuma to serve out his internment. Undaunted by all this turnabout of affairs, Mowry brought with him a private secretary, a servant, and a mistress. Some say that the real reason for arrest was an old feud that occurred when both he and Carleton were in the service. However, it has never been proved that they'd even met before. Whatever the reason, Sylvester Mowry was known as everything from a first-rate promoter to "an egotist, braggart and a shameless liar." As is usually the case with a controversial character, he was probably a combination of all of these. Mowry cooled his heels at Yuma, officially as a military prisoner, although he spent most of his time riding, renewing old acquaintances, and generally entertaining friends. A few months later he returned to his mine and found it had been pretty well cleaned out by Carleton, or at least so Mowry claimed.

Ironically, none of the early-day promoters for territorial status became prosperous from their endeavors. Mowry did recover his mine, although most of the riches had been mined out. He went to England, where in 1871 he died of Wright's syndrome. Heintzelman rose to the rank of general during the Civil War, fought at both Bull Runs, and died in 1880. Poston held numerous government jobs, including that of Territorial Delegate and Superintendent of Indian Affairs. However, none proved lucrative. He died penniless in Phoenix in 1902.

The first gold rush in Arizona occurred in 1858, some 20 miles up the Gila from its junction with the Colorado, when Colonel Jake Snively, erstwhile adventurer from Texas, discovered rich deposits of placer gold. It wasn't long before a town sprang up, boasting a population of some twelve hundred Argonauts. Gila City, as it was called, was somewhat lacking in abundance of moral character. One traveler passing through candidly noted that it had "everything but a church and a jail."

The gold was there. Even an inexperienced prospector could make $20 from just a few pans of dirt. In 1861 men were making from $20 to $125 a day. But the balloon burst and the rich pockets soon played out. In 1864 J. Ross Browne, while making a tour of the new territory, noted that the town consisted of "three chimneys and a coyote." Lumber being scarce in that part of Arizona, it was not uncommon to strip a town bare when leaving in order to have a sufficient supply of timber to construct the next boomtown. Without the framework, the adobe soon erodes—a good reason why it is sometimes nearly impossible to find any traces of former boomtowns today.

In 1862, Lady Luck smiled once again on southwestern Arizona, this time up the Colorado River a few miles from Yuma. La Paz far outstripped Gila City in people and gold. She boasted a population of five thousand and there was talk of making her the next capital. Merchants, including Joseph and Mike Goldwater, arrived and began supplying the miners. The yellow metal seemed limitless, but after $8 million worth had been taken out, there was no more and La Paz faded into oblivion.

Joseph Reddeford Walker was a mountain man who had led exploring parties in the earliest days of the beaver trade. He had first come to Santa Fe in 1821 with the Becknell Expedition, which opened up the famous Santa Fe Trail. At a time when most men his age had resigned themselves to a rocking chair, recalling wild Indian fights for anyone who cared to listen, "Uncle Joe" was looking for gold. His whole life had been a series of adventures. In 1833 he had led a carefully planned and superbly organized expedition of fur trappers into California, the first white men to cross the Sierra Nevada in wintertime. At that time, he was thirty-four years old, stood 6 feet tall, and weighed over 200 pounds. He was perhaps the best wilderness trailblazer of them all. There was a time when Daniel Conner, a young man in search of wealth and adventure, was trying to locate the old pathfinder in the southern Rockies. He asked another old mountain man if he knew which trail Walker had followed. "He don't follow trails," the old man replied. "He makes them." Conner's written chronicle in the 1860s with Walker in and around Prescott presents a classic account of the early mining history of the region.

The Walker party, organized in California in 1861, prospected for a time, and after facing the usual vicissitudes in the Colorado Rockies, found themselves in Santa Fe a year later. General James Carleton was the military commander of the district and also a man interested in mining ventures. On Carleton's instructions, the party headed toward Arizona. On the way they stopped to do some prospecting in the vicinity of the old Santa Rita copper mines near Silver City, New Mexico.

Apache harassment was a constant source of irritation to the prospectors. The idea occurred to Walker that if Mangas Coloradas, the old chieftain causing the trouble, could be induced to pay a visit, then be taken prisoner and held as a hostage, he could ensure safe passage through Apachería.

Jack Swilling, erstwhile Confederate officer during the occupation of Tucson, had recently joined the group. Swilling was elected to serve as captain of a detail of miners to carry out the plan of capture. At this time a party of federal soldiers arrived and were invited to join the caper. The Americans then went to Piños Altos, where a parley with Mangas was arranged. When the Apache entered the camp under a flag of truce he was immediately taken prisoner. Mangas Coloradas, the greatest of all Apache, had unwittingly walked into an old familiar trap. The crafty chieftain should have known better. Only two years before, his son-in-law Cochise had done a similar thing at Apache Pass with grave consequences. Daniel Conner described the great warrior vividly in his narrative following the capture:

> His dress consisted of a broad-brimmed small crowned chip or straw hat of Mexican manufacture—a checked cotton shirt, breech cloth or clout, and a high pair of moccasins or moccasins with legs to them like boots, only that they fit the legs closely. Mangus [sic] was apparently fifty years of age and a large athletic man considerably over six feet in height, with a large broad head covered with a tremen-

dously heavy growth of long hair that reached to his waist. His shoulders were broad and his chest full, and muscular. He stood erect and his step was proud and altogether he presented quite a model of physical manhood. If Mangus ever had any or many peers amongst his people in personal appearance, I never saw them during the five years experience in their country.

The miners had intended to release Mangas Coloradas after they had passed safely through. However, the Army took custody of the prisoner and the next day Mangas Coloradas was dead. "Shot while trying to escape," was the official Army report. However, Conner, who was present that night, saw it differently. He heard Colonel Joseph West tell two soldiers that he wanted that old devil "dead, do you understand me, dead." That night Conner saw the soldiers sticking the old man with bayonets which had been heated in the fire. When Mangas protested, they shot him. Later they removed his head, boiled the flesh off the bones, and sent the skull east, where it was displayed for a time. Several years later, charges were brought against West but after he denied them the matter was dropped.

Meanwhile, the Walker party journeyed on to Tucson and after picking up a few supplies, moved on toward the Hassayampa River. Within a few miles of today's Prescott they made their strike. Claims were filed and a mining district was established with laws regulating size of claims and locations.

Prosperity had arrived in northern Arizona. Soon Fort Whipple would be built and the community was destined to become the first territorial capital. From 1863 to the 1970s, some $6 million in gold and silver would be taken from the entrails of the Bradshaw Mountains.

On the heels of the Walker party came the Weaver-Peeples party, guided by Paulino Weaver, another old trapper-guide turned Argonaut. In August of 1863 they made camp near Antelope Hill, just east of today's Congress Junction. A Mexican party was also camped nearby. Sometime during the night, some mules wandered off, causing an early morning search. Climbing to the top of Antelope Hill for a better look-see, one of the searchers noticed the ground all around him was covered with gold nuggets. It was said that the men picked up $4,000 each before breakfast, though it's doubtful that they even bothered with victuals at a time like that. The Mexicans, exuberant over their find, went back to Mexico, while the Weaver-Peeples party stayed on. Within three months, over a quarter of a million dollars' worth of gold had been either picked up or pried out with a jackknife. On just one acre, over half a million dollars in nuggets was found. This was said to be the richest placer gold discovery in Arizona's history.

Rich Hill is still a popular place for today's weekend prospector. During unusually wet seasons, it is said that in order to get down to the stream to pan, you first have to take a number and wait. Such are the times in which we live.

Henry Wickenburg had been frustrated in his attempts to find the yellow metal. He had missed the Walker party, arrived too late to catch the Weaver-Peeples party, and was at that time ranching and prospecting in the Weaver district. Henry had come from California with Carleton's Column and like too many others in that group, he was first, last, and always a prospector.

There are several variations of the story of the discovery of his fabulous mine, and one can almost take one's pick. It is said that Wickenburg grabbed a stone to chuck at some vultures that were hovering nearby, and discovered that the stone which he was about to throw was laden with gold ore. A similar story is told, except that the creature on the receiving end was a recalcitrant burro. These stories and others are good for the tourist business today. They even used to amuse Wickenburg. In reality he just simply located the mine and called it the Vulture because he liked the name. Henry decided to sell his ore for $15 a ton to the local prospectors and let them transport it to Jack Swilling's arrastra for milling on the Hassayampa, a few miles to the east. It goes without saying that a lot of high-grading was going on. It is said that Jacob Waltz, a "Lost Dutchman" of some renown, worked at the Vulture at one time and was fired for high-grading. There are some today who believe that the Lost Dutchman mine was really a cache of ore high-graded from the Vulture mine and taken to the Superstition Mountains.

Wickenburg finally sold out for $85,000 and a one-fifth interest. However, he was swindled out of most of that by the new owners. The Vulture became one of the most productive gold mines in the West before it played out. Some say that the gold vein hit a fault and for the lucky one who finds where the vein picks up again . . . That's the stuff from which legends (and the tourist business) are born.

The buildings at the mine were constructed of stone gathered nearby. Some of these buildings, torn down in 1879, yielded $20 to the ton. It is known that one vein was 27 to 39 feet wide and went 350 feet into the earth from an outcropping. Before the Vulture played out, some $20 million had been extracted. Actual figures are hard to come by because of the large amount of high-grading. Henry's luck didn't improve with time. A flood wiped out his farm several years later, leaving him penniless. In 1905, he shot himself to death in the town that had been named in his honor.

In the years following the Civil War, silver was king. Up until 1873, the price of silver was at a premium. The government was purchasing at a price ratio of sixteen to one (gold was worth sixteen times the value of silver). Silver was selling for $1.29 an ounce and gold for $20.64. Present-day collectors of silver dollars will note that a few years are conspicuously absent. The government stopped minting silver dollars between the years 1873 and 1878. There was nearly another Civil War, this time between the East and the West. Western miners had no place to sell their silver, threatening the economy of many western silver-producing states, including Arizona. The government began purchasing the silver again in 1878 and the amount purchased was doubled by the Sherman Silver Act in 1890. Prosperity returned to the silver-producing regions once again. However, the hard feelings which developed between the western states and the East would be a factor in the delaying of Arizona's statehood in the years to come.

In 1873 a great silver discovery was made near what later became the town of Superior. A group of soldiers was constructing a military road up the Stonemen Grade to Camp Pinal when one of the workers, a man named Sullivan, picked up a piece of heavy black rock and examined it. Curious about the softness, he later showed it to a friend in Florence. Sullivan's enlistment was up about the same time and he left the area without revealing any more information about his discovery, except that he had found it at the foot of the grade. The friend, Charles Mason, along with Isaac Copeland, Bill Long, and Ben Reagan, farmers in the Florence area, decided to investigate. While on this prospecting trip, they were jumped by Apache and during the skirmish one of their burros wandered off. It was later found standing on an outcropping of chloride of silver, the same "black rock" as Sullivan's. The four men thought they had found the king of all silver mines, and the name Silver King was born. The burro has been as closely identified with the discovery of mineral in the West as the prospector himself.

The four men were farmers and not miners. They did as farmers who were not miners might be expected to do. They threw the good silver into the dump and packed the low-grade ore off to San Francisco. This exercise in futility cost them $12,000 in freight charges and other expenses. Discouraged, they offered the whole thing to a local merchant as payment for grubstaking them and he refused. At this time some more experienced miners saw the rich ore in the tailings and made arrangements with the four farmers to work it for half the profits. The first shipment netted $50,000. A merchant from Yuma, James Barney, offered to buy out the partners. He bought Copeland's share for $30,000. Mr. Long was harder to deal with. He wanted $100,000 for his. Eventually, Barney got control of the stock. He incorporated in 1877, and before the boom ended in 1888, the Silver King had produced more than $6 million in silver.

There were other great silver strikes in the same general area. Some, like Globe (thanks to its copper deposits), live on. Others, like McMillanville, had their day and died as rapidly as they had sprung up.

Ed Schieffelin had been prospecting in the West since the late fifties when he and his father came to the Rogue River country. When he arrived in Arizona in 1876, the $1.25 in his pocket was all he had to show for a lifetime of prospecting. Except for the fact that he neither drank nor gambled, Ed was a typical prospector, a dyed-in-the-wool optimist, always nursing the hope that the next one would be the big pay-off. For most, the hope was not necessarily to develop the mine, but just to stake a rich claim, sell to some large mining interest for a good price, and then move on.

Schieffelin, in need of funds to grubstake his next venture, took a job doing assessment work for the new owners of the old Brunchow mine, some 30 miles east of Fort Huachuca. This area had first been worked by Fred Brunchow, an engineer for Charlie Poston back in 1857, but he had been killed by Apache before he had done much to develop it.

Assessment work, according to federal mining law, requires that whenever one stakes a claim on public land, he must do $100 worth of laborious effort at the claim in the first ninety days, and $100

worth of work per year thereafter. It was in meeting this require-
ment that Schieffelin was hired. His own time was his to prospect
wherever he pleased. He surveyed the nearby hills and liked what
he saw. He checked the faults, knowing that the same upheaval
that caused the faults would also inject that which fulfills the
dreams of all wandering Argonauts.

That first year, 1877, did not yield much and Schieffelin went out
on his own. Always the optimist, he began looking for promising
prospects, picking up bits and pieces here and there, and not getting too much encouragement from the locals around Tucson. Some
even went as far as to tell him they would advance him money on a
ranching venture in the same area. However, for mining, they just
weren't too impressed with his ore samples. Ironically, these were
the same ones that had come from what would prove to be the
richest of the mines in the district. Not one to be discouraged easily
—after all, he'd only been looking for a little over twenty years—
Schieffelin took his samples to his brother Albert, who was working
at the McCracken mine over in Mohave County.

Albert was by far the more conservative of the two. His idea of
being a miner was steady employment with a large company for
$3.00 or $4.00 a day in wages. It took some persuasive talking on
the part of Ed before Albert finally became convinced. It was also
at this juncture that they met and teamed up with Dick Gird. Gird
had recently gone to work for the company as an assayer and when
he saw the samples Ed had been carrying around so diligently, he
could hardly conceal his enthusiasm. With a handshake they sealed
a partnership. It was a prophetic bit of counsel from the famed
scout Al Sieber that gave title to Arizona's last great silver strike.
"That's Apache country. You go out there and all you'll find will be
your tombstone," he had warned. The Tombstone mines were to be
the granddaddy of them all in the Southwest.

Legends have been created around the gunfight at the O.K. Corral, but the big show in Tombstone was silver—silver so soft you
could press a dollar against it and "read the mint mark on the im-
pression." By 1888 $30 million worth had been taken from eleven
major mines.

At a time when the economic situation in Arizona was getting
desperate and the world wasn't quite ready for copper, the gold in
the Walker district was about gone, and the Silver King was playing out, Tombstone arrived. Like all robust mining camps, Tomb-

stone attracted people in droves, all looking for a piece of the action. On one street were the girls, gamblers, and saloons. On the next block were the lawyers, doctors, and engineers. They all mingled together in the saloons on Allen Street, Tombstone's "Barbary Coast."

By and large they were not the romantic prospectors of lore, equipped with burro and gold pan. Rather they were the hard-rock miners who spent most of their lives underground. They lived in small houses, raised families, and didn't make more than $6.00 for a ten-hour shift.

These "bindle stiffs" or "cousin jacks," and their "cousin jennies," as the Cornish miners and their wives were called, were the salt of Tombstone's earth. It was they and the riches they uncovered that pulled Arizona out of the economic abyss, caused the Southern Pacific to build a railroad across the Territory, and brought merchants and settlers to the land. The Hollidays, Earps, Clantons, and McLaurys have contributed in recent years only in that they have made the erstwhile boomtown a colorful tourist attraction, and kept Tombstone from going the same route as her predecessors.

Tombstone's demise was slow but steady. Eventually the Schieffelins and Dick Gird sold out to the Corbin brothers of Connecticut for a handsome profit, though Ed never did give up his search for another great discovery. He died while searching for his next bonanza several years later.

The mines started to flood in 1883. In 1903 new pumps were installed, but by 1909 it was all over. Strikes and flooding had taken their toll. Only the myth remained.

Tombstone at her peak had a population of about fifteen thousand, not a small place as cities went at that time in the West. Her notorious reputation and wealth were sure to attract a following of unique individuals. Ed Schieffelin, Buckskin Frank Leslie, John Clum, Doc Goodfellow, C. S. Fly, Big Minnie, Nellie Cashman, Wyatt Earp, and Marcus Smith all walked her streets. Some were bad and some were good; all had character and style. Some worked hard for their money, others didn't. Most spent lavishly, lived fast, loved hard—and some died young. Her time in the limelight was brief and her reputation was checkered but all the old-timers agreed, for better or for worse, Tombstone was one of a kind.

THE UGLY DUCKLING MAKES OUT

OF ALL THE PRECIOUS METALS mined in Arizona, in the final analysis it was copper that would prove to be the biggest bonanza of them all. Today, Arizona produces more of the red metal annually than any other single nation in the free world. She has marketed more than twice as much as her nearest competitors in this country—Montana, Michigan, and Utah.

By the 1920s, most of the known high-grade ore deposits had just about played out. Traditional underground mining, with its restrictions on equipment, proved too costly for successful mining of the low-grade ores. A way had to be developed to concentrate the billions of tons of low-grade copper-bearing rock. A pioneer in the field of open pit mining was Dr. L. D. Ricketts, an engineer from Globe. He reasoned that by moving and concentrating large volumes of low-bearing ore in an open pit operation the business could be profitable. Today successful open pit mines are taking a theoretical average of only 7.2 pounds of the red metal from 1 ton of ore.

In the years that followed, great open pit mines began operations at Bisbee, Ray, Globe, Morenci, Ajo, Bagdad, and Tucson. There are still some profitable underground developments in operation. The Hecla Mining Company's Lakeshore mine near Casa Grande is an example. The Magma Copper Company still runs a successful mine at Superior and her ultra-modern operation at San Manuel became the state's largest producer in 1972.

Although Arizona does not have any high-grade gold or silver mining operations of a large scale, she produces as a by-product some 200,000 ounces of gold and 5.5 million ounces of silver annually from her huge copper productions, making her one of the nation's leaders in the field.

Most of Arizona's rich mineral deposits run diagonally across the state. The belt is some 450 miles long and 70 miles wide. It runs generally from the vicinity of Kingman over to Bisbee. There are a large number of faults along this line and it is considered by some scientists as one of the most unique and complicated mineral regions in the world. Since the 1880s, most of the surface mineral has been removed and the low-grade ore below was left. Modern techniques and machinery have made it possible to mine even this ore at a profit. Most of the mining done in Arizona today is open pit.

Other than a few minor operations by the Spaniards, the first major effort in mining the ore in Arizona occurred in 1854, when Captain Peter R. Brady reported finding rich silver-copper ore deposits. The American Mining and Trading Company was organized to explore the area.

The first ore mined at Ajo was transported by mule for $105 a ton to L. J. F. Jaeger's ferry landing at Yuma. From there it was taken down the Colorado River to a waiting ship and thence around the Horn to Wales for smelting. Amazingly enough, the operation was temporarily profitable. Lack of water and low-grade ore caused business to slow. The high-grade surface stringers were not rich enough in silver to make the operation profitable and the district lay idle until around 1900. At that time a smooth-talking promoter named A. J. Shotwell appeared on the scene. Taking a few rich samples to St. Louis, he located a pigeon of unquestionable integrity named John R. Boddie and convinced him of the opportunities in the Ajo area. Accentuating the positive and eliminating the negative (the absence of water), Shotwell's adroit use of rhetoric soon brought forth large amounts of investment capital. Boddie and his wealthy friends were fed a grandiose picture of the ore-laden country around Ajo by the avaricious Mr. Shotwell, and all had visions of some bottomless pit of wealth. When profits were slow coming in and the investors grew uneasy, Shotwell lavishly spent $45,000 to gather in $36,000 worth of rich ore to display. It wasn't long before the company was bankrupt and Shotwell again approached Mr. Boddie seeking new investors. Soon another group of prospective investors was lined up and a committee was selected to go West for a firsthand look at Ajo. Shotwell wisely chose the brief rainy season for the inspection tour as most of the year there was no water in which to operate the mill. He had spent weeks arduously gathering rich ore specimens and accumulating water. His diligence paid off. Every rock which the committee cracked open was green with copper carbonate. The attentive con man then showed the investors how to pulverize their samples. Using sulfuric acid, he dissolved the powder and when the visitors dipped their knife blades into the solution, they emerged from the caldron with a pure copper coating. It was an impressive demonstration. However, what the committee didn't know was that one could get the same coating from 1 per cent ore as from 5 per cent ore. This bit of chicanery was enough to convince the investors. On the way back to St. Louis, they organized the Cornelia Copper Company. Soon after the visitors left, the land did what it has done for the past several thousand years. It dried up and it wasn't long until the Cornelia Copper Company went the way of her predecessor.

In 1911 former Roughrider and manager of the Calumet and Arizona Company at Bisbee John C. Greenway and some associates became interested in and acquired an option on the stock. They called the new venture the New Cornelia Copper Company. Using astute mining technology and geological know-how which included the use of open pit mining and the discovery of a large, inexhaustible source of underground water, Ajo was soon on her way to becoming one of the richest of copper camps. She arrived just in time for the copper boom of 1917–18. The adroitness of geologist Ira Joralman and metallurgist Dr. L. D. Ricketts, along with the sagacious leadership of Greenway, did much to ensure the success of the operation. At last, the faithful Boddie realized his dream. The mine eventually yielded a fortune. However, the sudden death of General Greenway in 1926 seemed to take the heart out of the company. In 1931, Phelps-Dodge acquired the property and the operation has been profitable ever since.

In eastern Arizona, along the San Francisco River, lie some of the richest mineral deposits in the state. This was also a favorite habitat for the marauding Apache in the early days. Henry Clifton stopped there in the mid-1860s after spending some time prospecting in the Prescott area. He saw lots of promise and reported it to friends in Silver City, but it was several years before the area was worked.

In the mid-1870s, Jim and Bob Metcalf, while on a scouting expedition against the Apache, found ore so rich that it was "quarried rather than mined." Two of their claims especially, the Metcalf and the Longfellow, turned out to be rich bonanzas. They later sold out the Longfellow to the Lesinsky brothers, who did most of the developing of the property. To increase the profits, the Lesinskys decided to build a railroad line down the hill to Clifton, where the smelter was located. It was a 20-inch narrow-gauge and ran only 4 miles, but it was the first railroad line in Arizona. Mules were used to pull the ore cars up the hill to Morenci; the system worked on gravity, and the mules got a free ride back down the hill, riding in the empty ore cars. As in most mining camps, the homes were built on the steep hills near the mines. It was said that the front yards of these modern-day cliff dwellers slanted so that when mothers let their children out to play, the youngsters had to be tethered to the house by rope lest they fall out of the yard.

Clifton's first city jail was most unusual, yet compatible with the ethnic environment of the area. It was hollowed out of a mountain in 1881. Legend has it that the miner who contracted to do the job was so pleased with his work that upon completion, he took his pay and headed for the nearest watering hole, where he proposed a toast to the "best jailmaker in the world." Apparently the other patrons weren't that impressed with the idea of a jail in their community, for they refused to toast. The "world's greatest jailmaker," his dignity affronted, commenced shooting up the place. He was carted off to jail and hence the Clifton jailmaker also had the dubious distinction of becoming its first inmate.

Clifton was once victimized by an audacious bank robber who, after holding up the bank, circled around town where he casually asked for a fresh horse so that he could join the posse that was forming to pursue the bandit. He must have felt that he was much too clever to keep the caper a secret, for he got drunk one night and told some friends. Shortly thereafter he was arrested.

In 1877 Sergeant Jack Dunn, a government scout from Fort Bowie, was winding his way down what later became known as Tombstone Canyon in southeastern Arizona in pursuit of hostile Apache when he noticed an interesting outcropping and stopped to investigate. As was common in those days, the soldiers spent one eye looking for Apache and the other looking for mineral. Sergeant Dunn couldn't have known at the time, but this location would become known as the Glory Hole, and the Bisbee district in which it was located was destined to become one of the richest copper areas in the world.

Later, Sergeant Dunn recorded his name and the names of two others in his party, Lieutenant J. A. Rucker and T. D. Burne. The location was called The Rucker and was filed on August 2, 1877. Lieutenant Rucker was later drowned in a cloudburst in the canyon that today bears his name, just east of Sulphur Springs Valley.

Apparently Dunn told his story to one George Warren upon his return to Fort Bowie. He grubstaked Warren and sent him on his way to the Mule Mountains with instructions to stake out claims for both parties. As far as is known, this agreement was never kept, as Warren drank away his grubstake at Brunchow. He was "refitted" by the unscrupulous proprietors of a local drinking establishment.

Warren, with some companions, located the Mercey mine on December 27, 1877. His name also appears on several other claims either as locator or witness. Two years later, the original Mercey was relocated and renamed the Copper Queen. George Warren either sold or lost most of his mining properties over the next few years. In one drunken wager he bet he could travel up Brewery Gulch faster on foot than another man could on horseback. George lost. The stakes he had placed to cover his bet were none other than his interest in the Copper Queen. His share in the mine later turned out to be worth some $13 million. In 1881 George was charged with insanity and a guardian was appointed to look after him. His total worth was estimated at $925. Later he slipped over into Mexico, where he sold himself into peonage. Judge G. H. Berry learned of the situation and ransomed Warren back across the line by paying the Mexican debt. He lived out his remaining years in Bisbee doing odd jobs and subsisting off a small penison given him by the Copper Queen.

James Reilly, an eastern lawyer, though recently engaged in mining operations in Elko, Nevada, arrived in Bisbee in 1879. Through shrewd maneuvering he was able to buy up the rich claim Warren had lost in his infamous race. Reilly, in turn, sold it to the Copper Queen Mining Company for $1.25 million.

The Copper Queen began active operations in 1880. The camp had already been named for Judge DeWitt Bisbee, who incidentally never visited the town named in his honor. His son-in-law,

John Williams, and Williams' two brothers were owners of the Queen.

It was in 1880 that a small eastern mining firm known as Phelps-Dodge and Company sent Dr. James Douglas to Arizona to check out the prospects for a venture. Douglas, a physician turned geologist, sent back favorable reports on the region. He would later solve the difficult problem of extracting low-grade ore at a profit. Low-grade ore is less than 5 per cent copper to the ton.

Dr. Douglas moved to Bisbee in 1889, becoming assayer for the Copper Queen. He married the daughter of Lewis Williams, one of his partners, in 1891. In the years that followed Dr. James Douglas would become one of the most respected men in the mining business.

Bisbee was never a "bad" town in the way that Tombstone was. The company always was careful not to let things get too far out of hand. However, it did have a considerable amount of licentious activity, mostly around Brewery Gulch, so named in honor of the Mulheim Brewery built at the entrance to the gulch in 1904.

Old-timers in Bisbee say that the brewery kept a bear chained to a tree just outside the front entrance to act as a sort of "watch bear" to prevent burglaries. The bear had cultivated a taste for the Mulheim product and the miners used to accommodate the beast by getting him drunk every night. After the miners had all gone home and everything was quiet, the bear would crawl up into the tree and spend the rest of the night in deep slumber. However, much to the dismay of all, the bear got himself overloaded one night, fell out of the tree, and hanged himself.

Brewery Gulch was lined with saloons and the farther up the gulch one went, the rougher the clientele. The elevation of Bisbee is 5,000 feet and it was said that for some of her residents that was as close to heaven as any of them ever got. At the far end of the road were the sporting houses. All that remains today are the concrete stairs that led up to the little shanties where the girls worked. Symbolic, perhaps, of a way of life that, for most, led nowhere.

The houses along the gulch were almost all built on the hillsides. It was said that the hills were so steep in Bisbee that if a resident were to fall off his front yard he would land on his neighbor's rooftop. The social rule was usually the higher up the hill he lived, the more status had the resident. In the most affluent part of town, called Quality Hill, lived the most affluent of the high-ranking company officials. This hill was even equipped with a cave, into which company officials could lock themselves during times of serious labor unrest.

Bisbee had its first lynching in 1882. A drunken Mexican, offended over being kicked out of a local saloon, returned and shot up the place. One man died as a result of the melee and two others were wounded. The culprit was captured the next day. The angry miners took him up the canyon near Castle Rock and hanged him from a tree. A company owner, visiting Bisbee from the East, happened by just in time to see the body swinging from a limb. Horrified by these primitive acts, he decided that what the town needed was more diversification of leisure activities. When the official returned to New York he sent back a large number of well-chosen books for the miners to ingest. This was the beginning of the Copper Queen Library.

Not all of the women who came to the boomtowns were of the "notorious" variety. Some were a bit eccentric and some displayed other incongruities with what was considered normal behavior for women. However, they all added color to the social happenings. One of the most remarkable ladies to grace the mining camps of the West was an attractive young woman from Ireland named Nellie Cashman. Full of wanderlust, she spent the major part of her life in search of some rainbow's end.

There was one time when she and a party of male Argonauts went off in search of a lost gold mine in Mexico. It wasn't until they were hopelessly lost in the Sonoran desert that it occurred to them that they had been hoaxed. All their party would have perished under the burning hot sun had it not been for Nellie's formidable stamina. After the others had stopped to die, she continued on, finally reaching an old Catholic mission.

This wasn't the first nor would it be the last dream Nellie would chase. Born in Ireland, she came to this country shortly after the Civil War. She and a sister traveled across the United States, arriving in San Francisco in 1869, where her sister met and married Thomas Cunningham. He died ten years later and she passed away three years after, leaving Nellie with the five Cunningham children to raise.

Nellie seemed to have little use for money, although she was fascinated with the challenge and complexities of making it. She made and tossed away several small fortunes to hospitals, missions, prospectors down on their luck, and last but not least, the magical lust for some new mining venture.

She had her pick of several wealthy men who were seeking her hand in holy matrimony, but nonetheless she stayed single all her life.

Her wanderlust led her from Alaska to Mexico. In Virginia City, Nevada, she ran a boardinghouse for miners, and the miners of Cassiar, British Columbia, nicknamed her the "Angel of the Sourdoughs," a name that stuck the rest of her days.

During the great silver strikes in Arizona, Nellie headed for Tucson, where she ran a fancy restaurant by the name of Delmonico's. A year later, 1880, she was in Tombstone, where she acquired the Russ House. In this fine establishment Nellie served not only the best of culinary delights, but also plenty of good cheer to all the local bindle stiffs who worked in the mines. When charity was needed, she was always there, collecting money or selling tickets. No self-respecting man could refuse her. Once she raised $500 in a couple of days for the benefit of a lone miner who had fallen down a shaft and broken his legs.

Her last years were spent in the frozen north, where she was known as the champion woman musher of her time. She could pilot those turbulent Alaskan rivers in a kayak as well as any man. One of her last mining claims was staked out at the edge of the Arctic Circle in the northernmost camp in Alaska.

She died on January 4, 1925, and if one might rephrase an old adage, she was truly a woman who matched the mountains.

Bisbee was a company town and did not have the tempestuous reputation of many of her contemporaries. However, there were occasions when violence did occur. On December 8, 1883, the notorious and oft-written-about Bisbee Massacre shocked the district during its usually quiet Christmas season. It started out as a robbery of the Goldwater-Castenada store on Main Street, when five men entered the store and leveled their guns on Pete Dall, the bookkeeper. Two of the men covered Dall while the other three kept an eye on the shoppers. Joe Goldwater, one of the owners and a member of the pioneer merchant family, opened the safe.

Meanwhile, a passer-by saw the holdup in progress and started to give the alarm. He never got his chance, as three shots rang out, killing him instantly. The next victim was Deputy Sheriff D. T. Smith, shot in the head as he rushed up the narrow street. By this time, the gunmen were firing at anything and everything that moved. Usually the presence of a woman would cause some hesitation in such a situation, but apparently the robbers panicked as they shot and killed Mrs. Anna Roberts, a young restaurant keeper. She hadn't even been aware of the robbery when she fell, mortally wounded. The fourth victim, James A. Halley, was fatally wounded as he ran for safety.

Inside the store the men emptied the contents of the safe into their jackets. José Castenada, Goldwater's partner, was ill in the back room. He had hidden a sack of gold under his pillow when the robbery began. However, the robbers quickly found it and relieved him of the contents.

The five men, Dan Dowd, Bill Delaney, Dan Kelly, Tex Howard, and Red Sample, mounted their horses and rode out toward the lower end of town, firing occasionally to discourage any would-be heroes from interfering with their getaway.

James Kreighbaum rode 28 miles to the county seat at Tombstone in less than two hours to inform the sheriff. A posse was on the trail shortly thereafter.

Deputy Billy Daniels was assigned to lead one of the posses trailing the outlaws into the Chiricahua Mountains, where they found signs that the robbers had brutally run their exhausted horses off a cliff. Stealing fresh mounts from a nearby ranch, they had continued in a northerly direction.

Among the first to offer his services to the posse was a Bisbee saloonkeeper named John Heith. Heith kept trying to lead the posse up the wrong trail, finally arousing the suspicions of the posse members. They became even more suspicious when a man fitting his description and another fitting that of Tex Howard were reported to have been seen together a few days before. After some intimidation and coercion, Heith confessed to his part in the robbery. The others were taken into custody after an extensive manhunt—the chase covered hundreds of miles on both sides of the border. Deputy Daniels arrested Dowd in Mexico and smuggled him back into Arizona. Delaney was apprehended in Sonora by a Mexican officer who, without extradition papers, delivered him to the Arizona lawmen. Kelly was sitting in a barber's chair in Deming, New Mexico, when he was recognized and arrested. He had one close shave too many. Sample and Howard were captured near Clifton. Howard had taken a gold watch from the safe during the robbery, and in order to gain certain favors from one of the local soiled doves, had offered it to her. She later paraded the gift in front of her boy friend, who recognized it from a description of stolen goods that had been sent out from Bisbee. He was all too ready to deliver Mr. Howard to the proper authorities and collect said reward, not to mention the elimination of a potential rival for the affections of his sweetheart.

The five men were tried at the county seat at Tombstone immediately and sentenced to hang. The date set for the hanging was March 8, 1884. Heith demanded a separate trial on grounds that he was not present at the robbery. He turned state's evidence and was sentenced to twenty years at Yuma. However, the verdict was unacceptable to the residents of Bisbee. On the morning of February 22, 1884, Washington's birthday, a mob from Bisbee paraded over to Tombstone, entered the jail, and took Heith out. A rope was strung over the crossarm of a telegraph pole on Toughnut Street. The mob waited patiently as the doomed man took out a handkerchief and tied it over his eyes. He had just one request and that was that his body not be riddled with bullets, as was often the custom. His request was granted and the execution was carried out. The body hung there all day and was viewed by thousands.

It was Tombstone's only real lynching. The inimitable Dr. George Goodfellow, who later became a worldwide authority on the treatment of gunshot wounds, acted as coroner. He summed up the feelings of most when he issued this report: "I can't see but one ruling possible here. It's my opinion that this man died from emphysema, which might have been and probably was caused by strangulation, self-inflicted or otherwise as is in accordance with the medical evidence."

Meanwhile, the rest of the gang waited uneasily in the Tombstone jail for March 8. It was during this time that John L. Sullivan, the world heavyweight champion, paid a visit to Tombstone. When the condemned men learned of this they requested that the champ come visit them at the jail. Sullivan agreed to the request and was somewhat taken aback when Dan Dowd dryly admonished the champ with these words: "John Sullivan, you think you are a great man because you can knock out one man in five rounds, but our sheriff here, who is much smaller than you, can knock out five men in one round." Whatever John L.'s reply, it was not recorded.

During this time, Nellie Cashman was operating the Russ House in Tombstone. She fed the hungry and was a friend to all. It is no surprise that she became the mother-confessor to the doomed men at the jail. When they learned that some enterprising carpenter had obtained a permit to build a grandstand and charge admission to the hanging they asked her if something couldn't be done to prevent their last earthly moments from becoming a commercial spectacle. She obliged; she rounded up some of her friends the night before the hanging and the next morning the would-be entrepreneur found his grandstand torn down and the boards scattered in the gulch below.

She also saw to it that the men were given a decent burial. Plans had been made to give the bodies to science—not by choice of the men but by the authorities. She gave the ill-fated men assurances that this would not happen without their permission.

At 1 P.M., March 8, 1884, with only "invited guests" in the courtyard, Sheriff J. W. Ward prepared the men for their trip into eternity. All five wore smiles on their faces—some waved to friends in the crowd. They shook hands with priests and officers. Sheriff Ward asked them if they had any last words. Dowd replied, "It's getting pretty hot so you might as well go on with it." Tex Howard looked at Dowd and pensively replied, "Dan, it's liable to be a whole lot hotter where we're going."

Today in Tombstone's famous Boot Hill are the five graves of the men, saved from the laboratory by a kind woman who, regardless of past offenses, felt that the men had paid their debt to society and deserved a decent burial.

THE BILLION-DOLLAR
COPPER CAMP

SITTING ON A SLOPE at the foot of Cleopatra Hill, Jerome was once the third largest city in Arizona and the pride of the Territory. The area was rich in minerals, a fact that had been known a long time. The Indians had used her copper, mostly for the pigment. The Spanish explorers found it too, for they left some of their tools behind to be discovered almost two hundred years later. The mineral was there; the problem was how to transport it from that remote area.

Army Chief of Scouts for General Crook, Al Sieber, had staked a claim there in the 1870s. However, he never realized its value and sold out cheap. Others also tried, including Frederick Tritle, popular governor of the Territory. In 1883, Tritle and his partner, William Murray, were short on capital, so Murray contacted financier Eugene Jerome in New York. Jerome wasn't too interested, but his wife and sister-in-law, both wealthy in their own right, convinced him to invest. He invested $200,000 and insisted that the town be named in his honor.

Later that year they struck a large vein of silver and copper, but after taking out some $80,000 worth the vein played out. The partners were plagued with other problems also. Freight wagons were charging $20 a ton to transport the ore to the nearest railroad, which was at Ash Fork. It was 60 miles over rough road to Prescott by wagon. The town was isolated and prices began to drop.

A fall guy was needed and Tritle was the man, for, after all, could Jerome lay the blame on his wife and sister-in-law? Nevertheless, Tritle did try again three years later, but transportation and labor problems stopped him. He died in Phoenix in 1906, a broken man. He wouldn't be the last to be smitten at the hands of the fickle lady. Others would try and fail, victims all of Cleopatra Hill.

In 1888 Phelps-Dodge sent Dr. James Douglas to tender an offer to Jerome for the mine. The frugal Douglas offered $30,000 and Jerome grandiosely countered with $300,000.

Meanwhile, a copper magnate from Butte, Montana, William Andrews Clark, had been secretly looking at the property, and satisfied with his findings he decided to meet Jerome's price. Meanwhile, after doing some thinking on the subject, Dr. Douglas finally decided to meet Jerome's demands. He arrived one day late. His stubbornness had proven costly.

Clark, who stood only 5 feet, 2 inches in height, became a giant among the industrial magnates of his time. Nothing could stop the diminutive man with the red beard from getting anything he desired. He was a secretive man, and he loved intrigue. Nobody ever knew for certain how much he was worth. He kept the left-hand side of the ledger in New York and the right-hand side in Jerome. Only he was allowed to read both sides. This secrecy was even carried over into the mines. Those miners working topside were not allowed to go below, and those working below were not allowed to discuss their work under threat of dismissal.

No philanthropist, Clark did, however, run for the United States Senate from Montana in 1899, spending over a million dollars in bribes on his campaign. Not unsurprisingly, considering his investment, he won the election, although his son Charlie was run out of Montana and his lawyer was indicted and jailed. Through it all, Clark seemed unruffled, but when he went to Washington, the Senate Elections and Privileges Committee refused him a seat. Undaunted, he ran again in 1902. This time he was seated, but only stayed one term, apparently feeling that he was not cut out to be a public servant.

Clark maintained a permanent residence in Butte, and since he rarely delegated authority, a private railroad car transported him to his various holdings. He had little or no fear of local territorial governments. From time to time the idea of a bullion tax on the mines would spring up in the legislature. When it did, Clark would send his superintendent, Henry J. Allen, down to the Jerome bank to make a large withdrawal and announce to all that he was going to Phoenix to buy some mules and jackasses. A few days later he would return, without the money and also with no livestock. Shortly thereafter, the tax bill would die in some committee. Allen was instrumental in the nicknaming of one particular legislative session, the "Mule Legislature." It was said that some of the territorial legislators in early Arizona were some of the best that money could buy.

Charlie Clark, the senator's son, was unlike his dad in many ways. He loved the fast life, pretty women, and high-stakes poker games. The higher the ante the better. There were card games in which a million dollars was on the table when Charlie was in town. But like his father, he could also be a shrewd businessman. Young Charlie was a rare combination of capable business tycoon and playboy. In years to come he would play a major role in the family's United Verde mine operation at Jerome.

Dr. Douglas' stubbornness and the losing-out to Senator Clark on the United Verde must have grieved the old man in his later years. However, in 1912, his son "Rawhide" Jimmy Douglas did much to refurbish the family reputation. He and a man named George Turner bought out the Little Daisy mine and in the first year spent half a million dollars and found nothing. In 1914, they tried again and this time struck a vein of copper 5 feet thick, the richest ever found in American copper mining. In 1916, they took out $10 million worth, of which three quarters was pure profit. They called the mine the United Verde Extension and soon they were smelting more in one furnace than Clark was in three. The townspeople loved the competition. If they found working conditions unpleasant at one company, they could go to work for the other.

In 1893 Clark built a narrow-gauge railroad line to Chino Valley intersecting with the Ash Fork-Prescott Line. The United Verde and Pacific was said to be the "crookedest railroad in the world"— meaning the tracks, not the company. The 27 miles were traveled not exactly as the crow flies but then the crow didn't haul a whole lot of ore either. With switchbacks, loops, and more kinks than a cheap lariat, the tracks doubled back on themselves so much that the passengers could look out the windows and see the engine going the opposite way.

In 1912 Clark advanced the Santa Fe Railroad $3.5 million to build a standard-gauge line into the Verde Valley. A new smelter town was built in the valley, costing the senator another $2 million. It was a model community named Clarkdale, in honor of its benefactor, and employees could buy or rent on easy company terms.

Like all boomtowns, living quarters were hard to find in Jerome. Construction could never keep up with demand. Hotels and rooming houses were always filled to capacity. Local residents began fixing up spare rooms and everybody became a landlord.

Until it burned in 1915, Clark's Montana Hotel was a landmark. It was the "pride of Jerome," and four hundred people could be served in the main dining room. A miner could rent one of the two hundred rooms for only $5.00 a month. Still there was a shortage of room space. Sometimes the winter nights got so cold that the miners walked the 4-mile road from Jerome to Clarkdale just to keep warm.

Jerome was a male-dominated society and, like all boomtowns, the social parasites were not long in discovering it. The city sported fifteen saloons when the population was fifteen hundred, or roughly about one saloon for every hundred persons. Each month, right after payday, the mines would close down for a couple of days. When this occurred, alcoholic stimulant flowed freely as all concerned went on a two-day whizzer.

Nothing was too good for the customer on the old "Tenderloin," as the district was called. One house went so far as to provide an escape hatch to prevent embarrassing situations. It was called Husbands' Alley and, no doubt, saved many a promiscuous spouse. During one of Jerome's many fires, a madam named Jennie Banter rushed up to the firehouse and offered lifetime free passes to the boys if they would save her establishment. It was said that the men rose to superhuman efforts that day and Jennie's place was saved. A smart businesswoman, Jennie was reputed to be the richest woman in Arizona.

Fires destroyed Jerome with such regularity that some religious fanatics proclaimed that God was punishing the wicked city for its sinful ways. Each time it burned, they shouted with great alacrity, "God did it." A representative of the Salvation Army named Mrs. Thomas, was the most vociferous in the campaign. After one fire she declared that "God isn't done with Jerome yet. Since He has commenced He will regenerate the town or He will have no town here. He's started in to make Jerome a Christian town and it'll be a Christian town or nothing."

There were a few more fires but none as serious as the ones that had brought on the onslaught of the fatalistic prognosis. Perhaps wicked Jerome was repenting a bit after all.

In 1894 a fire broke out in the United Verde mine that burned for more than twenty years. The area was flooded with both water and carbon dioxide in hopes of drowning the blaze. Because of the numerous cracks and vents, all attempts were unsuccessful. In the 1920s, when the open pit operations became profitable, the area was opened up and the fire extinguished.

During the years the fire was out of control, the only people able to work the mine were a group of Spanish specialists who became quite legendary around Jerome. Their skills were handed down, father to son. They were the only ones able to withstand the tremendous heat—temperatures rose to over 150 degrees with the rock temperatures much higher.

During slack economic periods when the price of copper was down, the local merchants caught in the squeeze would get together and insist that the gamblers, girls, and booze be banned to "make Jerome a decent place to live." More likely they were protecting their own interests by decreeing that what money there was to spend should be spent on more respectable items. During one period it was forbidden even to watch a card game of any kind.

In 1920 the Prescott highway over Mingus Mountain was completed. Prescott now was only 30 miles away. The price of copper in 1920 dropped to $.12 a pound and by the end of the year the government stopped buying it altogether. Even though Jerome was no longer isolated from the rest of the world, the bubble was about to burst.

In 1925 came an end of an era. Senator William Andrews Clark died. There was a long court battle over his estate between his two daughters and his sons. Both sons passed away before the dispute was settled, and in 1935 Phelps-Dodge purchased the company for $21 million.

"Rawhide" Jimmy Douglas died a multimillionaire in 1949. His "Little Daisy" mine produced over $150 million in gold, silver, and copper. He had avenged and made amends for his father's stubbornness many times over before he cashed in.

Not only were copper prices on the downslide, but so was Jerome itself. There were several reasons why the "great shift" occurred. The city was situated on a fault. Whatever vegetation had not been removed from Cleopatra Hill for timber and firewood had been destroyed by the sulfurous smelter smoke. Without this foliage, erosion set in, eating away at foundations and retaining walls. Manmade faults played no small part in the slide. Literally millions of tons of explosives had been set off in the tunnels beneath Jerome. One single charge used 260,000 pounds of dynamite and black quarry powder. It is not surprising that Jerome slowly began to give way.

The city had a new motto, as Mayor Harry Mader proudly proclaimed, "Jerome is a city on the move."

It certainly was—all downhill.

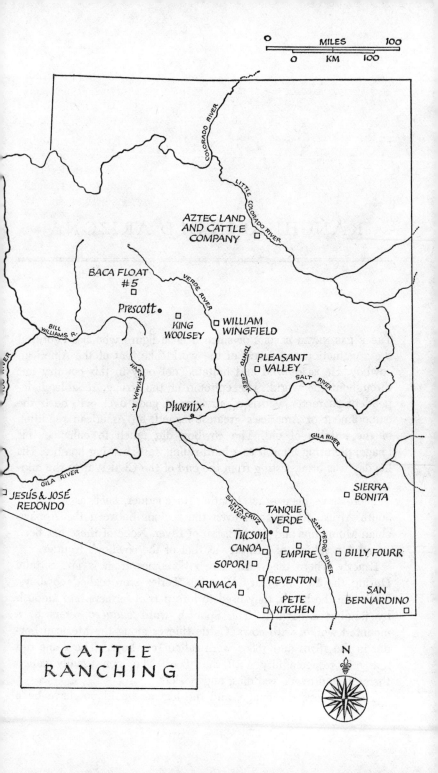

MILES 100

0 KM 100

COLORADO RIVER

LITTLE COLORADO RIVER

AZTEC LAND
AND CATTLE
COMPANY

BACA FLOAT
#5

VERDE RIVER

Prescott

KING
WOOLSEY

WILLIAM
WINGFIELD

PLEASANT
VALLEY

TONTO CREEK

SALT RIVER

BILL
WILLIAMS R.

HASSAYAMPA R.

Phoenix

GILA RIVER

GILA RIVER

JESÚS & JOSÉ
REDONDO

SANTA CRUZ RIVER

SIERRA
BONITA

TANQUE
VERDE

SAN PEDRO RIVER

Tucson

CANOA

EMPIRE

BILLY FOURR

SOPORI

ARIVACA

REVENTON

PETE
KITCHEN

SAN
BERNARDINO

CATTLE
RANCHING

N

RANCHING IN OLD ARIZONA

THERE HAS NEVER BEFORE or since been a figure who has captured the imagination or interest of the world like that of the American cowboy. He is idolized and imitated not only in this country but throughout the world. The epitome of the strong, reliable, independent character who is a purveyor of good over evil, he is the embodiment of America's greatest legend, an American rendition of the knights of old. The cowboy did much to enhance this image, picturing himself as a hard-riding, fast-shooting hombre. His heyday was brief, lasting from the end of the Civil War to the mid-1880s.

There have been other frontiers to conquer, such as Australia, South Africa, Alaska, and even the regions between the Appalachian Mountains and the Mississippi River. None of these has been as much a subject of curiosity as that of the cowboy's frontier.

Exactly where the word "cowboy" comes from is not certain. During the Revolutionary War the Tories were called cowboys. Hiding in the brush, they used to lure patriot-farmers into ambush by jingling a cowbell. The Spanish word *vaquero* refers to a mounted worker with cows. Cattle thieves along the Mexican border in the 1870s and 1880s were called "cowboys." The name did not gain respectability until the 1890s. The men usually called themselves drovers, waddies, and peelers.

The business, the image, and the legend would not have been

possible had it not been for one necessary item, the cow, or, to be more specific, the Mexican longhorn. The longhorn, like the cowboy, is a legend, the "bedrock on which the history of the cow country of America is founded." They were a natural breed for the arid Southwest, where in some areas the grazing land only received some 4 inches of rain a year. The longhorn possessed an incredible amount of stamina and the ability to survive everything from freezing blizzards to hot, blazing deserts. Drovers oftentimes had to sleep booted and spurred, ready to ride at a moment's notice. The unpredictable beasts were responsible for the deaths of more than a few cowboys.

Cattle were first brought to the shores of North America by the Spanish conquistadors. The beasts were lifted off the ships by a hoist with a long rope attached around the base of the horns. Once up in the air, they were swung out and lowered into the water and pointed toward the shore. At first the cattle weren't branded, although their shepherds were, as natives captured in war did the work of watching the herds. Each had branded on his cheek the letter "G" for *guerra* or war prisoner. In the evolutionary process of the cowboy it's an ironic curiosity to note that the first cowboy was an Indian and the first cattle weren't branded, whereas the first cowboys were.

The original cowboys, as we know them today, were the Mexican *vaqueros*. From Texas to California these superbly skilled men could ride and rope with such adroitness that visiting spectators were astounded. There seemed to be no feat which the *vaquero* couldn't perform from the hurricane deck of his Spanish pony. Like the Plains Indian, he only got off his horse to dance or to die, but he'd rather do both astride his *caballo*. In early California it was not unusual for a man to ride 60 miles for a *baile,* or dance, and home again afterward. Firewood was gathered by roping it with his rawhide *reata* and dragging it home. To kill a man, you didn't need to shoot him, just rope him and drag him to death. With *reatas* as long as 110 feet, the *vaquero* could take a dally on a running steer from 60 feet.

Most of the language that the American cowboy uses today is derived from some corruption of the Spanish-Mexican language. "Buckaroo" comes from the Spanish word *vaquero*, while "lariat" is derived from the words *la reata*. Spanish-Mexican influence is seen in other words like corral, rodeo, remuda, and bronco, all of which are almost pure Spanish. Other words were Americanized by the English-speaking cowboys north of the border. *Chaparreras* was shortened to "chaps." The *jáquima* became "hackamore," while the *mesteño* was corrupted into "mustang."

The colonization of Texas in the 1820s opened up a whole new way of life to the American. The techniques of ranching in the Southwest were like nothing he had ever seen. However, it wasn't too many years before the newcomers adapted to the life-style and were as skillful as the Mexicans. A whole new breed of man was born and destined to become the root of western American folklore, legend, and myth. He was the last grand image of adventure and romance, the rugged human spirit from which legends are made.

There are no records of how many young boys took it upon themselves to walk or hitchhike west to fulfill a lifelong dream of becoming a real-life cowboy. They said that all you needed to become one was guts and a horse, and if you had guts, you could steal a horse. The work was arduous and the hours were long. Death could occur at any time from stampede, swollen rivers, rustlers, or Indians. The pay ranged from $25 to $40 a month and the food consisted of a regular diet of beans, biscuits, and coffee.

There was little glory in getting up at four in the morning, cleaning screwworms out of some cow's sore or pulling a cow out of a boghole and having to run for one's life to escape the wrath of the ungrateful beast. While on the trail, the drover's job consisted of sitting in the saddle all day, seven days a week, for months on end. It's no wonder that he took the lid off any town he might happen to pass through, for discipline on the trail was always strict. An infraction of the rules might cause the loss of the herd or the death of some unfortunate drover, as those Texas cows were as ornery and unpredictable as anything that tramped the West. Down in south Texas the cattle were so wild that they could only be roped at night when they came out to water. The cowboys would sometimes have to stitch their eyes closed with gut-string and drive them, blind, up the trail. In a few weeks, when the stitching rotted away, it was said that they were somewhat more docile and easier to drive.

In the early days of the long drive, some of the cattle had run loose for so long that they were fifteen or twenty years old before they went to market. Since the horns continue growing for the entire life of the beast, many were known to reach a length of 8 to 9 feet across. The results of a man or horse being gored by one of these is obvious.

To say that the longhorn was pernicious would be a gross understatement. The Mexicans used to match him against the grizzly and wager on the outcome. European big-game hunters used to stalk and hunt the wily beast for trophy. More than one no doubt found its way to the den or game room of some foreign marquis.

There was an old saying, probably originating in some cow camp, that "Cowboys was noisy fellers with bow legs, brass stomachs, that ride horses and hates any kind of work they can't do on one." They were flamboyant in their actions and dress. A man earning $25 a month would spend all of that amount on a new Stetson and twice that on a new pair of boots. It was not unusual to see a cowboy with a $40 saddle cinched around a $10 horse. Normally inclined to be reticent, the cowboy let his tongue run free when swearing. One claimed his cussin' was so strong it could "peel the hide off a Gila monster or grow hair on a Mexican dog." He was also fiercely independent. "If you tossed one of 'em in a river he'd just naturally float upstream," one old-timer said. The mere suggestion on the part of the boss to perform some kind of work that the cowhand considered beneath his dignity would be enough to send him packing his bedroll and moving on to a new job.

The cowboy also had his own personal string of ponies to use while going up the trail. Most cowboys developed genuine affection for their mounts and spent a great deal of time extolling the abilities of their ponies around the evening campfire. There was his swimming pony, used when crossing swollen rivers, and his running pony for friendly wagers. Perhaps his favorite pony was his night pony. Sure-footed and alert, the night pony carried the tired cowboy through his two-hour watch. It was said that a good night pony would walk the entire two-hour watch smoothly enough so as to allow the waddie to sleep the entire time. Still, others claimed that their pony would even go so far as to deliver the cowboy back to his blankets at the end of two hours and kneel down so as not to wake the man while gently depositing him back on the ground. Better yet, others claimed, their night pony would not only do all those things but would even go over and wake the next cowboy who was to go on watch.

The early cattle drives, prior to the Civil War, did not go up to

Kansas but went instead to California during the gold rush. It didn't take long for the thousands of head of cattle there to be depleted as Argonauts rushed in from all over the world in search of the yellow metal.

Down in Texas, cattle could be purchased at $2.00 a head and driven to California, where in 1849 they sold for $300 a head. Prices later stabilized, but still there was tremendous profit, enough to justify driving them through Apachería and risking some losses to the natives and the deserts as well. Cattle were driven across Arizona mainly over two trails in those early years. One route went across northern Arizona, following the Beale Camel Road, while the other crossed southern Arizona along the Gila Trail. During these trips, wild cows were also gathered and driven to market.

Early Spanish land grant ranches in Arizona included the Arivaca, Reventon, Sopori, and Canoa along the Santa Cruz River and the San Bernardino, in the southeast corner. These huge ranches operated well into the Mexican period before the Apache finally drove them out. Large numbers of cattle were left behind to be rounded up at a later date by the newcomers from east of the Mississippi River. Descendants of these Spanish families still reside in the southern part of Arizona today and many still practice the cowboy skills of their ancestors. There was much intermarriage between the families and on occasion when one ranchero decided to throw a party, literally hundreds of his relatives would show up. The rancheros always entertained in grand style; guests were always sent home with "their bellies full and their hearts happy."

William Kirkland was the first American to become formally engaged in ranching in Arizona. He began his long tenure in the new acquisition in 1857 at Canoa, about 20 miles north of Tubac. He and his wife were the first American couple to be married in Tucson. Kirkland also fathered the first Anglo-American child in Tucson, raised the first American flag over that city, and helped develop the first canals in Tempe. One of his daughters, Ella, married Wayne Ritter and later became one of Tempe's most illustrious citizens. Ritter School in Tempe is named in her husband's honor. Another daughter married Jim Roberts, one of Arizona's most famous lawmen.

In 1863 Kirkland and his wife and two children moved to the valley that today bears his name. During these years he was engaged in mining, and built one of the first arrastras at the famous Vulture mine, near Wickenburg. He also did some farming and ran a stage station which was noted for its cuisine. Later he moved his family to the Salt River Valley. It was said that Kirkland was such a wanderer that even his chickens knew of his wayfaring habits, for whenever he walked toward them they just naturally turned over on their backs and extended their feet into the air to be tied.

Another famous Arizonan, William S. Oury, is credited with bringing the first purebred cattle into Arizona in 1862. He ranched at Tanque Verde, just east of Tucson. He was the first "resident" cattleman in the Territory. Some historians have been highly critical of Oury over the infamous massacre of Apache that occurred at Camp Grant in 1871; however, his good deeds far exceed his bad. He was the first Anglo mayor of Tucson and one of her leading citizens until his death in 1887.

When the Apache attempted to drive the Mexicans and Americans out of Apachería during the early days of the Civil War, there were virtually only two places to seek refuge in the entire land of Apachería. One was Tucson, and the other was Pete Kitchen's ranch. Located on Potrero Creek, along the Santa Cruz River just north of present-day Nogales, Pete's ranch sat right on a main Apache plunder trail. With the Apache on one side and Sonoran bandits on the other, Kitchen's ranch was turned into a veritable fortress. In the end, neither foe could scare the indomitable rancher off. The old adobe house still stands and has most recently been used as a restaurant. Kitchen's ranch had over a thousand acres of rich bottom land, raising corn, cabbage, potatoes, fruits, melons, and most important of all, hogs. "Pete's Hams" were famous throughout the southern part of Arizona and New Mexico.

Kitchen married a Mexican girl named Doña Rosa and it has been said that she was nearly as good a shot with a rifle as he was. That must have been pretty good, as he once put a bullet through the head of a hostile Apache at a distance of more than 600 yards.

The Apache made many all-out attacks in an attempt to drive him out, including cutting the throat of his stepson and killing his foreman. They once made three major attacks within a twelve-hour period. Finally, in frustration, the Apache did something that must have chagrined Pete more than anything else they could have done. They started shooting arrows into his hogs, turning them into veritable pincushions. But still he fought back ruthlessly until finally, in 1867, they decided to ignore him. Pete Kitchen had beaten them at their own game and they knew it.

Yavapai County's King Woolsey is perhaps best remembered for his raids against the Apache in the 1860s. Woolsey served as a territorial legislator as well as a guide and military leader. He was also an important rancher and miner in the area, his ranch being along the upper Agua Fria River. At the time of his death at the early age of forty-seven, King Woolsey was one of the most influential private citizens in Arizona.

In the years following the Civil War, ranching increased in Arizona as the military forces followed the miners into the area. The miners had to eat and their teams needed feed. The government let contracts on beef and forage for both the soldiers and their new wards as the reservation system began to take effect. Ranching was good business for anyone tough enough to face not only the harsh elements, but the rustlers and Indians as well.

One man got his start in Arizona by driving a flock of turkeys over the Sierra to the Comstock mines. Henry Clay Hooker purchased the fowls in California for $1.50 apiece and headed for Nevada with his flock. On the way they approached a high cliff. Suddenly the turkeys disappeared over the edge. Fearing that his investment was lost, Hooker rushed down to find the entire "herd" in fine condition at the bottom. Reaching Nevada, he sold them for $5.00 apiece, took his grubstake, and headed for Arizona Territory.

Setting up his headquarters in the Sulphur Springs Valley, Hooker worked for improved breeding of the stock he had purchased with his turkey profits. Soon he was known throughout the Territory for his prize herds consisting of Hereford, Durham, and Shorthorn cattle. He once paid $30,000 for two Hereford bull calves, an unheard-of sum in those days. Along with cattle-raising, Hooker also had a collection of purebred stallions. A track was built and before long his racing horses were as famous as his cattle. It was said that the Chiricahua Apache in the area wouldn't steal his stallions, but preferred instead to pilfer the offspring. The Apache, being practical, would allow the colonel to handle the breeding and raising, which would give the Apache a never-ending supply of excellent bloodlines to filch whenever needed.

Colonel Hooker could also be humane. Only recently, Tom Jeffords and General Howard had set up a reservation for the Chiricahua, or "cherry-cows" as the cowboys called them, in the vicinity. Hooker boldly rode into the stronghold and informed Cochise that he and his people were welcome to come down to his ranch and butcher a beef whenever they needed, as he was certain the Apache wouldn't be wasteful. This benevolent gesture on the part of the colonel was reciprocated by the Chiricahua, for when other ranchers were suffering from deprivations and rustling, Hooker's place was virtually left alone.

Hooker's ranch, called the Sierra Bonita, or "Beautiful Mountain," was the largest ranch in Arizona at the time. Consisting of over 800 square miles, it also served as a stopover for weary travelers, as the cuisine and hospitality were excellent. It became a kind of storybook ranch of the West, with many famous personalities stopping over. Army officers and their wives from nearby Forts Grant, Bowie, and Huachuca attended many festive occasions there. Perhaps most unusual for that remote part of the Southwest was the colonel's rule that each man must wear a coat to dinner. This rule was always enforced even if the colonel had to loan the guest a coat to wear for the occasion. Two rather notorious men of the West, Wyatt Earp and Doc Holliday, spent the night at Hooker's ranch while on their vendetta following the shooting of Wyatt's two brothers, Virgil and Morgan. One particular eastern traveler didn't fare so well with the colonel's hospitality, however. Thinking the ranch to be some local hotel, he spent the evening ordering everybody around, including Hooker, and insisting that his every desire be satisfied. The next morning as he was leaving, he handed the colonel a twenty-dollar bill and was about to turn away when the rancher spun him around, tore up the twenty, and with a few blistering words that must have taken the curl out of the Easterner's topknot, sent him down the road talking to himself.

Henry Clay Hooker's "Crooked H" brand is the oldest continuous one in Arizona. The ranch is still in operation today. In 1960 Hooker was given the highest honor accorded to cowboys and ranchers of the Old West when he was inducted into the Cowboy Hall of Fame in Oklahoma.

Other ranchers followed Hooker into the southern part of Arizona during those years. Uncle Billy Fourr set up in the Dragoon Mountains in 1878, where he took the brunt of the Apache and the local rustlers. He later sued the government for damages suffered at the hands of the Apache but never collected as the government told him he needed witnesses to the crimes. Nobody ever saw an Apache steal anything.

Fourr had come to Arizona during the gold rush days of the 1860s and stayed when the gold played out. He typified the Arizona rancher perhaps more than any other man. He never killed a white man though he confronted rustlers on several occasions when threatened. He was never a lawman or public official, just a rancher trying to survive and carve out a living in a hostile land. He was a crack shot with both pistol and rifle but not a gunman. A modest man, he preferred not to talk of his exploits against hostile Apache, though once he was in a battle where twenty-seven hostiles were slain. He seemed to have no animosity toward the Apache except in battle where he was known to friend and foe alike as a fierce fighter. Bill Fourr lived to the ripe old age of ninety-four, weathering the Apache and rustler storm of his early years to see the fulfillment of a dream and the rewards that come from a life of hard work.

The most adaptable lands for ranching in the southern part of the Territory were the valleys of the Santa Cruz and the San Pedro rivers. The lower Gila was the poorest. In northern Arizona the valleys along the Little Colorado River were the richest.

The first large herd in Yuma County was brought in from California by the Redondo brothers, Jesús and José in 1874. They supplied beef to the military post and later to the Southern Pacific during construction of the rail line.

William Wingfield settled in the Verde Valley in 1879 after spending a number of years traveling in the West seeking his fortune. His cattle, carrying the "Hatchet" brand, roamed far and wide in the fertile valley. Like many other ranchers during those years, most of his cattle were sold to the government for feeding the reservations and military posts. Descendants of the Wingfield family still inhabit the Verde Valley area and have played a significant role in the history of that region. During this period cattle raising was one of the largest industries in the Territory.

Great droughts in Texas in the 1870s and 1880s brought many ranchers into the new range lands of Arizona. The most famous of these was John Slaughter. Not a large man, Slaughter didn't need size to accomplish what he set out to do. He generally carried a shotgun and didn't hesitate to use it. He settled on the old San Bernardino Land Grant in the extreme southeastern corner of Arizona.

The land was a natural for the Apache on their forays to the south and also for the bandits and rustlers along the border with Mexico. Slaughter, a man of action and not many words, was soon feared by hostile Apache and rustler alike. It's not surprising that his contemporaries drafted the diminutive Texan for the position of sheriff of Cochise County when rustling was running rampant in the 1880s. He, more than any other man, cleaned the rustler element out of southeastern Arizona.

The Aztec Land and Cattle Company, better known as the "Hashknife" because of its peculiar brand, operated on land bordering the Atlantic and Pacific railroad line near Holbrook. Starting in 1883, this eastern-owned enterprise ran some sixty thousand head of cattle on a range that ran 40 by 90 miles. Though it was owned and operated by legitimate businessmen, they were far away from the scene and the local operators working out of the headquarters at Joseph City ran things pretty much as they pleased. The country was rough and remote, thus allowing the hirelings the opportunity to go into business for themselves, and many did just that. The company was on the verge of bankruptcy in 1897 when a Scots-Irishman named Burt Mossman was made superintendent. Mossman was a man of great ability, but even he could not stem the tide. The Aztec Land and Cattle Company, like many other big outfits throughout the West in the waning years of the nineteenth century, failed three years later. Mossman moved to Bisbee, where he went into the cattle business with another of the giants of the industry, Ed Tovrea. In 1901 he became first captain of the newly organized Arizona Rangers.

Just how and when the term "rustler" came into use is subject for speculation; it's generally considered a synonym for the word "hustler." A young wrangler might be told to go out and "rustle up the horses" or "rustle up some wood" for the fire. This probably carried over onto the range when cowhands were paid by their bosses to "go out and rustle up a few mavericks." It didn't take the cowboys long to figure out that it was just as easy to "rustle up" a few for themselves. This is basically how many of the great cattle ranches in the West got their start.

Young cowboys could "steal a start" just as their bosses did in their own younger days. However, many of these same ranchers now righteously considered it to be a hanging offense.

There were many clever witticisms directed toward ranchers

whose herds seemed to be growing too rapidly. Remarks like, "His calves don't suck the right cows," or, "His cows have twins," or better yet, "His cows have a calf every washday."

To steal a cow and change the brand took a great deal of skill. Ranchers used hidden brands and other such devices to catch the unwary rustler. In order to stay healthy, the rustler had always to be one step ahead of the rancher and a bit more cunning.

The rustlers stole mostly from the large ranches, especially foreign or eastern-owned, and during the winter months. Detection and pursuit were less likely under these conditions.

Separation of the mama from the calf was not always easy but there were ways to do it. Some rustlers would put sand in the calf's eyes and drive it away from the mama. Others would cut the muscles around the eyelid, temporarily blinding the calf. When it healed, the eyelid would sag. Calves with what was called the "droops" were always a telltale sign of stolen cattle.

Since a mama cow would follow her unbranded baby to the rustlers' hideout or ranch, the thieves would sometimes place a hot coal between her toes, making her too sore to follow.

There were many reasons for failures of the large cattle outfits during the 1880s and 1890s. The days of the open range were fast drawing to a close. Overgrazing and droughts were costly. Between 1885 and 1893 it got so bad that there wasn't enough grass on the ranges for a "bird to build a nest." The Great White Disaster, or blizzard, that ravished the Great Plains took its toll in 1885–86, nearly wrecking the industry. Homesteaders were coming in and fencing off the land with barbed wire. Following the surrender of Geronimo and the shipment of Apache to Florida, along with the reduction of troops, there was a decline in the market. The open range became a thing of the past. New methods of raising beef cattle had to be tried. The day of the feed lot was not far off.

Much to the chagrin of cattlemen, the sheep business seemed to prosper through good times and bad, as the market didn't seem to fluctuate as violently as did the cattle market. Sheep were not new to Arizona as the missionaries had brought flocks in early in the seventeenth century. Also, the Navajo had stolen tens of thousands of the woollies from the Spanish along the Rio Grande and driven them up on the plateau.

The first white man to run sheep in Arizona was Juan Candeleria in 1866. He was located near the present site of Concho. Candeleria was mostly interested in raising sheep for their wool rather than the meat. In 1868 Isadore Solomon took the first flock into what later became Graham County. That same year, James Baker of California brought a herd into Yavapai County. A severe drought in California in 1873–74 brought in the Daggs brothers. Settling near Flagstaff, they had one of the largest sheep-raising operations in Arizona, running some fifty thousand head. Mormons near Tuba City and Sunset City also got into the act.

The sheep business took a major step forward with the coming of the railroads to the Territory.

By the 1880s, competition between cattlemen and sheepmen for land grew. Stories of battles between the two in the Old West are legend in both book form and Hollywood and need not be retold in this chronicle. However violent the times were, common foes such as conservationists and homesteaders brought them closer together, as did the dispelling of the old myth that cattle and sheep would not graze together. It wasn't long before dyed-in-the-wool (no pun intended) cattlemen were raising flocks of sheep of their own.

The life of the farmer has never been the subject of romantic lore as was that of the rancher. A man in overalls slopping the hogs just never seemed to fit the image of a Gary Cooper or John Wayne. By and large, all ranchers had to raise their own feed with the closing of the open ranges. Ridicule the farmer as he might, the rancher needed the farmer. Either he bought feed from him, or, as in some cases, the rancher would build a home for the farmer and hire him to raise feed for the livestock, thus saving himself from the humiliating experience of being classified a farmer. Much of the dry cowboy humor today is directed toward the poor, beleaguered sodbuster. Some of it is well deserved and some of it is not.

Though the Indians had been farming by irrigation for thousands of years in the river valleys of Arizona, with the exception of the Mormon colonists irrigation was a new experience to most of the early Anglo-Americans in the area. Because of the limited amount of water available in the arid land laws had to be enacted to provide the most efficient use of the precious commodity. The Spanish laws concerning prior appropriation were used as a model for the new ones. These laws will be discussed in detail later.

The founding of Phoenix in 1867 was directly related to irrigation and farming. The high prices of food in the Territory coupled with a spirit of enterprise led Jack Swilling, a colorful soldier, miner, and entrepreneur, along with John Y. T. Smith, a farmer and sutler at Fort McDowell, to begin the task of cleaning out the old Hohokam canals.

Swilling convinced others, including Henry Wickenburg and L. J. F. Jaeger, to invest in his new enterprise, the Swilling Irrigation Canal Company. The first man actually to establish a farm in the valley was Frenchy Sawyer, in 1868. A small plaque commemorates that early venture at its location on what is now Twenty-fourth and Washington streets in Phoenix.

Phoenix continued to grow and prosper. On October 15, 1870, its citizens got together and selected an official townsite. City lots were expensive. Some sold for over a hundred dollars apiece, but those who bought and held on made a fortune in real estate. In 1889 the capital was moved from Prescott to Phoenix, where it has since remained.

In 1933 William Arthur Rogers of Tempe began operating the first pickup hay balers in the Salt River Valley. He ran two crews of six men each. One shift worked days and the other nights. John Deere and Company sold him the equipment and provided all replacement parts free of charge as it was an experimental machine and Rogers was its first promoter. In those pioneer days of farm machinery it took a crew of a half-dozen men to bale hay. Today, the same task can be performed in a fraction of the time by one man operating the baler.

In the early days of Spanish conquest, all the land conquered by Spain belonged to the king personally and he doled it out as he saw fit in what was termed land grants. These grants were immense in size and notorious for their ill-defined boundaries. During the Mexican period these policies were continued. As a part of the agreements between the United States and Mexico in the Treaty of Guadalupe Hidalgo and the Gadsden Purchase, the Americans agreed to recognize these grants. Because of the turbulent times that followed, nothing much was done about these claims until 1870. There were obviously many claimants and many cases of fraud and attempted fraud by heirs and would-be heirs. However, there were several legitimate claims recognized, including the Babacomori, Canoa, Boquillas, San Bernardino, Sonoita, and the Baca Float. The latter was a rather curious grant in that it involved an exchange with the federal government. In 1860, Luis María Baca traded some land near Las Vegas, New Mexico, to the government for five separate parcels, two of which were in Arizona. These grants were to be 100,000 acres each and were supposed to be non-mineral and unsettled. The two areas Baca selected in Arizona were near Prescott and in the southern portion near the Santa Cruz River. The latter included Tubac, Tumacacori, and Calabazas, and contained both minerals and settlers. The residents took their case all the way to the Supreme Court, where in 1914 the claim was upheld and the settlers were removed. The northern grant, called the Baca Float #5, was later purchased by William C. Greene, rancher and mining magnate.

Modern-day land swindles seem minuscule when compared to the grand scheme nearly carried off by one James Addison Reavis in the 1880s. Reavis, a streetcar conductor in St. Louis, was a man of many talents, one of which was forgery. Feeling that his skills were wasted on such perfunctory duties as running a streetcar, Reavis plotted to lay claim to nearly 11 million acres of land in a region that stretched from Silver City, New Mexico, on the east, to a point west of Phoenix, Arizona. The claim included some of the richest agricultural and mineral lands in Arizona.

Amazingly enough, he nearly carried it off. Traveling from Mexico to Spain, Reavis exchanged his forged documents for genuine ones in the archives. He left no stone unturned. Taking as a wife a young mixed-blood Indian girl of questionable heritage, Reavis changed her name to Sophia Loreta Micaela de Peralta de la Córdoba. Reavis then coached her on manners and other finer points of Spanish aristocracy. Filing for the land, Reavis produced masses of documents, wills, and papers supporting his claim. The claim was convincing enough and soon they were collecting royalties from such "squatters" as the Silver King mine and the Southern Pacific Railroad. The two would-be land barons occupied beautiful homes in St. Louis, Chihuahua, Washington, and just east of Casa Grande, Arizona, where Reavis made his headquarters. Royalties from the scheme were netting him nearly $100,000 a year.

It was too good to last, for the baron had made a minor, but fatal, error which led to his undoing. A newspaper printer noted that the print on one of Reavis' documents was dated 1784, yet the type face used was not invented until 1875. A Wisconsin watermark was found on another of the "ancient" documents. After years of investigation by land agents headed by Pete Brady of Florence, Reavis was brought to justice. In evidence of the fact that the world loves a thief who thinks on a grand scale, the Baron of Arizona served a prison term of less than two years.

One of the most unusual yet lucrative types of farming came into fashion around the turn of the century in the Salt River Valley. With a head-'em-up, move-'em-out, and a yippie-ti-yi-yay, cowboys on horseback were actually driving herds of ostriches.

It wasn't that the cattle business had fallen off so much, but rather that women's fashions of the time dictated the wearing of ostrich feathers on the hat or dress. Those die-hard cattlemen who originally scoffed at such an enterprise no doubt reconsidered when it was reported in 1910 that 4,023 ostriches were sheared of their feathers and the crop was valued at $1,365,000. Ostrich farms became as common as convenience markets are today.

The first ostriches arrived in Phoenix sometime around 1885. Prior to shipment from California, their bald heads were covered with hoods to discourage escape and perhaps to prevent sunburn. Of the two adults and eleven chicks that started the trip, only one adult and one chick survived the crossing of the desert. Luckily, one was a male and the other a female, and soon the eggs began to hatch. One man paid more then $16,000 for twenty-one pairs of breeding birds. Two years later he had realized some $31,000 from the sale of young chicks. Feathers were selling for around $75 a pound. The ostriches required less water than did other types of livestock and whereas full-grown cattle ate from 30 to 60 pounds of alfalfa a day, an ostrich ate only 4 pounds. Ostriches also sold for more than cattle—a young chick cost $100 and a four-year-old bird went for around $800. An adult ostrich might weigh from 300 to 400 pounds and stand 8 feet tall. They could run up to 60 miles per hour, taking 25-foot strides. They could leap over a 6-foot fence with little or no effort. The ostrich had about the same disregard for fences as he did for his valuable eggs, which he sometimes stepped on or carelessly kicked around. Since the success of the operation depended on the number of ostriches, the eggs were prized. Hired hands with long shepherd-like staffs gathered the eggs for incubation. The ostrich also provided the farmers with eggs and meat as well. One ostrich egg was equivalent to some thirty-three hen eggs. The eggs were good, but the meat was rather coarse and stringy. Equipped with a brain the size of a small pea, the ostrich must be placed somewhere near the bottom of the scale of vertebrae intelligence.

The industry was not without its hazardous moments. In 1914 a man and his wife suffered fatal injuries when their horse and buggy collided with a herd of stampeding ostriches.

It was women's styles that created the boom and she that giveth can also taketh away. Women's fashion was as fickle then as it is today, and in 1916 feathers were no longer in, and the business boom died as quickly as it had started.

With the market closed, most of the ostriches were ground up, feathers and all, into fertilizer. However, like the camel of an earlier era, some were released to roam free in the desert—their fate prolonged somewhat.

Gazing from the top of a modern building on Central Avenue in downtown Phoenix today, one can't help but reflect on how far the city has come in the past forty years or so. However, from time to time a legacy from the past comes forth to remind us that maybe we are closer to the near-distant past than we sometimes think. This became apparent recently when a huge hole suddenly appeared in the middle of a downtown high school football field. It seems that the 18-foot hole had been used as a "dressing" hole for animal refuse many years before when the land on north Central had been a cattle ranch. Later, the hole was covered with wooden planks and 4 feet of dirt. It remained in that state until nature finally took its course. Fortunately, the incident occurred during a time when a game was not in progress.

The rugged human spirit of the old-time cowboys is reincarnated over and over again in the cattlemen of today. There is more than enough material to fill a volume on the deeds and mischievous misdeeds of today's cowboy. However, a couple of brief anecdotes will be related herein just to give the reader an idea of the inimitable character of the cowboy.

Located in Phoenix is an eating establishment decorated along the lines of an old English manor. Befitting the atmosphere of the restaurant, the management saw fit to dress the parking attendant in a suit of armor. His duty was to direct traffic in and out of the establishment on horseback. Our hero, whose name shall remain anonymous, had just come down from Springerville and after a busy season of keeping the cattle company was in a festive mood. Following an evening of joyous partaking of the local beverages, he walked out into the parking lot, where he chanced to encounter the armor-clad attendant on horseback, facing the opposite direction.

The temptation was too great. He gave a run and bolted upon the back of the animal, causing immediate stupefaction to both horse and knight. The horse did a natural thing under the circumstances. He reared up and pitched, unloading both his passengers, one of which landed on the pavement with a resounding clatter. The management, failing to see the humor in the event, recommended several rival establishments that the pernicious adventurer might frequent the next time he visited Phoenix.

Until a few years ago, one of the largest ranches in northern Arizona was operated by Frank and Gene Campbell, headquartering at Ash Fork. They were the first cattlemen to bring the Charolais cattle from France into that part of the state. Just how much the two men were worth was anybody's guess. Unpretentious, they never wore anything but Levis, Stetson hats, and work shirts. A stranger could easily mistake either one for a saddle bum or some poor ranch hand. Once on a cattle-buying trip to the East, dressed in their customary fashion, they were arrested for vagrancy by the Chicago Police Department.

Frank usually drove an old pickup; even his new pickups looked old after a few weeks of driving over those makeshift roads south of Ash Fork and Seligman. His wife preferred riding in the family Cadillac and the comforts of an elegant home to the rigors of dusty pickup trucks and Spartan-like ranch life and she always stayed in town. One day the two were returning from a business trip to Prescott in the Cadillac when Frank chanced to see one of his sheep outside the fence and running along the highway. Stopping the car, he got out and chased it down. Picking it up he carried it over to the car and started to deposit it in the back seat. "Wait a minute," his wife admonished. "He can't ride in here." "He can if he wants to," Frank replied indignantly. "He helped pay for it."

. . . and the sheep rode into town sitting proudly in the back seat of a new Cadillac.

In closing, it somehow seems apropos to present a prayer attributed to rancher Daniel Houston Ming as he spoke before a group at a cattlemen's convention during one of Arizona's frequent prolonged dry spells. His plea epitomizes the salt-of-the-earth character of a man who has spent a lifetime in the out-of-doors close to nature, a proud man reluctantly asking a higher being for a little help.

"O Lord, I'm about to round you up for a good plain talk. Now,

Lord, I ain't like these fellows who come bothering you every day. This is the first time I ever tackled you for anything and if you will only grant this I promise I'll never bother you again. We want rain, good Lord, and we want it bad, and we ask you to send us some. But if you can't or don't want to send us any, for Christ's sake don't make it rain up around Hooker's or Leitch's ranges, but treat us all alike. Amen."

THE PLEASANT VALLEY FEUD

FEUDS BETWEEN FAMILIES or groups were not uncommon in the West. They started usually for a variety of reasons, occasionally some of the combatants not even knowing the true reasons for hostility. Modern-day grass-roots historians can still encounter difficulties when trying to interview the descendants of some early-day feuders. Perhaps one of the most distinguishing characteristics of all feuds is that no one is allowed to declare neutrality. One has to join one side or the other. Another option, of course, is simply to move on to newer, more peaceful surroundings.

One of the most notorious of these feuds occurred in Arizona around the Mogollon Rim country near where the town of Young stands today. Known as the Pleasant Valley War, it lasted from 1887 until 1892.

There have been numerous versions as to how the feud began, although no one knows for certain. One theory proposes the involvement of a woman. The theory does lend some credibility as most gun fights and feuds both then and now seem to involve the fairer of the sexes in one way or another. Another version has it that two of the families involved, the Grahams and the Tewksburys, were both stealing cattle from a rancher in the valley named Jim Stinson. Actually the entire area was so remote that it was a natural haven for every horse thief and rustler in the Southwest. On the plateau just to the north was the famous eastern-owned Hashknife outfit. A young cowboy, intent on starting out in the cattle business, merely had to rustle a few head from that big outfit on the Rim and drive them down into Pleasant Valley.

The Grahams and the Tewksburys apparently had some falling out, perhaps over the dividing of the spoils. For whatever the reason, there was bad blood between the two families and the Daggs brothers, sheepmen from Flagstaff, seized upon the opportunity to secure more range land for their sheep. A deal was made with the Tewksburys to allow the sheep to be driven over the Rim and into Pleasant Valley. In return for giving protection, the Tewksburys would share in the profits from the venture.

The first blood was shed in February 1887, when a Navajo sheepherder was murdered on the northern edge of the valley. Shortly thereafter, the sheep were removed from the area, although open hostilities had already begun.

As usual in these feuds, there were no neutral parties. When questioned by one faction or another it was fruitless to attempt to stay out of the fracas. For one to claim neutrality was tantamount to saying you favored the other side and that could be fatal. Innocent bystanders found it safer to pack up and move from the valley. Others, looking for action or an excuse for violence, went into the area and sided with one or the other. The first to die from the immediate families was Billy Graham, twenty-two-year-old half brother to the leader of the Graham clan. Shortly thereafter, Andy Cooper and the Blevins Gang, along with several Graham men, surprised a number of Tewksburys and besieged them inside a ranch house. John Tewksbury and Bill Jacobs had been shot and killed during the first moments of the battle and lay some distance from the house. During the melee some hogs began devouring the bodies of the two men. Local legend has it that when the men refused to stop shooting long enough to allow the party inside to drive the hogs away, Mrs. John Tewksbury grabbed a shovel and walked outside. The action stopped momentarily and the stillness of the September day was broken only by the crying of a baby inside the cabin. She scattered the swine with her shovel and then buried her husband and Jacobs. Finishing her unpleasant task, she returned to the confines of the cabin and her baby. Luckily for the Tewksburys, a posse from Payson arrived in time to save the rest of them. The Blevins Gang rode to their lair in Holbrook, a move which would prove fateful to members of the gang, and set the stage for one of the West's greatest gun fights.

When the new sheriff of Apache County first rode into Holbrook, he immediately found himself the subject of somewhat restrained amusement on the part of the local citizenry, for he was a most unusual sight for those parts. Holbrook was a tough little cow town in the 1880s and not used to seeing lawmen such as Commodore Perry Owens. A handsome man, he wore his hair long, reaching past his shoulders, and he wore his pistol with the butt forward. This ostentatious style might have been popular in towns such as Dodge City or in the dime novels of Ned Buntline, but Holbrook's residents considered Owens a bit of a dandy. His arrival coincided with the arrival of the Cooper-Blevins Gang and the locals anxiously awaited the inevitable meeting.

Owens might have been unaware of the shootings in Pleasant Valley when he arrived in Holbrook, but he was carrying a warrant for the arrest of Andy Cooper, or as he was sometimes called, Andy Blevins. The warrant was for horse-stealing rather than murder.

Arriving at the Blevins home on North Central Avenue, Owens stepped up to the door and asked to speak to Andy Cooper. Inside the house were John Blevins, Mose Roberts, Sam Houston Blevins, a youth of about sixteen, Cooper, and four women. After a short discussion between Owens and Cooper concerning the warrant, both men reached for their guns and fired. Cooper missed with his shot and reeled back into the house from the impact of Owens' Winchester. Next it was John Blevins' turn. He came around the side of the house and fired at the long-haired sheriff, but in his rush to fire, the shot went wild, hitting Cooper's horse. Owens spun around and fired at Blevins, wounding him. The lawman then moved off the porch and into the street for a better view. The next man who came out firing was Mose Roberts. Another shot from Owens' rifle mortally wounded Roberts. The last male in the house was young Sam Houston Blevins. He wrestled the pistol from the dying Cooper's hand and following a brief struggle with his mother he leaped through the door. Owens cut him down with a bullet in the heart. In less than sixty seconds it was all over. Three men were dead and one seriously wounded. In almost unbelievable fashion, the quiet-spoken sheriff had quickly dispatched the entire Blevins Gang, and even more miraculous, he had not even received a scratch. Here on a street in Holbrook, in one crowded minute, a man alone had seen fit to do his duty against seemingly impossible odds and had come away unscathed.

There are those today who praise Owens for his courageous stand and there are others who say he was a hired killer, hiding behind a badge. It was said he was hired by the Daggs brothers and other political nabobs in northern Arizona to open up the area for the sheep ranchers. Whichever is true, it cannot be denied that Owens made perhaps the most remarkable one-man stand in the history of the western gunfighters.

Recently, a researcher was trying to locate the graves of the Blevins Gang in the Holbrook cemetery. After many fruitless hours of search, it was learned that a road had been constructed right over the graves of the outlaws, rendering them impossible to relocate. Even in death some men find no peace. The old Blevins home is still standing. Today it houses the Historical Society of Holbrook.

In Pleasant Valley, the feud continued, sometimes with most tragic results for innocent parties who just happened to be passing through and found themselves caught in the middle. In August 1888 three men, Jim Scott, Jim Stott, and Billy Wilson, were making camp when a party of Tewksbury partisans, led by Jim Houck, a known assassin, rode up, conversed with them, drank their coffee, and then lynched the trio. None of the three were involved in any way with the feud.

The death toll from the five-year vendetta has been estimated at from seventeen to fifty. The correct figure is probably somewhere in between. The last of the Grahams, Tom, finally decided to call it quits. Following much persuasion by his young bride, Anne, he left his cattle with S. W. Young in 1889 and moved to Tempe, where he took up farming. Tom Graham never packed a gun from that time forth. For three years there was no violence. The vendetta seemed ended. On an August day in 1892, Tom Graham was driving a team of horses near the Twin Buttes, south of Tempe, when two men ambushed him. He was carried to the home of W. T. "Bud" Cummings where he soon expired, but not before identifying his assailants as Ed Tewksbury and John Rhodes.

There had been other witnesses to the murder also. Betty Gregg, the daughter of Tempe's first medical doctor, John Gregg, and friends Ed and Molly Cummings, testified later they saw the men waiting in ambush.

The trial that followed was the most sensational in the history of the Territory up to that time. Ed Tewksbury and John Rhodes were identified as the killers and brought to trial for murder. The testimony of the children tended to be discounted by some of the jurors because of their youth. However, many years later Betty Gregg, then Mrs. Emmett Adams, told this author's father in Tempe that one of the men was Ed Tewksbury. "I'm just as sure of that today as I was the day it happened."

Ed Tewksbury was found guilty although he was defended by a group of high-powered attorneys who got him a second trial on a legal technicality. In the second trial, Tewksbury gained his release. The man who supposedly pulled the trigger, John Rhodes, was not held over for trial. Rhodes had maintained that he was somewhere else when the murder was committed. In a surprise move on the part of the judge, W. O. Huson, who apparently believed his alibi, the Tewksbury man was released.

There was a large public outcry with threats of lynching but the most sensational incident occurred when Anne Graham, Tom's twenty-two-year-old widow, walked up behind Rhodes in the courtroom during the hearing and attempted to fire a pistol point-blank into the back of his head. The weapon failed to fire, preventing further bloodshed. Tewksbury later went to Globe, where he worked for a time as deputy sheriff. However, the ghost of the past eventually caught up with him too, for he died a few years later from tuberculosis. He had contracted the disease while in jail awaiting trial for the killing of Tom Graham.

One of the most interesting characters to emerge from the Pleasant Valley War was Jim Roberts. Considered to be the best man with a gun on both sides, Roberts found himself an unwilling participant at first. A taciturn man by nature, and content just to mind his own business, which was the breeding of fine horses, Roberts avoided the conflict as long as he could. One day he found some of his horses missing, including a prize stud. He tracked the thieves down and killed them. The three men were a part of the Graham faction, and in retaliation, they burned his house. That was probably the most foolish blunder committed by the Grahams in the entire war, for Roberts proved to be a most deadly adversary. Just how many of the Graham casualties Roberts was responsible for will never be known, for such was his reticence to discuss such matters that even his closest associates in later years never knew that he had participated in the conflict.

In 1889 Roberts took a job as deputy sheriff under the famed Buckey O'Neill, then sheriff of Yavapai County. Two years later, he married Jenny Kirkland, the daughter of Arizona pioneer William H. Kirkland. Bill Roberts, one of his sons, told this author that his father never talked at all of the early days. Concerning his life prior to arriving in Arizona, Mrs. Roberts only knew that her husband had "come from Missouri." Jim Roberts, according to his son, never carried his pistol in a holster as did many old-time gunfighters, but packed it in his hip pocket.

During his tenure as deputy at Jerome, Roberts became a legend in the community. When two miscreants, Sid Chew and Dud Crocker, killed Deputy Joe Hawkins and another man, Roberts tracked them down and in a gun fight shot and killed both men. In 1904 he took a job as deputy sheriff in Cochise County, a position he held for the next several years. He returned to the Verde Valley in 1927, this time as a deputy for the United Verde mine, stationed at Clarkdale. Tom Rynning, of Arizona Rangers fame, had held the same job before him.

By now Jim Roberts was seventy years old and known affectionately as "Uncle Jim" to his admirers and friends. Still he never discussed his past, even with his sons, who were now grown. He claimed to know the real reason for the Graham-Tewksbury feud and said everybody else had it wrong, yet he never revealed this information. His reputation as a gunfighter attracted many of the curious, but old Jim refused to give them a show. Not a few went away disappointed. The last of the old-time shooting sheriffs remained his quiet, calm self. He wouldn't even quick-draw for them. Some of the younger ones even began to doubt the stories of this living legend who walked the streets of Clarkdale with a nickel-plated .45 in his hip pocket. However, an incident in the spring of 1928 erased forever any questions that the dubious might raise. Fate had decreed that old Jim would once again be given a chance to demonstrate his courage in a gun fight.

On the morning of June 21, 1928, Earl Nelson and Willard Forrester, two notorious Oklahoma bank robbers, held up the Bank of Arizona in Clarkdale, taking some $40,000 in the heist. The two men ran outside the bank and jumped into the getaway car just as Roberts arrived on the scene. As the car sped away, the old lawman pulled his gun and fired two shots at the speeding automobile. The driver jerked and the car careened into a schoolyard, coming to rest against a guy wire leading to a power pole. The driver, Forrester, was dead with a bullet in his neck. The other man, Nelson, wisely surrendered without a fight.

Jim Roberts was late coming home for lunch that day and the biscuits had gotten cold. When he walked in the door his wife asked what kept him. True to character clear up to the end, old Jim just looked at her and replied in his calm manner, "Oh, nothing. There was just a little trouble downtown." That was all he ever said to her concerning the incident.

The "last fighting man" in the Pleasant Valley War died with his boots on, while walking the beat in Clarkdale on January 8, 1934.

The annals of Arizona lawmen are full of daring exploits and well-known personalities. Cochise County had John Slaughter and Harry Wheeler. Yavapai County had Buckey O'Neill, George Ruffner, and Roberts. Apache County had Commodore Perry Owens and Maricopa boasted the legendary Henry Garfias and Carl Hayden. There were many others, mostly forgotten except by local county historians. Perhaps one day the state will see fit to erect a hall to commemorate those men who pinned a badge on and swore to uphold the law. Not a few paid the ultimate price in the performance of duty for a sometimes apathetic citizenry.

FROM WHICH LEGENDS ARE MADE

TRAIL DUST HAS SETTLED and false-front saloons are seen only on movie sets or in tourist towns, but the legend of the gunfighter lives on. Was he really a defender of the innocent and helpless and a noble protector of decency, or was he some purveyor of evil, a gun-toting rogue who used his prowess with a Colt revolver or sawed-off shotgun for personal gain? They were a product of a tumultuous period unparalleled in American history. The violent and lawless years following the Civil War spawned an era of lust for riches, land, and power. It was a time of range wars, feuds, and man killings. The result was a new figure in American folklore—the gunfighter.

Some men such as Wyatt Earp and Bat Masterson lived to ripe, respectable old ages and were able to provide later generations with firsthand accounts of "how it really was," although one might question the memories of a man recalling his exploits some fifty years earlier. This is especially true if all other witnesses to the affair have long since departed.

As the West became settled the era of the gunfighter passed into romantic nostalgia and into the hands of novelists such as Owen Wister and Zane Grey, whose heroes came to resemble the mythical knights of old. Early wild West shows such as Buffalo Bill Cody's made a full-scale production of what was the new stereotype of the West and took it around the world, thus giving the western gunfighter a universal appeal. Edwin S. Porter's *The Great Train Robbery*, filmed in the wilds of New Jersey in 1903, thrilled audiences, who demanded more of the same. Ironically, during this time, trains were actually being robbed in the West and men were still dying in gun fights. The public loved it and thus launched the movie careers of dozens of real and pseudo cowboys, including William S. Hart, Tom Mix, Gary Cooper, and John Wayne. Through the medium of motion pictures the world was given its grand image of the American West.

Certainly one of the most controversial characters ever to appear in Arizona was Wyatt Berry Stapp Earp. Born in Monmouth, Illinois, in 1848, he went west to California with his family in 1864. During the next few years he occupied his time with an assorted number of jobs including buffalo-hunting, freighting, Indian-fighting, and professional gambling. Not all of Wyatt's activities were on the side of the law. He has been accused of being, at one time or another, a bunko artist, a horse thief, a con man, a bigamist, and a pimp. On the other side of the ledger, he was also a church deacon, a miner, and a lawman. Earp is not an easy man to stereotype. His checkered career was not at all unlike many others of his breed. The picture-book image of a western gunfighter, Wyatt was tall, blond, and strikingly handsome; he sported a heavy, drooping mustache that nearly hid his mouth. He dressed well, as befitting a man of his profession. Wyatt had few friends but the ones he had were extremely loyal. Rarely showing a hint of emotion, he spoke in a low tone, and his cold, deep-set blue-gray eyes struck fear into his enemies and would-be enemies. His outstanding virtue was his courage, something even his modern-day detractors cannot deny.

Wyatt was not the only member of the Earp clan to come to Arizona during those turbulent years in search of fortune. His older brothers James and Virgil as well as younger siblings Morgan and Warren all made their appearance in Tombstone. James had been crippled during the Civil War and did not take an active part in the escapades of his younger brothers, and Warren, in his early twenties, did not play a prominent role in the forthcoming feud.

While doubling as a police officer and gambler in Dodge City in 1876, Wyatt made the acquaintance of such notables as Luke Short and Bat Masterson. Not long afterward he struck up a lasting friendship with a sardonic, tubercular dentist turned gambler named John Holliday.

By 1880 Wyatt, Doc, Bat, and Luke, along with Wyatt's wife Mattie and Doc's girl, Kate Fisher, were all in Arizona to seek their fortunes. Stopping at Prescott, they picked up Wyatt's older brother, Virgil, who had been able to secure a commission as deputy U.S. marshal at Tucson. Soon the entire gang headed for Tombstone with visions of grand schemes.

For a time, Wyatt worked as a deputy for Pima County sheriff Charles Shibell, but for some reason he was dismissed in favor of Johnny Behan. A long-lasting hatred between Wyatt and Johnny Behan ensued over this affair. Wyatt took another job, this time as a shotgun rider for Wells Fargo and for the next few months life was dull and unprofitable.

Being a law-enforcement officer could be quite lucrative in those days when the citizenry was more tolerant of certain extracurricular activities. For example, the boys received "protection" money from saloon owners as well as a percentage of the money from the "soiled doves." Even the sheriff of the county could increase his salary by several thousand dollars a year by collecting taxes, a percentage of which he received for services rendered. However, tax collecting could be dangerous work, especially in towns like Galeyville which were run by an outlaw element. Perhaps it was the belief that some semblance of law is better than no law at all that made the people accept lawmen with questionable integrity. Generally speaking, however, the tough mining and cow towns of Arizona found it necessary to hire law-enforcement officers tough enough to get the job done. The moral standards of these "enforcers" were of secondary importance.

While the Dodge City Gang operated in town, another group known locally as the "cowboys" were rustling cattle. The Indian reservations, military posts, and mining camps were a lucrative market for beef. The close proximity to the Mexican border and the lack of law and order made southeastern Arizona a haven for outlaws, smugglers, and rustlers. The leader of this element was Newman H. "Old Man" Clanton, who with his sons, Ike, Phin, and Billy, ran a ranch in the San Pedro Valley. At a nearby ranch were the McLaury brothers, Tom and Frank. These two ranches served as strongholds for a gang of more than a score of border ruffians. Serving as chief lieutenant for Old Man Clanton, and later succeeding the old chieftain, was William Brocius Graham, better known as Curly Bill Brocius. Another member was Johnny Ringo, reputed to be a cousin to the Younger brothers of Missouri.

This gang of rogues feared nobody, even bragging about its escapades in public places and stealing cattle in the middle of the day from the local ranches. When things got quiet on the U.S. side they merely went south and stole from the vast herds of Mexican cattle or the silver-laden pack trains from the mines, killing indiscriminately as they went. It was such an incident that led to the demise of Old Man Clanton in the summer of 1881.

A band of Mexican smugglers was making its way through the Peloncillo Mountains in the extreme southeastern corner of Arizona when it was ambushed by Curly Bill, the Clantons, and some others. Some $4,000 in silver bullion, coin, and other valuables was taken and the bodies were left where they fell. To this day the place is called Skeleton Canyon, and is better remembered as the place where Geronimo made his final surrender in 1886.

The smuggler-train massacre occurred early in August 1881. A few days later, while driving some cattle through Guadalupe Canyon, some vindictive Mexicans took revenge, killing five "cowboys," including Old Man Clanton.

With this nefarious activity going on outside of Tombstone, combined with the caliber of men running the town itself, the inevitable clash between the Earps and Clantons was not long in coming.

Trouble between the two had actually begun nearly a year before the killing of Old Man Clanton, when Curly Bill and some of his friends had come to town in search of fun and frolic. City Marshal Fred White asked the Earps to accompany him while he made his rounds. Curly Bill, feeling the effects of the local spirits, was discharging his pistol into the ceiling of one of the local establishments when Marshal White approached and attempted to take his gun. In the struggle that followed, the weapon discharged, mortally wounding White. Wyatt pulled his gun and conked Curly Bill on the head, sending him to the floor, knocked senseless. Brocius was saved from justice when Marshal White, just before he died, exonerated the rustler, saying that the shooting was an accident. Needless to say, Brocius left town with bad feelings, both in his head and in his heart, for the Earps.

Virgil Earp was appointed to fill the vacancy temporarily but later lost the post in a special election. By now, all five brothers, Virgil, Wyatt, Morgan, James, and Warren, along with cohorts Doc,

Luke, and Bat, were working on Allen Street. The locals called them the Dodge City Gang, an obvious improvement over the moniker given them by the drovers up from Texas in their Kansas cow town days, the Fighting Pimps.

By now, even the political parties were beginning to get into the act, with each side accusing the other of cavorting with the outlaw element. Even the newspapers couldn't agree on the matter. The Republican *Epitaph* and its editor, John Clum, had a great admiration for the Earp brothers, while the Democratic *Daily Nugget* saw it the other way around.

The Earps received good news in their quest for power when on January 4, 1881, their admirer Clum was elected mayor. With a Republican mayor and Republican Governor John C. Frémont in the territorial capital, it looked like a sure bet that Wyatt would be appointed sheriff of the newly created Cochise County. What the Earps didn't count on was that the Territory itself was still staunchly Democratic and Democrat John Behan received the appointment over Wyatt. To Wyatt this meant a loss of some $30,000 to $40,000 a year in tax collections and fees. Understandably, Wyatt was bitter and a lot of his ill feelings were channeled toward the new sheriff.

More events occurred in the next few months which would bring the two sides closer to open conflict. On March 15, 1881, the Benson stagecoach, carrying some $25,000 in silver, was held up. The driver, Bud Philpot, and a passenger were killed. However, Bob Paul grabbed the reins and foiled the attempted heist by giving the robbers the slip. Ironically, Paul and Philpot had changed positions on the coach just a few minutes earlier. A posse consisting of the Earp brothers, Masterson, and others went in pursuit. Following a trail to a nearby ranch they captured Luther King, who also implicated Jim Crane, Harry Head, and Bill Leonard in the killings. King was taken to Behan's jail, from where, under rather unusual circumstances, he soon escaped. Rumors were now being spread that the man who actually did the killing was none other than Doc Holliday, and that Wyatt had planned the whole thing. When questioned about the matter, the erstwhile dentist remarked wryly that if he had been the culprit it wouldn't have been merely an attempted robbery. However, Doc was out of town at the time of the incident and was seen by at least one reliable witness, John Slaughter.

The Earp brothers now suffered a major loss to their ranks when Luke Short and Bat Masterson suddenly decided to leave town. The breaks evened somewhat when City Marshal Ben Sippy left town suddenly and Mayor Clum and his "Law and Order" Council appointed Virgil to the vacant post. Wyatt, desperately trying to put an end to rumors implicating the Earps in the attempted holdup, approached Ike Clanton, the most loquacious of the opposing faction, and offered a deal. If Ike would set up the wanted men for the Earps, they would see to it that he would receive the $2,000 per-man reward offered by Wells Fargo. Ike later testified indignantly that he refused the offer, which is understandable, in view of the fact that to have testified any other way would have been tantamount to committing suicide, feelings being as they were.

The proposed setup plan, if there was one, never got a chance to be implemented, for it was learned that Bill Leonard and Harry Head had been killed during a robbery in Eureka, New Mexico.

Doc and his girl friend, Big-Nosed Kate, had been quarreling of late and Sheriff Behan seized on the opportunity to get Kate drunk and question her. Kate was mad enough at Doc to tell Behan just about anything he wanted to hear, including Doc's role in the attempted stagecoach heist. When the interrogation was finished, a warrant was issued for Doc's arrest. When Kate sobered up enough to realize what she had done, she wasted no time in leaving town. Wyatt testified at the hearing on behalf of his friend and Judge Wells Spicer released Doc Holliday on bond.

The town's two newspapers followed the chain of events with great interest, the Democratic *Daily Nugget* giving its version with a propensity toward one faction and John Clum's *Epitaph*, staunchly Republican, favoring the other.

The rivalry between Wyatt and Johnny Behan began to take on new dimensions. Behan had been courting for some time a young actress named Josephine Marcus and Wyatt suddenly took a shine to her and began escorting her around some of the finest restaurants, much to the chagrin of the sheriff.

It was during this same period that Old Man Clanton was killed and several more robberies had taken place. Somewhat suspiciously, the Earps had been making periodic trips to visit their parents in Colton, California. Once again rumors were being spread implying, perhaps, that the brothers were taking more to California than just their good will.

On September 8, 1881, the Bisbee stage was robbed and Frank Stilwell, along with Pete Spence, was arrested. Again accusations and counteraccusations were leveled by the Clantons and Earps as to who actually planned the robbery.

On October 25, the night before the confrontation, several of the boys got into a poker game. Participants included Virgil Earp, Ike Clanton, Doc Holliday, and John Behan. An argument took place between Virgil and Ike; this was not unusual, for Ike was constantly arguing with somebody. That same morning he had had an unpleasant encounter with Doc in a restaurant.

The following day, Ike and Virgil met again. This time, Virgil conked Ike over the head with his pistol and hauled him off to court, where Clanton was fined for violation of the local gun ordinance. That same morning Wyatt had performed a similar feat on Tom McLaury for allowing his horse on the sidewalk. The two men exchanged unpleasantries, McLaury finally taking his horse over to the O.K. Corral. It was now one-thirty in the afternoon and tempers were getting hot.

Sheriff Behan had a reputation for being friendly with some of the rustlers, and when the fracas began he made a halfhearted attempt to disarm the cowboys. When the Earps and Doc Holliday learned of this they stepped out on Fremont Street and faced the out-of-towners. It's not likely that any of the participants had any inkling of the historic significance of this meeting, at least from the standpoint of the movie industry, for what was to follow became the fodder for countless movie and television scripts.

There have been many versions describing the action down through the years, depending on whether the so-called witnesses were pro-Earp or not. One has it that the Clantons and McLaurys were not as heavily armed as were their adversaries and that one or two of them were unarmed. This seems rather difficult to explain as they had been making threats of shooting the Earps on sight for the past two days. There was also some discrepancy over who shot first but not over who was the first to fall. Frank McLaury tumbled down off his horse mortally wounded. Before cashing in, he got off a shot that wounded Virgil, the leader of the Earp faction. When the shooting started, young Billy Claibourne ran to seek refuge in Fly's Photography Studio, and Sheriff Behan ducked behind a building to watch. Ike Clanton, the man whose remarks had done much to provoke trouble, was still in a mood to talk rather than fight. He rushed up to Wyatt pleading for his life. The latter told him to start shooting or get away for the fight had begun. As Ike ran away, Doc fired in his direction but missed. Behind the cover of his horse, Tom McLaury reached for his rifle, still in the scabbard, and the animal bolted, thus exposing McLaury to the guns of Wyatt and Doc Holliday's shotgun nearly cut the cowboy in two. The last one left alive on the Clanton-McLaury side was eighteen-year-old Billy Clanton. The kid, game to the end, had six bullets in his body but was asking God to give him just one more shot when C. S. Fly walked over and took the pistol from his trembling hands. Dr. George Goodfellow was summoned, and Billy lived long enough to request that the doctor remove his boots: he had promised his mother he would not die with his boots on.

The fight had lasted less than thirty seconds, but for Billy Clanton and Tom and Frank McLaury it was a lifetime spent. Morgan and Virgil Earp were both seriously wounded and Doc had suffered a crease. Wyatt, standing in the open through the entire fracas, ironically had not been hit. Thirty-four shots had been fired in the time which had elapsed; the cowboys had scored three out of seventeen shots, while the Earps and Doc hit on eleven. Friends of the deceased removed the bodies to a hardware store, where they were decked out in fine clothes and placed in the store window. A sign was placed in the window with them saying: "Murdered in the Streets of Tombstone."

When the shooting ended, Sheriff Behan attempted to place the Earps under arrest but was unsuccessful. A few days later, Virgil was dismissed from his position as city marshal by the council. Even their staunchest admirer, Mayor Clum, couldn't help.

The Earp Gang was then brought up before Judge Wells Spicer for a hearing that lasted a month. Spicer ruled that there was insufficient evidence to bring murder charges against the Earps and that they were carrying out their duties as appointed and deputized lawmen.

Emotions and tempers were running hot in the days following Spicer's decision. The judge received threatening letters and John Clum was fired upon outside of town. A few days later, Virgil, who was still recovering from wounds suffered in the battle, was shot from ambush. The wound permanently crippled the leader of the Earp faction. Ike Clanton, Frank Stilwell, John Ringo, and Hank Swilling were all seen toting shotguns that night although all were released when they said they were miles away. Some three months later, Morgan Earp was shot to death as he and Wyatt were in Hatch's saloon. Morgan was shooting pool with the proprietor when a shotgun blast cut him down. Another shot narrowly missed Wyatt. The assassins had fired through the windowpanes of a side door, hitting Morgan in the back. One innocent bystander also met death that night. George Berry was slightly wounded when the bullet passed through Earp's body striking Berry in the thigh. Berry collapsed on the floor and never regained consciousness. Dr. Goodfellow, the attending physician and county coroner, recorded dryly that Berry had "died from shock. The simple fact was that the man was scared to death." Frank Stilwell, Hank Swilling, Pete Spence, and Florentino (Indian Charlie) Cruz were in town that night and were named by a coroner's jury as the culprits. Spence's vindictive wife told of the plot after her husband had slapped her around a bit just prior to the murder.

A few days later, the Earps boarded a train for California, taking along with them the body of their slain brother, Doc Holliday, and a couple of other members of the gang. When the train reached Tucson all exited except for Virgil, who with his wife went on to California. In the railroad yard, they encountered Frank Stilwell, where they dispatched him in short order. Later his body was found with "four rifle balls and two loads of buckshot."

Wyatt and Warren Earp, Doc, Sherman McMasters, and Turkey Creek Jack Johnson returned to Tombstone. Knowing that a warrant for their arrest would be forthcoming from Tucson, the boys packed and prepared to leave. They also knew that since they were now operating outside the law, they would have no protection if caught.

Anticipating a warrant for the arrest of the Earps, Sheriff Behan attempted once again to take the men into custody. Again, he backed off when Wyatt scoffed at his request. Contrary to some who later said that the gang was "chased out of town," the Earps and their followers defiantly mounted their horses and rode out of town at a slow walk.

The entire nation was beginning to sit up and take note of the happenings in the Arizona Territory. Finally, in desperation, President Chester A. Arthur threatened martial law on the entire area should the violence continue. Local residents rose indignantly against not only the President's proclamation and the eastern press for their sensationalism, but also the general disrespect for law and order on the part of the locals.

Meanwhile Wyatt was still at work. He found Indian Charlie Cruz and killed him after Cruz admitted standing watch outside Hatch's saloon while Morgan was assassinated. Before dying Cruz admitted his fee for this had been $25. Next they went to Iron Springs, where, according to Wyatt, they encountered the "cowboy" leader, Curly Bill Brocius. Wyatt later claimed he killed Curly Bill, although others have said this isn't so. Whether one believes Wyatt's version or not, Curly Bill was never seen in Arizona again. Heading up the Sulphur Springs Valley, they spent the night at Colonel Hooker's ranch. Feeling that things were getting too hot in Arizona, they left the Territory and went to Colorado. Later, Sheriff Behan, at the head of a posse made up largely of Behan's "cowboy" friends, arrived at Hooker's ranch looking for the Earp Gang. The colonel took one look at the ignominious posse and told Behan rather unceremoniously to get off his land. Afterward, when an attempt was made to extradite Wyatt from Colorado to stand trial in Tombstone, Governor Pitkin of Colorado refused, knowing that Earp would never receive a fair trial anywhere in Arizona Territory.

In the aftermath, somebody killed the notorious Johnny Ringo. Billy Claibourne believed that Buckskin Frank Leslie did it and said so. He challenged Frank and got himself killed instead. Young Billy was no match for the professional gunman. Others blamed Wyatt for the killing, and no doubt Wyatt would have liked to have been responsible; however, Wyatt was in Colorado and that would have taken some kind of shooting. It is generally believed that a chap named Johnny-Behind-the-Deuce killed the drunken, sleeping Ringo over near Turkey Creek.

For the others life went on. Big-Nosed Kate went to Globe, where she opened a boardinghouse. Mattie Blaylock, Wyatt's wife, was left behind. She later committed suicide with an overdose of laudanum at Pinal City. Doc died with his boots off at Glenwood Springs, Colorado, of tuberculosis in 1887, at the age of thirty-five. Virgil never fully recovered from his wounds and worked as a deputy and prospector. He died at Goldfield, Nevada, in 1905. Bat Masterson finally went East, where he became a famous newspaperman. Warren Earp, the youngest, was murdered at Willcox under mysterious circumstances around 1900.

On the other side, John Behan later became superintendent of the territorial prison at Yuma. Ike Clanton was killed a few years later by a correspondence school detective, a fact which must have chagrined Clanton greatly in his final moments on earth.

Wyatt spent the next several years wandering throughout the West. He married again, this time Josephine Marcus, the actress he had courted and won from Behan. In 1886 he refereed the Tom Sharkey-Bob Fitzsimmons heavyweight fight. He gave the fight to Sharkey on a foul, although Sharkey had fouled Fitzsimmons throughout the fight, lending some credence to suspicions that Wyatt had wagered his money on Sharkey. In 1911 he was arrested in Los Angeles for fleecing one J. Y. Patterson out of $25,000 in an alleged con game involving a fake gold brick. Apparently the years had not changed him much. Later on he had held hopes that William S. Hart would play him in a movie based on past exploits but this never came to pass.

In the late 1920s author Stuart Lake interviewed Wyatt for a book and it is from these interviews that much of the legend and myth arose around Wyatt Earp and the O.K. Corral. Up to that time it had not created much excitement, but now the Old West was fading rapidly and the public wanted more of the "stuff that legends are made of." Through Stuart Lake's book *Wyatt Earp: Frontier Marshal,* the legend was born. When Wyatt told his story to Lake it was from the thoughts and recollections of a man in his eighties. Most, if not all, of the major characters were long gone and understandably Wyatt saw himself in the role of some saintly preserver of law and order and that was pretty much the way he told his story.

Billy Breckenridge, a deputy for Behan, wrote a different version to the episode in his book *Helldorado.* Breckenridge had few kind words for the Earps. Other exceptional works on Tombstone during this period are Frank Waters, *The Earp Brothers of Tombstone,* Odie Faulk, *Tombstone, Myth and Reality,* and Walter Noble Burns, *Tombstone.*

Perhaps one of the Earp women, Allie, summed up best the attitude of the folks in Tombstone toward the Dodge City Gang during those years the Earps preserved law and order in the town: "No one in Tombstone ever spoke to us," she said.

A SPLENDID LITTLE WAR

During time of war special volunteer groups have always captured the fancy and imagination of the American public. Often, to the eternal chagrin of other military units, they also become the focal point of a hero-worshiping press. No body of American fighting men has ever appeared on the scene, before or since, that caught the imagination of the American people like the hell-bent-for-leather cowboy cavalry, better known in the books of history as the Roughriders.

It was the end of an era for the American people. Following a disastrous civil war, the nation had turned her attention westward until there was no more frontier to conquer, no more West to win. The rash of westward activity combined with recovering from the war had kept the Americans away from any imperialist activities outside their own boundaries. However, that was all in the past and now the country was able and eager to join the rush to empire.

There was also a new generation of young men, men who had listened to tales of glorious battles between Rebels and Yankees at the knees of their grandpappies or stories of heroic deeds by their daddies fighting hostile Indians before the frontier had closed. How in these modern times would they ever have the opportunity to partake of the same tasks as had their elders? Those times had ended forever within the boundaries of the continental United States. However, a series of events was taking place a short distance to the south of Florida that would culminate with the youngsters getting their once-in-a-lifetime chance for adventure on the battlefield. The war was brief, casualties were light, and the mere presence of the ebullient figure of Teddy Roosevelt created an aura of excitement. All in all, it was a "splendid little war." For the young men, their time had finally come.

Causes for the 1898 war with Spain are still subject to debate. For years the Cubans had been struggling for independence from the Spanish government, and their plight had gained the sympathy of many Americans. This was also the period of so-called "yellow journalism" whereby newspapers were more interested in sensationalism and lurid tales to stimulate sales rather than sticking simply to the news of the day.

On the night of February 15, 1898, the battleship *Maine* blew up in Havana harbor, taking nearly 250 American lives. Even though blame for the explosion has not been determined to this day, the newspapers and jingoists of the day were clamoring for war. William McKinley, President of the United States for less than a year at the time of the incident, sent a message to Congress asking for authority to intervene in the Cuban revolution. On April 25, 1898, the United States declared war on Spain and the call went out for volunteers. For the first time, American boys would be fighting over another nation's internal problems. The twentieth century had brought about a new dawn in American policy, a policy that, once committed to, would entangle America for many years.

The same day war was declared, Secretary of War Russell Alger called upon Arizona territorial governor Myron T. McCord to respond to a request for the enlisting of a regiment to be raised under the command of Colonel Leonard Wood and Assistant Secretary of the Navy Theodore Roosevelt. Enthusiasm for the adventure brought hundreds of applicants. In ten days, Arizona's two-hundred-man quota was filled, leaving some eight hundred disappointed aspirants behind, and the Roughriders were on their way to San Antonio for training.

The official name was the 1st United States Volunteer Cavalry. However, when Governor McCord referred to the men in a speech as "Colonel Brodie's regiment of Arizona roughriders," the name stuck. The moniker was slow catching on with the men themselves, as they felt that it suggested some slur on their riding ability, but it was popular with the eastern newspapers and soon enough the men were referring to themselves as Roughriders.

The men were not, by any means, all cowboys. They came from all walks of life, from schoolteacher to miner. Only eight were native Arizonans. Their ages ranged from eighteen to forty-four, with an average age of twenty-eight, and they were led by a doctor and a dude. The doctor was Leonard Wood, a man who had distinguished himself in the final stages of the Geronimo campaign in the Sierra Madre by winning the Congressional Medal of Honor. The dude was the inimitable Teddy Roosevelt, an impetuous Easterner who had overcome seemingly insurmountable handicaps. Nearsighted and wracked with asthma, the frail Roosevelt spent his youth almost completely kept in confinement. Following a youthful altercation when he was beaten by two bullies, Teddy went on a vigorous body-building campaign. His voracity for health and physical fitness never waned from that day on. He boxed in college and when he was twenty-five he went West to the badlands of Dakota, where he became a cowboy. This experience no doubt prepared him for the responsibilities he was soon to undertake. At first the Southwesterners were skeptical of the "four-eyed tenderfoot," but Roosevelt's strong personality, enthusiasm, and friendly manner soon prevailed. Before long he was one of the boys.

All other officers were selected at the local level and it was no surprise that Governor McCord nominated Alexander Brodie as regimental major. Brodie had graduated from West Point in 1870 and fought in Arizona with General Crook's command during the Apache campaigns in the early 1870s. He had served with distinction, being wounded once in an Apache ambush. Above all others, the men considered him the backbone of the regiment. Brodie had earlier given up a promising Army career after his young wife died in childbirth. He went into the cattle business in Kansas for a time, returning to Arizona in 1887. For the next three years he was chief engineer at Walnut Dam. This dam on the Hassayampa broke during heavy rains in the winter of 1890. Many lives were lost in the flood, still considered Arizona's greatest disaster. In 1891 Brodie was appointed commander of the Arizona National Guard but resigned to dabble in politics and mining in Yavapai County for the next few years.

By far the most popular of the officers was the dashing, swashbuckling mayor of Prescott, William O. "Buckey" O'Neill. He picked up the nickname with his flamboyant style of "bucking the tiger" at faro. The women were taken by his charm and men admired him. Had he never gone to Cuba, Buckey's name would still have found its place in history books.

O'Neill had come to Arizona in 1879, where he worked for a time as a typesetter for the Phoenix *Herald*. He later joined the rush to Tombstone and worked for the *Epitaph* during the era of the Earps. In 1888 Buckey was elected sheriff of Yavapai County; his most famous exploit, perhaps, centered around a Santa Fe train robbery at Canyon del Diablo, just east of Flagstaff. O'Neill and a posse tracked the train robbers into Utah, where they captured them. Another side of Buckey's character was revealed one day in Prescott when he was called upon to witness a hanging. Just as the trap was sprung, the future Roughrider captain fainted dead away. It was a long time before the gregarious O'Neill lived that down.

Much to the disappointment of the young men in Arizona Territory, the Secretary of War authorized the enlistment of only 780 men into Colonel Wood's Roughriders. This number was later raised to 1,000 but still less than 200 of the more than 1,000 applicants from Arizona were accepted, the others coming from New Mexico, Oklahoma, and the Indian Territory. The Arizonans were a natural for a regiment of this type. They could already ride, shoot, and make camp. Many had seen action in the late Apache wars, were already acclimated to the hot climate, and most could speak at least a little Spanish.

Eventually the regiment would be divided up into three squadrons of four troops each. Each troop would carry some 80 men on the roster, making a total of 320 men to the squadron. Colonel Brodie's Arizonans were divided up into three troops, the squadron's fourth troop being made up from Oklahoma Territory.

Senior captain of the regiment Buckey O'Neill was appointed commander of "A" Troop, while Captain James H. McClintock, a newspaperman-schoolteacher and later historian of renown, commanded "B" Troop. "C" Troop was led by Captain Joseph Alexander, a lawyer from Phoenix, and "D" Troop consisted of the Oklahomans. One of McClintock's lieutenants, Harbo Tom Rynning, was a veteran of the Geronimo campaign. He would later command the colorful Arizona Rangers. Lieutenant John C. Greenway of "A" Troop quickly won the respect among both officers and enlisted men. Teddy Roosevelt later called him "one of the finest and most aggressive officers in the Regiment." He became a mining magnate and one of Arizona's most well-known citizens. Another Arizonan who had gained fame during the Geronimo campaign was Chief Packer Tom Horn. Horn would later be hanged under questionable circumstances for murder in Wyoming.

By May 4 the preliminaries of induction were completed and the Arizonans were ready to board the train for San Antonio, Texas. They had the distinction of being the first group of volunteers in the United States to mobilize, a factor that became crucial in the weeks to come, in view of the Army's seniority system.

Before boarding, the ladies of the Phoenix chapter of the Grand Army of the Republic presented the boys with a flag that they had hand-sewn. Little did they know at the time that the banner would be the first to fly on Cuban soil and be carried into Santiago. Today the flag rests proudly in the State Capitol Building in Phoenix, tattered, weather-beaten, and carrying three bullet holes.

Other tokens were handed out to the boys that day. Buckey was given an engraved pistol and holster, and the men were given distinctive hatbands. The local citizens raised some $500 to buy treats and food for the trip to San Antonio. A puma, named Florence, went along as official mascot. Morale was high as the train wound its way across the Southwest, bound for Texas. Crowds of well-wishers lined the stations along the way. At one point the boys attempted to cajole a comely young miss to board the train and go to Texas. She had just reached the agreeable stage when an officer happened along and put an end to the escapade.

When Teddy Roosevelt first arrived in San Antonio, he was viewed with skepticism by the Arizonans, but any doubts as to his ability were quickly expunged once the training began. Teddy had been offered the full command of the regiment by President McKinley when the war began but he felt he had not enough experience and suggested Leonard Wood for the position and himself as second-in-command. His indefatigable spirit and enthusiasm engulfed all the volunteers. Before training was over, most referred to the troopers as "Roosevelt's Roughriders."

The uniforms worn by the Roughriders consisted of a blue flannel shirt, brown trousers with canvas leggings, shoes, a brown canvas jacket, and a gray campaign hat. The familiar khaki didn't come into popular use until after the war. For weapons they were issued Colt .45 pistols and .30-.40 Krag-Jörgensen rifles. Their horses were purchased locally according to prescribed government regulations, although this didn't always seem to be the case: as one man wrote, "some of the damn horses bucked like hell." The cowboys in the regiment earned extra money by breaking the horses for the inexperienced troopers at $10 a head. Needless to say, there was much raiding and counterraiding at night during those first days in camp for a more desirable mount.

By and large, the training went smoothly. The hours were long but that didn't seem to keep the boys from going into town with or without authorization. It wasn't long before they knew every hole in the fence that surrounded the camp.

The citizens of San Antonio were, for the most part, tolerant of the antics of their colorful guests. Shooting out the lights in a San Antonio streetcar earned for William Owens of Globe the nickname "Smoke-'Em-Up-Bill" among his fellow troopers. One AWOL group avoided the task of trying to sneak past the guards late one night when one of its members formed the inebriated soldiers into a squad formation and marched them through the gate. Once inside, the men scattered like quail to their respective quarters.

On May 28 the regiment received its orders to move out. It had been only thirty days since they had first gathered at Prescott. Training had been rigorous and the men were anxious to get on to Cuba and the business at hand. They had joined to fight the Spaniard and all seemed to sense that the hour was near. After a shaky train ride accompanied by a food shortage of such proportions that the volunteers took to rustling chickens and other such things at each stop, the Roughriders finally reached Tampa, Florida.

Since they were a special force, it is understandable that the press anxiously watched their every move. No doubt the Spanish intelligence anxiously awaited each daily copy with as much interest as the locals.

They found southern hospitality to be in excess of their fondest expectations, especially among the ladies, as they traveled across the southland of America. Apparently their reputations as midnight flyers and wild bull riders had preceded them along the line as the people turned out to get a glimpse of "Roosevelt's cowboy cavalry."

Tampa was one of the major embarkation ports for the war effort and by the time the volunteers arrived it was a den of activity. It was at Tampa that the Arizonans met their commanding officer, General William Shafter. Shafter was an old-time soldier, winning the Medal of Honor in the Civil War and later serving with Ranald Mackenzie in the Indian wars. By 1898 he was a portly 300-pound man who at times during the campaign would have to be carried around by a detail of men on a door. They also met another man at Tampa who reminded them very much of their own commander, Alexander Brodie. He was former general of the Confederate Army "Fighting Joe" Wheeler. Wheeler had fought in 180 Civil War skirmishes and battles including Shiloh, Murfreesboro, and Chickamauga. Robert E. Lee had called him one of the South's two best cavalry officers—the other being Jeb Stuart.

The location chosen for the amphibious landing was Daiquiri, 24 miles from Santiago. The unopposed landing was marred by the capsizing of a landing boat carrying members of the 10th Cavalry, the Black Buffalo Soldiers of Indian war fame. Buckey O'Neill jumped into the water in an attempt to save two soldiers who were pulled under by their heavy equipment. However, rescue efforts were in vain and the two men drowned.

Another near tragedy was averted when some of the officers' horses became confused when they were lowered into the water. The mounts began swimming out to sea. An alert bugler blew "recall" and the well-drilled horses reversed their direction and headed toward shore.

It was at this time that the Arizonans' home-sewn flag went ashore with the first landing craft and became the first American flag on Cuban soil. Six-foot-six-inch Color Sergeant Albert Wright of Yuma, the tallest man in the outfit, carried it to a nearby hill to signal the fleet that the American forces had landed. When the Arizonans recognized their flag with its tricolors blowing in the breeze they let forth with a long series of cowboy yells. Pistols were fired in the air, reverberating off the island. Somebody tied down the ship's whistle and the band struck up "A Hot Time in the Old Town." That song would be sung with such alacrity in the next few months that the Spanish believed it to be the American national anthem.

On June 24, the Roughriders had their baptism of fire at Las Guásimas; and when the smoke had cleared two officers were among the casualties. Captain McClintock lay wounded with two bullets in his leg and Major Brodie had his wrist shattered by a Spanish Mauser.

There remains today somewhat of a myth about San Juan Hill. Artists have mistakenly painted the cavalry charge, horses and all, failing to note that only a few horses made the trip. Something else misunderstood about San Juan Hill is that actually the hill itself was only a part of a mile-long ridge called the San Juan Heights. Another part of the Heights, separated by a small pond, was Kettle Hill, somewhat higher than the others. It was here that the "Crowded Hour" really began.

By now the men had learned easily to distinguish the flat, brittle cracks of the Spanish Mausers from the deeper, more resonant boom of their own Krags, and as the Americans formed at the base of Kettle Hill the Spaniards began raining fire down upon them.

Buckey O'Neill was walking up and down in front of his troops oblivious to the bullets flying about him, just as he had done previously at Las Guásimas. "An officer should never take cover," he had said many times before. He had also said jokingly that "the Spanish bullet has never been molded that will kill Buckey O'Neill." Buckey paused now and then to joke with his men. Understandably the men were nervous as the Spanish bullets began to take their toll. No doubt, O'Neill's intrepid manner had its effect. He had then gone over to talk to another officer when a Mauser slug hit him right in the open mouth.

The death of Captain O'Neill had a demoralizing effect on all the men of "A" Troop. They had all identified with the gallant officer, the entire troop becoming a veritable reflection of Buckey's colorful personality. To see their commander lying dead on the ground, a mortal being, left them stunned. "A" Troop ceased to function as a unit after that. Some of the men joined other units while others just went "off on their own."

It has been said that Tom Rynning stepped in when O'Neill fell and took command. However, the records show that the future Arizona Rangers captain was at sick call during the time and did not participate in this part of the battle. Many of the Arizonans, including Albert Wright, rallied around Roosevelt.

Mounted on his horse, Little Texas, Teddy took his men through the regular troops who were waiting for orders to be passed down. The sight of the volunteers moving into battle was a little too much for the regulars, however, and many joined the charge. The tempestuous Roosevelt cut quite a figure with his blue bandanna tied around his hat, the tail streaming behind. The familiar cavalry saber was conspicuously absent, as Teddy had discarded it prior to the battle. He had tripped over it at Las Guásimas and didn't intend to do so again. With a great show of gallantry Roosevelt mustered his troops and prepared to do battle. To the men he seemed to be in several places at once as he rode up and down the line, cajoling them to rally around him. The ubiquitous Roosevelt was easily the most noticeable figure on the entire battlefield. On one occasion he charged, to find that only five men were following. He quickly recovered, and riding back, retrieved the others. The battle was short and furious. The casualty rate was highest in the cavalry division: eleven Roughriders were killed outright and sixty-five were wounded. Fred Bugbee was wounded in the head prior to the charge and was ordered by Roosevelt to the rear for treatment. The young cowboy from Safford replied, "You go to hell. We are not going back." That was the kind of spirit that Teddy had implanted into the unit from the time of their first meeting. No doubt he was proud of them all as he smiled and walked away.

The spectators, watching from a vantage point at El Poso, later described the gallant force of men as "a glorious, almost incredible sight."

It was hard to believe that just sixty-seven days earlier they had been civilians reading about a war that had just been declared. Now the weary combat veterans sat on top of San Juan Heights, the personal glory of a lifetime crowded into just a day.

The real enemy in Cuba had not been the Spanish. Disease took a higher toll. With yellow fever, dysentery, and malaria cutting the men down daily it was with no regrets that the men boarded the *Miami* for New York City some forty-seven days after the battle.

Nearly one half of the regiment had remained behind at Tampa with the horse detail, where some had died of the same jungle diseases that had taken their comrades in Cuba. They had joined to fight and the only fighting they had seen had been in the Tampa saloons. To make matters worse, they would have to bear the burdensome anxiety of facing the inevitable question at countless anniversaries in the years to come: "Were you left behind with the horse detail?"

The troops were all reunited at Long Island, New York, though it was not the same outfit that boarded the train out of Prescott on that spring day that now seemed so long ago. Captain McClintock would walk with a limp for the remainder of his life, Major Brodie had a shattered right arm, and the gallant Buckey O'Neill would rest at Arlington Cemetery, the only commissioned Arizonan to die in battle. The men had not fared much better, for the disease had taken its toll. A cheering crowd had gathered to greet the volunteers when they landed in New York, but the mood of the home folks faded into stunned silence as the condition of the men became evident. Of "A" Troop, only thirty men were able to march off the ship without assistance.

They were still the darlings of the press and the public, as hospitable folks came from miles around, bringing food baskets and inviting them into their homes. Recovery under these conditions was rapid and it wasn't long before the men were readied for discharge. Before leaving, the boys gave Colonel Roosevelt a bronze reproduction of Remington's "Bronco Buster" as a symbol of their feeling for the "dude who had arrived."

On September 15, 1898, the regiment ceased to exist and its troopers were discharged. The Arizona boys took their flag and returned home. Some of the Roughriders had gambled away their mustering-out pay and couldn't afford train fare, but like the benevolent fathers they were, Teddy and Major Brodie bought one-way tickets back to Arizona for their boys.

Teddy Roosevelt carried on in American politics pretty much the same way he conducted himself in the battle for the San Juan Heights. Many political bosses found him extremely offensive and decided that the best place to hide Teddy, where he could do the least amount of harm, was in the office of the Vice-President of the United States. "Don't any of you realize there's only one life between this madman and the White House?" erupted G.O.P. National Chairman Mark Hanna. A year later, following McKinley's assassination, Hanna cried, "Now look, that damned cowboy is President of the United States!" With Teddy's zest for life, several robust children, and an entourage of animals ranging from a pet bear named Jonathan Edwards to a Shetland pony, the White House took on the air of a multi-ringed circus. It seemed to epitomize the times and the country loved it.

In 1902 a vacancy occurred in the office of governor of Arizona and Roosevelt persuaded his old comrade in arms Alexander Brodie to fill the post. Brodie later resigned and re-entered the Army.

Several former members of the Roughriders became Arizona Rangers. Two of the three Ranger captains were former Roughriders. Tom Rynning of "B" Company was one and Harry Wheeler, who rose from the rank of private to captain of the Rangers, was the other, though not from the Arizona squadron.

In 1907 the citizens of Arizona paid the group its greatest tribute. A bronze statue portraying a Roughrider in action was unveiled in Prescott. Down through the years this statue has come to be known as the Buckey O'Neill statue, although it was not supposed to represent any one man but to honor all the men who served with the regiment.

THE PROFESSIONALS

Doctors, Journalists, Lawyers, Judges, Preachers, and Teachers

LEADING THE MOVE WESTWARD in the footsteps of the mountain men and prospectors during the latter half of the nineteenth century came many types of newcomers including immigrants, merchants, and mechanics. Accompanying them were the "professionals," lawyers, doctors, teachers, and preachers. However, not all came to implement their chosen profession. A great number went off to the gold fields seeking that proverbial rainbow's end.

Of the early doctors who came to Arizona, most were military surgeons or contract physicians who practiced their profession on the remote military posts. Not a few spent a good deal of time prospecting and leaving the hospital work to some green steward. Most moved on at the first opportunity. Since the demand was much greater than the supply, a large number of quacks intermingled with the legitimate physicians.

The first "doctor" of record to pass through Arizona was an adventurous part-time miner, sometime mountain man, and full-time itinerant named James Ohio Pattie. Pattie, who crossed Arizona in the 1820s with his father, claimed to have inoculated some 22,000 Californians for smallpox in return for which he gained his freedom from the San Diego jail where he and his father were doing time for trespassing into Mexican territory. The father, Sylvester, died while in captivity, but James returned to the States, where several years later he recalled many hair-raising adventure stories for his readers.

Dr. John S. Griffin, traveling with Kearny's Army of the West in 1846, was the first legitimate doctor to cross Arizona into California, although Dr. John Marsh had passed through some eleven years earlier on his way to California. Marsh was on the run from an unsavory past. A warrant had been issued for his arrest in St. Louis for various indiscretions. Upon reaching California he presented his Bachelor of Arts degree from Harvard to Spanish authorities and passed it off as a medical degree. It was printed in Latin, which the officials couldn't read, but they passed him anyway. "Dr." John Marsh became one of the first Anglo-American practitioners in California and played a major part in political activities during the turbulent years prior to statehood.

Some early doctors opened saloons and pool halls while practicing medicine as a sideline, while others were not always law-abiding. In 1871 Dr. Edward Phelps, also U.S. marshal for the Territory, absconded to Mexico with $12,000 in government funds. He was later reported killed near Mexico City. However, another source mentions that his death was falsely reported and that Dr. Phelps collected several thousand dollars in life insurance for his timely "death."

Dr. John C. Handy became one of Tucson's finest physicians and was instrumental in the legislation to prevent unlicensed practitioners from setting up business in the Territory. Unfortunately, he was shot and killed in a fight with his estranged wife's attorney some years later.

Dr. Jack McDonnell, colorful physician at McCabe around 1900, was a constant source of entertainment to clients and friends with his sometimes unorthodox manner of diagnosing injuries. He once repaired the nearly severed toe of a miner, and in telling another physician of it later he remarked, "I sewed it back on and it grew just fine. The only thing was, I sewed it on upside down." He died under somewhat mysterious circumstances in Jerome. Ironically, the final diagnosis on Doc McDonnell is rather ambiguous. His doctor said the appendix ruptured, while rumor persisted that the rupture had been brought on by a stab wound.

Florence was the scene in 1888 of the so-called "Six-gun Classic." Joe Phy and Pete Gabriel, personal and political enemies of long standing, opened fire on each other in a local saloon. When the smoke cleared away, Joe Phy had three bullets in his body. He was treated by his good friend Dr. William Harvey, but died anyway. Pete Gabriel had two wounds, one in the groin and one in the breast. Dr. Harvey refused to treat Gabriel, whom he did not like, and another doctor some 18 miles away was summoned. Gabriel lived another ten years after recuperating from the battle.

Dr. Nancy Miller Pickens was the first woman to practice in Phoenix, specializing in "diseases of women and children." In 1883 she was accused of performing an abortion. Dr. Pickens apparently moved on, as nothing more was ever heard of her.

Dr. John L. Gregg, Tempe's first physician, once had the difficult task of performing surgery on himself. Following a gunshot wound, Gregg amputated his own leg, obviously suffering much pain as he did so. However, this in no way curtailed his ability to perform, as he was quite active in that city for many years.

Another Tempe physician, Benjamin Moeur, later became governor of the state. It was said that the ten thousand babies the doctor had delivered all grew up and voted for him, thus guaranteeing his election. He was a gruff, country-type doctor who was said to possess a rather crusty bedside manner.

The author's grandmother came to Arizona from Texas in 1917 for her health and assisted Dr. Moeur in delivering babies around Tempe for several years. An indefatigable woman, she loved to pick cotton, spending many a day laboring in the rows, towing that long sack. Dr. Moeur told her many times to stay out of those cotton fields, but she persisted in signing on each season when picking time came.

Years later she was taken into Tempe with a hernia that was strangulating and the doctor in attendance was unable to do anything with it. Dr. Moeur, who was now Governor Moeur, was visiting the office at the time and took the situation in hand. Adroitly manipulating her abdominal region, he straightened it out in short order. Finishing, he stepped back and regarded his old assistant for a moment and then with typical bedside manner said, "There, old woman. Now you can go back to pickin' cotton."

One of the most famous of all the territorial doctors was George E. Goodfellow. Doc Goodfellow gained notoriety shortly after he began his practice in Tombstone in the early 1880s. That city, a great place for practical experience, did much to enhance Goodfellow's reputation as the foremost authority on gunshot wounds and their treatment. Many of his articles on the subject were published nationally. To the Mexicans he was "El Doctor Santo"—"the blessed doctor"—after his work among them during the earthquake at Sonora in 1887. Whether it was a lonely outlaw hideout treating some lead-poisoned rustler or in the home of a poor Mexican family, Doc Goodfellow always responded no matter what the inconvenience. He could run a locomotive steam engine as well as any engineer or crawl down into a smoke-filled shaft to rescue trapped miners. During waking hours, the doc could usually be found in either of two places, his office, or downstairs at the Crystal Palace saloon, where he was promoting some wager or sporting event. In a city full of colorful characters, Doc Goodfellow ranked with the best of them. Goodfellow remained in Tombstone for eleven years, moving his practice to Tucson in 1891 following the death of his friend Dr. John Handy. In 1898 Goodfellow joined General William Shafter's staff as a civilian volunteer and went to Cuba. His astute knowledge of the Spanish language made him an invaluable aide to the general. It was Goodfellow who negotiated the Spanish surrender. Following the capitulation, the Spanish general gave the doctor credit for talking him into it.

Doctors during territorial days were called upon to perform some rather unusual tasks. The rough terrain in which they practiced oftentimes called for much improvisation. This was true also in the means used for transportation, as illustrated by the following:

Dr. John Lacy served the communities of Clifton and Morenci during the 1880s for the Arizona Copper Company. Lacy, an innovative genius, used a velocipede—a railway handcar—to cut down on travel time while making his calls. Traveling at speeds up to 20 m.p.h. Dr. Lacy traveled up and down the narrow-gauge railroad tracks between the two communities. The trip up to Morenci was most difficult, while the ride back down the hill to Clifton was always easy rolling.

One day when Doc Lacy was making his return journey he chanced to meet a train coming from the other direction. The terrain through which he was traveling consisted of a steep cliff on one side and the San Francisco River on the other. No doubt feeling much anxiety over the precarious situation in which he now found himself, the doctor took advantage of the only exit available. He leaped over the side, landing in the river, followed close behind by the battered handcar. It is presumed that Dr. Lacy discontinued this highly speculative means of transportation or afterward confined himself to some less hazardous mode of travel.

A story is told about a farmer whose mule was suffering from some incurable ailment. It was decided that nothing could be done and the beast might just as well be destroyed. The doctor, lacking the necessary tools to administer the final *coup de grâce*, asked the farmer for a gun, but the farmer, having none, offered instead the only weapon available. He had some dynamite left over from some recent excavation work. It should have been an easy task to accomplish. Merely insert the stick in the headstall section of the mule's halter, light the fuse, and wait at a safe distance for the final result. Something the two forgot to consider after lighting the fuse was that this was rattlesnake country, and that mule might not have known what the tubular instrument beside his face was, but he instinctively knew that any hissing sound meant danger and he didn't mean to stand still for it. The frantic mule charged first north, then south, then east, then west. The two would-be executioners didn't know which way to run next, as it seemed that each direction they scurried, the mule always seemed to be coming from the opposite direction. Fortunately for all except the mule, the charge went off a safe distance from the panic-stricken twosome.

Most of Arizona's early surgeons were military men and some went on to greater fame. Others showed prowess in military operations outside medicine. Dr. B. J. D. Irwin, who gained recognition for his articles on amputations, was the first to implement the idea of a large field hospital. At Shiloh, 2,500 patients were attended to as a result of Irwin's inspiration. No less skilled on the field of battle, Dr. Irwin won the Congressional Medal of Honor for his performance at the Bascom affair involving Cochise and an alleged kidnapping at Apache Pass in 1861.

One of the first duty assignments of Dr. Walter Reed was the Territory of Arizona. He first became interested in the dreaded yellow fever and its possible cure while stationed at Fort Lowell, near Tucson. Dr. Leonard Wood began his military career at Fort Whipple. He won the Medal of Honor in the campaign against Geronimo, was commanding officer of the famed Roughriders in Cuba, and was Army Chief of Staff before his brilliant career ended.

When the nationally famous Carlisle Indian School football team arrived in Phoenix to play against the Phoenix Indian School in January 1900, they brought along as team physician and friend Dr.

Carlos Montezuma, a full-blooded Yavapai. Dr. Montezuma had experienced a unique experience in cross-culturization when, as a
small boy, he survived a savage battle between a band of Pima and
Yavapai in the Four Peaks area. The heavily outnumbered Yavapai
were defeated and all the adult males and several women were
slain. Carlos, only four years old at the time, was taken by the Pima
and sold to a white man, named Stedman, in Florence for $20. The
boy was taken to Chicago and given an education. He graduated
from the University of Illinois with high honors, just thirteen years
after his capture. He was to become one of the most noted physicians in Phoenix.

His visit to Arizona in 1900 marked the first time he had been in
the Territory since that tragic day some twenty-eight years earlier
when he had witnessed the death of his entire band at the hands of
their traditional foes.

During those years of school in Illinois, Carlos developed an interest in medicine and eventually graduated from medical school.
He also became a crusader for Indian rights. He went to work for
the Bureau of Indian Affairs but this paradox of a man found himself resented by both Indian and white, especially bureau personnel. The Indians considered him too white and the whites considered him too noisy. Finally he resigned and started a practice in
Chicago, where he soon became wealthy and prominent. In 1906
Teddy Roosevelt offered him the post of Director of Indian Affairs.
However, he refused, preferring instead to work among his people
than to sit at a desk in Washington.

Once again he returned to Arizona to encourage the Yavapai to
stand up for their rights. They would only laugh at and ridicule
him. Returning to Chicago and his practice and loneliness, he
sought comfort in matrimony.

After several years had passed, he decided to return once again to
his homeland, this time to die. He had not been well and had cor-
rectly diagnosed his ailment as tuberculosis. He might have recovered in a rest home in the dry southwestern climate; instead, he
had himself taken to Fort McDowell reservation. Discarding his
"white man's clothes," he dressed once again as an Indian and
awaited his inevitable end. Many of the causes he embraced eventually did come to pass, though not as rapidly as he had hoped. Carlos
Montezuma never lived to see the day when his people would once
again walk with pride.

Our history is filled with stories of great Indian leaders, many of whom are from Arizona tribes. However, all things considered, perhaps the greatest of them all was this brilliant man who was born in a primitive existence and lived years ahead of his time. Carlos Montezuma had completed the cycle, evolving from a nomadic Yavapai band to become one of Chicago's leading physicians and back again to die a lonely death in an old wickiup on a reservation.

In the years immediately following the Civil War, the mineral wealth of the West brought large numbers of immigrants from foreign lands. These foreigners also brought their alien diseases with them. In a land where dysentery, diarrhea, and malaria had always been a problem, diphtheria, scarlet fever, smallpox, and that scourge of the last half of the nineteenth century, typhoid, were added. They would all prove devastating.

Poorly planned military posts built downwind from open latrines, pigpens, and stables caused an effluvial of decaying, noxious material that spread over the forts. The unsanitary conditions caused by this spread were dangerous and resulted in much illness.

The problem of sanitation was a source of constant consternation among city fathers. On at least one occasion, a newspaper article criticized Phoenix saloons for putting their spittoons in the irrigation ditches to soak when others farther down had to drink and cook from the same water. Cases of smallpox and hospital gangrene had to be separated in the hospitals, as the clothing of the patient and bed could transmit the disease. Pesthouses were constructed, and sometimes people had to be taken in at gunpoint. One night in Tombstone, a passer-by was hailed by a patient who said they had no food to eat. The Samaritan went immediately to the mayor's house and reported the situation; food was obtained shortly. Local newspapers would sometimes play down an epidemic or not print cases of smallpox, hoping somehow that it would disappear by ignoring it. However, other towns were not reluctant about informing their residents to avoid the city in question.

In 1869 Gila and Graham counties disagreed as to who was at fault for an outbreak of diphtheria. Gila County blamed Graham for carelessness and neglect in treating the disease, adding that peddlers and traders were transmitting it. It was even suggested that a deep ditch or high wall should be constructed between the two counties. The feud and the epidemic lasted intermittently for two years. Over forty children died of diphtheria in the tiny community of St. Johns in 1888.

Attempts at quarantine were sometimes successful and sometimes not. Three doctors in Tucson visited a questionable case of smallpox and all pronounced it positive. A quarantine was placed. Two more doctors were called in on the case and they diagnosed it as inflammatory rheumatism and removed the quarantine flag. The former three had the latter two arrested. The case came before a judge and in the middle of the proceedings the patient walked into the courtroom and inquired as to how matters stood.

Gargling sulfur and brimstone was a favorite home remedy for diphtheria, as it would kill every fungus in man, beast, or plant. Inhaling fumes of tar and turpentine set afire in an open pan was another. For scarlet fever, ointments made of butter without salt added to oil of citronella were used. Quinine was the standard treatment for malaria for all who could afford it. The going price was $3.00 an ounce in 1885.

Typhoid was a scourge until water supplies were protected from contamination from sewage. Diarrhea and dysentery were treated with opium, beef tea, and ammonia and brandy as stimulants, but the usual remedies were lead, bismuth, and quinine.

Addiction to drugs and alcohol was fairly common and many unfortunates were committed to asylums and jails. No small number died as wards of the county in these institutions. The sale of opium and laudanum was only slightly regulated, and along with morphine these drugs could be purchased at any drugstore. It wasn't until 1899 that the purchase of drugs was restricted to prescriptions, except for the Chinese section of the community, where opium was available in laundries and restaurants owned by Orientals.

In the 1890s the Bichloride of Gold Institute claimed that they could cure a patient's taste for alcohol or drugs in just a short period with injections of bichloride of gold. People were encouraged to interview the patients undergoing treatment. Many other institutes were formed and did have some success. Some of the most notorious drunks were loud in their praise of the treatment.

The desert dwellers also took their toll on the early settlers. The sting of the scorpion, though not always fatal, was always serious as a threat to infants. Mothers placed screens over cribs so that scorpions crawling on the ceilings might be prevented from falling into bed with the child. Usual treatments were applications of ammonia, baking soda, or vinegar to the sting to draw the poison out.

There was a great deal of controversy even among doctors as to the seriousness of the Gila monster bite. Dr. H. C. Yarrow of the Smithsonian Institution thought the reptile to be non-poisonous. He said that the Arizona whiskey used in the treatment was what killed the victims. Dr. Yarrow's theory received a severe jolt when Walter Vail, a non-drinker, was bitten on the finger. After using a stick to pry it off, Vail was hurried to Dr. Handy in Tucson. He suffered considerably and nearly lost his arm. Believers on the other extreme tried to point out that the residual effects of poison killed Vail ten years later, until it was pointed out that he had met death by getting run over by a streetcar in Los Angeles.

For snakebite, the experienced traveler always carried ammonia or baking soda. That panacea for all ailments, whiskey, was ever present also. Home treatments for snakebite were sucking, applying ammonia or baking soda to the wound, and application of a tourniquet above the wound. Ammonia was sometimes given internally. A Yuma man was bitten on the little finger by a rattler. He grabbed a hatchet and chopped off his finger just above the bite. Later, the doctor found the bone shattered, amputated the rest of the finger, and pronounced his patient as good as new and went so far as to say that the man traded his "finger for his life."

Skunks normally do their fighting with the other end. However, when the normally timid skunk bit a person, rabies was the fear. Wild dog packs and coyotes, as well as bats, were other common carriers of the dreaded hydrophobia. Stray dogs were sometimes shot on sight, thus incurring hard feelings between neighbors. Many untreated cases died a miserable death, as once the symptoms appeared, it was too late for treatment. In 1893 suspected rabies victims were sent to the Pasteur Institute in Chicago for the painful eighteen-day treatment.

The *Arizona Gazette,* on July 26, 1899, reported that an old gentleman named Cox, living near Jerome, was bitten on the nose by a skunk while he slept. The startled man choked the skunk to death but couldn't unfasten the dead animal's teeth from his nose. Finally, the jaw was pried open with a stick, and the skunk released his "death grip." The citizens of Jerome took up a collection and Mr. Cox left for Chicago.

One early doctor advised that the victim's wound be cleansed with soap and hot water, then a tincture of cedron seed applied into the wound and carbolized Vaseline ointment placed on the wound. "Rabies might develop, but the wound would heal," he concluded.

Although screwworm is not normally associated with humans, a few cases had been discovered. The screwworm fly, similar to the housefly but gray in color, is capable of laying hundreds of eggs in a matter of seconds. After a few days' incubation, the maggots are born and reach maturity in about a week. They thrive on both diseased and live tissue, emitting a deadly toxic property. A deep-sleeping or heavily intoxicated person in slumber around these flies is a susceptible target. The most likely place for the fly to lay the eggs would be the nose, where it is attracted by the odor of nasal discharge or nosebleed. The ears and any open sore are other likely locations. One victim complained of a severe headache and was dead a few days later. Another was reported to have died in "excruciating agony." The cause of death was unknown until the worms began dropping out of his nose. Another doctor reported extracting 110 of the worms from the nose and soft palate of a prospector at Tombstone. In treating screwworms, the doctors used forceps for extracting the worms. Chloroform in dilution or combined with olive oil was the most common treatment.

An early authority on the hazards of the screwworm to humans was Dr. Clarence E. Yount of Prescott. In 1906 Dr. Yount published an article, "Human Myiasis from the Screwworm Fly," in which he identified twenty-three cases of screwworm in humans the previous year. Yount also noted that some 78 per cent of screwworm cases occurred in the nose, 17 per cent in wounds, and 4 per cent in the ear. Dr. Yount was also noted for his recognition of the occurrence of rabies in skunks.

Whenever friends got together in territorial times, the subject of illness and its treatments invariably came up. Many people were superstitious and, no doubt, tried many unusual remedies before finding themselves "cured." The human body has an amazing ability to recover on its own and the patient most likely would have recovered in spite of the treatment. However, one could never convince the patient that the last thing used as a "cure" hadn't performed the miracle. The worse the ailment, the more violent the treatment. For those old enough to remember Grandma's castor oil and other such things, it simply meant the worse something tasted, the better it was for you.

These were times when going to the local drugstore meant several days' journey, so each individual home became a veritable drugstore on its own. Such things as calomel, turpentine, laudanum, castor oil, paregoric, and Seidlitz powders were always kept on hand. Also, many people had their own favorite "remedies," and though they may seem ludicrous, or tongue-in-cheek, some really did have medicinal value. For coughing, coal oil and sugar were recommended. Pungent chest rubs were considered helpful. For those who could stand the smell, asafetida bags tied around the neck prevented the spread of communicable diseases as the odoriferous conditions made close human contact impossible.

Cow manure was used to treat foot rash, to pack wounds, and as a poultice for pneumonia. For rope burns, cowboy urine was recommended.

Suffering from anemia? Drive several iron nails into an apple and leave it overnight. Take them out the next morning and eat the apple.

Warts were then, as today, considered bothersome and unsightly. One suggested method of removal was to rub them with a potato. Beans, corn, pebbles, and pennies were other suitable implements to rub off warts. Perhaps the most unique treatment for warts was to wet the hand, pour salt over it, and let a horse kick it. At least the specific problem of warts was forgotten by following this rather dubious remedy.

Rheumatism called for the wearing of copper bands, a method still highly thought of today. Another treatment was to drink tea made from cactus roots or cockleburs.

Sufferers from dysentery took the roasted pulp from prickly-pear cactus. Another recommended treatment was the painting of the abdomen with egg white.

Teas seemed to be a popular remedy. The leaves of the creosote bush were a favorite among many, as was the brew made from a bush called Mormon tea. Both are highly unpalatable unless sweetened. Drinking tea made from cockroaches was supposed to be a cure for lockjaw, while the grinding up of beetles was thought to be of great medicinal value. The philosophy again being, of course, the more unpalatable for the taste buds, the better for you.

In the days before the so-called "germ theory" became fact, hospitals operated oblivious to the problem of germs. Patients were operated on with unclean instruments adding, no doubt, to the high rate of peritonitis and the spreading of deadly germs among the patients. This is not to say that there was a disregard for cleanliness in the medical profession, but simply a lack of awareness of the dangers of germs. By and large, carbolic acid was most commonly used for surgical cleanliness.

Medicine has changed drastically in the past century. This is most noticeable when one considers that the stethoscope didn't come into use until 1850, the thermometer until 1870, and the X-ray machine until 1895. The Arizona Territory did not even have a microscope until the arrival of Dr. C. E. Yount in Prescott in 1902.

Early doctors were attracted to Arizona primarily for three reasons. Most of them came with the military as contract surgeons. The lure of wealth attracted others, not so much through the practice of medicine but from the involvement in mining ventures. Others came as health-seekers. The pay was not excessive. A physician in Prescott in the 1890s could earn around $300 a month at his practice.

As with any profession, there were a few incompetents and impostors. The great majority were dedicated to the profession and were a welcome addition to any community.

Reading, writing, and arithmetic, like many other cultural conveniences, were late in arriving on the Arizona frontier. The lifestyle for young people residing in the Territory was not conducive to learning the arts. Some communities were so rough that the citizens could assume no responsibility for any pranks their offspring might choose to play upon the teachers. One teacher in Tombstone came home from school one day to find his house had been painted with polka dots, while another took a pistol away from an impish cherub and tossed it into the stove. In her anger, she forgot to remove the bullets. A reminder to check such things in the future was driven home in a resounding manner shortly afterward.

When the Sisters of St. Joseph stopped briefly in Yuma prior to journeying across the desert to Tucson, locals there warned of the dangers of travel through Indian country. It should be noted that the sisters also received several proposals of marriage from the town's bachelor element. Undaunted, the fearless ladies trekked on to the Old Pueblo, where they established a school for girls.

Students and teachers attending school along the Mexican border in the early 1900s found studies occasionally disrupted, particularly when some revolutionary battle was taking place nearby. Attendance was always poor during those times as the youngsters flocked to the border to watch the fireworks. One school at Palominas was so near the action that the cannons were easily heard. One time a group of revolutionaries pulled a cannon to the top of a hill overlooking Naco, where they fired down into the city below. Unable to anchor the gun properly, the recoil from each shot caused it to roll back down the opposite way, not stopping until it reached the bottom. The soldiers would then trot down the hill and tow the cannon up the hill once more. This, of course, limited the action to just a few shots a day.

Funds were not always available for a school and the teachers had to make use of whatever materials and structures were at hand. Josephine Brawley Hughes opened the first public school for girls in Tucson in an old brewery, while Mary Elizabeth Post taught pupils at Yuma in a three-room adobe building that had formerly served as the city jail and courtroom. Graffiti scratched on the walls gave mute testimony as to the previous occupants, along with serving to broaden the educational horizons of the pupils.

One of the most versatile and articulate of the early Arizonans was a Swiss named John Spring. Spring came to Arizona in 1866 with the Regular Army and decided to stay. At different times he was a brewer, farmer, court translator, artist, writer, and schoolteacher.

He began his pedagogic duties in Tucson in 1872 in an adobe building with a dirt floor that had to be sprinkled with water to hold down the dust. The parents, in anticipation of some future need, brought Spring a supply of ash flogging sticks. School opened with 138 students ranging in age from six to twenty-one. Most couldn't speak English. Among the pupils was a young man named Ignacio Bonillas. Ignacio had captured the interest of Governor A. P. K. Safford, who was a frequent visitor to the school. He had been absent for several days and when the governor asked his whereabouts he was told that the boy had no money to buy books and other supplies. Governor Safford offered to buy his books and any other supplies that the boy might need. The lad could come over to the governor's place each morning and feed his mules and perform other tasks in payment. This enterprise seems to have worked well, for Ignacio continued his education and went on to become

Mexico's first ambassador to Washington. A school in Tucson is named in his honor today. A. P. K. Safford is recognized today as the father of the public school system in Arizona.

John Spring's school was a great success. At the time he was making $125 a month. He went to the board and asked for an increase to $150 a month in order to hire an assistant. The board informed him that they could hire two female teachers, called "schoolma'ms," at the price they were paying him. After Spring resigned, the board hired two ladies to teach. However, they failed to meet the first prerequisite for teaching in Arizona. They couldn't speak Spanish, and their students couldn't speak English.

By and large, women were preferred as teachers because they were more patient, and worked for less money. On the other hand, in a male-dominated society, few remained teachers, or single, for long. The bachelors grabbed them up as fast as they arrived.

Not all were qualified in their profession either. In Florence a prospective lady failed the qualification test administered to her by a member of the school board. She was allowed to teach anyway, as the board member confessed he couldn't pass the test either.

An embarrassing oversight nearly delayed the opening of the forerunner of Arizona State University at Tempe. It seems that in the rush to construct someone forgot to erect outhouses for the students and faculty. The error was discovered just two days prior to the opening of school and a special meeting was called to remedy the situation. A committee of one board member, Charles Trumbull Hayden, saw to it that the proper facilities were added and the first term in 1886 opened on schedule.

There were many preachers who came to Arizona during her territorial days in hopes of salvaging a few of the many lost souls. But none was more liked and respected by men and women of all walks of life than blue-blooded New Englander Endicott Peabody, who came to Tombstone during its legendary heyday. A big, burly 200-pounder, he quickly won the respect of the miners with his athletic prowess. In a boxing match he could hold his own with the best of the tough mining camp pugilists. He was as much at home on the baseball diamond as he was standing in the pulpit of the Episcopalian church that he helped to build. His friends and admirers ranged from mining magnates and superintendents to gamblers and saloonkeepers. He once preached a sermon against cattle rustling and drinking in Charleston. It aroused the ire of one cowboy, Billy

Claibourne, friend of the Clantons and McLaurys. Claibourne sent word to Tombstone that if the minister ever preached again in Charleston, he would make him dance. Peabody then sent word that he would be in Charleston in a couple of weeks and would look forward to meeting Mr. Claibourne. Just as he had done a few months earlier at the O.K. Corral fight, Billy decided he had more important business elsewhere.

Peabody frequently visited the saloons and gambling palaces in Tombstone, informing the locals that he would be preaching against the evils of sin and vice the following Sunday. Interestingly, employees and customers alike respected him enough to give up a little of their time to attend church and hear the big man speak.

It was unfortunate for Tombstone that the Reverend Mr. Peabody only served the town for six months before his tenure ended. They realized that they had not only lost a preacher, but also their baseball umpire, boxing referee, and a colorful companion.

Sometime later he established a church-affiliated boys' school at Groton, Massachusetts, which he headed until his retirement in 1940. Among his many protégés was a young lad named Franklin Delano Roosevelt.

The emotional pulse of a community was largely regulated by the local newspapers. Subscribers were fed a steady diet of news coverage that included much editorializing by the staff. Competition between newspapers was keen for both advertisers and subscribers. Each considered itself the guardian of humanity and deliverer from the wicked wages of sin that gravitated upon the community in one form or another. Editorials were of a highly emotional nature, laced with raw vitriol, mincing neither words nor opinions. Fear of libel never held a frontier journalist back, even though there were codes and fines against such things. The lack in factual material to substantiate claims many times culminated in physical violence for the parties involved. Then, as now, newspapers exerted a powerful influence over the populace. Whether this was a positive force or otherwise depended upon the journalistic propensities of the editor and his staff.

The frontier editors were an intrepid breed. The mighty pen became a potent weapon in the journalistic arsenal of a man bent on a cause, and there were plenty of causes toward which one could bend. More than one editor had to resort to something more mighty than the pen in defense of some printed material that stirred the ire of some citizen or competitor.

John Clum's Tombstone *Epitaph* fought a running battle with the Tombstone *Nugget,* not only over political issues of the day but over the Earp-Clanton feud as well. On one occasion the editor was fired upon from ambush by parties who had taken offense at his editorials.

Ed Cross of the Tubac *Weekly Arizonian* fought a famous duel with promoter Sylvester Mowry over remarks the former had made in reference to the latter's schemes. Fortunately this turned out to be a bloodless affray as both men missed their target.

There were several alternatives open to an important man in public life who found himself the victim of journalistic lies and innuendoes. It was not unusual for an offended person to demolish printing presses in the course of silencing the venomous pen of some insolent writer. He could also attempt to silence the mischievous journalist by bribing him. More subtle was the practice of removing a newspaper that had become a nuisance by stopping the advertising. Since this was the lifeblood of a newspaper, an editor who incurred the wrath of the controlling nabobs in a community could expect to see his list of advertisers dwindle to nothing in a short time.

This form of intimidation is exemplified in the case of Lindley Branson and the Jerome *Sun.* During World War I Branson's fledgling newspaper took on both the powerful United Verde mine and the *Arizona Mining News,* an established paper with a circulation of more than six thousand subscribers. At first the company and the *News* ignored the verbal assaults aimed at them from the brash young upstart, but when the *Sun* accused the United Verde of being a slacker in the war effort, when in fact the mine was operating at full capacity, it was more than the officials could stand. Adding to this were vindictive attacks on other citizens in the town who were friendly to the mine. Shortly afterward, the presses belonging to the *Sun* mysteriously disappeared. Using a borrowed press, the paper continued to publish for a short time, while a shortage of advertisers created further financial problems. On April 9, 1918, the Jerome *Sun* published its last edition and the frustrated editor was forced to call it quits and move on.

News reporters played significant roles in the uncovering of the many scandals that plagued Arizona during her territorial days.

When master forger James Addison Reavis, better known as the Baron of Arizona, schemed to claim a parcel of real estate that included nearly 11 million acres and extended from Silver City, New Mexico, on the east, to a point west of Phoenix, Arizona, it was a group of Arizona newspapers who raised an indignant cry, calling upon citizens to rally against the claims of the "Baron." Tom Weedin, editor of the Florence *Enterprise,* played a significant role in bringing Reavis and his henchmen to justice. The sharp-eyed reporter noted that the "ancient" documents bore Wisconsin watermarks and the type of print used on the forgeries was not in use during the period Reavis claimed they were written.

"Doc" Richard Flower was making a fortune selling stock in an imaginary gold mine called the Spendazuma, supposedly located near the San Carlos Reservation. Reporter George Smalley of the *Arizona Republican* became suspicious, traveled to the fictitious mine, and subsequently exposed the 10-million-dollar nefarious dealings to the public.

Both of these frontier journalists exposed these scandals under threats of bodily harm.

Modern-day editors and journalists are not immune to threats of violence, yet they continue to be watchdogs for the public interest in exposing shady political dealings and land fraud schemes. The tragic murder of investigative reporter Don Bolles in the spring of 1976 is an example of the ultimate price that is sometimes exacted from a reporter in the performance of public service.

The two most significant publishers in twentieth-century Arizona have been William R. Mathews of Tucson's *Arizona Daily Star* and Eugene C. Pulliam of the *Arizona Republic.* Mathews was publisher of the *Daily Star* from 1924 to 1969. He purchased the struggling paper from Phelps-Dodge and changed its image from that of a "copper-collared" journal to one of the finest newspaper publications in the West. Mathews' crowning achievement perhaps was the establishment of a medical school for the University of Arizona at Tucson. Pulliam acquired the *Republic* and the Phoenix *Gazette* in 1946 and was largely responsible for the growth of the Republican party in the state, the realization of the Central Arizona Project, and university status for Arizona State College at Tempe. Today the *Republic* is the state's leading newspaper, its circulation reaching even the most remote sections of Arizona.

The immense mining regions with their intricate laws concerning ownership of claims brought lawyers and judges to the Territory by the score. Like the doctors, many were self-appointed and practiced accordingly. Others were brilliant men dedicated to the betterment of the profession. Judge Joseph P. Allyn, Arizona's first "health-seeker," wrote many articles about the new territory. Allyn came to Arizona with the first territorial officials in 1863. Judge Joseph Kibbey rendered several monumental decisions concerning water rights in Arizona, becoming known as the foremost authority on irrigation law. Both Kibbey and Judge Richard E. Sloan became territorial governors of Arizona.

Many towns really had no official judge and usually a man respected for his knowledge would be asked to arbitrate disputes between two parties. If the man's decisions appeared wise to the populace, he would simply evolve into the role of justice of the peace. One such man was Charles H. Meyer of Tucson. Born in Hannover, Germany, Meyer came to Arizona with the U. S. Army. He settled in Tucson in 1858, and opened a drugstore. His Army experiences in the Hospital Corps had taught him a great deal about mixing medicines and he was soon known in the Old Pueblo as Dr. Meyer. He was elected justice of the peace in 1864 and held public office until the turn of the century. Charlie Meyer owned two books in those early days, likely the only two books in the city. One was *The Technique of Setting Bones*, and the other was called *Materia Medica*. Both were German, and in times when a decision needed to be rendered, Judge Meyer would consult the *Medica* and a decision would be forthcoming. These decisions were apparently never questioned, as nobody else could read German, and who would dare question such a high authority as the *Medica?*

Judge Meyer became a terror to not only the transgressors of law in Tucson, but to their lawyers as well. On at least one occasion he passed sentence upon both attorney and client when the former questioned his decision.

Another of Judge Meyer's contributions to Tucson was the initiation of a "chain gang" system, whereby a convicted person could work off his sentence by performing some civic function such as sweeping the streets.

Judge Meyer had the uncanny ability to guess just how much money the accused person was carrying. This would usually constitute the amount of the fine imposed.

One intractable miscreant named "Olive Camp Johnnie Divine"

40. Charles T. Hayden, Santa Fe trader, freighter, merchant, and judge. He operated a ferry on the Salt River where Tempe is today. His son Carl served in the U. S. Congress longer than any other man. *Arizona State Lib*.

41. Commodore Perry Owens, sheriff of Apache County; remembered mostly for his shoot-out with the Blevins gang at Holbrook in 1887. *Arizona State Lib*.

42. Harry Wheeler, Roughrider, Arizona Ranger captain, and sheriff of Cochise County. *Arizona Historical Foundation, Barry Goldwater Photo Collection.*

43. Left to right: Ed St. Clair, Carl Holton, William "Buckey" O'Neill, and James Black, the posse from Prescott who captured the gang that held up the train at Canyon del Diablo. *Arizona State Lib.*

44. George W. P. Hunt, first governor of the state of Arizona. Nicknamed "Old Roman," he was elected governor seven times. *Arizona Historical Foundation, Hunt Collection.*

45. Marcus A. Smith,
Tombstone lawyer,
territorial delegate, and
one of the first two
senators from Arizona.
*Arizona Historical
Foundation.*

46. Peter Brady, miner,
surveyor, legislator,
merchant, and lawman.
Sharlot Hall Museum.

47. Carl Hayden during his first political campaign. Scion of a pioneer family and sheriff of Maricopa County, Hayden served in the U. S. Congress longer than any other man. *Arizona Historical Foundation.*

48. Estevan Ochóa, Tucson pioneer, politician, and freighter. *Arizona Historical Foundation.*

49. Nellie Bush, riverboat pilot, politician, and airplane pilot, one of the state's most colorful characters. *Arizona Historical Foundation.*

50. Senator Barry Goldwater, Arizona's most famous citizen. Writer, photographer, and avid historian, the senator discusses some of his family's pioneer history with the author in 1974.

51. Warrant Officer Fred Ferguson, U. S. Army helicopter pilot who won the Medal of Honor when he flew his ship through heavy enemy fire to rescue and bring to safety the passengers and crew of a downed helicopter during the Tet Offensive, January 1968. *U. S. Army photograph.*

found himself brought up before Judge Meyer once too often for mischievous behavior. Johnnie was known in mining circles as a steady, hard-working miner. However, on rare visits to town he displayed a proclivity for being a bit too destructive for Tucson's more refined inhabitants. His favorite stunt was to rent a horse at the local stable and race up and down Congress Street. After being hauled in several times for the same offense the judge warned him that the next race would cost him $50. Sure enough, the next day Johnnie was up before the bench again. "Well, what have you been doing now?" the judge asked, in his strong German accent.

"Painting the town red," was the reply.

"Well, I charge you $50 for the paint," the judge said as he brought down his gavel.

One of the most humorous episodes in his courtroom happened when the judge and a companion were ticketed for speeding in a buggy. When the matter came up before the court he fined his companion $15. Then he got down off the bench and coming around to the other side faced the now vacated seat, gave himself a stern admonishment, and pronounced a $25 fine upon himself. He then reached into his pocket, withdrew the money, and paid his fine. With that, Judge Meyer walked back around and seated himself upon the bench. All this was done to the delight and applause of the courtroom audience.

Over at Ehrenberg there was a judge of a different character. In the waning days of the river traffic on the Colorado, a crippled, autocratic man named Tom Hamilton handed out justice to the local miscreants. In addition to his positions as postmaster and ferryman, Hamilton owned a saloon and small store. It was said he was his own best customer, spending many hours in blissful sleep following a night of debauchery. During these times the store and bar were kept open on a serve-yourself basis.

Not all of the territorial justices were of an amicable nature. One such character was Jim Burnett of Charleston. Taking livestock as payment in lieu of money for fines levied on cattlemen, Burnett stocked his own ranch with the proceeds. Charleston was a hangout for many Cochise County rustlers and smugglers, and Burnett seems to have been no better than most of the people brought before the bench. He was even known to have dispensed justice at gunpoint, collecting said fines.

Burnett's pernicious behavior finally caught up with him when he was alleged to have blown up a dam built by Colonel William C. Greene on the San Pedro River. Greene had built the dam for water storage and Burnett apparently felt that not enough water was flowing on down to his own place so he blew the dam up. Unfortunately two children, one of them Greene's, died in the flood that followed.

Shortly after, Greene gunned down Burnett on the streets of Tombstone in broad daylight in front of witnesses. Greene was exonerated of charges, lending no doubt to the fact that the general public was glad to be rid of the justice from Charleston.

Jerome had Lewis St. James for a justice of the peace. He was totally deaf and never heard any of the testimony presented him, but he knew most of the men personally, as well as all their past transgressions. With this knowledge in mind he rendered his decisions and fines accordingly.

Though the acts of the judges were colorful at times, they were occasionally outdone by the buffoonery of the attorneys. C. L. Sonnichsen's classic work on the characters of Tombstone, *Billy King's Tombstone*, vividly describes the antics of some of these lawyers. On Fourth Street between Allen and Tough Nut in Tombstone was a row of one-story adobe structures that housed Tombstone's inimitable attorneys. To the local citizenry, the area was known somewhat affectionately as "Rotten Row." The offices were located auspiciously between the courthouse and the saloons of Allen Street. Perhaps the most famous to graduate from that group of barristers was Marcus Aurelius Smith, who later served as territorial delegate eight times in Washington and in 1911 was elected as one of the state's first senators.

Mark, as he was called by his friends, had few equals an an orator. His dynamic personality and character made him one of Tombstone's most illustrious and popular citizens.

Another "member of the bar" was William C. Staehle. No one knew for sure what the middle initial "C." signified. His associates claimed it stood for "corkscrew," attributing it to his favorite pastime. He referred to himself as the "German warrior." One night after causing some disturbance in one of the local drinking establishments, the stately Teuton was escorted out the back door and given a friendly kick in the seat of the pants. Recalling the incident later, he replied indignantly, "I didn't mind so much being kicked, but the dirty son of a gun kicked me with a pair of dollar-and-a-half shoes."

A partner of Mark Smith's in Tombstone was Allen R. English. Old-timers in Cochise County say that he was the greatest orator of them all. He had an adroit command of the English language and was known as a great persuader of juries. He could shed great tears, cajole, be sentimental or indignant. At times he was even poetic and the audience loved to hear him orate. However, John Barleycorn had gotten the best of him. The mining companies used to retain him as their attorney on important trials. When a case was coming up, they would send a special detail over to sit with English in his hotel room, keeping him as dry as possible.

A story is told about a time when, during a recess, he got so drunk that he had to be carried back into the courtroom. He had gone to have lunch in one of the local saloons. At the end of two hours he was so stiff that he had to be stretched out in the back of a wagon for the return trip. However, once before the jury, he steadied himself and launched an oratory of poetry and logic that held the audience spellbound. Observers said it was his greatest speech. Some two hours later, his client cleared, the great elocutionist was still too drunk to go home by himself.

THE POLITICOS

THE RICH MINERAL STRIKES in Arizona in the nineteenth century brought to the Territory more than just the desert rat prospector and the hard-rock miner. Settlers, farmers, ranchers, and soldiers all followed in the footsteps of those early Argonauts. It would have been impossible for these people to sustain life for an extended period during those years had it not been for the freighter, the merchant, and his predecessor, the traveling drummer.

Many of these early freighters and merchants, ranchers, farmers, and miners played significant roles in Arizona's political future in the years to come. One of the most noteworthy was Peter Brady.

Arriving in Texas in 1845, Brady joined the Texas Mounted Volunteers, where he made the acquaintance of William S. Oury, another man destined to play a major role in the history of southern Arizona. Following a brief sojourn in California in 1848, he returned to Texas by way of Tucson. In Texas he served as a lieutenant in "Big Foot" Wallace's Texas Rangers for over a year, distinguishing himself in several battles with the Comanche.

In 1853 Brady was in Arizona with Andrew B. Gray, leading a survey team along the 32nd parallel. While mapping the area he became interested in the mining possibilities around Ajo. The next year he organized the Arizona Trading and Mining Company and began shipping high-grade ore to Swansea, Wales, for smelting. This is believed to be the first commercial mining development in Arizona. Because of his fluency in Spanish and several Indian dialects, Brady spent the next few years as an interpreter for the Army at Fort Mohave. During his free time he published a newspaper, the *Mohave Dog Star,* the first in northern Arizona. According to historian James H. McClintock, the paper was "issued more for pastime than otherwise, its ostensible object being to correct the free love tendencies of the Mohave Indians."

Following the Civil War, during which time he did intelligence work for the Union in Mexico, Brady returned to Pima County, where he tossed his hat into the political ring, becoming that county's first elected sheriff. In 1870 he ran for territorial delegate, but lost to Governor Richard C. McCormick. A later recount showed that Brady had actually won.

In his autumn years, Pete Brady served in the territorial legislature as representative from both Pima and the newly created Pinal counties. Taking up residence in Florence, he was also sheriff of Pinal County and operated a flour mill. At the time of his retirement from politics, Brady was the oldest member of the legislature.

Many of the early pioneers of the Southwest were either on the run from something or opportunists. Others were typical border riffraff, as mentioned in early accounts by writers such as John C. Cremony and J. Ross Browne. Pete Brady belonged to none of these dubious elements. He was well educated, a natural leader of men, strong, and able. In short, he was the prototype of the ideal pioneer.

One of Arizona's most distinguished political families traces its beginnings in the Territory to those early days when supplies were either hauled across the desert on the Bradshaw Road from California or transported by ocean voyage around the Baja to Yuma, thence up the Colorado to the various river ports.

Michael Goldwater came to Arizona Territory in 1860 from California, where he opened a store at La Paz, on the Colorado. He and his brother Joseph supplied the miners during the early gold rushes in that region. They later opened other stores in Ehrenberg, Prescott, Bisbee, and Phoenix, becoming well-known as merchants and freighters throughout the Territory.

Joe Goldwater got his start in the mercantile business with a grubstake from his friend Levi Strauss. The famous pants-maker from San Francisco financed him with $25,000 worth of merchandise. It is said that Joe was slow in paying this debt to Levi but eventually the matter was settled.

There was always the danger of violence by either outlaw or Apache on those lonely roads. On one occasion Joe was severely wounded during a running gunfight with some hostile Apache on a road outside of Prescott.

Michael Goldwater had two sons, Baron and Morris. Morris was one of the most influential men in early Arizona politics, serving as mayor of Prescott for twenty-two years, territorial legislator, and vice-president of the Arizona Constitutional Convention in 1910. He was the man who, perhaps, did the most to establish the Democratic party in Arizona.

The other son, Baron, opened a store in Phoenix in 1872, followed by a second store in 1895. Throughout the territorial and statehood periods they have remained two of Arizona's most popular department stores.

An interesting story is told concerning the building of one of the Goldwater stores in Phoenix. It seems that when the Goldwaters erected their building, they accidentally built past another party's property line. When this error was pointed out the building was moved, at no small expense, to well inside the property line. Sometime later, when the party earlier mentioned decided to erect a building of his own, he built right up to what he thought was the property line. Not realizing that the Goldwater brothers, taking no chances this time, had plenty of space between their building and the property line, said party built on the Goldwater property. Much embarrassment was suffered by the party when he learned of his mistake.

Political vexations are commonplace in a democratic society. Some are humorous and some are not; some are just plain old horse-trading and others are more ignominious in nature.

Following the war with Mexico, Arizona had come into the Union as a part of New Mexico. Feeling isolated and so far from the territorial capital at Santa Fe, the locals began clamoring for separate status. Legal and military aid was limited and justice was served by those who were strong enough to administer it. The Arizonans differed politically from the New Mexicans, who tended to be much more conservative than their neighbors to the west.

Interestingly, the original shape of Arizona was oblong, extending from the 103rd meridian westward along the 34th parallel to the Colorado River. A compromise with Santa Fe over boundary lines gave Arizona the familiar profile she has today. New Mexico forfeited some of the rich minerals of her western regions for the fertile Mesilla Valley.

Separate territorial status from New Mexico had been difficult to achieve. In 1860 a convention was held in Tucson setting up a provisional government with Dr. Lewis S. Owings as first governor. The following year a rebellious convention at Mesilla severed all ties with the Union and declared Arizona a territory. In February 1862 Colonel John Baylor declared the oblong version of Arizona to be a territory of the Confederacy. In June 1862 General James Carleton of the California Volunteers proclaimed the reoccupied area a territory of the Union. Finally, on February 24, 1863, thanks to the political groundwork of promoters Charlie Poston, Sylvester Mowry, and Sam Heintzelman (in years previous), Arizona officially became a United States Territory. In this case, the fourth time was the charm.

The Territory was plagued by a shifting capital. Tucson seemed the likely choice, but her large Mexican population and the recent embracing of the Confederacy caused many to withdraw support. The Mexican war was still fresh in the minds of many, and the war with the Confederacy was still in progress. Thanks to the recent mineral discoveries in the Bradshaw Mountains and the prodding of General Carleton, the territorial delegation selected the site of Prescott as first capital. At the time, there was no village on Granite Creek, so the party, led by Governor John Goodwin and secretary Richard McCormick, set up temporary quarters in Chino Valley, the original location of Fort Whipple. In May, both soldiers and politicians moved southward to Granite Creek, where Fort Whipple was relocated and a capitol building was erected. The new community was named Prescott by McCormick in honor of the great American historian William Hickling Prescott.

The two-room log cabin which served as capitol building had no windows, so the legislators worked by candlelight. The walls had not been calked and the cool autumn breezes kept the rooms ventilated. No one objected when the tobacco chewers spat on the floor, as it was dirt anyway. All in all, it was a far cry from the eastern luxury which the newcomers were used to enjoying. Justice William T. Howell, who drew up the first code of laws for the Territory, left Arizona in disgust after a year, complaining of the harsh conditions in which he had to conduct court. He found the adobe shack with a dirt floor and the upturned crate for a rostrum not to his liking.

Most of the early administrators left Arizona for the more comfortable environs of the East at the first opportunity.

In 1867 the capital was shifted to Tucson, where it remained for ten years. Prescott secured the prize in 1877, and held it for a dozen years. Finally, in 1889 the so-called "capital on wheels" was moved to Phoenix, where it has remained. Phoenix, at this time, was a bustling agricultural community of some three thousand residents. It should be mentioned that all these shifts were not without a certain amount of chicanery and vote-buying.

The legislature was by and large Democratic. The national administration was Republican during the territorial years. Therefore the appointed governors were usually Republican and the legislators were Democrats. Since the legislators were in session for a brief period, the governors seldom saw them. Communication was lacking. Thanks to the political spoils system in Washington, each time there was a change in the administration Arizona's federal officialdom was revamped in the "house cleaning."

The territorial legislature met for sixty-day sessions annually and legislators were paid $4.00 a day plus travel expenses. All legislation was subject to review in Washington, thus allowing for the rise to power of several special-interest groups including mining, railroads, cattle, and farming. It was said, perhaps satirically but with a certain amount of credibility, that the makeup of the representatives in the territorial legislature consisted of the following: twenty representatives for the mines, fifteen for the railroads, ten for the cattlemen, utilities, and farmers, five for organized labor, and five for the rest of the populace.

Arizonans would soon learn that statehood would be a much more difficult plum to achieve than territorial status. It would be forty-nine years and many political battles later before Arizona would add her star, the forty-eighth, to the national colors. In her early struggles for statehood, which began in 1871, Arizona had many internal problems. Poor roads and lack of suitable transportation kept her isolated from the rest of the Union. The mail service was inadequate and the mines needed capital to expand their operations. It was nearly 1890 before the roving bands of hostile Apache were tamed, and well into the 1900s before most of the rustler-outlaw elements were driven out of business. The political question of the federal purchase of silver also delayed statehood. The eastern establishment was not interested in adding any more representatives from the western territories to the U. S. Congress. Populism had become a popular issue among Westerners and this also frightened the congressmen.

Early political observers of Arizona went away with misconceptions or were disillusioned by what they saw. One senator remarked of Arizona in the early 1900s, "You cannot have statehood. You have some Indians and Mormons down there." Teddy Roosevelt spoke in favor of joint Arizona-New Mexico statehood. He so enraged locals in Phoenix that a vote was called to change the name of Roosevelt Street to Cleveland Street. There was no way the Populist-Democrats of Arizona wanted a joint venture with the conservative Republicans from New Mexico. Albert Beveridge, senator from Indiana, conducted a whirlwind tour of Arizona in the early 1900s—so rapid, in fact, that delegate Mark Smith remarked that he couldn't catch up to it. After locating some Mexicans who couldn't speak English, Beveridge, referring to Arizona as a "mining camp," concluded (perhaps satisfying some preconceived notion) that there were not enough English-speaking people in Arizona. Therefore the state would be controlled by the minority Anglo-Americans. He recommended a joint venture with New Mexico. Others, such as newspaper nabob William Randolph Hearst, came to the Territory and reported favorably. To these, Washington turned a deaf ear, preferring instead to use the issue as a political football for the next several years.

The Territory did have several things going for it in its quest for statehood around the turn of the century. Traditionally statehood had always followed a neophyte period of territorial status. The Salt River project had begun and water for irrigation would be forthcoming. There was prosperity in the mines and the population was growing. The natural resources such as copper and lumber were available in abundance. Thanks in part to the Arizona Rangers, law and order had come. Last, but certainly not least, the Arizonans had played a significant role in the recent war with Spain not only as members of the Roughriders, but in other regiments as well.

Most of the territorial governors were capable men, although some hated the place and made no bones about it. The early governors were carpetbaggers. In later times the chief executives were selected from Arizona residents. All were subject to the political whims of the party in power in Washington. They ranged from skillful politicians like Richard McCormick and brilliant men the caliber of Judge Joseph Kibby to political retreads and opportunists like John C. Frémont, an old "pathfinder" who spent most of his tenure pathfinding in the lairs of eastern capitalists, promoting various mining schemes.

Conrad Zulick, who served from 1885 to 1889, was the first Democrat to act as governor. Zulick is unique in the annals of territorial governors in that he has the dubious distinction of sitting in a Mexican jail at the time of his appointment to the office. He had to be rescued somewhat dramatically by a U.S. marshal to assume the duties of governor. Myron McCord had three wives, as did A. P. K. Safford. Safford divorced one of his wives by territorial legislation. On the other end of the marital spectrum was Lewis Wolfley, who was Arizona's only bachelor governor. Wolfley had a terrible disposition, which may account for his bachelor status. He was removed from office in the middle of his term.

Irregularities at the polls during territorial days were evidenced by an election in 1870 at Yuma when the local Indians were used to cast votes. Clad only in breechcloths and stovepipe hats (the latter no doubt a bribe for services rendered), the natives awaited their turn at the polls. When the clerk asked their names the Indians replied, in mock innocence, Sullivan, O'Toole, or some other such sobriquet which they had been previously instructed to give. It was said that some four hundred ineligible voters of both sexes turned out at the polls. Two years earlier "Slippery Dick" McCormick carried Pima County 932 votes to 71 over John Rush in the race for delegate to Congress. The Prescott *Miner* charged that soldiers from Fort Crittenden and many non-citizens from Mexico voted as many as three times. The motto was, "Vote early and vote often."

Politics at the county and local level in territorial Arizona sometimes sparked events that created national interest. It also did much to enhance the wild frontier image that the West held for those in the eastern part of the country. Those who only knew what they read in the papers were the gullible ones.

Three candidates threw their hats into the ring for the office of sheriff of Maricopa County in the fall of 1869. Of the three, Jim Barnum was the least conspicuous. He seemed content just to sit back and let his two adversaries fight over the issues of the day. The other two, "Whispering Jim" Favorite and J. M. Chenoweth, proclaimed vociferously the incompetence and low morality of each other. The names of the noisy twosome were on everyone's lips while the silent candidate was nearly forgotten, although it was said that he contributed subtly to the growing political feud, occasionally feeding the flames. The battle of words reached such proportions that open hostility was inevitable. When the smoke had cleared, "Whispering Jim" lay dead on the ground and Mr. Chenoweth was advised to leave town immediately.

When election day rolled around, the unopposed candidate, silent Jim Barnum, was elected. As one might surmise, he was elected by a landslide vote, thus becoming the first sheriff of Maricopa County.

The territorial legislature had perhaps its most memorable session when it met for the thirteenth time at Prescott in 1885. Its misdeeds have become classic. Tax money was squandered on lavish entertainment and outlandish travel expenses. Tucson raised some $4,000 in bribe money to have the capital relocated to that city. "If that isn't enough another sack will be forthcoming," they boldly declared. Willcox sent another sack of money to promote the creation of a new county, to be called Sierra Bonita. Opponents of this in Cochise County sent another sack to counter the offer. The railroads were said to have another sack. It should be mentioned that as far as is known, no member of the legislature was found guilty of taking a bribe. This money was to be used strictly for out-partying the opposition, thereby influencing the votes.

Claims for expenditures set all kinds of records for the session. One member hired his wife and kids as clerks. Several others employed women of "questionable background" whose only duty was to entertain their employers. The members were paid $.15 a mile for travel expenses, and Pima County delegates, who came by train via California, claimed $330 per member. Dr. Frank Ainsworth, delegate-at-large from the northern section of the Territory, put in a mileage claim covering the distance from the northernmost area of Arizona, asking $225 in expenses for the trip. Dr. Ainsworth actually lived just down the street within easy walking distance from where the delegates met. Over $40,000 was spent for clerks and publicity alone. This figure seems astounding when one considers the legal limit for expenditures was only $4,000. Perhaps the delegates allocating funds simply misplaced a decimal point. It should be mentioned that there were an equal number of Democrats and

Republicans present so neither party had the opportunity self-righteously to cast stones at some later date.

There were several battles of a physical nature. J. A. Brown and Lafayette Nash of Yavapai County engaged each other in a battle of fisticuffs. Another delegate swung a wrench at a fellow member. Fortunately he missed. A duel was averted when one of the adversaries chose as weapons French poniards, and as the only poniards available were hundreds of miles away, the duel was called off and drinks were served instead.

Each populated area had gone to the session hoping to gain certain things for its respective constituents. Tucson wanted to regain the lost territorial capital. Phoenix wanted an insane asylum, Tempe a normal school, and Florence was hoping for a bridge to span the Gila River. Pima County, or Tucson, was late for the session. Traveling by train to California, thence to Ash Fork, the delegates had boarded a stagecoach at that community for Prescott. The stage encountered a blizzard at Hell's Canyon midway to Prescott, and was delayed. Undismayed by all this inconvenience, council member R. N. Leatherwood borrowed a donkey and completed the trip to the capital. Unfortunately for Tucson's members, the parties had already begun and most of the rich political plums had already been handed out. They were given a university as compensation for their efforts. Upon his return home, one of the Tucson delegates was greeted with a shower of rotten vegetables and eggs from irate citizens. One particularly disgruntled Tucsonian threw a dead cat at the hapless politician.

Florence was given her bridge. But as nature would have it, the fickle Gila changed her course shortly after the dedication ceremonies and left the bridge standing some distance from the river's edge.

So much has been said about the misdeeds of the so-called "Thieving Thirteenth" that it would be unfair not to mention some of her good deeds. Among them are included charters for today's Arizona State University, the University of Arizona, and a hospital for the insane.

When the uproar had died down, two U.S. grand juries were called upon to investigate the conduct of the delegates. All were given a clean bill of health. Nevertheless, out of its entire thirty-six-member body, only one was re-elected to attend the following session.

ENTER THE LAW—
THE ARIZONA RANGERS

THE CLOSE PROXIMITY to the Mexican border has, to this day, made Arizona a prime target for lawlessness and smuggling of contraband. Even the Apache utilized it with his infamous plunder trails up the river valleys into Mexico. Today many of those ancient trails are still used, but for a different kind of contraband. Since its beginning in 1924, the U. S. Border Patrol has had the difficult responsibility for keeping law and order along the international border.

In the latter part of the nineteenth century, cattle rustlers were operating on a major scale, especially in southeastern Arizona. The remoteness of the terrain made pursuit and apprehension close to impossible. The local ranchers, for the most part, lacked the facilities to combat the rustler gangs. Many feared the outlaws so much that when a posse did enter the stricken area, they refused to help. They even gave warning to the outlaws of the approaching lawmen. In some areas the outlaws operated in broad daylight and bragged about it openly.

Finally in 1901 Governor Nathan Oakes Murphy decided to take strong action against the smugglers and rustlers. He organized a company of lawmen patterned after the famed Texas Rangers. Their history was brief, August 1901 to February 1909. They were probably the only police force in history to be disbanded because they were too efficient. The newspapers loved them. The pages were full of their heroic exploits. This, of course, was bound to cause resentment and jealousy among the local police agencies. One has only to read the collection of newspaper accounts of the day to appreciate how an overeager, hero-worshiping press could and did cause bitter feelings locally.

Governor Murphy's first chore was to hire a leader for the new organization, a man with proven ability to handle the difficult task that lay ahead. He was able to persuade Burt Mossman, erstwhile superintendent of the Aztec Land and Cattle Company, to take the job.

Using the old adage "It takes a thief . . . ," Mossman set about putting together a tough bunch of lawmen. Not that all were former outlaws, but many had, at one time or another, taken a step or two on the wrong side of the law.

The Arizona Rangers started out with twelve men and were never allowed to have more than twenty-six men on the force at one time. They were not federal agents, but worked for the Territory. The average age was thirty-six, and the pay ranged from $175 a month for the captain to $100 for the privates, of which there were twenty. In between were four sergeants at $110 a month and a lieutenant who was paid $130 monthly. The men signed on for one-year enlistments. The captains and lieutenants were allowed to ride free on trains, while the rest covered the Territory on horseback. Each man averaged some 390 miles per month on horseback, mostly in southern Arizona. Once apprehended, suspects were turned over to local authorities and the Ranger's task was accomplished. He filed a report and moved on, returning later if needed to testify.

The Rangers' counterpart on the south side of the international border was the Guardia Nacional. Their elite force was called the Gendarmería Fiscal and was commanded by an unlikely character named Emilio Kosterlitzky. Perhaps nowhere in the annals of southwestern history has a more improbable figure loomed, and the Southwest had more than its share of improbable figures. The son of a Russian cavalry colonel, Kosterlitzky himself was a Russian naval cadet. He jumped ship in South America and worked his way north. Arriving in Guaymas in 1872, he joined the Mexican Army as a private and worked his way up through the ranks.

When he served under dictator Porfirio Díaz, Kosterlitzky's star began to rise in the 1880s. He headed the dreaded border Rurales, or Cordada, a truculent band of rogues, recruited from Mexican jails and prisons and officered by the cream of the Mexican Army. The Gendarmería Fiscal was considered the most efficient police organization in the world at the time. To a captured outlaw, vengeance was swift and harsh, though some were given a choice of meeting a firing squad or joining Kosterlitzky's Cordada.

For more than a quarter of a century, Kosterlitzky's law was the only law on the northern Mexican frontier. It was said you could "trundle a wheelbarrow loaded with diamonds from the border to Mazatlán without fear of molestation" during his long reign as head of the Cordada. However, as violent as Kosterlitzky's reputation was, Díaz was never able to persuade his "mailed fist" to assassinate political enemies of the state. Once, during Madero's brief tenure as president, Kosterlitzky was asked to go south to Morelos to gain the confidence of famed revolutionary leader Emiliano Zapata and then kill him. Kosterlitzky resigned his position instead. When Huerta seized power, the Russian was made a general. However, after his defeat at the hands of General Obregón in 1913, he crossed over the international border and surrendered his sword to U. S. Army officer Cornelius Cole Smith, Sr. Afterward the two officers became long-time friends, and Smith's son, Dr. Cornelius C. Smith, Jr., has written a very interesting and definitive account of the famous Cossack entitled *Kosterlitzky.*

Some of his methods might have been questionable, but Kosterlitzky's bravery and prowess on the battlefield have never been disputed. He had the battle scars to prove it. Once, in a chase with Pancho Villa, he observed that the rebel chieftain, mounted on a faster horse, was pulling away. In frustration, the Cossack threw his saber at Villa. Still not satisfied, he then threw his empty pistol in the direction of the quickly disappearing rogue.

On another occasion, his command scattered, Kosterlitzky rode over a hilltop right into the middle of an enemy force. Looking back over his shoulder and ordering his imaginary army to halt, he boldly rode up to the enemy and ordered them to throw down their arms. The Russian bluff worked and he singlehandedly captured the entire enemy command. He once had Geronimo and his band surrounded in the Sierra Madre but backed off in order to allow U.S. troops to negotiate a surrender.

Kosterlitzky only backed down once, and that was to Captain Tom Rynning and the Arizona Rangers at Cananea in 1906. The trouble began at an American mining operation, headed by Colonel William C. Greene, when Mexican employees struck for a wage increase up from $3.00 a day to $5.00, plus an eight-hour work day. When told these demands could not be met without the consent of Mexican governor Yzabal, they turned their frustrations loose on the Americans and their families. Several Americans were shot in cold blood and others were wounded. Colonel Greene wired the United States for help. "For God's sake send us armed help at once," he pleaded. Americans north of the border rallied to the cause, gathering at Bisbee. One group tried to advance across the border, which resulted in a shoot-out with Mexican troops.

In an attempt to restore order to the beleaguered city of Cananea, Governor Yzabal appointed Rynning and his Rangers as temporary officers in the Mexican Army and sent them by train to Cananea. No sooner had they arrived and taken position than Colonel Kosterlitzky and his Cordada arrived to take control. Knowing full well he was at a disadvantage strategically, he still attempted to bluff the Ranger captain. "Get the hell out of Mexico, Tom, or I'll shoot you out," he shouted to his old friend. There was tension in the air, both sides watching their commanders intently. While waiting for orders, Rynning told the Russian to get his troops into the rocks and he would show him a fight like he had never seen before. For several tense moments the colonel weighed the situation. No one was more surprised than Rynning when Kosterlitzky withdrew.

The refugees, numbering some three hundred, were safely escorted to Bisbee by train. Kosterlitzky later recalled the incident, saying he had taken the strong stand mostly as show for the effect it would have on the morale of his men. Still, the ominous presence of the Norteamericanos, with their rifles cocked and aimed down on Kosterlitzky and his men, must have had some effect on his decision also.

After moving to the United States, Kosterlitzky's vast knowledge of Mexican politics enabled him to render an invaluable service to U. S. Intelligence. He was able to provide much information on the German spies operating against the United States in Mexico. During World War I, Kosterlitzky, who spoke eight languages fluently, posed as a doctor and infiltrated a German organization in Los Angeles. As an undercover agent he provided the Department of Justice with a continuous stream of information on that group's activities.

Earlier, in 1903, the Rangers had another close call from striking workers. This time it was on the American side of the border. The workers, mostly Mexican and Italian, numbering some 3,500 in all, rioted in the neighboring towns of Clifton, Morenci, and Metcalf. It was the miners who held the high ground. Captain Tom Rynning and his nineteen Rangers found themselves in a tight situation, surrounded by a well-armed army of angry miners. A tragedy was averted when Colonel James McClintock and 230 Arizona National Guardsmen, along with 800 regular troops from Forts Grant and Huachuca, arrived.

Perhaps the thing that prevented further rioting was not man-made, as nature chose this moment to cast her lot into the sequence of events. A cloudburst flooded the San Francisco River, killing some twenty to thirty people. During this diversion, further rioting was averted and eventually a settlement was reached.

It was during the Morenci riots that the Rangers posed for a now famous photograph. Some fifty years later, the Winchester Arms Company published the photo in an advertisement. By some oversight, they captioned it "Texas Rangers." The mistake was soon corrected as a perturbed citizenry, mostly old-time Arizonans, responded to the *faux pas*. The arms company remedied the situation by throwing a party in honor of the corrected error and all seems to have ended on a happy note.

Burt Mossman was the first Ranger captain. Born in 1867 of Scotch-Irish ancestry, he came to Arizona in 1893 and worked as a cowman. In 1897 he was appointed superintendent for the near-defunct Aztec Land and Cattle Company. Following this venture he went into business with Ed Tovrea at Bisbee, where in 1901 he was asked to form the Rangers. A year later, following a minor scandal involving one of his men, Mossman resigned and went into business with Colonel Greene. He died in Roswell, New Mexico, in 1956 and is today one of that state's honored pioneers in the Cowboy Hall of Fame in Oklahoma City.

Tom Rynning, of Douglas, was appointed next. A native of Norway, he came to the United States in 1866, when he was only two years old. In 1885 he enlisted in the U. S. Cavalry, and fought in some seventeen battles during the Cheyenne and Apache campaigns. When war with Spain began, he joined Teddy Roosevelt's Roughriders, where he rose to the rank of lieutenant.

Following Rynning's incursion into Mexico during the riots there in 1906, there was a good deal of clamor for bringing charges against him. But his old commanding officer now sitting in the White House could only exclaim proudly, "Tom's all right, isn't he?" The matter was dropped.

In 1907 Rynning was appointed warden of the new prison at Florence as a reward for his efficient work as a Ranger captain. He later became a U.S. marshal and co-authored a book called *Gun Notches*, based on his life. He also spent his later years around the Hollywood sets acting as an adviser for Western movies. He died at San Diego in 1941.

The third and final Ranger captain was Harry Wheeler, who rose from the rank of private all the way to the top of the organization in just four years of service. Wheeler and his father both served with distinction in the Spanish war, where Harry was a member of the Roughriders, though not with the Arizona group. Not a big man, he was good with a gun, which made him an equal to anyone along the border. The famous Texas lawman Jeff Milton once called Wheeler the best he'd ever seen, and he'd seen the best, including the legendary John Wesley Hardin.

One of the most unusual gun fights in the history of the Southwest occurred in 1906, when a man named J. A. Tracy decided to shoot it out with the Ranger.

It all started when Tracy recognized a woman from his past on the arm of another man, D. W. Silverton. Apparently the woman informed Tracy that she was now married and would just as soon forget any past relationship. This was not good enough for the erstwhile lover, who followed them to Benson, where he threatened their lives. As fate would have it, Ranger Wheeler was in town and just as Silverton was relating his dilemma to the lawman, Tracy was seen approaching the two men from across the street.

When Wheeler called out to Tracy, the man drew his weapon and fired. All in all, both men fired four times. Tracy missed on all four while Wheeler scored four hits. "I am all in, my gun is empty," Tracy called out as he dropped his arm down to his side. For reasons known only to himself, the Ranger dropped his own pistol on the ground and walked toward the man. Tracy raised his gun and fired twice more, hitting Wheeler in the foot and the leg. Years later Wheeler recalled, "I'll never know how it happened, but only four cylinders of my gun were loaded. So when I was out of ammunition I dropped my gun and started throwing rocks at the fellow."

Tracy soon collapsed. Whether it was from loss of blood or shock from the reaction to his adversary's hurling of rocks in his direction is not recorded.

Wheeler later became sheriff of Cochise County, a post he held for many years. His most memorable task, perhaps, was the famous Bisbee deportation in 1917. Members of the Industrial Workers of the World, the I.W.W., a group known for its proclivity toward violence and radicalism, gathered in Bisbee. These "Wobblies," or as the old-timers still call them, the "I Won't Work Union," were in town for the purpose of disrupting American war-making capabilities. Sheriff Wheeler and two thousand deputies rounded up the radicals and others, then herded them to the baseball park in Warren. There were more than one thousand in all. They were then forced aboard freight cars and escorted across the New Mexico line with orders to keep moving in an eastward direction. There were no more I.W.W. problems in Bisbee.

The Rangers operated against outlawry in Arizona until 1909, when politics finally ended them. They had been too efficient; expenditures had been light and interestingly enough, not many desperadoes died at their hands. However, too many political nabobs and lawmen, especially in the southern counties, considered them an unnecessary arm of the territorial governor.

All in all, a colorful chapter of Arizona history came to an end with the demise of this peerless band of lawmen.

THE LAST CAMPAIGN

THE CALM THAT APPEARED on the surface of Mexico belied the turbulence that was seething within. For decades foreign investors had exploited her natural resources. American capitalists alone had invested a billion dollars in railroads, oil, and mining. If Mexico was richly endowed with natural resources, she was destitute in many other ways. By far the majority of her 15 million inhabitants were landless peons. A small handful of wealthy landowners and foreign capitalists controlled the wealth. The inevitable explosion came in 1910, bringing an end to the long, despotic dictatorship of Porfirio Díaz the following year. Francisco Madero, a California-educated visionary, became president after Díaz. Madero was unable to control the pernicious forces within the revolution and was murdered in 1913. The next to ascend to the position was a full-blooded Aztec Indian, General Victoriano Huerta. Huerta had been a member of the clique that had murdered Madero. At this same time Mexico's neighbor to the north had also gotten a new President, a highly moralistic former educator named Woodrow Wilson. Wilson steadfastly refused to recognize Huerta's "government by murder," and took steps to pressure the military strong man to resign. "I am going to teach the South American republics to elect good men," he righteously proclaimed. He began by allowing arms to flow freely through American ports to revolutionaries such as Francisco "Pancho" Villa and Venustiano Carranza. At the same time Wilson resisted pressure on the home front from businessmen and journalists with interests in Mexico who cried, "Morality is all right but what about the dividends?" The tension between the two republics was brought to a head in April 1914 when an insignificant incident was blown into a full-scale international show of muscle. A short time earlier a small landing party of American sailors was arrested at Tampico after accidentally landing in a war zone. The sailors were going ashore to pick up supplies when the incident occurred. After a short delay the matter was cleared and the Mexicans apologized, allowing the sailors to return to their ship. When word of the misunderstanding reached Admiral Henry Mayo tempers flared. The tempestuous Mayo demanded a formal apology and a twenty-one-gun salute immediately. Huerta stubbornly refused to offer a salute to the flag of a country that didn't even recognize his government. National pride was at stake for both nations and neither side wanted to back down. Although Wilson would just as soon not have been faced with open confrontation, he nevertheless did not fail to see the opportunity of bringing down the "unspeakable Huerta" once and for all. The American President asked for and received permission from Congress to intervene in Mexico. On April 21, 1914, U. S. Marines and sailors captured the coastal city of Vera Cruz.

Casualties were light, as war hysteria swept both countries. A shooting war seemed inevitable. Fortunately the A.B.C. powers of Argentina, Brazil, and Chile intervened and prevented hostilities from getting out of hand. In July 1914 Huerta finally succumbed to the pressure from without and within and resigned.

With Huerta out of the way, the aristocratic, white-bearded Carranza attempted to take over the reins of government. It appeared that Wilson's policies had been successful. Peace did not prevail. There was still the matter to be resolved between the forces of Villa and Emiliano Zapata, who refused to declare for Carranza. The personable Villa had many friends and supporters in the United States, where his image was that of a Mexican Robin Hood. Zapata, from southern Mexico, was a revolutionary in the truest form. He desired neither titles, pesos, nor power. "He was perhaps the purest revolutionary who ever lived," wrote American historian T. R. Fahrenbach. During the fighting against Huerta, Carranza had refused to give Villa supplies with which to carry on the struggle. After Huerta resigned, Carranza attempted to get the two popular rebel chieftains to disband their armies. Neither Villa nor Zapata desired the presidency for himself, but they were able to get one of Villa's generals, Eulalio Gutiérrez, named as a counter *el presidente* at a convention that Carranza had refused to recognize. The provisional government was short-lived and shortly thereafter the forces of Villa and Carranza went to war.

Naco, Sonora, a little border town just south of Bisbee (and separated from Naco, Arizona, by a dusty street, and wire fence) was the scene of a bloody confrontation between the forces of Villa and Carranza in October 1914. The famed American 9th and 10th Negro Cavalry units lined red flags along the border in hopes of confining the activities to the Mexican side. This was not to be. After two months and some fifty-four American casualties, mostly from stray bullets, the State Department decided to act. Army Chief of Staff General Hugh Scott, a former border commander, met with Villa. The end result negotiated was that the two warring armies would vacate Naco. Scott and Villa, locked in conference like "two bull elk," parted as good friends.

Wilson could and probably should have thrown his support toward Villa at this time, as the man Villa supported for the presidency was General Felipe Angeles, a respected and educated man. Above all, he was the most capable leader in all of Mexico at the time. Once again the American President delayed, and this indecision proved costly.

World events at the time did much to shape the situation in Mexico. Like some political chess game, the players studied the moves and maneuvered for position. Germany was firmly entrenched in the affair. She hoped to keep the United States busy on her southwestern border and out of the European war. Carranza wanted arms, but no guidance-counseling from her northern neighbor. Villa and Zapata wanted to put an end to the ruling classes altogether.

The two rebel chieftains momentarily delayed their offensive. In doing so, they inadvertently allowed Carranza and General Álvaro Obregón time to arm themselves and prepare for fighting. After a series of battles, Zapata was driven back to his home state, Morelos. With the help of imperial German artillery officer Maximilian Kloss, Obregón set up a series of trenches and machine-gun nests at Celaya, a city 130 mlies north of the Mexican capital. It was reminiscent of the Western Front. On April 6, 1915, Villa and his famed Dorados, or "Golden Cavalry," attacked and met with devastating results. Three times the armies met, and Obregón emerged the victor on all three occasions. Villa seemed unable to grasp the mechanics of trench and machine-gun warfare. His once proud army, cut to pieces, finally retreated into Chihuahua to regroup.

It was at Celaya that Obregón had his arm shot away while observing the battle. He later remarked, "When I came to I found that members of my staff had already taken my watch and my pocketbook."

Back in his favorite haunts of northern Mexico and back to some of his favorite old tricks, Villa confiscated some mining properties, putting a strain on his American relations. Once again the State Department sent troubleshooter Scott to confer with the chieftain and once again the two conversed amicably. However, on October 19, 1915, Wilson gave recognition to Carranza's government, recognition to a man whom he had earlier described as "impossible to deal with on human principles."

When the Americans had landed at Vera Cruz, Villa was the only revolutionary general who didn't condemn the action. He quelled all opposition within his ranks when he remarked, "It is Huerta's bull that is being gored." He refused to join the federales or Carranza in any action against the United States. There is evidence to indicate that he convinced Zapata to do the same. Without the help of Zapata and Villa, Huerta had no choice but to resign.

Wilson now put into effect his famous "elastic embargo," whereby the United States reluctantly began shipments of arms to Carranza but not to Villa. When Villa attacked the border city of Agua Prieta, south of Douglas, in 1915, the United States allowed Carranza's troops to board American trains and cross over American territory to intercept Villa's army. When Villa mounted a night attack from the south side of Agua Prieta, huge searchlights from the north side blinded his troops. Hundreds of Villistas were slaughtered in the merciless machine-gun fire. Many blamed the Americans for their severe setbacks at Agua Prieta. Once again, Villa faded into the wilds of Chihuahua.

The years of revolution had a telling effect on the Mexican economy. To stimulate activity in northern Mexico's mines, Carranza's government offered "full protection" to Americans who would enter the area to operate them. One such party of Americans, eighteen in all, were taken off the train at Santa Isabel on January 10, 1916, by a force of Villistas under Colonel Pablo López. Seventeen of the men were lined up outside the train and murdered in cold blood. One man survived by playing dead. Villa later denied having ordered the killings, but the damage was done.

On the night of March 9, 1916, Villa attacked the small American community of Columbus, New Mexico, 3 miles north of the border. They left seventeen dead Americans behind. It was the last time the continental United States has ever been attacked by a foreign power.

Reasons for the attack are not certain. Perhaps Villa was hoping to pull the United States into the conflict. It was a well-planned and executed raid, but Villa had not anticipated the fierce resistance offered by the 13th Cavalry stationed at Columbus. The stable hands grabbed pitchforks and used them with deadly effect on the Villistas, as did the cooks. They greeted the invaders by dousing them with caldrons of scalding water as they tried to crowd through the narrow doorways. Villa suffered some 140 men lost in a running fight with the tenacious Americans.

By the following morning hundreds of troops were arriving by train, much to the relief of the local citizens. President Wilson acted swiftly this time. Something Carranza dreaded even more than the despised presence of Villa was about to occur. American troops were preparing to advance upon Mexican soil.

The man chosen to lead the difficult expedition was General John Pershing. Pershing had graduated from West Point in 1886, and had come West just in time to participate in the final battles of the Geronimo campaign. Later he had served with the Black 9th Cavalry at the San Juan Heights, picking up the nickname that lasted throughout the remainder of his life. "Black Jack" Pershing turned down the Congressional Medal of Honor in the Philippine campaign, saying he didn't deserve it, as his presence on the line was "necessary." Teddy Roosevelt passed him over 862 senior officers in 1906, promoting him to general. He was the type of officer who could be friendly and affable, but at the same time demanded strictest obedience and loyalty. Serving on the lines with the troops, he had a proclivity for appearing at odd hours in order to inspect the troops and see that his instructions were being carried out.

For the next several months, the U.S. troops scanned the northern Mexican frontier in search of the elusive Villistas. The campaign trail was hot and dusty by day, freezing cold at night. Cooperation on the part of the Carranza forces was non-existent in the operation. Many times the Carranzistas opened fire on the Americanos as readily as did the Villistas. With the Americanos cast into the role of the "bullies of the north," Villa's popularity began to rise. Mexican folk singers sang his praises in the local cantinas, and the local citizens viewed the Americans with open contempt.

Finally, the campaign ground to a halt. It became only a matter of time until the Americans would be ordered to withdraw. Orders finally came and on February 5, 1917, the last soldier left Mexico. It had been a most difficult task to accomplish successfully, and it has been a matter of controversy to this day as to just what the campaign did accomplish. Its detractors say that the mission was a failure because Villa was never captured or killed. On the other hand the U.S. border was never seriously threatened again. It's also said that the United States had no right to impose upon the sovereignty of Mexican soil. Still, Carranza had been either unable or unwilling to take action to prevent the raids along the border. It was also learned that a so-called Plan of San Diego existed that called for a general uprising of all border Mexicans against the United States. The states included were Texas, New Mexico, Arizona, California, and Colorado. This was not a "madman's dream," as several disturbances and raids did occur early in 1915. The fact that Germany was busy keeping the two republics at each other's throat, was evidenced by the famous Zimmermann Note. The note outlined on a grand scale a course of action that was to be taken along the Mexican border in the event of war between the United States and Germany. The note was written by the German Foreign Secretary and intercepted by British naval intelligence. Its contents were startling. Germany proposed an alliance with Mexico which would return Texas, Arizona, and New Mexico in return for Mexican support. The note also proposed that Japan was to be invited to join the scheme. This note, more than anything, rallied the previously lukewarm Southwesterners for action against Germany.

The men who took part in the last campaign were to form the hard core of the American force that fought in Europe the next year. Its commander, John J. Pershing, became commander of the American Expeditionary Force. His aide-de-camp in the Mexico campaign was George Patton, a man destined for greater glory in another war.

It was the first time the Americans used an air force and mechanical vehicles. Sadly for the old veterans, it was the last real campaign for the horse cavalry.

The lessons learned in the punitive expedition, as it was called, in tactics, testing of weapons, and logistics, coupled with the mobilization of American troops for the First World War, would pay rich dividends in the trying months to come. Perhaps most ironic was that the imperial German government was much amused by the apparent ineptness of the Americans in the campaign. Discounting them as a military threat, the Germans boldly decided to resume their U-boat warfare on American shipping.

THE MEN IN THE
FLYING MACHINES

WITH THE COMING OF trench warfare and machine guns the old horse cavalry was relegated to a role of secondary importance in the mission of U.S. military forces. From her early beginnings on the Plains in 1833 to the Pershing expedition in 1916–17 she played an integral role in the government military. The horse cavalry was used mostly in parades and around the garrisons for the remainder of its active career, though there was some cavalry action in the Philippines during the early part of World War II prior to the surrender of U.S. forces stationed there.

The tools of war were changing. An armored vehicle with the unlikely name of "tank" would soon replace the horse. George Patton, who was a superb equestrian, would go on to the next war, and the next, riding atop an iron horse. But even more revolutionary was the airplane, or as the public dubbed it, the flying machine. Little did people realize at the time just how important the plane would become in warfare. Its early escapades in warfare, no doubt, gave little testimony to its future capabilities, as man and machine were required to put forth an epic struggle just to stay aloft.

During the Mexican revolutions American barnstormers were hired as pilots by both sides. In 1911 Hector Worden, an American, was hired by Madero's army to fly missions against Díaz, perhaps making him the first aviator in the world to participate in warfare with an airplane. In 1913 another pilot, Didier Masson, flew for

Obregón's rebels and attacked a federal gunboat at Guaymas using homemade bombs of pipe filled with dynamite. Apparently Masson didn't score a hit on the boat, but the moral effect of his attack was considerable as the sailors leaped overboard and paddled for shore. Pancho Villa, quick to see the advantages of aerial warfare, tried to organize his own air force. This, too, ended in failure as the students all fled after witnessing the landing techniques of pilot Ed Parsons. The bumpy crash landing on a rocky field drained the remaining courage of the would-be pilots and the Villa Air Force, so to speak, never got off the ground.

The American military lagged behind in its acceptance of the newfangled machine as a weapon of warfare. During one period, the United States ranked fourteenth in the world in air forces. Finally, in 1916, under the leadership of Captain Ben Foulois, our air force was put to the supreme test. There were only eight Curtiss JN2 machines, and Foulois's pilots were subjected to such indignities as having their planes blown down by the strong Mexican winds, and worse. One pilot was forced to land in a cow pasture in the dead of night. He barely escaped after being pursued by the unfriendly beasts. Still another had to prevent some of the locals from burning holes in his craft with cigarettes after he crash-landed near their village. What with local citizens throwing rocks at the hapless pilots upon landing and propellers that wouldn't keep the planes in the air, our air force was literally blown out of the sky in Mexico. The amazing thing about the whole episode is that there were no fatalities suffered by the pilots during the entire conflict.

One of the most remarkable incidents in southwestern lore occurred in March 1929 and dealt with the flying machines. The residents of Bisbee found themselves with ringside seats to a revolution that year as the Mexicans were once again locked in one of their periodic struggles. Railroad cars were pulled up alongside the international border town of Naco and the locals climbed on top to view the contest. Except for an occasional stray bullet which scattered the spectators, the Mexicans put on quite a show. Usually when daylight ended, the combatants also had good sense enough to put aside their differences and quaff down *cerveza* in one of the local cantinas until dawn and the revolution once again called upon the gladiators to report for duty at the trenches. It's been said that on occasion the two opposing factions even frequented the same cantinas during off-duty hours and exchanged war stories together.

With the federales entrenched on three sides of Naco, the rebels saw fit to hire an American mercenary pilot named Patrick Murphy and an old nondescript airplane to bomb the defenders. It should be noted that American soldiers of fortune were taking part in the revolution against the expressed wishes and desires of the U. S. Government.

Since merely keeping the plane aloft was a full-time job, the pilots took on young Mexican boys as bombardiers. The bombs were leather bags full of nuts, bolts, screws, and explosives. A fuse was attached and when the mini-bomber made its run over the trenches, the lad merely had to touch his cigarette to the fuse, drop the bag over the side, and wait for the expected result. Like the bombing raids of earlier times, it was extremely doubtful if any significant conclusions could be drawn from the blasts but they did put on quite a show for the spectators. As for the bombs, surely there were better, more efficient ones available, but not to the impoverished rebels.

There is no great monument or physical barrier to mark the international boundary between Naco, Arizona, and Naco, Sonora, beyond an old fence and a dusty street. It came to pass that aviator Murphy, in his zealousness, strayed over to the American side, where he dropped several of his suitcase bombs, one landing in Newton's Garage, where it destroyed a Dodge automobile, and another hitting in front of the Phelps-Dodge store. It is said that one of the local sharpshooters stepped out and shot the plane down with his rifle just as it was making another run. Pilot Murphy was later arrested but no charges were pressed and the luckless soldier of fortune faded into obscurity.

This epic air battle marked the only time the continental United States has ever been bombed from the air by a "foreign power." Such were the ways of aerial warfare when pilot and aircraft were in the formative years and each flight was an adventure in itself.

Not all the early flying in the Arizona country was confined to the military. Pilots like Charles Lindbergh and Amelia Earhart spent some time navigating the southwestern deserts. Isabella Greenway, wife of the old Roughrider and mining magnate, and Bill Gilpin teamed up to form Gilpin-Greenway Airlines, one of the first commercial airlines to operate in Arizona. Mrs. Greenway was skeptical of flying until Gilpin took her up for a ride. The colorful Mrs. Greenway took to the skies with the same finesse as she later did when, as U. S. Representative in Washington, she roller-skated on the steps of the Capitol Building with her son. Gilpin and Greenway owned and operated the airline together until he was killed in a crash near Mexico City in 1932. After Gilpin's death Mrs. Greenway sold her interest in the business.

The most famous of the early Arizona barnstorming pilots was Charley Mayse. Mayse performed his skills wherever and whenever he could draw a crowd. Charley's personal life dramatically changed when he crash-landed in a rancher's field near Safford. The rancher's daughter was among the curious spectators who gathered around the plane. During the next few days while he repaired the craft he also found time to court the already engaged Lola Carter. When the plane was ready to fly again, he took her up, up and away, landing in El Paso. With her ears still ringing from the roar of the engine he once more proposed, and this time she accepted. The two took what was perhaps the first aerial honeymoon in history.

No history of aviation in Arizona would be complete without the telling of Mesa's famous yuletide story, sometimes known as the legend of John McPhee, the man who killed Santa Claus.

It was Christmas season, 1930, and times were rough in Arizona. The Great Depression had just begun and local businessmen were looking for something to take the shoppers' minds off hard times and into the spirit of spending. Usually the season was kicked off with a festive parade but this year the usual luster was lacking. It was the local newspaper editor, John McPhee, who came forth with a novel approach to stimulate interest. Why not have Santa drop into town from a parachute? He could leap from a plane, land gracefully, and distribute gifts to the children. McPhee became an immediate hero, especially to the merchants, who knew that crowds would naturally stimulate business, and to the children, who gleefully anticipated the actual dropping from the sky of old St. Nick. If one keeps in mind that these were still the formative years of aviation and parachuting, it was truly a novel idea.

McPhee's near-perfect plan for yuletide festivities went awry when the stunt man hired to pose as Santa got himself some private Christmas cheer and found it impossible to maneuver his body off the bar stool, much less bail out of an airplane in a Santa suit. Undaunted by this setback, McPhee borrowed a department store dummy, dressed it in the Santa suit, and announced to his anxious supporters that the show would go on. The pilot would push the dummy Santa out of the plane, pull the cord, and Santa would float to earth 'neath the billowing canopy. McPhee would then pick up the dummy, change into the suit, and emerge as a real-life Santa. The plan was flawless and foolproof.

The people came from miles around, gathering to watch the epic descent. Children climbed up to rooftops for a better view. Parents held their small children skyward as the distant drone of a single-engine airplane came nearer. Suddenly the door opened and "Santa" jumped out. All eyes were upon the figure in red as he started his free fall. Down.

Down.

Down.

Just as on that fateful day in Mudville when mighty Casey went down swinging, there was no joy in Mesa. Santa was last seen plummeting from the sky . . . his malfunctioning canopy following limply toward earth.

The stores were empty and the streets were deserted that afternoon except for a few merchants and bawling children standing in a state of shock and disbelief.

Editor McPhee left town for a few days in hopes that the event might be forgotten. However, it never was. When he died nearly forty years later the fact was mentioned prominently in his obituary. McPhee will always be remembered by old-timers in Mesa as "the man who killed Santa Claus."

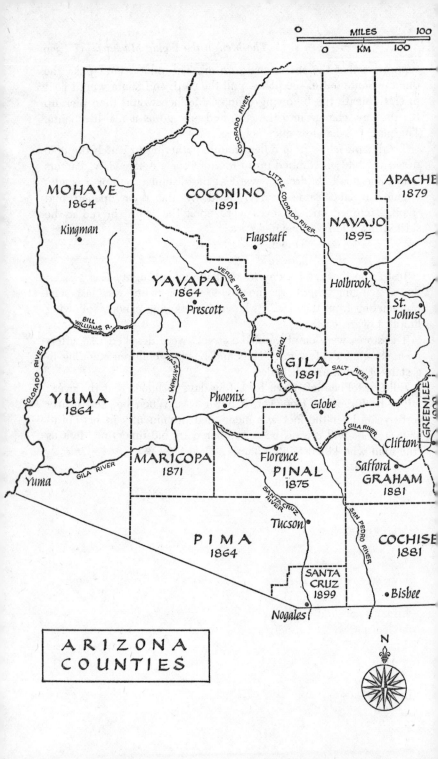

ARIZONA COUNTIES

THE VANISHING FRONTIER

GREAT CHANGES WERE TAKING PLACE in Arizona around the turn of the century and not all were of a political nature. Prices were going up. A ton of hay now cost $8.00; beef was $.10 a pound; potatoes sold for $.02 apiece; a pair of Levi's cost $.75; men's suits sold for $5.00; and the price of a shave went up to $.25. The people were wondering where the inflation would end. In 1905 irate Tucson citizens petitioned the city council to prohibit spitting on sidewalks. Gambling was voted out in 1907. Two years later the Prescott school board proclaimed that it was putting an end to the smoking habit among the students. Arizona's progressive spirit was demonstrated in the election of 1912 when the male voters approved woman suffrage eight years before Congress got around to adding the Nineteenth Amendment to the U. S. Constitution. Arizona went "dry" in 1914, as the electorate voted for prohibition, although it should be mentioned that the law seemed to be "abided only by those who were already abstaining from demon rum and john barleycorn." For the rest it was "business as usual." In 1917 the public drinking cup and the common towel were banned. That same year the legislature established a $10 a week minimum wage for women. Women had come a long way since 1907, when an act was passed preventing them from loitering in saloons.

In 1912, after years of political hassle over such issues as hostile Indians, outlaws, free silver, bigotry, and myopic-visioned eastern politicians, Arizona took her place as the forty-eighth state in the Union. The first governor was George Wiley Paul Hunt, a rotund, bald-headed man with a big walrus mustache. Hunt, a master politician, had come to Arizona in 1881, penniless, and riding a jackass. Within ten years, this frontier-style Horatio Alger was president of a bank, a commercial store, and first mayor of Globe.

In 1910 Hunt was elected president of the Democrat-dominated constitutional convention, a group whose job it was to draft a constitution prior to proposed statehood. The document they drafted was liberal, almost to the point of being radical for the times. The chief executive would have little appointive or executive power. Future governors would learn to their dismay that the framers of the constitution intended for the lawmaking branch to have the controlling power. The governor and the legislators would serve two-year terms and there would be a popular election of judges. Controversial were three liberal provisions allowing for the initiative, the referendum, and the recall of public officials. The latter included the recall of judges. The initiative allows the people to make laws directly, without action of legislature. The referendum reserves to the people the right to approve or reject any law passed by the legislature. Both of these have to be proposed and then voted upon. The recall allows for the removal of public officials by popular vote.

President William Howard Taft took exception to all three liberal provisions. Taft, a former judge, was especially unhappy over the subject of recall of judges. The bill was approved overwhelmingly by the voters of Arizona, and in August 1911 Congress passed a joint resolution admitting Arizona and New Mexico to the Union. The President considered the recall detrimental to the independence and integrity of the judiciary and let it be known that he would veto the measure if the recall were not withdrawn. It was not, and true to his word, the bill was nixed. The provision for recall of judges was withdrawn and Congress resubmitted the joint resolution. This time Taft signed, fully realizing that once statehood was achieved the recall would be put back in the constitution. To him it was simply a matter of principle and as long as he could influence the makeup of the constitution he would do so. On December 11, 1911, the Arizonans approved the constitution without the recall. It would later be reinstated and the locals would take their wrath out on Taft in the next election, where he would finish fourth in a field of four.

The electorate also selected Hunt as first governor; Sidney P. Osborn, who was destined to become one of the state's greatest governors, was named Secretary of State. The two senators were Marcus A. Smith, erstwhile Tombstone lawyer and territorial delegate, and Henry F. Ashurst, former cowboy turned politician. The representative was Carl Hayden, former sheriff of Maricopa County and son of pioneer business political leader Charles Trumbull Hayden.

On the morning of February 14, 1912, Taft signed the proclamation declaring Arizona a state. The event was recorded for posterity with a motion-picture camera, the first time a President had been filmed signing a bill into law. In Arizona there was much cause for celebration. Nearly fifty years of political struggle had ended. Pistols were fired in the air and mine whistles screamed as festivities began in earnest. Promising to operate the state efficiently and economically, Hunt walked from the downtown Ford Hotel out to the capitol. Later he decided it was much more economical and comfortable to make the trip in an automobile. It was a gala celebration, with William Jennings Bryan on hand to welcome the baby state. Later in the day the three-time Democratic nominee for President enthralled the audience with one of his patented two-hour speeches. The forty-eight-gun salute honoring the occasion was shortened to thirty-eight when windows started cracking and horses began shying. Arizona, sophisticated as she might pretend to be, still had a lot of frontier left in her.

G. W. P. Hunt would be elected governor of Arizona off and on six more times, and his tenure would span clear into the Depression years. He was colorful, adroit, and clever, his familiar features easily recognizable by all. Once a person had seen the portly chief executive he never forgot him. Hunt reciprocated by keeping a list of people, facts, and data about each place he visited. He would study these just prior to another visit. He prided himself on the number of people he could call by name, and his constituents were obviously impressed by his uncanny ability of recall.

A proponent of liberal legislation and opponent of big business, especially the mines, he said he wore no "copper collar." Hunt claimed to be a friend of the working man and his front door was always open to him. His political adversaries said that this was true and that his back door was always open to businessmen. However,

Hunt was a shrewd enough politician to know when he had to compromise, and therein was the key to his success.

Politics in Arizona for the first fifty years after statehood was, by and large, one-party. With few exceptions, the Democrats were in control of the state's political system. Republican Tom Campbell of Prescott became governor in 1919, when Hunt chose not to run. Campbell served two terms and then was defeated. His old political adversary, Hunt, returned to the scene. The "Old Roman" had been appointed Minister to Siam by President Woodrow Wilson when Hunt had let it be known he was planning to seek Mark Smith's senatorial post. Friends of Smith's persuaded the President to appoint the Arizona governor to the foreign post. While he was away he kept in touch with the electorate by sending postcards back home. When he returned he was more popular than ever.

Hunt held the governorship again until Republican John C. Phillips defeated him in 1928, the only time he lost in a general election. Phillips inherited a $285,000 deficit and found that all except $1.00 of the money appropriated for the governor's office had been spent by the previous administration. When he left office, he left over $11,000 to the incoming governor, Hunt, who also had preceded him. A Republican, he worked in harmony with the Democratic legislature, a fact he prided himself on. Ironically, when Phillips had moved to Arizona in 1898 he was broke and secured a job as a common laborer at $1.50 an hour in construction of the state capitol.

The Democratic landslide in 1930 saw the return of G. W. P. Hunt for the seventh time. The old campaigner's last campaign was in 1932, when he lost out to fellow Democrat Dr. Benjamin B. Moeur of Tempe. Dr. Moeur was a crusty physician who had, at various times, practiced medicine in Tombstone, Bisbee, and Tempe. Moeur, known as the Depression governor, marshaled the National Guard along the Colorado River to protect the state's rights to river water during construction of Parker Dam. The federal government finally backed down and ordered a halt until the matter could be settled in court. Moeur served as governor until 1936, when he lost in the primary to Rawghlie C. Stanford. Judge Stanford, a native of Buffalo Gap, Texas, had come to Arizona at the age of two and had been a miner, cowboy, and soldier before settling down to the practice of law. He later became a member of the State Supreme Court, where he served until 1955.

In the election of 1938, former state senator Bob Jones won in a bitterly contested election. Jones was assisted in his quest for the Democratic nomination when C. M. Zander, a skilled political craftsman and former member of the Hunt machine, was killed in a plane crash. Jones, a businessman, urged a more businesslike approach to state government. However, the former senator had problems with members of the house and retired after one term. He later owned a western store in Phoenix and raised cattle.

Jones's successor was Democrat Sidney P. Osborn, only the second native Arizonan to hold the post. His father, Neri Osborn, had been a page at the first territorial legislature back in 1864. Osborn's regime saw economic boom during the World War II years, a population explosion, and the ratification of the Colorado River Compact. Realizing the political clout of public pressure, Osborn went before the public on radio urging the people to support him in his battles with the legislature. These acts did not endear him to certain members of that body. He defeated Republican Jerry W. Lee in 1944 by nearly 75,000 votes, the most one-sided gubernatorial race in the state's history. A few months later there was an attempt to impeach him over misuse of public funds in the river dispute. The charges were quickly disproved and he was easily vindicated.

Sidney P. Osborn died in office on May 25, 1948, of lateral sclerosis, a paralysis that affects both speech and limbs. His last days were sad ones for those who had worked closely with him the last few years. His head was bowed over his chest, the neck having lost the strength to support it, and he had lost control of one arm and leg. His speech had failed so badly that he had to resort to using phrase and alphabet cards, on which he pointed out the words and phrases he wanted to use with a pencil in his mouth.

Osborn's years in office were exhilarating ones for Arizona. He was a proud, vain man yet he was respected by friends and foes alike for his devotion and duty to public service. He was elected to office four times and is considered by political experts to be one of the state's greatest governors.

Osborn's successor, under Arizona law, was Secretary of State Dan E. Garvey, a man who never really desired the post. Garvey was too much the non-aggressive type for the fierce political infighting that others before him relished. However, he was elected in his own right that November. He lost in the primary of 1950, and happily retired from the political wars. His greatest accomplishments came later when he served as state examiner, a post he held from 1955 to 1969.

The gubernatorial election in 1950 marked the first time a woman had sought such a high position in Arizona politics. Former state auditor Ana Frohmiller made a race of it, although she lost out to Republican Howard Pyle. Pyle became the first Republican governor elected since John Phillips in 1928. Up to this time most of the excitement in Arizona's gubernatorial races had been the Democratic primaries. However, this time the Republicans provided a formidable combination in Pyle and his campaign manager, photographer and adventurer Barry Goldwater. The two made a sensational barnstorming tour across Arizona in Goldwater's plane to overcome a vast majority of Democratic registrations. Pyle won over his opponent by some three thousand votes. A native of Sheridan, Wyoming, Pyle had originally wanted to become a singer. He came to Arizona in 1925 and gained a wide reputation in radio with his popular show "Arizona Highlights." He later originated the Easter sunrise services at the Grand Canyon. Pyle also gained wide popularity during World War II when, as a reporter, he sought out and interviewed Arizonans in the Pacific campaigns for the folks back home. He was the first radio reporter to land in conquered Japan at the war's end. The most significant accomplishment of Pyle's administration perhaps was the creation of the Underground Water Commission to control excessive pumping of the water table. Attempts at governmental reorganization met stubborn resistance from legislators and the suspicious populace, who feared that more appointive offices would lead to machine politics. Pyle was successful at first because of his bipartisan approach; however, he would learn as did his predecessors that in the final analysis it was the legislators who had the upper hand in these matters, and they were not about to relinquish control.

Pyle lost his bid for re-election primarily as a result of a grandiose raid on a polygamist community named Short Creek, up on the Utah border, in 1953. The governor, a warm, compassionate man, had tried to handle the matter delicately. However, the raid was overpublicized and the sensitive religious nature of the incident offended many Mormon voters in the state, some of whom had descended from polygamist families. Pyle went to Washington after his defeat and served as administrative assistant to President

Dwight D. Eisenhower and as president of the National Safety Council.

Next to govern was Ernest W. McFarland, former senator and majority leader until his upset in the 1952 Republican landslide. A lawyer in Florence, he rose to county attorney, then judge. In 1940 he unseated Henry F. Ashurst, one of the state's two original senators, for the Washington seat. Although not the accomplished orator that his predecessor was, "Mac" earned a reputation as a hard worker among his colleagues, who elected him majority leader in 1952. After serving two terms as governor, McFarland decided to regain his lost seat from Barry Goldwater, who had beaten him in one of the state's greatest upsets. Losing his bid, he returned to his law practice. In 1964 he was elected to the Arizona Supreme Court. After retiring from that post, he became principal owner of a television station in Phoenix.

Arizona's fourth Republican governor since statehood was a political novice although he was well-known as a sports figure and businessman. Paul J. Fannin surprised the experts in 1958 by gaining the Republican nomination and going on to win the general election. Lacking experience as a speaker and the charisma of school chum Barry Goldwater, Fannin was nonetheless a tireless worker. He did more than any of his predecessors to bring industry to the state. He chose the best men available to aid him regardless of political affiliations, sometimes incurring the wrath of his own party. Fannin served as governor for three terms and was rewarded for his work in 1964 when he was elected to fill the vacated seat of Goldwater in the U. S. Senate.

The Democrats regained the gubernatorial post in 1964 with the election of Sam Goddard, a Tucson attorney. His regime was marred by scandals and political maneuvering within his party, causing the "roadrunner" to lose his bid for re-election after only one term.

Another popular radio personality took the governor's chair in 1966 with the election of Jack Williams, long-time Phoenix resident and former mayor. During his administration the court-ordered redistricting of the legislature changed the political complexion of that body. Control of the state's politics passed from the rural communities to Maricopa and Pima counties, where some 70 per cent of the population resides. In 1966 the Republicans gained control of both houses for the first time in the state's history. Two other firsts occurred in the legislature, signifying an increasing minority involvement in politics. Clovis Campbell became the first Black and Wing Ong the first Chinese-American to serve in the state senate.

The Democrats had always been plagued by factionalism and it was not uncommon for conservative Democrats, called "pintos," and Republicans in the legislature to form a coalition against liberal Democrats. The years following World War II brought many new residents to Arizona, many of them Republicans. The G.O.P. shifted into high gear in the 1950s with strong candidates like John Rhodes, Barry Goldwater, Howard Pyle, and Paul Fannin to equalize the state's political structure. After years of liberal politics a latent conservative surge, coupled with the influx of new residents, awakened the Republican party, which converted its operations from part-time to full-time politics.

Arizona, now on an even keel politically speaking, went Democratic in a close race in 1974 as former ambassador and judge Raul Castro won the gubernatorial race and the Democrats regained control of the senate by taking a more moderate stand on the issues. With his election, Castro, an outgoing, personable man, climaxed a long, brilliant, rags-to-riches career that began in a shack along the Mexican border in the early 1900s.

Arizona has had a congressional delegation down through the years of which she can be rightly proud. Some have made international reputations for themselves while others have earned the highest respect from their colleagues in the Congress.

The state's first full-term senator was Henry F. Ashurst, an erstwhile cowboy who served in the Senate for twenty-eight years and was known for his silver-tongued eloquence. He lost out in a surprising upset to Ernest W. McFarland in 1940. The death of his wife a year earlier had much to do with the halfhearted campaign that cost him the election. McFarland remained in the Senate, becoming Senate majority leader until 1952, when he too was defeated in a stunning upset at the hands of Barry Goldwater. Goldwater held the post until 1964, when he was drafted to accept his party's nomination as candidate for President. His seat was then taken by former governor Paul Fannin. Fannin served Arizona well in Washington, especially in the promotion of new energy sources, until his retirement in 1977. A "work horse" senator, Fannin had one of the best attendance records in the Senate. His seat was won by Democrat Dennis de Concini, scion of an old Arizona political family.

The other senatorial seat was first occupied by Marcus A. Smith, former Tombstone lawyer and perennial territorial delegate to Congress. His handsome appearance and persuasive personality along with his adroit use of the English language did much to win friends and enhance the chances for statehood around the turn of the century. Elected to the short term in 1912, he ran again in 1914, this time winning a full six-year term. He was defeated in 1920 by Ralph H. Cameron in a Republican upsurge following World War I. Cameron, from Coconino County, was a former sheriff, mine developer, builder of Bright Angel Trail at the Grand Canyon, and politician. He served only one term, losing to Representative Carl Hayden in 1926.

Carl Hayden's seven terms in the House and six terms in the Senate gave him a total of fifty-six years in Congress, the longest of any man in history. Hayden, the son of Tempe pioneer Charles Trumbull Hayden, was sheriff of Maricopa County and representative before running for the Senate. His tenure ran from 1912 until he voluntarily retired in 1968. His father had arrived in Tucson in 1858, on the first Butterfield Overland Stage. This father-son combination spanned nearly the entire Anglo-American history in Arizona. Hayden, while in the Senate, was considered a "work horse" rather than a "show horse," a fact on which he prided himself. A quiet, reserved man, he was universally respected. When he retired, he was chairman of the powerful Appropriations and Rules Committee, and president pro tempore of the Senate. An entire history of Arizona could and probably will be written someday just around the senator. He worked tirelessly in committees down through the years, watching his state grow from raw adolescence to maturity. The final, crowning achievement of his brilliant career was the approval of the Central Arizona Project just before his retirement.

Barry Goldwater, unsuccessful in his presidential bid in 1964, was elected to fill Hayden's seat in 1968. Goldwater, one of the most respected men in the U. S. Senate, is also the best-known Arizonan in the world. He is still the spokesman for the conservative philosophy in American national politics.

In the House, Arizona has had only twelve congressmen representing her interests. In the first thirty years of statehood Arizona had only one seat in the Congress. Lewis Douglas replaced Carl

Hayden in 1926, when the latter ran for the Senate. Douglas, the grandson of Dr. James Douglas, the mining engineer of territorial days, served with distinction in the House for three terms. He resigned in his fourth term to accept a position in Franklin D. Roosevelt's New Deal. However, he became disenchanted and resigned after eighteen months. In 1947 he was appointed Ambassador to Great Britain. Following a long and distinguished career, Lew Douglas resigned in 1950 to pursue business interests in Tucson.

In the special election to fill the vacancy left by Douglas, Isabella Selmes Greenway, the widow of General John C. Greenway, emerged the winner. A colorful woman with much political acumen, she was quite popular around the Washington set. Retiring in 1936, she was replaced by John R. Murdock, long-time professor of government and history at Arizona State College at Tempe. Murdock worked long and hard for Arizona's cause in the Colorado River dispute until his defeat in the Republican landslide in 1952.

When the state gained a second seat in 1942, the man chosen to fill it was former teacher and attorney Richard F. Harless. His most noteworthy achievement was the work in gaining for the Indians the right to vote. He dropped out of Congress after three terms to make an unsuccessful bid for the governor's job.

Harless' successor was Harold A. Patten, former football star and coach at the University of Arizona. He also served three terms.

Arizona's first Republican representative was attorney John J. Rhodes of Mesa. He is known for his support of the right-to-work law as a check on unions. Since his election in the Eisenhower landslide in 1952, Rhodes's political stock has risen steadily. In 1974 he was elected Senate minority leader, replacing Gerald Ford.

When Patten chose not to run in 1954 his post was won by Stewart L. Udall, member of a prominent pioneer Mormon family. Udall, from St. Johns, went to school at the University of Arizona, where he starred in basketball. After serving as gunner on bombing missions in World War II, he returned to the U. of A. to study law.

His grandfather, David King Udall, came to Arizona from Utah in 1880 as a missionary. His father, Levi S. Udall, was a justice in the Arizona Supreme Court. An astute politician, Stew Udall resigned during his fourth term to accept a post as Secretary of the Interior in John F. Kennedy's New Frontier. He was the first Arizonan to serve in a Cabinet post.

When Stewart Udall vacated his post to become Secretary of the

Interior, his brother and law partner, Morris King Udall, won out in a special election. Like his brother, Mo is a skilled politician, known for his wit and homespun humor. In 1976 he made a strong bid for the Democratic nomination for the presidency.

In 1960 Arizona gained a third seat in the House. The first man to fill the position was George Senner, a Democrat from Miami. In 1966 he waged a campaign and lost to Sam Steiger, former airplane wing-walker, rodeo cowboy, colorful and sometimes controversial rancher from Prescott. Steiger remained in the House of Representatives until 1976, when he ran for senator after Paul Fannin's announced retirement. In the general election Steiger lost his bid for Fannin's seat to Democrat Dennis de Concini.

The state's fourth and newest congressional district seat was filled by John Conlan, son of popular Hall of Fame baseball umpire Jocko Conlan. Conlan had a most unique and popular method of keeping in touch with the voters of his district. When in Arizona he maintained an office in his mobile home allowing him to get out into the neighborhoods and converse with his constituents on a person-to-person basis. Conlan, a right-wing conservative, vacated his seat in 1976 to run unsuccessfully against Sam Steiger in the Republican senatorial primary.

OVER THERE

WHEN WORLD WAR I BROKE OUT in Europe, many Arizonans strapped on their guns and prepared for another campaign. No doubt many old ex-Roughriders heard the distant bugle call as Teddy Roosevelt offered his services to lead another regiment. However, this would be a different kind of war than the old-timers had known. It would be fought with different stratagems and weaponry, vastly different from the style of the old campaigners. Teddy and his Roughriders were obsolete. However, another old cavalryman would be chosen to lead the American Expeditionary Force in Europe. John J. Pershing's life on the campaign trail would span the era of Apache with bows and arrows to the era of atom bombs over Japan.

Frank Luke and John Pruitt were the state's most famous soldiers in the war. Pruitt, a Marine, was killed at Mont Blanc in 1918, shortly after he had killed several enemy soldiers and captured another forty. For this he was decorated with the Congressional Medal of Honor. Frank Luke lived in the combat zone for just seventeen days and flew only ten combat missions, but during his brief career this scion of a pioneer Phoenix family shot down nineteen enemy planes and balloons. On September 18, 1918, he shot down three balloons and two aircraft, all in only ten minutes. After the skirmish, his plane was shot down behind German lines. Luke crash-landed the craft and with an aura of coolness that would have done the old gunfighters proud, he pulled his service pistol and shot it out with the German Army. He was the first aviator to be awarded the Congressional Medal of Honor. In 1975 Luke was enshrined in the Aviation Hall of Fame. Today his statue stands in front of the State Capitol Building in Phoenix.

Patriotic fever ran high in Arizona in 1918. It was with great pride that the newest state in the Union sent her sons off to fight the "war to end all wars." However, not all the boys answered the call when the draft notices were posted. A still disputed incident occurred in 1918 when a posse in Graham County went into Rattlesnake Canyon of the Galiuro Mountains with intentions of bringing two draft evaders in. The two men, Tom and John Power, lived with their father in a cabin at the end of the canyon. Another man, Tom Sisson, worked at the ranch and was there at the time of the battle. The posse was made up of Graham County Sheriff Bob McBride, deputies Martin Kempton, Kane Wootan, and U. S. Deputy Marshal Frank Haynes.

It was dark when the shooting started. The officers claimed that the family resisted and the brothers testified that the posse fired without giving the men a chance to surrender. According to the Powers' version, it started before dawn when the men inside the cabin heard a noise outside. Grabbing his rifle, Tom Power, Sr., the boys' father, headed for the door. Just as he opened the door somebody yelled, "Throw up your hands," and started shooting. Tom Sr. fell to the floor, mortally wounded. It was still so dark "that you couldn't tell a man from a stump at thirty feet," Frank Haynes later testified. When the fight was over, both brothers had fragments of glass in their eyes and their father was dying. On the other side, three of the four men, Bob McBride, Kane Wootan, and Martin Kempton, were dead. The lone posse survivor, Frank Haynes, rushed over to Klondyke in Aravaipa Valley for help. Ranch hand Tom Sisson, who claimed to be an old Army scout, took the boys into the Chiricahua Mountains, where for twenty-nine days they evaded lawmen. It was the largest manhunt in Arizona's history as three thousand men scaled the rough terrain searching for the wanted men. They finally surrendered to a platoon of Army troops a few miles south of the Mexican border. It was fortunate that an Army unit captured them, for feelings were running so high, especially in Graham County where the dead lawmen lived, that a lynch mob would certainly have prevailed. There was such a furor over the prisoners in Graham County that the trial had to be moved to Clifton, in Greenlee County. People waited in line for blocks just to get a glimpse of the two brothers as they awaited trial.

All three received life sentences. The only thing that saved them from the gallows was that a short time before, Arizona had abolished the death penalty. Shortly after the trial, it was reinstated, and has been on the books ever since.

The Power brothers spent forty-two years in prison for the killings. They have always maintained that they didn't know that they had been drafted and that the posse outside their cabin that fateful day never identified themselves as lawmen. When they saw their father shot, they grabbed rifles and returned the fire. Tom Sisson died in prison in 1957. The brothers maintained that he had no part in the fight, although one old Arizonan who knew him laid the blame right on his doorstep. Frank Gilpin, brother-in-law of one of the slain deputies, and former lawman himself, told the author, "Tom Sisson never was an Army scout. He served time in Texas before coming here. He was a troublemaker who told the Power boys they didn't have to report for the draft."

To this day, no one knows for sure what happened that morning. As when there are many witnesses to an accident, there are many versions. In 1918 feelings were definitely against the brothers. The Power brothers served longer prison terms than any other men in the history of Arizona. An attempt to free them in 1952 was thwarted by relatives of the slain lawmen. Finally, in 1960, Tom and John were paroled. Ten years later, they were pardoned. Tom died a short time later and John passed away in 1976. They had both paid their debt to society, with interest.

In her first years as a new state, Arizona suffered the many vicissitudes of adolescence. However, no year was more traumatic than 1917, as the following will illustrate: In the election for governor, Tom Campbell defeated George W. P. Hunt by some thirty votes. However, Hunt vehemently contested the election and on January 1, 1917, both men were sworn in as governor in their own separate ceremonies. Hunt refused to vacate the governor's office so Campbell set up his office in the kitchen of his home. The state treasurer and state auditor, both Democrats, refused to honor checks signed by the Republican, Campbell. Matters took on comic-opera proportions when the legislature met and both men decided to address it. Several months later, Superior Court Judge R. C. Stanford ruled that examinations of the ballots revealed that Campbell had defeated Hunt by thirty to fifty votes and the five-month legal battle was thought to be ended. However, on December 22, the Supreme Court reversed the decision and declared Hunt the winner, ordering the state to pay him his salary for the entire year. Tom Campbell had served as governor of Arizona for eleven months and three weeks, part of that time as "co-governor." He did, however, manage to serve a couple of terms on his own later.

It was several years after statehood before Arizona officially had a state flag. When one was finally designed and approved in 1917, there was much criticism. Many people felt it looked too much like the rising sun of Japan. This same criticism would reappear during World War II. The bill finally approving the flag sneaked through the legislature on a fluke and sat on Governor Campbell's desk unsigned until it automatically became law after five days. A new flag was presented to the 1st Arizona Infantry at Naco on September 11, 1917, just before they left for Europe.

The year 1917 was also a bad year for the city of Nogales. Not only was the close proximity of the Mexican revolutionaries a source of constant consternation, but now authorities complained that the city jail was overflowing with draft dodgers taken into custody while trying to slip across the international border.

In April 1917 fire destroyed all but two buildings in the mining town of Ajo. Citizens were able to salvage a phonograph from one store. While Ajo burned the phonograph played "A Hot Time in the Old Town" for the fire fighters.

Patriotic feelings of the time were in evidence when a German-born foreman of a Tucson dairy was indicted on charges of disloyalty and espionage. The federal court convicted him and the judge sentenced the man to two years for saying the United States would lose the war and Liberty bonds would be useless.

The Arizona National Guard stationed along the Mexican border no doubt received some sardonic looks from the Regular Army when Company "M" was charged with parading up and down the company street shouting that it wanted to go home. The Arizona Guard later proved its mettle when it was chosen as the guard of honor for President Wilson during the peace conference. The same unit would win even greater glory during World War II fighting the Japanese in Southeast Asia.

In 1918 Arizona was besieged by a great flu epidemic. The situation was so desperate that citizens were required to wear protective masks in public. Phoenix and Tucson police arrested scores of citizens for failing to wear the flu masks prescribed by city ordinances.

Poor roads were a hindrance to development in the early statehood days. Road races were promoted as a gimmick to attract attention to the problem. In 1908 the Cactus Derby, a strenuous race across the desert from Los Angeles to Phoenix, tested both men and machines. The race was run for several years, attracting racing men like Barney Oldfield, Louis Chevrolet, Olin Davis, and Louis Nikrent. The course varied, running sometimes by way of San Diego and Yuma and other times via Needles and Prescott. The people came from miles around to witness these sporting events. The last race was run in 1917, World War I bringing the derby to an end.

The promotions to dramatize the need for better roads were successful. Still, by 1929 Arizona still had less than 300 miles of pavement. Government programs during the Depression were responsible for many new paved roads throughout the state. The Federal Highway Act in 1944 established a national system of highways and led the way for the completion of Highway 66 across northern Arizona and Highway 80 across the southern half. The Interstate Defense System, a controlled-access, multi-lane freeway-building program, began in 1956, and is nearly completed. The latter has been met with mixed emotions by Arizonans.

The air age officially arrived in Tucson on October 15, 1930, when the first transcontinental mail plane arrived. It was exactly seventy-three years from the day that the first coach of the famed "jackass mail" reached Tucson.

On Sunday morning, December 7, 1941, aircraft from imperial Japan hit the United States forces stationed at Pearl Harbor in a sneak attack and created a rallying cry for all Americans, who up to that time had been divided on the war issue. One of the major tragedies of the attack was the sinking of the battleship *Arizona*, sending 1,102 sailors and Marines to the bottom of the bay, where they still lie entombed. Six of those were native Arizonans.

World War II brought a boom to the economy of the state and created a great many changes. The demand for copper sent prices skyrocketing. The weather was instrumental in the creation of several military training bases. The Arizona National Guard, dubbed the "Bushmasters" during their training in Panama, went off to Southeast Asia, where they won many battle honors. Sylvestre Herrerra was the state's only winner of the Congressional Medal of Honor during the war, fighting in the Italian campaign.

A tragic incident centered around the Pima Indian from Bapchule, Ira Hays. Ira came off the reservation, joined the Marines, and found himself on top of Mount Suribachi, Iwo Jima, in February 1945. During a lull in the fighting, a combat photographer asked him and four others to pose for a photo, raising the flag. Although other photos were taken at the same time, the flag-raising scene captured the imagination of the American public. It has become the most famous photograph ever taken in battle. The public demanded to meet the boys who raised the flag. However, three of the five were killed before the battle was over. The two survivors were shipped home to promote war bond drives. One of the survivors was Ira Hays.

Ira Hays became a celebrity for reasons he never really understood. He was escorted around the country, the subject of much public adulation. He soon requested to be sent back overseas to rejoin his outfit. When the war ended Ira came home and the pomp and ceremony began all over again. He was wined and dined by celebrities, treated as a novelty or curiosity. The famous photograph became an albatross around his neck. He began drinking heavily, making the front pages of newspapers each time he landed in jail. Ira Hays returned to the Pima reservation still plagued by personal problems. He was found dead one morning lying in an irrigation ditch, but his memory lives on in monument and song.

Other tragic figures during the war were the Japanese-Americans who were uprooted from their homes and property in what must go down in history as one of the more shameful acts ever perpetrated by the government. The panic following Pearl Harbor is ofttimes given as the reason for the incarceration of the Japanese-Americans. However, it went much deeper than that, as many cast wanton eyes upon the properties of the industrious Orientals. Other prejudices, dating back to gold rush days, were obvious. Two of the so-called "relocation centers" were in Arizona, one at Gila near Maricopa and the other at Poston, along the Colorado River. Poston, sporting a population of eighteen thousand, was Arizona's third largest city during those years. Several military units of American-Japanese or Nisei fought on the side of the Allies during the struggle. The most famous of those units was the 442nd Regimental Combat Team, the "Go for Broke" guys, who went on to become the most decorated

American combat unit in the entire war. About twelve hundred of these men signed up for the Army while still behind barbed wire, and many died on some distant shore while their parents were still locked up in the camps. Their casualty rate was one of the highest in the Army and since they were a segregated unit, many felt that they were being given suicidal missions.

On the other side of the coin were many Japanese who came to the United States, secured an education, and returned to the homeland. Many of them spoke English fluently and could rattle off everything American from the latest fads to baseball players. It was rather disconcerting for American military communication personnel to be talking strategy over the radio only to find out later that they had been conversing with the Japanese Army, informing them of all the latest developments on the American side. It remained a serious problem until Phillip Johnston, the son of a missionary in Arizona, remembered listening to the Navajo carrying on conversations on the reservation prior to the war. The problem was solved when some 375 Navajo "code talkers" were recruited by the U. S. Marines and trained as radiomen. No doubt the Japanese linguists were mystified when they tuned their radios to the American frequency and picked up two American Indians speaking their native tongue. The "code" was never broken by the Japanese. The same program was offered to the armed forces during the Vietnam War, when messages were being intercepted with a great deal of success. For reasons known only to Pentagonian bureaucracy, the offer was refused.

Arizona did not have another winner of the Congressional Medal of Honor until the 1968 Tet Offensive in Vietnam: helicopter pilot Fred Ferguson was awarded the medal when he flew a daring mission through heavy enemy ground fire to rescue and bring to safety the passengers and crew of a downed helicopter.

ANGELS IN THE DESERT

By AND LARGE, SINCE prehistoric times women in Arizona have been relegated to a relatively minor role. The earliest were, of course, the countless, nameless Indian women who spent most of their lives herding animals, weaving, making pottery, grinding corn, and having babies. They were as durable as the land itself. In the more nomadic tribes, they endured the same hardships as did the men. Nearly half the band that made up the final Geronimo campaign were women. Early visitors described some of the agricultural tribeswomen as by far the "most industrious" of the two genders.

When the Spaniards brought their women into Arizona in the 1750s it marked the beginnings of permanent white settlement. The early-day Anglo-American and Spanish women are, perhaps, best epitomized by a statue of the Madonna of the Trail in Springerville. Women of all religious faiths and races faced the frontier with as much aspiration and intrepidness as did the men. Because of their role in society, they actually faced even more insurmountable tasks.

Many of these women have been discussed earlier, although there have been many others who made their presence felt in one way or another in the more recent past. One was Josephine Brawley Hughes, who used her husband's influence to push her feminist and anti-temperance views upon society. The wife of Louis C. Hughes, a Tucson newspaper publisher and territorial governor of Arizona, this indomitable woman also set the editorial policies of his newspaper. She is sometimes referred to as the "Mother of Arizona."

Isabella Selmes Greenway, widow of General John C. Greenway, went into politics after his death and to date is the only woman to have represented Arizona in the U. S. Congress.

Nancy Hayden, wife of the long-time senator, was Arizona's "first lady" for nearly fifty years. She is also reputed to have designed the first Arizona flag, thus earning for her the title "Betsy Ross of Arizona."

Ana Frohmiller, long-time state auditor and "watchdog of the treasury," ran for governor in 1950, and nearly won, just barely losing out to popular radio personality Howard Pyle.

The first woman elected to the Arizona senate was Frances Willard Munds of Prescott. Mrs. Munds was elected to represent Yavapai at the second Arizona legislature in 1914, making her the first woman elected to that body and only the second woman in the United States to be elected a state senator. Mrs. Munds's most important achievement was the woman suffrage bill which passed on the referendum vote in 1912. She had been an advocate of woman suffrage for fifteen years and was chairman of the Arizona Women's Suffrage Organization which led the campaign to its successful conclusion.

Nellie Bush, "admiral of the Arizona navy," riverboat and airplane pilot, also served in the state legislature. She entered law school in Tucson, and recalled, "They wanted to keep women out of the classes when they discussed rape cases. I asked if they had ever heard of a rape case that didn't involve a woman. They let us in after that." In 1924 this "Queen of the Colorado River" became the second woman elected to the Arizona senate.

The first woman elected to the Navajo tribal council was Annie Dodge Wauneka. She was also the recipient of the Presidential Medal of Freedom, the highest civilian award given to individuals in peacetime, for her work in Indian affairs. A granddaughter of the first Navajo tribal chairman, Chee Dodge, Mrs. Wauneka was named American Woman of the Year for Education in 1976.

The first woman in the country to become chief justice of a State Supreme Court was Lorna Lockwood of Phoenix. This outstanding jurist had previously been the first woman superior court judge in Arizona.

There were many others: Ellen Brophy, who founded Brophy

College in Phoenix and returned the Jesuits to Arizona; Maie Bartlett Heard, museum founder and donor of the library site in
Phoenix; Sharlot Hall, territorial historian, author, poet, and Prescott museum founder; Sara Herring, Arizona's first woman lawyer;
Sister Monica, founder of the Convent of St. Joseph at Tucson; Ida
Redbird, famous Maricopa Indian potter; Grace Gil Olivares, the
first woman to graduate from the law school at Notre Dame, and
the first woman to direct the Office of Economic Opportunity in Arizona; Margaret Hance, the first woman mayor of Phoenix; Carolyn
Warner, State Superintendent of Public Instruction; Margarite Cooley, Director, State Library, Archives and Records; Sandra O'Con-
nor, superior court judge and former Arizona senate majority
leader. And these are just a few. They were all leaders and pioneers
in one sense or another. The impact of women in Arizona has been
significant, for it was they who in their own fashion helped tame
the frontier as much as the men.

DAMMING THE RIVERS

FROM THE TIME MAN FIRST set foot in the rich, fertile valleys of Arizona, water has been the key to his survival. The original farmers, the Hohokam, built canals and irrigated the land from the source of the Salt River. When the surplus water was not pumped out of the canals, the water table rose, along with the alkali, and the crops were destroyed. The next serious attempt at harnessing the Salt did not come for several hundred years after the Hohokam.

In 1867 Jack Swilling, erstwhile adventurer, gold seeker, and Confederate officer, organized the Swilling Irrigation and Canal Company. The old canals were cleaned out and the Salt River Valley was back in business supplying the miners in the Bradshaw Mountains and the soldiers at Fort McDowell. The dams were made of brush and worked well until the Salt flooded, tearing the barriers loose and creating general havoc as the water continued uncontrolled to the Sea of Cortez. Ironically, most of the rain in Arizona seemed to fall at one time. During the dry summer months, the Salt would dwindle down to a trickle and crops would die. The settlers knew that if they were to survive and prosper in the valley, a better way of harnessing the river's flow and the elimination of bitter disputes concerning the limited water supply must be found.

In 1902 the Newlands Act came into being, a grand design for irrigating the West, setting the stage for the Salt River Project. The first major irrigation project in the nation financed by the federal government was the Roosevelt Dam, located at a point where Tonto Creek meets the Salt. The site was discovered in 1889, by Billy Breckenridge, former Tombstone deputy and Maricopa County surveyor. The dam was begun in 1905 and completed in 1911, although its reservoir didn't fill for four more years. The dam was built at a cost of $11 million, the government loan finally being paid in full in 1955. The arduous task of building the road from Mesa to Roosevelt was done in part by Apache labor. It was while building this road that Al Sieber, famed Apache scout for General Crook, was injured fatally when a rock fell on him.

The first water over the spillway was bottled and used to christen the greatest new battleship in the Navy, the U.S.S. *Arizona*. In the years that followed, other dams, including the Horse Mesa, Mormon Flat, and Stewart Mountain, were constructed on the Salt. A tributary of the Salt, the Rio Verde, has two dams, Bartlett and Horseshoe. Enough water is held in storage to irrigate 1.5 million acres of cotton, citrus, lettuce, and other crops. Still, from time to time the Salt goes on a rampage and the residents of the Salt River Valley feel the effects. The Salt has a history of cycles of major flooding and there is no reason to suspect that she will change her ways.

The history of the Colorado River has been much the same. One great flood around the turn of the century was responsible for the creation of the Salton Sea in California. The great river of the West was finally tamed with the building of Boulder, Parker, Davis, and Glen Canyon dams.

The scarcity of water during dry spells was cause for some violence and much court action during territorial times. Men protected their valuable brush dams with shotguns. The eastern sections of the United States never had to contend with such an uncertain water supply. They operated under the riparian doctrine, whereby the landowner was entitled to use water flowing through his property as he saw fit. Obviously this law was unsuited to the Southwest, which held with Spanish law in decreeing that the first user of the water had the first right to it as long as he was using it in a productive way. This was upheld by the Anglo-Americans in the Howell Code of 1864. It was later refined as many interpretations were vague and water users used the law as they saw fit. The foremost authority on irrigation law, Judge Joseph H. Kibbey, ruled in 1892 that water rights were permanently attached to the land.

This meant that the sale of water rights was forbidden except in regard to a specific piece of ground. This decision became known as the doctrine of "prior appropriation."

Prosperous farmers had been buying up the rights to somebody else's land as the irrigation companies considered the water rights separate from the ownership of the land. A lot of avaricious people were cleaning up on water deals until Kibbey's doctrine came forth. A few years later, another significant decision, the Kent decree, clarified water rights on every parcel of land in the Salt River Valley. Generally, the decree states that the land where the water was first used has the first right to water flowing in the river. When the river flows were low, only the lands with the earliest water rights could make use of the normal flow. Even if it necessitates drying up of a stream, the water can be consumed as long as it is not wasted. "Arizona streams are public, but the right to use of water is valid only when the rights of prior claimants are not violated. Latecomers must defer to earlier appropriators." Even today those who hold the older lands are entitled to the normal flow water ahead of the latecomers.

In 1903 in another landmark decision, Kibbey ruled that domestic water has dominance over agriculture. During times of water shortage the needs of the public would prevail over farming.

The irrigation period in Arizona passed through three stages. First were the private individuals with dams, ditches, and wells. Next came the irrigation companies, and third came the federal government, the latter building major dams and canals on a grand scale. The scarcity of water was not confined to Arizona alone. Other western states had also become aware of the importance of harnessing the rivers to meet growing needs.

The greatest river in the Southwest, the Colorado, crosses or borders several states, and a co-operative effort was required if the water was to be distributed fairly. Colorado, Utah, New Mexico, and Wyoming comprise the upper basin, while Arizona—which drains some 95 per cent of her runoff into the Colorado—and Nevada and California make up the lower basin. Representatives from the states along with federal representative Herbert Hoover met at Santa Fe in 1922 to discuss the problems of damming and distribution. The agreement that followed, called the Colorado River Compact, allotted half the estimated 15 million acre-feet to the upper basin states and the other half to the lower. Even though the Arizona delegate signed the pact, the state legislature refused to ratify it, making Arizona the lone dissident. G. W. P. Hunt had just become governor again and he was opposed to the agreement. With some adroit maneuvering, he was able to persuade the legislature to refuse it. When the Swing-Johnson Act was passed in 1928, authorizing the building of Boulder Dam on the Colorado, Arizona took the case all the way to the Supreme Court. Ruling that under the Constitution the Congress had authority over navigable streams, the Court decided against Arizona. The state feared, and with good reason, that their more populous neighbor to the west would grab up a lion's share of the water, since at the time there was no facility for Arizona to take the 2.8 million acre-feet allotted it. The dam was built and named Boulder Dam (later changed officially to Hoover Dam in 1947). The spectacular structure was 730 feet above bedrock, created a lake 115 miles long, and held more than 30 million acre-feet of water. Once again Arizona went to court to obtain more water and once again the ruling went against her.

When a California utilities company began constructing a diversion dam on the Colorado in 1934, Governor Moeur, Tempe's "horse and buggy doctor," sent members of the National Guard to patrol the area. Using a couple of antique steamboats called the *Julia B* and the *Nellie T*, the soldiers tried surreptitiously to reconnoiter the site. In doing so, the two craft got themselves tangled in a cable and had to be rescued by their adversaries. There was much national news coverage of this incident, much to the chagrin of the Arizonans and their "desert navy."

It was not until the administration of Sidney P. Osborn that Arizona decided that the only sure way to obtain the benefits of both electrical power and water was to join the Compact. The Arizona Interstate Stream Commission was then organized to consolidate the efforts. The duties of the Commission were to secure water for Arizona, plan irrigation projects, and oversee the welfare and interests of the people concerning water. All this gave birth to a new program that became known as the Central Arizona Project. The grandiose scheme of the Project was to channel water from Lake Havasu into the interior of Arizona by a system of aqueducts and reservoirs. Originally known as the Highline Project, it began as a grand dream of Fred T. Colter, who proposed channeling water from above the Grand Canyon through tunnels in the mountains, including the Mogollon Rim, to the interior basins. This plan was later revised to the above-mentioned one.

A court victory for Arizona in 1956 limited the amount of water that California might take; coupled with another decision in 1963, when the Supreme Court upheld the earlier decision, it guaranteed the state's allotment of 2.8 million acre-feet. This did not include the water from the Gila, which was ruled not a part of the Colorado River drainage.

Other dams were built along the Colorado, including the Glen Canyon Dam, which created a lake some 200 miles long. The battles between the environmentalists and proponents go on.

Most recent was the proposed Orme Dam site at the confluence of the Salt and Verde rivers 30 miles northeast of Phoenix. The dam is a part of the Central Arizona Project to bring water into the interior of the state from the Colorado by the 1980s. Environmentalists and wildlife enthusiasts opposed the site vehemently. Chief complaints were the removal of the Indians at the Fort McDowell Reservation, endangering wildlife in the area, and a dangerous situation created because of faulting in the region on which the dam is to be built. The Bureau of Reclamation began studying several other sites as possible alternatives. Historically, when the need for more energy reaches the critical stage, the proponents of such projects emerge the victors.

One of the great energy hopes of the future, nuclear power, arrived in Arizona in the 1970s. The station, located west of Phoenix, will have three large pressurized water nuclear reactor units and will be in service to meet peak demands of the 1980s. The cooling water supply is expected to be obtained from treated sewage effluent from the greater metropolitan Phoenix area. The proposed nuclear plant has met with much opposition from groups fearing a nuclear catastrophe.

Another power source is solar energy, which Arizonans as far back as the nineteenth century made use of to heat their homes. In 1976 a consortium of Arizona utilities proposed to build a $100 million experimental solar plant at Gila Bend. There is no more suitable spot this side of the Sahara Desert than Gila Bend, which is in a region considered by experts to have the best sunlight in the United States. The solar plant would no doubt enhance the image of the little desert city known heretofore as the "fan belt capital of the world." Solar energy could become the best source of energy yet conceived to serve mankind. It's clean, safe, and natural. Who could argue with these points?

BUT IT WAS ALL IN THE PAST . . .

NEARLY SEVENTY YEARS have passed since Arizona became a full-fledged member of the United States, becoming the last of the continental territories to do so. The days of rustlers, range wars, hostile Apache bands, and armed citizens seemed a thing of the past although it might be noted that much of the highly publicized gunplay of territorial times seems a bit overrated in view of some of today's nefarious activities.

We relish the re-creation of famous gun fights and territorial events both social and violent. Tourists come from distant places with many preconceived notions of life here. Expecting to see stagecoaches rolling down dusty roads and wild painted savages, they are sometimes disappointed when they view our southwestern lifestyle in person for the first time. However, those who stay and take the time really to explore Arizona in depth will find, much to their enjoyment, that there is still a great deal of the past to savor.

When writers and historians extol the progress of civilization in Arizona over the last forty years credit is given to several sources, all of which contributed greatly. Her dry climate had attracted large numbers of health seekers since the 1880s. A new kind of rush, a "sunshine rush," brought out not only the sickly but the affluent as well. The 130-degree mineral water at Castle Hot Spring in the Bradshaw Mountains was one of the first American health resorts. Early-day prospectors used the warm water to do their laundry. It took just five minutes to wash out a shirt that a miner had worn for three months. Isabella Greenway's San Marcos Hotel in Chandler was a pioneer in the winter visitor business. Today tourism ranks fourth in the state's sources of income. The increased sightings of out-of-state license plates each November always signal the opening of a new winter season in the state.

The fear of a Japanese invasion on the West Coast during the early part of World War II caused the government to encourage industry to locate farther inland. War-related companies such as Garrett and Goodyear opened facilities in the Salt River Valley. The year-round climate with its clear atmosphere was cause for building airfields such as Luke Field, Davis-Monthan, and William Field to train pilots. The desert around Yuma was an excellent training ground for Patton's tank corps, training for the campaigns of North Africa, while black troops in the still segregated Army trained at Fort Huachuca.

The wartime demand for beef and cotton soared and ranchers were pressed to meet the needs. The economy had come a long way from the recent Depression when families were living in tents under the Central Avenue bridge in Phoenix while others set up residency on the lawn of the Capitol Building.

Following World War II large numbers of ex-GIs returned to Arizona, bringing their families with them. Many of the industrial complexes opened during the war converted to peacetime pursuits, while Motorola and General Electric opened new plants. The construction business boomed as the electronics industry gained impetus from the war. The population in Arizona in 1940 was less than 500,000 people. By 1950 it had jumped to nearly 750,000, an increase of 50 per cent. In the 1970s it had soared to over 2.5 million, more than two thirds of the new residents coming from outside the state. Manufacturing surpassed mining as the leading source of income, and agriculture slipped to third.

Still, there are serious obstacles to overcome. The tremendous growth in such a short period has brought with it the obvious technological and sociological problems. Only 15.5 per cent of the land is privately owned; 27 per cent is owned by the Indians, 13.5 per cent by the state, and a whopping 44 per cent by the federal government. This small amount of privately owned land creates a problem with the tax base that has yet to be worked out.

The last thirty years in Arizona have seen the advent of a

broader industrial base. No longer does a construction or copper strike seriously cripple the state's economy. Even more advantageous is the number of so-called clean air industries such as Sperry Rand, Greyhound Corporation, Armour Research, and American Express that have settled in the state and become an integral part of the economy.

For better or worse, it might never have come to pass had it not been for people like A. J. Eddy of Yuma, credited with inventing the evaporative cooler, and the Goettls of Phoenix, pioneers in the field of air conditioning. No matter how beautiful the land or how mild the winters, large-scale industry and its employees would never build a tolerance for the searing summertime temperatures without air conditioning.

The past few years have brought great changes to Arizona, and perhaps what best exemplifies the transition that has taken place is the tremendous growth in real estate. Those who were farsighted enough to see it coming no doubt struck it rich. However, many others are typified by this writer's grandfather, who in 1926 was offered 160 acres on north Scottsdale Road, on what is today's McCormick Ranch, for the sum of $600. His memorable (at least to his descendants) reply was, "What do I need with that worthless desert land?"

Town houses on lots measuring 52 feet by 106 feet were selling for an average of $70,000 on that same piece of "worthless desert land" in the mid-1970s.

Arizonans have played significant roles in many fields. Bill Mauldin spent his formative years in Phoenix before going off to war as a journalist. His GI cartoon characters, Willie and Joe, depicted the life of the average World War II foot soldier better than anything captured on camera. Jim Palmer of the Baltimore Orioles, a Scottsdale product, became one of baseball's greatest pitchers, three times winning the Cy Young award. Jimmy Bryan of Phoenix was a racing legend. The popular, cigar-chomping Bryan was a top driver on the speedway circuit for many years. His tragic death came just shortly after winning the Indianapolis 500 in 1958. Zora Folley of Chandler was a top heavyweight boxing contender in the 1950s and 1960s. A soft-spoken, scientific boxer, he was also one of the most popular fighters ever to step into the ring. In the field of science, Tucsonian Frank Borman, a pioneer on the New Frontier, was the first man to pilot a spaceship around the moon. In the entertainment field Rex Allen of Wilcox became one of Hollywood's most successful stars during the era of the singing cowboy. His familiar southwestern drawl is still heard on many Western documentaries. Flagstaff native Andy Devine was for years one of the best-known character actors in motion pictures. Phoenician Jack Elam, the "face that sank a thousand stagecoaches," has been one of the screen's most popular anti-heroes.

Roscoe Willson, whose weekly articles on Arizona history have appeared for nearly thirty years on the pages of the *Arizona Republic*, became one of the best-known writers of Arizona lore. A former cowboy, forest ranger, prospector, and miner, Willson arrived in Arizona in 1902. His colorful accounts, many of them based on personal experiences, have remained a favorite of all the features in that newspaper and have earned him not only the role of premier grass-roots historian of Arizona but rank him high among all historians as well. Roscoe Willson died in 1976, leaving behind a legacy of rich Arizona folklore.

Perhaps at some future date historians will write of these men's achievements in more detail to future generations in the same way this chronicle has depicted the lives of Charles Poston, Pete Brady, Buckey O'Neill, and all the others who arrived when Arizona was known as the last frontier.

An old Arizonan described it as a land that was "hell on horses, dogs, and women." Ranchers still gaze hopefully toward the heavens during the long dry spells that occur frequently in the arid Southwest. Cattle still perish by the score when the water holes dry up. Those few who hang on to the rugged life that gave the world its last grand image of adventure and romance still rope and brand wild cows in the high desert a few miles north of modern Phoenix. Out of place in a country that accepts only his legend, American cowboys and Mexican *vaqueros* brave the brasada or thorny brush and cholla cactus under the same conditions as their predecessors a century ago.

Prospectors searching for that rainbow's end are still found in the mineral-bearing mountains that abound in the state. Using a curious mixture of old and new ways in uncovering some undiscovered bonanza, their eternal optimism is as unshakable as that of the Argonauts of old. Cycles of change in a changeless land, the people still come and their indomitable spirit and will to survive prevail.

For years men saw the land and its wilderness as a challenge to overcome. The early pioneers braved sandstorms, droughts, hostile Apache, and blistering heat to carve out a living in the inhospitable environment. Building highways, cities, and dams, they learned to harness the rivers and create energy, thereby making the turbulent land inhabitable for large numbers of people. However, as with all things in the environs of nature, something is lost when something is gained. Man, in his quest to conquer the land, has nearly upset the delicate ecological balance that nature has developed over the past aeons. Man can live compatibly within the bounds of nature and still maintain a comfortable existence; however, he must play by the rules.

Today man faces perhaps an even greater challenge than did his predecessors, for on his shoulders rest the responsibility and obligation to preserve that which is left. There is so much of the past in the present Arizona. To lose it by default would be a crime not only to ourselves but to posterity as well. We must strive to preserve this unique wonder for future generations to savor and enjoy for we are its product and it is our legacy.

ARIZONA'S POLITICAL FIGURES

TERRITORIAL GOVERNORS OF ARIZONA

John N. Goodwin	Republican	1863–1865
Richard G. McCormick	Republican	1865–1869
Anson P. K. Safford	Republican	1869–1877
John P. Hoyt	Republican	1877–1878
John C. Frémont	Republican	1878–1882
Frederick A. Tritle	Republican	1882–1885
C. Meyer Zulick	Democrat	1885–1889
Lewis Wolfley	Republican	1889–1890
John N. Irwin	Republican	1890–1892
Nathan O. Murphy	Republican	1892–1893
Louis C. Hughes	Democrat	1893–1896
Benjamin J. Franklin	Democrat	1896–1897
Myron H. McCord	Republican	1897–1898
Nathan O. Murphy	Republican	1898–1902
Alexander O. Brodie	Republican	1902–1905
Joseph H. Kibbey	Republican	1905–1909
Richard E. Sloan	Republican	1909–1912

STATE GOVERNORS OF ARIZONA

George W. P. Hunt	Democrat	1912–1917
Thomas E. Campbell	Republican	1917–
George W. P. Hunt	Democrat	1917–1919
Thomas E. Campbell	Republican	1919–1923
George W. P. Hunt	Democrat	1923–1929
John C. Phillips	Republican	1929–1931
George W. P. Hunt	Democrat	1931–1933
Benjamin B. Moeur	Democrat	1933–1937
Rawghlie C. Stanford	Democrat	1937–1939
Robert T. Jones	Democrat	1939–1941
Sidney P. Osborn	Democrat	1941–1948
Dan E. Garvey	Democrat	1948–1951
Howard Pyle	Republican	1951–1955
Ernest W. McFarland	Democrat	1955–1959
Paul Fannin	Republican	1959–1965
Samuel P. Goddard	Democrat	1965–1967
John R. ("Jack") Williams	Republican	1967–1975
Raul Castro	Democrat	1975–

ARIZONA TERRITORIAL DELEGATES TO CONGRESS

Charles D. Poston	Republican	1864–1865
John N. Goodwin	Republican	1865–1867
Coles Bashford	Independent	1867–1869
Richard C. McCormick	Unionist	1869–1875
Hiram S. Stevens	Democrat	1875–1879
John G. Campbell	Democrat	1879–1881
Granville H. Oury	Democrat	1881–1885
Curtis C. Bean	Republican	1885–1887
Marcus A. Smith	Democrat	1887–1895
Nathan O. Murphy	Republican	1895–1897
Marcus A. Smith	Democrat	1897–1899
John F. Wilson	Democrat	1899–1901
Marcus A. Smith	Democrat	1901–1903
John F. Wilson	Democrat	1903–1905
Marcus A. Smith	Democrat	1905–1909
Ralph H. Cameron	Republican	1909–1912

UNITED STATES SENATORS FROM ARIZONA

Marcus A. Smith	Democrat	1912–1921
Henry F. Ashurst	Democrat	1912–1941
Ralph H. Cameron	Republican	1921–1927
Carl T. Hayden	Democrat	1927–1969
Ernest W. McFarland	Democrat	1941–1953
Barry M. Goldwater	Republican	1953–1965
		1969–
Paul J. Fannin	Republican	1965–1977
Dennis de Concini	Democrat	1977–

REPRESENTATIVES FROM ARIZONA

Carl T. Hayden	Democrat	1912–1927
Lewis W. Douglas	Democrat	1927–1933
Isabella S. Greenway	Democrat	1933–1937
John R. Murdock	Democrat	1937–1953
Richard F. Harless	Democrat	1943–1949
Harold A. Patten	Democrat	1949–1955
John J. Rhodes	Republican	1953–
Stewart L. Udall	Democrat	1955–1961
Morris K. Udall	Democrat	1961–
George F. Senner, Jr.	Democrat	1963–1967
Sam Steiger, Jr.	Republican	1967–1977
John Conlan	Republican	1973–1977
Eldon Rudd	Republican	1977–
Robert Stump	Democrat	1977–

COMMON WORDS, NAMES, AND PLACES IN THE LANGUAGE OF THE SOUTHWEST

Spanish	English	Spanish	English
acequia	ditch	bronco	wild
adiós	farewell	buena	good
agua caliente	hot water	caballo	horse
agua fría	cold water	cabeza	head
águila	eagle	cacique	political boss
ajo	paint— Papago word or garlic— Spanish	calabaza	pumpkin
		calabozo	jail
		calle	street
		camino	highway
álamo	cottonwood	cañada	dale
alcalde	mayor	canyon	deep hollow
alta	upper	casa	house
amargosa	bitter	cascabel	rattlesnake
ancha	broad	chaparral	scrub brush
aravaipa	girls— Pima word	charco	pond
		charro	cowboy
arroyo	gulch	cholla	skull
azul	blue	ciénaga	marsh
baile	dance	ciudad	city
blanco	white	concha	shell
bonita	pretty	diablo	devil
bosque	forest grove	escondida	hidden
escuela	school	palo verde	green stick
esperanza	hope	paso	pass

Spanish	English	Spanish	English
estrella	star	picacho	peak
fresco	cool	plata	silver
guerra	war	poco	little
jacal	cabin	prieta	black
jaula	cage	quién sabe?	who knows?
laguna	pond	ramada	porch
llano	plain	reata	lasso
madre	mother	rillito	creek
maraña	tangle	rincón	corner
mesa	table	rodeo	roundup
mesteño	wild stray	salado	salty
montana	mountain	sierra	saw-toothed (ridges)
muerte	death		
nevada	snow-covered	sombrero	shade (cowboy hat)
nogales	walnuts		
nuevo	new	tinaja	natural water hole
ocotillo	coach whip		
oro	gold	vieja	old
palo alto	high tree	viento	wind

BIBLIOGRAPHY

GENERAL

ARNOLD, OREN. *Arizona Under the Sun*. Freeport, Maine: Bond Wheelwright and Company, 1968.

BLAIR, ROBERT. *Tales of the Superstitions: The Origins of the Lost Dutchman Legend*. Tempe, Arizona: Arizona Historical Foundation, 1975.

BOURNE, EULALIA. *Nine Months Is a Year*. Tucson: University of Arizona Press, 1968.

——. *Woman in Levis*. Tucson: University of Arizona Press, 1967.

BRINKERHOFF, SIDNEY, and CROWE, ROSALIE, eds. *Early Yuma*. Flagstaff, Arizona: Northland Press, 1976.

BROWNE, J. ROSS. *Adventures in Apache Country*. New York: Harper, 1869.

CLINE, PLATT. *They Came to the Mountain: The History of Flagstaff*. Flagstaff, Arizona: Northland, 1976.

COOKRIDGE, E. H. *The Baron of Arizona*. New York: John Cay Company, 1967.

CORLE, EDWIN. *Desert Country*. New York: Duell, Sloan and Pearce, 1941.

——. *The Gila; River of the Southwest*. New York: Rinehart, 1951.

COZZENS, SAMUEL W. *Three Years in Arizona and in New Mexico*. Boston: Lee and Shepard, 1891.

DEDERA, DAN. *A Mile in His Moccasins.* Phoenix: McGrew Print and Lithographing Company, 1960.

DODGE, NATT N. *Poisonous Dwellers of the Desert.* Globe, Arizona: Southwest Parks and Monuments Association, 1975.

DUNLOP, RICHARD. *Goodfellow: Gunshot Surgeon of Tombstone.* Garden City, New York: Doubleday, 1965.

FARISH, THOMAS E. *History of Arizona.* 8 volumes. Phoenix: Manufacture Stationers, 1920.

FAULK, ODIE. *Arizona: A Short History.* Norman, Oklahoma: University of Oklahoma Press, 1970.

————. *Land of Many Frontiers.* New York: Oxford University Press, 1968.

FEENEY, FRANCIS. *The Incredible Story of Arizona.* Tempe, Arizona: Golden West Literary Enterprises, 1967.

GOLDWATER, BARRY. *Delightful Journey down the Green and Colorado Rivers.* Tempe, Arizona: Arizona Historical Foundation, 1970.

GRANGER, BYRD, ed. *Will C. Barnes' Arizona Place Names.* Tucson: University of Arizona Press, 1960.

GUSTAFSON, A. M., ed. *John Spring's Arizona.* Tuscon: University of Arizona Press, 1966.

HAURY, EMIL. *Hohokam: Desert Farmers and Craftsmen.* Tucson: University of Arizona Press, 1976.

HENSEN, PAULINE. *Founding a Wilderness Capital.* Flagstaff, Arizona: Northland Press, 1965.

HILL, MYLES E., and GOFF, JOHN S. *Arizona Past and Present.* Cave Creek, Arizona: Black Mountain Press, 1970, 1975.

HINK, HEINZ; MASON, BRUCE; and HALACY, DAN. *Arizona: People and Government.* Tempe, Arizona: H.M.H. Book Company, 1975.

HINTON, RICHARD. *Handbook to Arizona.* San Francisco: Payot, Upham and Company; New York: American News Company, 1878.

HODGE, HIRAM. *Arizona as It Was in 1877.* Chicago: Rio Grande Press, 1962.

JENNINGS, JAMES R. *Arizona Was the West.* San Antonio, Texas: Naylor, 1970.

KIDDER, ALFRED. *An Introduction to the Study of Southwestern Archaeology.* New Haven: Yale University Press, 1962.

LOCKWOOD, FRANK. *Arizona Characters.* Los Angeles: The Times-Mirror Press, 1928.

————. *Pioneer Portraits.* Tucson: University of Arizona Press, 1968.

LOVE, FRANK. *Mining Camps and Ghost Towns.* Los Angeles: Westernlore Press, 1974.

LOWE, CHARLES H. *Arizona's Natural Environment Landscapes and Habitats*. Tucson: University of Arizona Press, 1964.

McCLINTOCK, JAMES H. *Arizona*. 3 volumes. Chicago: Clarke Publishing Company, 1916.

McLAUGHLIN, HERB and DOROTHY. *Phoenix 1870–1970 in Photographs*. Phoenix: Photographic Associates, 1970.

MARION, JOHN. *Notes of Travel Through the Territory of Arizona*. Tucson: University of Arizona Press, 1965.

MARTIN, DOUGLAS. *Arizona Chronology*. 2 volumes. Tucson: University of Arizona Press, 1963–66.

——. *Yuma Crossing*. Albuquerque, New Mexico: University of New Mexico Press, 1954.

MARTIN, DOUGLAS, ed. *Tombstone's Epitaph*. Albuquerque, New Mexico: University of New Mexico Press, 1951.

MILLER, JOSEPH. *Arizona: The Last Frontier*. New York: Hastings House, 1956.

MILLER, JOSEPH, ed. *Arizona Cavalcade*. New York: Hastings House, 1962.

MOWRY, SYLVESTER. *Memories of the Proposal Territory of Arizona*. Washington: H. Polkinhorn, Printer, 1857.

O'CONNER, JACK. *Horse and Buggy West*. New York: Knopf, 1969.

OLIN, GEORGE. *Mammals of the Southwest Deserts*. Globe, Arizona: Southwest Parks and Monuments Association, 1975.

——. *Mammals of the Southwest Mountains and Mesas*. Globe, Arizona: Southwest Parks and Monuments Association, 1975.

PARÉ, MADELINE. *Arizona Pageant*. Tempe, Arizona: Arizona Historical Foundation, 1965.

PARKER, LOWELL. *Arizona Towns and Tales*. Phoenix: Phoenix Newspapers Inc., 1975.

POSTON, CHARLES. *Building a State in Apache Land*. Tempe, Arizona: Aztec Press, 1963.

PUMPELLY, R. *Pumpelly's Arizona*. Tucson: Palo Verde Press, 1965.

QUEBBEMAN, FRANCIS. *Medicine in Territorial Arizona*. Phoenix: Arizona Historical Foundation, 1966.

ROCKFELLOW, JOHN. *Log of an Arizona Trail Blazer*. Tucson: Acme Printing Company, 1933.

RUFFNER, LESTER. *All Hell Needs Is Water*. Tucson: University of Arizona Press, 1972.

SACKS, BEN. *Be It Enacted: The Creation of a Territory*. Phoenix: Arizona Historical Foundation, 1964.

SMALLEY, GEORGE. *My Adventures in Arizona*. Tucson: Arizona Pioneers' Historical Society, 1966.

SMITH, C. C. *William Sanders Oury: History Maker of the Southwest*. Tucson: University of Arizona Press, 1967.

SONNICHSEN, C. L. *Billy King's Tombstone.* Caldwell, Idaho: The Caxton Printers Ltd., 1942.

SPICER, EDWARD. *Cycles of Conquest.* Tucson: University of Arizona Press, 1962.

STRATTON, E. O. *Pioneering in Arizona.* Tucson: Arizona Pioneers' Historical Society, 1964.

STRATTON, R. B. *Captivity of the Oatman Girls.* New York: Carlton and Porter, 1857.

TEVIS, JAMES H. *Arizona in the Fifties.* Albuquerque, New Mexico: University of New Mexico Press, 1954.

THEOBALD, JOHN and LILLIAN. *Arizona Territory Post Offices and Post Masters.* Phoenix: Arizona Historical Foundation, 1961.

WAGONER, JAY. *Arizona Territory: 1863–1912.* Tucson: University of Arizona Press, 1970.

———. *Early Arizona: Prehistoric to Civil War.* Tucson: University of Arizona Press, 1974.

WALKER, DALE. *Death Was the Black Horse: The Story of Buckey O'Neill.* Austin, Texas: Madrona, 1975.

WALLACE, ANDREW. *Sources and Readings in Arizona History.* Tucson: Arizona Pioneers' Historical Society, 1965.

WATERS, FRANK. *The Colorado.* New York and Toronto: Rinehart and Company, Inc., 1946.

WATKINS, TOM. *The Grand Colorado: The Story of a River and Its Canyon.* Palo Alto, California: American West Publishing Company, 1969.

WILLSON, ROSCOE. *No Place for Angels.* Phoenix: Arizona Republic, 1958.

WYLLYS, RUFUS K. *Arizona: The History of a Frontier State.* Phoenix: Hobsen and Herr, 1950.

YAVAPAI COWBELLES. *Echoes of the Past.* 2 volumes. Prescott, Arizona: Yavapai Cowbelles of Arizona, 1955–64.

INDIANS

ADAMS, ALEXANDER. *Geronimo.* New York: Putnam, 1971.

ARNOLD, ELLIOTT. *Blood Brother.* New York: Duell, Sloan and Pearce, 1947.

ARNOLD, OREN. *Savage Son, The Story of Carlos Montezuma.* Albuquerque, New Mexico: University of New Mexico Press, 1951.

BAILEY, L. R. *Indian Slave Trade in the Southwest.* Los Angeles: Westernlore Press, 1966.

——. *The Long Walk, A History of the Navajo Wars.* Los Angeles: Westernlore Press, 1964.

BALDWIN, GORDON. *The Warrior Apaches.* Tucson: D. S. King, 1965.

BARRETT, S. M., ed. *Geronimo, His Own Story.* New York: Dutton, 1970.

BETZINEZ, JASON. *I Fought with Geronimo.* Harrisburg, Pennsylvania: Stackpole Company, 1960.

CREMONY, JOHN. *Life Among the Apaches.* San Francisco: A. Roman, 1868.

FORBES, JACK. *Apache, Navajo, and Spaniard.* Norman, Oklahoma: University of Oklahoma Press, 1960.

——. *Warriors of the Colorado.* Norman, Oklahoma: University of Oklahoma Press, 1965.

GOODWIN, GRENVILLE. *The Social Organization of the Western Apaches.* Chicago: University of Chicago Press, 1942.

——. *Western Apaches Raiding and Warfare.* Tucson: University of Arizona Press, 1971.

LOCKWOOD, FRANK. *The Apache Indians.* New York: The Macmillan Company, 1938.

MARTIN, PAUL S., and PLOG, FRED. *The Archaeology of Arizona.* Garden City, New York: Doubleday/Natural History Press, 1973.

OGLE, RALPH. *Federal Control of the Western Apaches.* Albuquerque, New Mexico: University of New Mexico Press, 1940.

PAUL, DORIS A. *The Navajo Code Talkers.* Philadelphia: Dorrance, 1973.

POWELL, JOHN W. *The Exploration of the Colorado River and Its Canyons.* New York: Dover, 1961.

SANTEE, ROSS. *Apacheland.* New York: C. Scribner's Sons, 1947.

SONNICHSEN, C. L. *The Mescalero Apaches.* Norman, Oklahoma: University of Oklahoma Press, 1958.

SPICER, EDWARD. *The Cycles of Conquest.* Tucson: University of Arizona Press, 1963.

THRAPP, DAN. *Victorio and the Mimbrés Apaches.* Norman, Oklahoma: University of Oklahoma Press, 1974.

UNDERHILL, RUTH. *The Navajos.* Norman, Oklahoma: University of Oklahoma Press, 1967.

WATERS, FRANK. *The Book of the Hopi.* New York: Viking Press, 1964.

WEBB, GEORGE. *A Pima Remembers.* Tucson: University of Arizona Press, 1959.

WELLMAN, PAUL. *Broncho Apache.* Garden City, New York: Doubleday, 1936.

——. *Death on the Desert.* Garden City, New York: Doubleday, 1954.

SPANISH / MEXICAN

BANDELIER, A. F. A. *The Gilded Man.* New York: D. Appleton and Company, 1893.

BANNON, JOHN. *Bolton and the Spanish Borderlands.* Norman, Oklahoma: University of Oklahoma Press, 1964.

———. *The Spanish Borderlands Frontier.* New York: Holt, Rinehart and Winston, 1970.

BOLTON, HERBERT. *Coronado: Knight of Pueblos and Plains.* New York: Whittlesey House, 1949.

———. *The Padre on Horseback.* Chicago: Loyola University Press, 1963.

———. *Rim of Christendom.* New York: Russell and Russell, 1960.

———. *Spanish Borderlands.* New Haven: Yale University Press, 1921.

———. *Spanish Exploration of the Southwest.* New York: Barnes and Noble, 1952.

BRINKERHOFF, SIDNEY. *Boots and Shoes of the Frontier Soldier.* Tucson: Arizona Historical Society, 1976.

BRINKERHOFF, S., and FAULK, O. *Lancers for the King.* Phoenix: Arizona Historical Foundation, 1963.

CASTANEDA, PEDRO DE. *The Coronado Expedition.* Chicago: Rio Grande Press, 1964.

CATHER, WILLA. *Death Comes for the Archbishop.* New York: Knopf, 1934.

CHAMBERLIN, SAM. *My Confession.* New York: Harper, 1956.

FORREST, EARLE. *Missions to Old Pueblos of the Southwest.* Chicago: Rio Grande Press, 1962.

HALLENBACK, CLEVE. *Land of the Conquistadors.* Caldwell, Idaho: Caxton Printers, 1950.

HAMMOND, GEORGE P. *Don Juan Oñate, Colonizer of New Mexico.* Albuquerque, New Mexico: University of New Mexico Press, 1953.

HORGAN, PAUL. *Conquistadores in North American History.* New York: Farrar, Straus and Company, 1963.

McCARTY, KIERAN. *Desert Documentary: The Spanish Years, 1767–1821.* Tucson: Arizona Historical Society, 1976.

SALPOINTE, J. B. *Soldiers of the Cross.* Banning, California: St. Boniface's Industrial School, 1898.

SMITH, FAY. *Father Kino in Arizona.* Phoenix: Arizona Historical Foundation, 1966.

WELLMAN, PAUL. *Glory, God, and Gold.* Garden City, New York: Doubleday, 1954.

WYLLYS, R. K. *Pioneer Padre Kino.* Dallas, Texas: Southwest Press, 1935.

AMERICAN TRAILBLAZERS

BARTLETT, JOHN. *Personal Narrative.* New York: D. Appleton, 1854.

BONSAL, STEPHEN. *Edward F. Beale.* New York and London: G. P. Putnam's Sons, 1912.

CARSON, KIT. *The Autobiography of Kit Carson.* Lincoln: University of Nebraska Press, 1966.

CHITTENDEN, H. *The American Fur Trade of the Far West.* 2 volumes. New York: Francis P. Harper, 1902.

CLELAND, R. G. *This Reckless Breed of Men.* New York: Knopf, 1950.

CONNER, DANIEL E. *Joseph R. Walker and the Arizona Adventure.* Norman, Oklahoma: University of Oklahoma Press, 1956.

EMORY, WILLIAM H. *Notes of a Military Reconnaissance.* Albuquerque, New Mexico: University of New Mexico Press, 1951.

FAULK, ODIE. *Destiny Road.* New York: Oxford University Press, 1973.

———. *The U. S. Camel Corps.* New York: Oxford University Press, 1976.

FAVOUR, ALPHEUS. *Old Bill Williams, Mountain Man.* Chapel Hill, North Carolina: University of North Carolina Press, 1936.

FOREMAN, GRANT. *Pathfinder in the Southwest: Lt. A. W. Whipple.* Norman, Oklahoma: University of Oklahoma Press, 1941.

GREGG, JOSIAH. *Commerce of the Prairies.* Chicago: R. R. Donnelley and Sons Company, 1926.

HAFEN, LEROY. *Broken Hand: The Story of Tom Fitzpatrick.* Denver: Old West Publishing Company, 1973.

HALL, SHARLOT. *Paulino Weaver.* Prescott Booklet, 1929.

HOBBS, JAMES. *Wild Life in the Far West.* Hartford, Connecticut: Wiley, Waterman, and Eaton, 1874.

JENNINGS, JAMES R. *The Freight Rolled.* San Antonio, Texas: Naylor Company, 1969.

LAVENDER, DAVID. *Bent's Fort.* Los Angeles: Cole-Holmquist, 1955.

LEONARD, ZENAS. *The Narrative of Zenas Leonard.* Norman, Oklahoma: University of Oklahoma Press, 1959.

LESLEY, STACY. *Uncle Sam's Camels.* Cambridge: Harvard University Press, 1929.

MAGOFFIN, SUSAN. *Down the Santa Fe Trail and into Mexico*. New Haven: Yale University Press, 1962.

PARKHILL, FORBES. *The Blazed Trail of Antoine Leroux*. Los Angeles: Westernlore Press, 1965.

PHILLIPS, PAUL. *The Fur Trade*. 2 volumes. Norman, Oklahoma: University of Oklahoma Press, 1961.

POWELL, JOHN W. *The Exploration of the Colorado River and Its Canyons*. New York: Dover, 1961.

RUXTON, GEORGE F. *Adventures in Mexico and the Rocky Mountains*. London: J. Murray, 1847.

STONE, IRVING. *Immortal Wife; Jessie Benton Fremont*. Garden City, New York: Doubleday, 1944.

———. *Men to Match My Mountains*. Garden City, New York: Doubleday, 1956.

VESTAL, STANLEY. *Kit Carson: Happy Warrior of the Old West*. Boston: Houghton Mifflin, 1928.

WEBBER, DAVID. *The Taos Trappers: The Fur Trade in the Far Southwest*. Norman, Oklahoma: University of Oklahoma Press, 1966.

WHIPPLE, A. W. *The Whipple Report: Journal of an Expedition from San Diego, California*. Los Angeles: Westernlore Press, 1961.

MILITARY

BIGELOW, JAMES. *On the Bloody Trail of Geronimo*. Los Angeles: Westernlore Press, 1968.

BOURKE, JOHN. *On the Border with Crook*. Chicago: Rio Grande Press, 1962.

BRANDES, RAY. *Frontier Military Posts of Arizona*. Globe, Arizona: D. S. King, 1960.

CLARK, DWIGHT. *Stephen Watts Kearny: Soldier of the West*. Norman, Oklahoma: University of Oklahoma Press, 1966.

CLENDENIN, C. *Blood on the Border*. New York: Macmillan, 1969.

CONNELLY, WILLIAM. *Doniphan's Expedition*. Topeka, Kansas: The Author, 1907.

COOKE, PHILLIP. *The Conquest of New Mexico and California*. Albuquerque, New Mexico: Horn and Wallace, 1964.

DAVIS, BRITTON. *The Truth About Geronimo*. New Haven: Yale University Press, 1963.

DOWNEY, F., and JACOBSEN, J. *The Red-Blue Coats: The Indian Scouts*. Fort Collins, Colorado: Old Army Press, 1973.

FAULK, ODIE. *The Crimson Desert*. New York: Oxford University Press, 1974.

——. *The Geronimo Campaign.* New York: Oxford University Press, 1969.

GRIFFITH, A. KINNEY. *Mickey Free; Manhunter.* Caldwell, Idaho: Caxton Printers, 1969.

HALL, MARTIN. *Sibley's New Mexico Campaign.* Austin, Texas: University of Texas Press, 1960.

HERNER, CHARLES. *The Arizona Rough Riders.* Tucson: University of Arizona Press, 1970.

HEYMAN, MAX. *Prudent Soldier: Biography of Gen. E. R. S. Canby.* Glendale, California: A. H. Clark Company, 1959.

HORGAN, PAUL. *Distant Trumpet.* New York: Farrar, Straus and Cudahy, 1960.

HUGHES, JOHN. *Doniphan's Expedition.* Cincinnati: The Author, 1848.

HUNT, AURORA. *Maj. Gen. James H. Carleton.* Glendale, California: A. H. Clark Company, 1958.

JOHNSON, V. W. *The Unregimented General: Nelson Miles.* Boston and New York: Houghton Mifflin, 1962.

LECKIE, ROBERT. *The Buffalo Soldiers.* Norman, Oklahoma: University of Oklahoma Press, 1967.

LUMMIS, CHARLES. *General Crook and the Apache Wars.* Flagstaff, Arizona: Northland Press, 1966.

MASON, HERBERT M. *The Great Pursuit.* New York: Random House, 1970.

RICKEY, DON. *Forty Miles a Day on Beans and Hay.* Norman, Oklahoma: University of Oklahoma Press, 1963.

SCHMITT, MARTIN, ed. *The Autobiography of George Crook.* Norman, Oklahoma: University of Oklahoma Press, 1946.

SMITH, C. C. *Emilio Kosterlitzky.* Glendale, California: A. H. Clark Company, 1970.

SUMMERHAYS, MARTHA. *Vanished Arizona.* Philadelphia: Lippincott Company, 1908.

THRAPP, DAN. *Al Sieber: Chief of Scouts.* Norman, Oklahoma: University of Oklahoma Press, 1964.

——. *Conquest of Apacheria.* Norman, Oklahoma: University of Oklahoma Press, 1967.

——. *Sierra Madre Campaign.* Norman, Oklahoma: University of Oklahoma Press, 1972.

UTLEY, ROBERT. *Frontier Regulars.* New York: Macmillan Company, 1967.

——. *Frontiersmen in Blue.* New York: Macmillan Company, 1967.

YOUNG, OTIS E. *The West of Phillip St. George Cooke.* Glendale, California: A. H. Clark Company, 1955.

MINING

ARIZONA BUREAU OF MINES. *Gold Placers in Arizona*. Tucson: University of Arizona Press, 1961.

ARNOLD, OREN. *Ghost Gold*. San Antonio, Texas: Naylor Company, 1967.

BURGESS, OPIE. *Bisbee Not So Long Ago*. San Antonio, Texas: Naylor Company, 1967.

BURNS, WALTER NOBLE. *Tombstone*. New York: Grosset and Dunlap, 1929.

CLELAND, ROBERT G. *A History of Phelps Dodge*. New York: Knopf, 1952.

CONNER, DANIEL E. *Joseph R. Walker and the Arizona Adventure*. Norman, Oklahoma: University of Oklahoma Press, 1956.

CRAMPTON, FRANK. *Deep Enough*. Denver: A. Swallow, 1956.

DOBIE, J. FRANK. *Apache Gold and Yaqui Silver*. New York: Bramhall House, 1939.

———. *Coronado's Children*. New York: Literary Guild of America, 1930.

DUNNING, CHARLES. *Arizona's Golden Road*. Phoenix, Arizona: Southwest Publishing Company, 1961.

DUNNING, CHARLES H., and PEPLOW, EDWARD H. *Rock to Riches*. Phoenix, Arizona: Southwest Publishing Company, 1959.

EDGERTON, KEARNEY. *Somewhere Out There*. Glendale, Arizona: Prickly Pear Press, 1974.

ELY, SIMS. *The Lost Dutchman Mine*. New York: Morrow, 1953.

FAULK, ODIE. *Tombstone: Myth and Reality*. New York: Oxford University Press, 1972.

GREEVER, WILLIAM. *The Bonanza West*. Norman, Oklahoma: University of Oklahoma Press, 1963.

HINTON, R. *1,000 Old Arizona Mines*. Toyahvale, Texas: Frontier Book Company, 1962.

PAUL, RODMAN. *Mining Frontiers of the Far West*. Albuquerque: University of New Mexico Press, 1963.

SONNICHSEN, C. L. *Colonel Greene and the Copper Skyrocket*. Tucson: University of Arizona Press, 1974.

STORM, BARRY. *Thunder God's Gold*. Chiriaco Summit, California: Stormjade Books, 1967.

WALTERS, LORENZO. *Tombstone's Yesterdays*. Glorieta, New Mexico: Rio Grande Press, 1928.

YOUNG, HERBERT V. *The Ghosts of Cleopatra Hill*. Jerome, Arizona: Jerome Historical Society, 1964.
——. *They Came to Jerome*. Jerome, Arizona: Jerome Historical Society, 1972.
YOUNG, OTIS E. *How They Dug the Gold*. Tucson: University of Arizona Press, 1967.
——. *Western Mining*. Norman, Oklahoma: University of Oklahoma Press, 1970.

THE CATTLEMEN

ADAMS, RAMON. *The Old-Time Cowhand*. New York: Macmillan Company, 1961.
BARNES, WILL C., and RAINE, WILLIAM M. *Cattle*. Garden City, New York: Doubleday, Doran and Company, Inc., 1930.
COOLIDGE, DANE. *Arizona Cowboys*. New York: E. P. Dutton and Company, Inc., 1938.
DOBIE, J. FRANK. *Vaquero of the Brush Country*. Dallas, Texas: The Southwest Press, 1929.
ELLISON, SLIM. *Cowboys Under the Mogollon Rim*. Tucson: University of Arizona Press, 1968.
ERWIN, ALLEN. *The Southwest of John H. Slaughter*. Glendale, California: A. H. Clark Company, 1965.
HUNT, FRAZIER. *Cap Mossman: Last of the Great Cowmen*. New York: Hastings House, 1951.
LOCKWOOD, FRANK. *Apaches and Longhorns*. New York: The Macmillan Company, 1938.
PROCTOR, GIL. *The Trails of Pete Kitchen*. Tucson: D. S. King, 1964.
SANTEE, ROSS. *Cowboy*. New York: Cosmopolitan Book Corporation, 1928.
SHARP, BOB. *Big Outfit: Ranching on the Baca Float*. Tucson: University of Arizona Press, 1974.
STEWART, JANET. *Arizona Ranch Houses*. Tucson: University of Arizona Press, 1974.
WAGONER, JAY. "History of the Cattle Industry of Southern Arizona." Tucson: University of Arizona Social Science Bulletin #20, 1952.

OUTLAWRY AND JUSTICE

BRECKENRIDGE, BILLY. *Helldorado*. Boston and New York: Houghton Mifflin, 1928.

FORREST, EARLE. *Arizona's Dark and Bloody Ground*. Caldwell, Idaho: Caxton Printers, 1936.

HALEY, J. E. *Jeff Milton: A Good Man with a Gun*. Norman, Oklahoma: University of Oklahoma Press, 1958.

LAKE, STUART. *Wyatt Earp: Frontier Marshal*. Boston and New York: Houghton Mifflin, 1931.

MILLER, JOSEPH, ed. *The Arizona Rangers*. New York: Hastings House, 1972.

MONAGHAN, JAMES. *The Last of the Bad Men: The Legend of Tom Horn*. New York: The Bobbs-Merrill Company, 1946.

MYERS, JOHN MEYERS. *Doc Holliday*. Boston and New York: Houghton Mifflin, 1955.

———. *I, Jack Swilling*. New York: Hastings House, 1961.

———. *The Last Chance: Tombstone's Early Years*. New York: E. P. Dutton and Company, 1950.

RYNNING, TOM. *Gun Notches*. New York: Frederick A. Stokes, 1931.

SONNICHSEN, C. L. *Alias Billy the Kid (Brushy Bill Roberts)*. Albuquerque, New Mexico: University of New Mexico Press, 1955.

WATERS, FRANK. *The Earp Brothers of Tombstone*. New York: Clarkson N. Potter, 1960.

INDEX

Page numbers in italics refer to map references.